Days of Revolution

Days of Revolution

Political Unrest in an Iranian Village

Mary Elaine Hegland

Stanford University Press

Stanford, California

Stanford University Press
Stanford, California

Printed in the United States of America on acid-free, archival-quality paper

Library of Congress Cataloging-in-Publication Data

Hegland, Mary Elaine, author.
  Days of revolution : political unrest in an Iranian village / Mary Elaine
Hegland.
      pages cm
  Includes bibliographical references and index.
  ISBN 978-0-8047-7567-0 (cloth : alk. paper) --
  ISBN 978-0-8047-7568-7 (pbk. : alk. paper)
  1. Villages--Iran--Case studies. 2. Political culture--Iran. 3. Iran--History
--Revolution, 1979. 4. Iran--Politics and government--1979-1997. 5. Iran--
Politics and government--1997- I. Title.
  DS318.81.H44 2014
  955'.72--dc23
                                        2013026629
  ISBN 978-0-8047-8885-4 (electronic)

Typeset by Bruce Lundquist in 11/13.5 Adobe Garamond

With gratitude, in memory of
  Rahmat Khanum
  Shaikh Naser
  Margaret Hegland
  Norval Hegland
  Richard Antoun
          and with many thanks to the people of "Aliabad"

Contents

Illustrations

Preface
Researching a Revolution: 1978–1979

WHEN I FLEW TO IRAN IN JUNE 1978, I did not know I would be conducting field research about a revolution. My study was originally to have been about agricultural credit systems in rural Iran to shed light on processes of change in social, political and economic relations in an Iranian village. The ten prospective village fieldwork sites I visited near Shiraz, capital of the southwestern province of Fars, seemed to fall into three categories. Villages close to Shiraz demonstrated a new prosperity due to employment opportunities in and near the city. Other villages prospered due to land reform and mechanized agricultural irrigation. A third category of village was characterized by poverty and the absence of able-bodied men. These settlements had not benefited from land reform and were far enough away from Shiraz to prevent villagers from commuting for work. Men moved away to find work, leaving mainly the elderly and less able living in the home village.

In one of these latter settlements, my family and I and the two staff members from Shiraz University kind enough to escort us were served tea and watermelon in an open area among the ramshackle mudbrick homes. We ate, swatting away the many flies, watched quietly by barefoot children in tattered clothing who knew the treat was not for them. The little group of villagers talked with us about their need for water and the inequity of the land distribution. One slight old man (actually probably about 55) pleaded insistently with us to convey the village's needs to the provincial governor, to ask him to at least give them a paved road. The road to the nearby town was impassible during the rainy season because of thick mud.

Women experiencing trouble in childbirth had died because they couldn't be brought to the town only a few kilometers away. I passed this plea on to the highest official I could, but with little hope of benefit.

In late summer we settled in Aliabad, a relatively prosperous village close to Shiraz. A bus line to the outskirts of the city meant my then-husband could get to Pahlavi University (now Shiraz University), where he had a Fulbright teaching position for the year. I was directed by the gendarmerie (rural police) office in Shiraz to present my letter of research permission to the captain of the Qodratabad gendarmerie station 2.2 kilometers (about 1.4 miles) from Aliabad. The captain took me to the home of Mashd[1] Musa Saedi in Aliabad with the suggestion that we reside in his home. When I explained that I wished to live in the "old village" within the village walls, he took us to the home of another government representative in the old village. Then I used the excuse that his courtyard was not tiled and I was concerned about my one-year-old child, Karima, playing in the dirt. When the gendarmerie captain took us to the home of Seyyid[2] Yaqub Askari, whose courtyard *was* tiled, I didn't know what to say. The appearance of his courtyard told me he was a member of the village elite. In fact, he was the *de facto* village boss and main government representative in Aliabad, I learned later, no matter who formally held offices. We rented three rooms in his courtyard[3] for the first half of our period in the village. After the Revolution, when the gendarmes were no longer in control and in fact no center of control in Shiraz was effective, I felt free to change my residence to another courtyard. The second half of my stay I lived with neighbors sympathetic to the local uprising against Seyyid Yaqub's powerful brother, Seyyid Ibn Ali Askari.

Because I wished to conduct research in a village in the midst of changing economic relations, I had hoped to live in a smaller and more remote settlement, but Aliabad, with its history of political significance and conflict and many residents' activism during the revolutionary period, turned out to be a fruitful site.

Aliabad was a village of some 3,000 then, a population in constant flux as villagers moved away and others returned. Many villagers came back from Shiraz and elsewhere to build urban-style homes in the "new village" across the highway from the old walled settlement. The convenient travel between Aliabad and Shiraz, as well as the nearby factories and construction sites, were among the reasons for the relative prosperity of residents. The plentiful availability of jobs in the late 1970s meant that few households in Aliabad were extremely needy. This relative economic prosperity resulted in a major research challenge for me. I could not find any girl living nearby whose family needed money enough to overcome the stigma against females working. Time available for interviewing was minimized and frequently interrupted while I gave attention to my still-nursing daughter and cared for my household. The 18-month grant, instead of the more typical 9-month research period, from the Social Science Research Council and the American Council of Learned Societies was all the more welcome to me—a mother as well as a researcher.

In addition to its relatively large size and its prosperity resulting from close proximity to Shiraz, Aliabad was unusual in having facilities not ordinarily found in Iranian villages. Aliabad had been chosen by the national government to be somewhat of a model village and had water piped into many courtyards, piped natural gas, electricity, a full elementary school and a clinic.[4]

In spite of the limiting and awkward position of living in the courtyard of the village boss, I attempted to get acquainted with villagers. Meeting the Askaris' relatives and associates was not difficult. Rana, social leader of the informal group of seyyid women and wife of Seyyid Yaqub's nephew Seyyid Enayat Askari, soon became a friend. Rana hosted the meetings led by personnel from the conservative Religious School of Zahra in Shiraz. In the nearby courtyard of Seyyid Ayyub, Seyyid Yaqub's father's brother, I became acquainted with Seyyid Ayyub's son Seyyid Kazem, a gifted political analyst, and with members of other households in the courtyard who in turn brought me into contact with still more relatives. Seyyid Ayyub's youngest daughter brought her nephew Hushang Amini, who attended Tehran University for a few months before it closed, to meet me. In this way, contact was established between me and Haidar Amini's family, several of whom proved to be important informants. This family was respected and connected to several village factions yet remained relatively neutral regarding the Revolution[5] and the post-revolutionary uprising against Seyyid Ibn Ali Askari. Family members were well-informed about village history and current conflicts. Because of their status and political neutrality, they did not seem to fear negative results from association with "the Americans." In retrospect, I suspect that the sight of Haidar Amini's son Behnam escorting the American family to his father's home at dinnertime must have helped shield us in the sensitive period right after the Revolution. The family of Haidar Amini was one of the few families who continued to associate with us during that time.

When I needed a *chador* (a semicircle of cloth used as an enveloping veil) and a couple of pairs of the loose pants worn by village women at home, Seyyid Yaqub's wife, Rezvan, sent for Esmat Ajami, a young widow and seamstress who did sewing for her, to come meet me. Esmat lived not far from the Askaris with her two sons; her widowed mother, who brought cloth from Shiraz to sell; and her married brother who ran a tailoring shop in Shiraz. The Ajami home was a center of activity; women dropped by to buy cloth from the mother, often sewed by Esmat into chadors; loose pants for men, women and children; infant layettes; and traditional women's clothing. Esmat's brother, who commuted to Shiraz, and relatives visiting from Shiraz kept Esmat informed about events in the city. The weekly visit from the religious narrative chanter was another source of information. With her quick, analytical mind and able verbal skills, Esmat questioned visitors about happenings in the village and in Shiraz. Sifting and combining stories, she could then produce a full, rich account of a particular event. Her experience and skills were most helpful to me, especially after the hostages were taken at the American Embassy in Tehran on November 4, 1979, and subsequently when those villagers who did not know me well hesitated to tell me about ongoing political happenings. Esmat's in-laws were important organizers in the local struggle against Seyyid Ibn Ali Askari, then the largest owner of Aliabad land, and she was frequently called upon to serve tea at meetings of the opposition. Although basically illiterate then, Esmat was a repository of religious stories and descriptions of village customs. Once she quietly confessed to me that she too was interested in asking older people about village history and social customs and had done so when she was young. As she matured, however, she was told this was not seemly, so she stopped her inquiries. Esmat Khanum[6] became one of my most important informants and, during my visits between 2003 and 2008, was a highly skilled and knowledgeable research assistant as well as my closest friend.[7]

Although I was discouraged by Seyyid Yaqub and his wife, I also sought out peasants and former heads of agricultural groups to interview. When I moved to another courtyard after the Revolution, it became easier to have contact with peasants and with members of the opposition to the Shah's government and to Seyyid Yaqub Askari and Seyyid Ibn Ali Askari. Several times I visited the home of Shaikh Rahim Kazemi, leader of the opposition and earlier a supporter of the Tudeh Party and Prime Minister Mosaddeq, and became friendly with his daughter. Especially after

Seyyid Ibn Ali was put in jail, villagers became more open and less fearful in describing for me their suffering at his hands. The effect of residing in Seyyid Yaqub's courtyard—and of being an American and thus connected whether I liked it or not with the Pahlavi regime and its agents and sympathizers—was never entirely removed. My association with the seyyids was regular whereas my interviews with the opposition were somewhat sporadic. Partly due to research conditions, contact with the members of current and earlier oppositional movements, peasants, commuters and migrants living in Shiraz remained relatively limited. Although I set eyes on Seyyid Ibn Ali Askari once or twice when he was visiting his brother's village courtyard and at one or two family picnics, I never conversed with him personally, nor was I even introduced to him.

During the first two or three months of my stay in Aliabad, I continued with my original research plans, interviewing people on the political and economic history of the village and learning something about current political and economic organization, divisions within the village, politically powerful persons and economic, political and social relations with persons outside the village. I visited men working in orchards, vineyards and wheat fields. I looked into both agriculture and trading.

By October 1979, though, it became impossible to avoid preoccupation with the state of the Revolution. Like many others in the village, I did not miss the BBC radio news broadcasts on Iran and could talk of nothing but the political situation. It was a strain to live under such circumstances, especially because of my long-time association with Iran and deep concern about many dear Iranian friends as well as the fate of the society. (I had served as an English high school teacher in the Peace Corps in northwestern Iran from 1966 through 1968 and had made several study trips to Iran since then.) The near future was fraught with uncertainty. There was a daily death toll during the months leading up to the fall of the Shah's regime, and a sad and frightening barrage of news about violent government encounters with revolutionary forces. Each day began with the short BBC morning report. All day long, thoughts and conversations centered on the uprising as I exchanged information and evaluation with everyone I encountered. The last thing at night before trying to sleep was listening to the 45-minute BBC Persian newscast—with the radio on battery power and in lamplight because employees of the government Office of Electricity turned off the electricity every night all over Iran to show their support for the revolutionary movement.

My previous experiences in Iran had left me predisposed to be sympathetic to the revolutionary movement. Repression and violence by Mohammad Reza Shah Pahlavi's[8] government against the Kurds, discussions with Iranian social scientists who suffered from persecution and lack of intellectual freedom, and observations and conversations during visits to Iran during 1966 to 1968, 1971 to 1972, and the summers of 1970 and 1977, as well as contact with Iranians in the United States left me anticipating a revolution at some point—but not this soon. Because of my sympathies, I participated in movement activities. I entered into conversations, listened to tapes and exchanged information. (I had learned to speak Persian in 1966.) I joined with other women in evening marches and in shouting political slogans in Aliabad, and then when some of the village women began going to Shiraz for marches, I went with them. There, to prevent me from getting separated from them, my friends tied corners of their chadors to mine or protectively formed a barrier by walking in a circle around me. I interviewed villagers about their experiences and attitudes about demonstrations and confrontations with armed forces in Shiraz, and recorded incidents in the village related to the Revolution, interviewing participants and others. Gradually it became clear my research would focus on the Revolution rather than on agricultural credit.

In January and February 1979, the period before the fall of Prime Minister Shapour Bakhtiar's[9] government, I was invited to come to the daily morning Qoran classes for females at the mosque, including discussions about Islam and the Revolution, taught by a prayer leader from the religious center of Qom stationed in the village at the time. Women took me to the mosque for evening prayers, often followed by a rousing speech on the revolutionary movement or Islamic government. Of course I took notes on everything.

For a long time it was difficult to communicate with the outside world. Employees of the postal service went on strike for several months before February 11, 1979, and employees of the government telephone and telegraph services were on strike too. Once in a while we could send a letter with someone leaving the country. Immediately after February 11, the day the Shah's government fell, I joined the long lines of people waiting at the telephone office in Shiraz, again open for service, to call and reassure loved ones outside the country. Even after the Revolution and the end of the strikes, mail was slow and erratic. For a time the borders were closed to adult males trying to leave the country, so even the use of personal couriers was restricted. In spite of their suffering during the revolutionary period, exacerbated by my inability to communicate with them, my supportive parents never once asked me to come home but left me to decide for myself what was safe and whether to continue my research.

My American citizenship and the revolutionary conditions of the fieldwork period restricted research in several ways. The greatest research challenge was the constant and overwhelming suspicion that I was a spy, probably a CIA agent, or that I was in Iran to work for American interests. This suspicion had a greater impact on my research during specific periods. The worst point was during the two or three months after the return of Ayatollah Khomeini from France to Iran on February 1, 1979, and the February 11 collapse of Mohammad Reza Shah Pahlavi's regime. Iranians sympathetic to the revolutionary movement were pleased to have the interest and involvement of foreigners before the fall of the regime, but immediately after the success of the Revolution, a main concern was the possibility that the CIA would assist other forces in bringing back the Shah. People remembered 1953 and feared a modified replay of the CIA-engineered coup that overthrew popularly elected Prime Minister Mosaddeq and returned the Shah to power. Revolutionary activists were preoccupied with fear that their hard-won Revolution would be reversed. Every American was suspected of being a CIA agent. This suspicion was encouraged by a barrage of anti-American propaganda on radio and TV and in the press. Villagers wondered why we had stayed in Iran when other Americans had been evacuated. A few Aliabad people thought I was indeed a sociologist or anthropologist but had been sent to study Iranian agriculture so the US imperialists could cause its further deterioration and create even greater markets for their own products. Or they thought I had been sent to study Iranian culture and society and help plan how to keep Iranians entertained with other activities and out of politics.

Just before the success of the Revolution on February 11, I had been attending evening meetings, including revolutionary speeches, and a morning Qoran class at the mosque. After the Revolution, I continued for a couple of weeks. Then a friend, Mohammad Amini, told us a group of villagers felt antagonistic toward us and wished to attack and burn our home, take our possessions and carry us bodily out of the village. Mohammad was able to persuade this group that if we could obtain a letter from the religious authorities in Shiraz certifying our harmlessness we should be allowed to stay. If we could not, he suggested to us—before he himself stopped interacting with us due to concern for his own revolutionary credentials and effectiveness in the revolutionary movement—we should leave. Through an American anthropologist married to a man from Shiraz, I was able to meet the daughter of an important religious figure. This woman trusted me and arranged an interview with her father. The two of them appreciated research on revolutionary Islam, a main focus of my research by then—and of my anticipated book—and promised to do what they could to obtain a letter for me.

While waiting for the letter, I did not attempt any research. One day at the height of the negative feelings against us, I packed all of my research notebooks into a big bag and left with my family to stay with friends in Shiraz for a couple of days. During these few months of our stay in Aliabad, we suffered the unhappiness of being suspected by those who had previously befriended us. Only three or four families in the village would talk to us. My then-husband especially was insulted and shouted at in the alleyways of the village and on the bus going into town, "Go home, American." He was heckled and threatened, usually by young men, while in Shiraz. In Shiraz, a young man on a motorcycle used a slingshot to shoot a bolt at an American woman, a friend of ours, while she was out walking with her husband and two young children, raising a great bruise. This incident, in addition to reports about the few Americans, high-level military and business officials, who had been killed in Iran, caused us some worry about our personal safety and that of our young child. Such experiences, plus the continual suspicion directed at us, had a detrimental effect on my research even after the situation had calmed down to some extent. I assumed a cautious approach, becoming immediately sensitive to any signs of hesitation in a potential informant.

Although my gender left me with the time-consuming "women's work" of caring for a child and household, and with less freedom for research, at this time, being a women was an advantage. Villagers were less concerned about my potential political harmfulness. I could continue to visit with my close female friends, who as women were also assumed to be apolitical. They were not suspected of collaboration but were rather seen as sympathetic and hospitable to the American woman in their midst. During these uncomfortable times, if a few days elapsed when I did not see the compassionate Rana, she would send her little daughter after me. (Sadly, when I returned in September 2003, after an absence of almost 24 years, this dear person was confined to bed and had trouble speaking; she had suffered a series of strokes.) Still welcome in several homes, I could at least sit and listen to conversations about ongoing national and local events. Driven to ask questions and take notes about something, I turned to customs. I asked women about their activities connected with life-cycle events and other social occasions and commemorations. Quite by accident, then, the major role of women in maintaining social relations, and thereby political alliances as well, was revealed to me.

Eventually, the letter Mohammad Amini had advised us to get was provided. I took it to Mr. Rohani, the visiting *mulla* (preacher, religious specialist) from Qom. The letter was posted in the mosque courtyard. Gradually, whether due to the letter or not, attitudes toward us began softening, and by the summer wedding season we had been reintegrated into village society and were invited guests at most marriage celebrations.

Some months later my Shiraz friend told me she had gone to the Islamic court, the Revolutionary Committee, and her uncle, an even more important religious figure than her father; no one was willing to sign a letter for the American woman researcher. Only her father could be persuaded to do this. As he handed her the letter, she told me, he said, "You know what a chance I'm taking, don't you?" I'm grateful to him and others who helped me stay in Aliabad for another ten months of research after February 11.

A second crisis occurred in early fall of 1979. Karima, who was now two, and I took a trip to Mahabad and Sanandaj in the Kurdish area of Iran. I thought it would be beneficial to get some idea about Sunni[10] attitudes toward the Revolution and Ayatollah Khomeini. Because I had lived in Mahabad for two years as a Peace Corps volunteer 12 years earlier, it was also an opportunity to see old friends. The Kurds as well as other ethnic groups had risen up against the government. Ayatollah Khomeini declared *jehad*, holy war, against the Kurds. He ordered a major government attack on Sanandaj on August 19, 1979, two days after I ended my two-week visit to Kurdistan. The army began its siege against Mahabad on August 20, 1979, and on September 3, took over this largest Iranian Kurdish city. Then the government began executing many Kurds. When villagers in Aliabad found out I had been in the Kurdish area, many of them jumped to the conclusion that I had been there as a CIA agent to signal the beginning of the Kurdish revolt. Their reasoning was not surprising as the government radio, TV and press often repeated that the CIA had instigated the "problems" in Kurdistan, to disrupt the revolutionary government and bring back the Shah as the British and the American CIA had done in 1953. I was again unable to conduct much research for two or three weeks, until this suspicion died down.

A third point of difficulty in conducting research occurred after radical students took over the American Embassy in Tehran on November 4, 1979, and seized 66 Americans as hostages. Government propaganda against America again began to have an effect. Although villagers did not change in their courtesy toward me, suspicion persisted. At a dinner celebrating the return from Mecca of a *haji*,[11] someone asked when I was leaving. A young woman, a relative of the haji now living in Shiraz, said quietly, "They'll let her know before they start bombing, and that's when she'll leave."

If villagers were not rude, fewer people were willing to talk openly with me. Toward the end of my stay I was relying almost entirely on close friends to provide me with information on the very interesting political events taking place in the village.

Several of the radically anti-American young men in Aliabad were apparently spreading rumors that I was working as a spy for the local landlord. Although pleased to have me present taking photos during the takeover of Seyyid Ibn Ali Askari's land on November 2, 1979, later on participants feared I would show the photos to the Askaris to identify those who had joined in this activity. Leaders of the village-level "revolution" were reluctant to discuss their strategies and activities in the battle against the landlord and his supporters. Although I was actually sympathetic to the local uprising, this problem was compounded by the fact that I had lived in the courtyard of Seyyid Ibn Ali's brother, Seyyid Yaqub, during the first half of my stay.

At the same time, by then I was not on good terms with Seyyid Yaqub and his family. Now that contact with Americans had become a political liability instead of an advantage, his son Seyyid Muslem and Muslem's wife, Mina, were not cordial to us as they had been before the Revolution. Just as for others, their association with us could only be detrimental to them at this point. As the local conflict escalated, some of Seyyid Ibn Ali's relatives developed resentment against me because of my apparent lack of sympathy for him. I did continue to occasionally visit several of the Askari women and others supporting the Askari faction, thereby leaving myself open to being called a spy by both sides, just as would anyone else who visited people on both sides of this local conflict.

People had to be concerned about their own reputations and standing in the view of others should they associate with me. Even those who trusted my motives feared divulging information and attitudes to me in case I would unknowingly or accidentally jeopardize their safety and welfare by passing on such information to other villagers or persons in authority. Ever since I had first lived in Iran in 1966, I had observed Iranians to be wisely cautious about revealing their political attitudes. Discussion of politics did become amazingly open in Iran during the few months before and after February 11, 1979. Many Iranians subsequently paid for their candor with their lives. This atmosphere of fear, insecurity and suspicion shaped my research procedures far more effectively than any plans of my own. From the beginning of my stay in Aliabad, I acted with restraint, leaving many questions unasked. Throughout, I felt almost like a human barometer, constantly evaluating the atmosphere for the current pressure of suspicion before making decisions about what subjects could be covered and what questions could be asked. I did not attempt a census, surveys or maps. My one attempt to use a questionnaire, about practices for celebrating the birthday of the Hidden Imam,[12] was unsuccessful. In answer to my questions about who did what and what amounts of money were involved, my prospective informant gave noncommittal, vague responses such as "whoever felt like doing it" and "whatever amount of money people felt like spending." He clearly did not want to give me any specific answers, even on such a seemingly innocuous subject.

Use of a tape recorder was likewise inappropriate. As reluctance to allow interviews to be recorded was obvious, most often I did not even ask. Once early in the research I did ask and was given permission, but during the discussion I sensed that the informant did not wish to touch on sensitive issues. He talked about vineyard tending practices. Somehow, Seyyid Yaqub Askari learned of the recording session and jocularly asked me to play the tape because, he said, it would be fun to hear how the man's voice sounded. As the man had made no incriminating comments, and refusing would cast suspicion on him, I played it. Later I learned that this informant had lost all of his agricultural land to the Askaris during the conflict described in Chapter 2 and that he was "retired" and unable to work because of psychological problems, probably a nervous breakdown and depression resulting from his failed struggle against the Askaris. This incident provided an illustration of why villagers were cautious about voicing their grievances and especially did not want interviews to be recorded. An exception was when I was given permission to tape a lengthy interview, quoted in Chapter 5, with Seyyid Mostafa Askari about the 1978 Tasua and Ashura demonstrations.

My research was relatively undirected and relied mainly on the traditional anthropological techniques of participant observation and informal, unstructured interviewing. At some points I felt the only way I could collect information was merely to take part in or listen to ongoing conversation, with no attempt to ask questions or even nudge the subject of conversation. Instead of using a questionnaire approach and gathering information from a large number of people, I used a small circle of informants who trusted me and I gathered case material and information on a large area of related subjects. To check the material, I asked the same questions of as many people as possible and elicited descriptions of incidents from several people, often members of divergent factions.

Also because of the sensitive conditions, I was not able to travel much, to go to government offices for information or visit research institutes and utilize the work of Iranian social scientists. It seemed best to stay right in the village as much as possible and avoid calling outsiders' attention to myself.

In spite of the strain, uncertainty and difficulties of conducting field research during this turbulent period, it proved to be a valuable and memorable experience and the most fascinating 18 months of my life. A Shirazi friend wrote to her sister in the United States, "You missed the best year of your life!" Observing the dedication, respect for others, selflessness, cooperation and unity displayed during the months of revolutionary fervor and the optimism and joy shown during revolutionary marches left an impact not entirely removed by subsequent developments.

I am grateful for the courtesy and kindness of Iranians toward me and my daughter, Karima, a lone American woman and child-in-arms, even while we were shopping near the American Embassy in December 1979, several weeks after radical students took 66 Americans hostage, before we left for the United States. (Karima's father had left in July 1979.) When, against the advice of friends, I replied truthfully to inquiries from strangers in Shiraz or Tehran about my nationality, the usual response was, "Oh, we like Americans. It's just their government we don't like." Back in the States, I could not help but note the contrast when I saw the great anger of many Americans directed against hapless Iranian students. Apparently Americans did not distinguish people from their government as easily as most Iranians did. During my visits between 2003 and 2008 as well, Iranians, even those who didn't know me, showed hospitality to and delighted interest in an American.

To protect anonymity, the names of village residents, the research site and neighboring villages are fictitious.

In the interest of easier reading, diacritical marks are not used. I have transcribed Persian words and names into English according to the way they are commonly spelled or the way they sound if not found often in English writing. Persian language words used often, such as *kadkhoda*, are left un-italicized after introduction and are included in the glossary.

Acknowledgments

MY GREATEST DEBT is to the residents of Aliabad who have shared their lives with me, allowing me to live in their midst during an anti-American revolution and generously giving me friendship and assistance. The people of Aliabad—and revolutionary Iran—provided me with some of my closest friendships and more gripping fieldwork experiences than most anthropologists enjoy. Since 1966, many other Iranians inside and outside Iran have taught and befriended me. Even today, my ever-present goal is to get back to Aliabad.

I would like to thank the following organizations for research and write-up funding: the Social Science Research Council and the American Council of Learned Societies for a research fellowship from June 1978 to December 1979 and a write-up fellowship from February 1980 to July 1980, the State University of New York at Binghamton for a write-up fellowship from September 1980 to January 1981, the Program in Southwest Asian and North African Studies of the State University of New York at Binghamton for a FLAS Assistantship award from August 1984 to June 1985, the American Association of University Women for an Educational Foundation Fellowship from July 1985 to July 1986, the National Endowment for Humanities for Summer Stipends in 1987 and 2012, and the American Institute of Iranian Studies and my own institution, Santa Clara University, for funding another six and a half months of research in Iran between 2003 and 2008. The conclusions, opinions and other statements in this book are those of the author and not necessarily those of any of these sources of funding.

Several people have read sections of or even the whole manuscript, offered suggestions and criticisms or helped in other significant ways: Ervand Abrahamian, Janet Afary, Richard Antoun, Bill Beeman, Anne Betteridge, Jane Curry, Laura Ellingson, Sima Fahid, Sue Frey, Erika Friedl, Steven Gelber, Jean Hegland, Patricia Higgins, Nikki Keddie, Agnes Loeffler, George Westermark and Ashraf Zahedi. Pat Higgins applied her anthropological and editorial expertise to the entire manuscript. Many improvements are due to her hard work. Remarkable Stanford University Press editor Kate Wahl, editorial assistant Frances Malcolm, production staff Patricia Myers and Judith Hibbard, cartographer William Nelson, and the rest of the Stanford team have provided excellent advice and assistance. My closest colleague, Erika Friedl, has—as always—been a great friend, advisor and editor. I am especially grateful for encouragement and direction from the late Richard Antoun, an excellent guide, humanist and friend.

Without the support of my parents, Margaret and Norval Hegland; my brother, Paul Hegland; his wife, Kristen Puckett; and my sister, Ruth Hegland, this book might well not have been written. Paul and Kristen gave me a year at their home during which I wrote half of the manuscript. My parents provided me with an adventurous and tenacious spirit, sustaining moral support and a computer.

The chairs of the Department of Anthropology at Santa Clara University, George Westermark and Lisa Kealhofer, provided support beyond the call of duty. So many people have helped, encouraged and inspired me along the way. I am grateful to all of them.

Cast of Characters

Names used for villagers, as well as for the fieldwork site and surrounding villages, are pseudonyms.

Seyyid Ayyub Askari   The old and, by 1978–1979, poor, formal head of the Askari taifeh.

Ezzat   Wife of Seyyid Ayyub Askari.

Seyyid Ayatollah Askari   Son of Seyyid Ayyub Askari; shopkeeper; one of the village peacemakers.[1]

Seyyid Ali Askari   Son of Seyyid Ayyub; guard at the gravel pit.

Akhtar Askari   Wife of Seyyid Ali.

Seyyid Morteza Askari   Son of Seyyid Ali; supported the peasants or people's faction against his father's cousin, Seyyid Ibn Ali.

Seyyid Kazem Askari   Son of Seyyid Ayyub Askari; gifted political analyst; usually unemployed, apparently due to back problems.

Seyyid Mostafa Askari   Son of Seyyid Ayyub Askari; often away from the village on his job with the Office of Malaria Control.

Sakineh Askari   Younger daughter of Seyyid Ayyub Askari.

Seyyid Ibn Ali Askari   Son of a deceased brother of Seyyid Ayyub Askari; richest and most influential person from Aliabad; became largest landowner of the village when he bought village land before land reform; lived in Shiraz in 1978–1979.

Seyyid Yaqub Askari   Brother's son of Seyyid Ayyub Askari and Seyyid Ibn Ali Askari's brother; *de facto* head of the village and main government representative in Aliabad.

Rezvan   Wife of Seyyid Yaqub Askari; not a native of Aliabad.

Seyyid Muslem Askari   Son of Seyyid Yaqub Askari; important figure in village politics and economics.

Mina Amini   Wife of Seyyid Muslem Askari and daughter of Mashd Yusef Amini.

Haj Ali Reza Amini   Son of deceased sister of Seyyid Ayyub Askari and Mashd Yusef Amini's brother; right-hand man of the Askari brothers.

Mashd Yusef Amini   Brother to Haj Ali Reza Amini and an important supporter of the Askari brothers.

Mohammad Amini   Son of Mashd Yusef Amini; teacher and important young leader of the revolutionary movement in the village.

Naser Amini   Son of Mashd Yusef Amini and Mohammad Amini's brother; policeman in Shiraz; married to daughter of the kadkhoda, Hamid Jehangiri; important supporter of the Askari brothers.

Haj Aqa Amini   Another brother of Haj Ali Reza and Mashd Yusef Amini; supporter of the Askari brothers.[2]

Fatimeh Askari   Daughter of a deceased brother of Seyyid Ayyub; sister of Askari brothers Seyyid Ibn Ali and Seyyid Yaqub.

Roqayeh Askari   Younger daughter of Fatimeh Askari.

Ehteram Askari   Daughter of a deceased daughter of Fatimeh Askari.

Jafar Askari   Younger son of Fatimeh Askari.

Seyyid Enayat Askari   older son of Fatimeh Askari.

Rana Askari   Wife of Seyyid Enayat Askari; leader of the social circle of seyyid women.

Seyyid Asadollah   Seyyid Ibn Ali Askari's and Seyyid Yaqub Askari's brother; in charge of Askari gasoline pump and natural gas installation controlled by the Askari brothers.

Seyyid Rahman Askari   Son of another deceased brother of Seyyid Ayyub Askari; employed as guard in gravel pit partially owned by Seyyid Ibn Ali and his supporter during the post-Revolution uprising against him.

Seyyid Akbar Askari   Distant relative of the Askari brothers; was a shoemaker and trader; began working for a nearby factory in 1979; capitulated to pressure from the anti-Ibn Ali faction, including his wife's father, and joined their side.

Seyyid Husein Askari   Local mulla; distant relative of the Askari brothers though he did not have much contact with them.

Haidar Amini   Son-in-law and former partner of Seyyid Ayyub Askari; trader and former sharecropper.

Behnam Amini   Son of Haidar Amini; employee of the Office of Electricity in Shiraz.

Hushang Amini   Son of Haidar Amini; accepted at Tehran University but returned to Aliabad during university strikes in support of the Revolution.

Kurosh (Cyrus) Amini   Son of Haidar Amini's brother; revolutionary leader among the local young men; stabbed in a crucial local incident before the Revolution; married Haidar Amini's only daughter.

Mohsein Saedi   Son of Kurosh Amini's mother's brother; also wounded in the knifing incident.

Mehdi   Married to the sister of Kurosh Amini and his assailant in the knifing incident.

Haj Khodabakhsh   Shopkeeper and husband of Ali Reza's and Mashd Yusef Amini's sister as well as their supporter; brother of Mehdi's mother.

Shaikh Karim Kazemi   Leading religious figure and head of pro-Mosaddeq and pro-Tudeh sympathizers in Aliabad; died not long after the Mosaddeq period in the 1950s.

Shaikh Rahim Kazemi   Son of Shaikh Karim Kazemi; not actually a Shaikh but a retired school teacher who, with his father, was active in supporting Mosaddeq; important figure in pro-revolutionary village activity; initially perhaps the main leader in the local movement against Seyyid Ibn Ali some months after the Revolution.

Haj Manuchehr Zamani   Last kadkhoda before the 1962 land reform; lived in Shiraz in 1978–1979.

Mulla Jamshid Ajami   Former kadkhoda; died shortly before 1978.

Haj Ali Hemmat Hashemi   Important leader of the pro-Mosaddeq movement in the village; lost his land during the peasant strike; called upon to perform religious functions in the village; important leader in the movement against Seyyid Ibn Ali after the Revolution.

Haj Sadrollah Hashemi   Owner of successful local construction company; supporter of the revolutionary movement and the post-Revolution movement against Seyyid Ibn Ali.

Haj Fazlollah Rezai   Trader from a family that fought against the Askaris during the land reform struggles; active supporter of the Revolution and a leader in the anti-Seyyid Ibn Ali movement after the Revolution.

Haj Baqer Rezai   Died during the land reform struggle. Though his death was accidental, the Rezais blamed Seyyid Ibn Ali Askari. According to villagers, the continuing bitter enmity of the Rezais toward the Askaris was due to Haj Baqer's death—that and land.

Esmat Ajami   Seamstress and young widow; her in-laws, the Saedis, were active in the land reform struggle and leaders in the post-Revolution movement against Seyyid Ibn Ali; articulate supporter of the Revolution and the anti-Seyyid Ibn Ali faction; the author's closest friend in Aliabad.

Haj Hamdullah Saedi   Brother-in-law of Esmat Ajami; from the Saedi family active in the land reform struggle and post-Revolution movement against Seyyid Ibn Ali.

Hamid Jehangiri   Kadkhoda during the fieldwork period.

Majid Jafari   From a family active in the struggle against Seyyid Ibn Ali during the land reform conflict; refused to join the movement against Seyyid Ibn Ali after the Revolution because his wife was related to him.

Mashd Musa Saedi   From a family active in the land reform resistance against Seyyid Ibn Ali; has since joined the village administration as a member of the village council and president of the cooperative.

Chronology of Significant Events

Important regional and national events are indicated in **bold**.

1800s   After first taking it on as a tax farm, the Qavams take over owner-ship of Aliabad.

1946   Seyyid Yaqub Askari is appointed bailiff, main agent of the land-lord in Aliabad.

1946   Tudeh Party representatives come to Aliabad.

August 1953   Prime Minister Mosaddeq is overthrown in a British and American CIA-sponsored coup. The Shah, who had fled, is brought back to Iran under British and American sponsorship.
     Pro-Mosaddeq and pro-Tudeh Party people in Aliabad are pun-ished for their support of the ousted Prime Minister Mosaddeq by beatings, humiliation, imprisonment and in at least in one case, exile.

1950s   The peasant strike occurs in Aliabad.

1958   Government officials attempt to seize Seyyid Ibn Ali Askari's large stash of opium in Aliabad.

1962   Implementation of land reform in Aliabad instigates peasant struggles against Seyyid Ibn Ali Askari.

August 10, 1978   Massacre by government forces at the New Mosque and other disturbances occur in Shiraz.

September 8, 1978   Martial law is imposed in Shiraz and other cities.

November 20, 1978   Massacre occurs at Habib Mosque in Shiraz.

December 7, 1978   Stone throwing is directed by Seyyid Yaqub Askari against a convoy of vehicles carrying mourners to a town farther up the valley.

December 8, 1978   Pro-Khomeini Kurosh Amini is stabbed by his brother-in-law Mehdi, followed by people marching and shouting "Death to the Shah" in Aliabad for the first time.

December 10, 1978   Tasua, anniversary of the eve of the martyrdom of Imam Husein, is commemorated with a large revolutionary march in Shiraz.

December 11, 1978   Many village men go to the large Ashura march in Shiraz, then return in a group to the Aliabad mosque.

January 5, 1979   The informal group of seyyid women initiate nightly marches against the Shah's government in Aliabad.

January 16, 1979   The Shah leaves the country.

February 1, 1979   Ayatollah Khomeini arrives in Tehran.

February 11, 1979   The government of the Shah and Prime Minister Bakhtiar falls. Mehdi and his supporters assault Kurosh Amini's stepfather-uncle.

March 21, 1979   On this Noruz (New Year's Day), no one visits Seyyid Yaqub Askari, demonstrating the decline in his influence.

March 30–31, 1979   A national referendum is held on whether to institute an Islamic Republic government, with possible votes of yes or no. The government reports the results as ⊤% in favor.

April 1, 1979   Ayatollah Khomeini declares Iran the Islamic Republic of Iran.

May 14, 1979   Seyyid Yaqub Askari's son Seyyid Muslem is attacked by the younger brother of Fazlollah Rezai, who goes unpunished.

October 2, 1979   Seyyid Ibn Ali Askari attempts to divide up some Aliabad land among "needy" villagers who are actually his own relatives and supporters.

October 6, 1979   Seyyid Ibn Ali Askari is imprisoned due to pressure by villagers. He is released four days later.

October 11, 1979   Seyyid Ibn Ali Askari is put back in prison after demonstrations and outraged protest by villagers.

November 2, 1979   Seyyid Ibn Ali Askari's land is taken over and planted by the peasant faction.

November 4, 1979   The American embassy is occupied by radical students, and American hostages are seized.

November 16, 1979   Several hundred members of the peasant faction clean out the ditch that brings irrigation water from Darab and are threatened by attack from residents of this neighboring village due to misinformation provided by Seyyid Yaqub Askari's faction. For the first time, there are opposition marches into Aliabad with people shouting slogans against the Askaris, followed by a violent confrontation and the subsequent arrest of some of the Askari faction by the gendarmes.

November 21, 1979   On this first day of the mourning month of Moharram, self-flagellation practices intensify in Aliabad.

November 28, 1979   Seyyid Ibn Ali Askari is again released from prison.

November 29, 1979   When villagers learn of the release of Seyyid Ibn Ali from prison, they drop their Tasua mourning commemorations to protest. Assured that he would be reincarcerated, they return from Shiraz to Aliabad late at night.

November 30, 1979   The opposition monopolizes Ashura commemoration activities in a forceful demonstration of political superiority. Upon conclusion of the mourning at noon, participants march to an orchard owned by Seyyid Ibn Ali Askari and tear down the walls, then return for feasts in three village homes sponsored by opposition sympathizers.

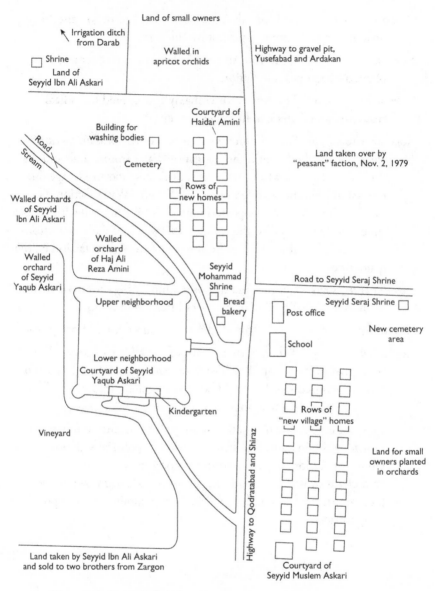

Land of small owners

Irrigation ditch from Darab

Shrine

Land of Seyyid Ibn Ali Askari

Walled in apricot orchids

Highway to gravel pit, Yusefabad and Ardakan

Road

Stream

Building for washing bodies

Cemetery

Courtyard of Haidar Amini

Rows of new homes

Land taken over by "peasant" faction, Nov. 2, 1979

Walled orchards of Seyyid Ibn Ali Askari

Walled orchard of Haj Ali Reza Amini

Walled orchard of Seyyid Yaqub Askari

Seyyid Mohammad Shrine

Road to Seyyid Seraj Shrine

Upper neighborhood

Bread bakery

Seyyid Seraj Shrine

Post office

New cemetery area

School

Lower neighborhood
Courtyard of Seyyid Yaqub Askari

Kindergarten

Rows of "new village" homes

Vineyard

Land for small owners planted in orchards

Highway to Qodratabad and Shiraz

Land taken by Seyyid Ibn Ali Askari and sold to two brothers from Zargon

Courtyard of Seyyid Muslem Askari

MAP 1. The walled village of Aliabad and its immediate environs, 1978–1979.

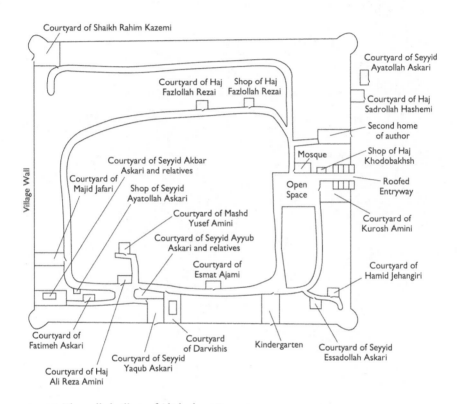

Courtyard of Shaikh Rahim Kazemi

Courtyard of Seyyid Ayatollah Askari

Courtyard of Haj Sadrollah Hashemi

Courtyard of Haj Fazlollah Rezai

Shop of Haj Fazlollah Rezai

Second home of author

Mosque

Shop of Haj Khodobakhsh

Village Wall

Courtyard of Seyyid Akbar Askari and relatives

Open Space

Roofed Entryway

Courtyard of Majid Jafari

Shop of Seyyid Ayatollah Askari

Courtyard of Mashd Yusef Amini

Courtyard of Kurosh Amini

Courtyard of Seyyid Ayyub Askari and relatives

Courtyard of Esmat Ajami

Courtyard of Hamid Jehangiri

Courtyard of Fatimeh Askari

Courtyard of Darvishis

Kindergarten

Courtyard of Seyyid Essadollah Askari

Courtyard of Haj Ali Reza Amini

Courtyard of Seyyid Yaqub Askari

MAP 2. The walled village of Aliabad, 1978–1979.

Introduction

A COMMON EXPLANATION for the 1979 Iranian Revolution was that "modernization" had proceeded too rapidly, that people had reacted against the changes related to modernization. Of course many Iranians, including religious figures, the conservative *bazaris* (shopkeepers, owners and wholesalers in the bazar) and the lower classes, did not like aspects of modernization promoted by the central government, such as women's European-style too-revealing clothing, lack of proper segregation between the sexes and the rule against girls and women wearing scarves or veils in schools and government workplaces. Mohammad Reza Shah Pahlavi seemed more interested in appearances, in a modern-looking style of living, than in real modernization in terms of more egalitarian and collaborative relationships in political process and other areas of life.[1] Many of the Shia clergy did not like their loss of power and the land reform they considered to be against Islamic law and that also made them lose sources of wealth.

I came to a different judgment about the connections between modernization and the Revolution.[2] Modernization led to the Revolution in other, more substantial ways. In the process of fieldwork in a community, while working closely with individuals, it was easy to see how the dynamics of economic and political change were related to people's decisions to join the revolutionary movement. I found that people were reacting not so much against modernization as against insufficient or uneven modernization. Why should other, richer Iranians have so much more of it than they did? Inequitable modernization kindled resentment.

Also, modernization in means of communication and transportation helped enable the Revolution. People could use literacy to write and read the ubiquitous graffiti and the revolutionary fliers. They could use loudspeakers to reach large audiences at shrines and mosques and demonstrations, cassette tapes and recorders to distribute revolutionary speeches, and radios and televisions to listen to foreign news broadcasts, especially the BBC. Roads and transportation could bring people from place to place, to talk and listen and demonstrate and march. Young people gathered with one another in schools and universities inside Iran and abroad and learned about other societies and political philosophies.

Modernization in the form of many new types of jobs, greatly improved transportation and communication, and expanding educational opportunities helped enable revolutionary action by freeing village people from the control of community representatives of the central government.[3] Villagers were no longer dependent upon local politicians for their livelihoods—for access to agricultural land—and thus were largely out of reach of their political control as well.

Modernization in the form of more effective means of force and control over the population also prevented kinship-based groups from organizing effectively. The central government could keep its local representatives in office rather than allow local contenders to fight it out and ratify the winner in office. Before land reform and the strengthening of the central government, community residents were able to have some effect on political administration, but without such a possibility, people found themselves unable to choose new local representatives, and their resentment could only grow. In the end, modernization of the armed forces, using them to quell dissention, resulted in the stifling of political action at the local level and therefore the diverting of political dissatisfaction to higher levels, leading ultimately to the rage and action against the Pahlavi regime.

Ultimately, a main reason for the Iranian Revolution was the *lack* of political modernization.[4] If political modernization had also taken place, if the central government had been more responsive to the population and allowed participation in government instead of using force to silence dissent, the Revolution might well have been avoided. Modernization, in the form of expanding and wielding against citizens the gendarmes (rural police), police, secret police (SAVAK) and armed forces, succeeded in damming up political action until resentment accumulated and gathered such force that it could overturn a regime. Also, in Aliabad, because of lack of political modernization and therefore lack of knowledge about alternative ways of approaching political process, villagers returned to their local *taifeh-keshi* (political competition and conflict among kinship-based factions), applying this political paradigm to the 1978–1979 revolutionary process.

A Taifeh-Keshi Struggle from Aliabad History

Shortly after I arrived in Aliabad, during the 1978 fall term, many Iranian university students and professors went on strike in support of the revolutionary movement against the government of Mohammad Reza Shah Pahlavi. Because the University of Tehran was basically closed, Hushang, son of Haidar Amini, came back from Tehran to Aliabad. He described to me a power struggle from village political history in which his family had been involved that had resulted in a change of *kadkhoda* (village headman). It may well have been the last time kinship-based factional conflict brought in a new kadkhoda in Aliabad.

A long time ago, before land reform, we had a fight with the Saedis over a little piece of land. It was when Mulla[5] Jamshid [Ajami] was kadkhoda. The Saedis were relatives of Mulla Jamshid because Mulla Jamshid's daughter was the wife of Haj Ali Panah Saedi, son of Haj Khodadad Saedi.[6] The Saedis thought that because the kadkhoda was on their side, they could do whatever they wanted.

One of my cousins, Am Aziz,[7] had placed stones around a piece of land that hadn't yet been planted to show that it was his. The Saedis wanted to take it. They claimed it was theirs.

One day Am Aziz was taking his cow out the village gate to give it water. Haj Khodadad Saedi's son hit Aziz and started a fight. Am Aziz left his cow there and went home to tell everyone. My father, Haidar—head of our *taifeh* [kinship-based political faction]—told everyone to get ready for a fight. Everyone went out. The fight was near Seyyid Rahim's shop.

We had a big taifeh. Mulla Jamshid had a large group too, and they helped the Saedis. A stone hit the back of Amu Ramazun's head. He fell down. My father— Haidar—shouted, "Bring him into the courtyard"—everyone was screaming that he'd been killed—"and then let's go and get revenge."

The fighting went on. My father gave Haj Khodadad a severe blow on the head with a cudgel, and he fell over.

The fight ended to our advantage. Our taifeh got the plot of land, for two reasons—one, because we were stronger, and two, because the right was on our side; we had put in the earlier claim. The Saedis thought that since they had the kadkhoda, and his taifeh was on their side, they'd be able to beat us.

The other side accepted Mulla Jamshid as kadkhoda, and our side supported Haj Manuchehr Zamani. Seyyid Ibn Ali Askari and Seyyid Yaqub Askari supported my father in this matter. Our side—Seyyid Ibn Ali, Seyyid Yaqub, Haj Manuchehr and so on—supported Arab, who was the landlord after all. [In formal terms, Asadollah Khan Arab Shaibani was not actually landlord. He was the agent, serving as intermediary with the kadkhodas, and husband of the absentee Qavam landlord, a female—Khanum Khorshid Kolah Qavam—who took over Aliabad from the previous Qavam family owner.][8]

After this incident, Arab invited everyone to the city and scolded and threatened Mulla Jamshid. He told him, "If you do this sort of thing again, I'll take over your land and kick you out of the village."

So this shows that Seyyid Ibn Ali and Seyyid Yaqub were on Arab's side, that the right was on our side and that Amu Aziz could cultivate that piece of land.

A person from Darab was sitting there too. Ali Panah, Mulla Jamshid's son-in-law, said to this Darabi, "We have more power than anyone else in Aliabad. We have so much power that we could even refuse Arab access to the village and refuse access to Seyyid Ibn Ali and Seyyid Yaqub—who are nothing compared with Arab, the landlord after all."

The people from Darab said back to him, "Then why did you lose?"

The night of the fight, the other side went to Arab and complained, saying, "There was a big fight, and they really beat up eight or nine of our people."

They went to complain, but when Arab found out that everyone realized the right was on the side of my father, he took our side.

Later on, Arab said to my father, "Have you opened a butcher shop?" He meant, "You've bloodied up *so* many people."

Another incident took place about a year later. A lot of rain had fallen and a large pool of water had collected in the open area just inside the village gate. The water was about to run into our courtyard. My father, Haidar, and my uncles who lived in the same courtyard decided to make a ditch through the gate passageway to the outside of the village to let the water out. Mulla Jamshid said, "If you dig a ditch, the water will get into the storage rooms lining the passageway."

At the time, the storage rooms were filled with Arab's wheat. But the rooms were one meter above the level of the road. Since the rooms were at a higher level, the water wouldn't reach them.

My father went ahead and dug the ditch. Mulla Jamshid wrote a long letter to Arab telling him about the situation and saying that the water was ruining his wheat. Arab sent for my father, who went to the city and explained to him that this wasn't the case. They planned to come to the village and together look into the matter.

FIGURE 1. Haidar Amini, head of the Amini taifeh, welcoming people to his home after returning from his pilgrimage to Mecca, fall 1979.

Arab came to the village. When he saw that the situation was not as Mulla Jamshid had written, he asked Mulla Jamshid, "Where is the key to the storeroom?"

Mulla Jamshid said, "At home."

Arab told him to send after the key. When the key was brought, Arab took it from Mulla Jamshid and gave it to Seyyid Yaqub. So Seyyid Yaqub became Arab's *ambardar,* his keeper of the grain storage rooms. Mulla Jamshid was finished. He was no longer kadkhoda. Haj Manuchehr became kadkhoda.

After I had lived in Aliabad longer and learned more about village politics, I could see how this story demonstrated many of the typical characteristics of conflict between kinship-based factions over power, position and resources.[9] In this story, as well as in other conversations, informants presented taifeh as the most significant political unit. Outbreaks between competing factions might be instigated by minor incidents or attempted encroachments on land. Members of the kadkhoda's taifeh felt entitled and people who enjoyed his backing acted with confidence. A large kinship group could make a strong faction, and in-law relations could cement political alliances. Belonging to a taifeh often meant reacting against any incursion or violence against the group, to demonstrate power. An outrageous act mobilized the taifeh, and violence prompted anger and determination for revenge. Taifeh members would attempt to demonstrate and persuade others of their power. The strongest group, the faction that won the fight, would gain access to village resources. Their taifeh head would be able to take over the position of kadkhoda, and with that, political power and control of village agricultural land. The winning side believed that justice was on its side; the victorious faction saw right and might as going together.

With the help of some gifted Aliabad political analysts, I continued to study taifeh and the taifeh-keshi political system during my research stay in Iran between June 1978 and December 1979. It was through taifeh-keshi, I learned, that political process took place in Aliabad while it was owned by the absentee Qavam landlord, before the 1962 land reform. (During the 1960s land reform in Iran, landlords were basically supposed to give up ownership of all but one or the equivalent of one village; the extremely powerful Qavam family lost ownership of Aliabad.) Through taifeh-keshi, villagers could try to bring about change in village administration, to improve conditions for themselves. Peasants who had become dissatisfied with a kadkhoda whom they judged too brutal, unjust and unresponsive could attempt to pull together a large taifeh, fight to get that kadkhoda out of office, and bring in a hopefully better substitute.[10] When I realized how much taifeh-keshi culture and political process, learned by Aliabad villagers through experiencing and hearing about taifeh-keshi, influenced their perceptions, decision making and actions regarding the 1978–1979 Iranian Revolution, I became all the more intrigued by taifeh and taifeh-keshi.

Researching a Revolution

When I went to live in Aliabad in late summer 1978, I was not prepared for the widespread use of the word *taifeh* and the taifeh worldview I encountered there. I didn't know that a system of taifeh-keshi had operated in the village. I was not even familiar with the word *taifeh,* except for a section of a tribal group. Anthropologists had done field research about lineage-based conflict over position and resources among tribal groups in Iran but had not focused on it in village settings.

I owe to my concern with village history and to the holistic nature of anthropology—the aim to learn as much as possible about various aspects of life in order to analyze how each might influence one's chosen subject—that I became aware of people's preoccupation with taifeh membership and balance of power and of how taifeh-keshi operated.[11] Then, as Aliabad people engaged with the revolutionary movement and later with the village-level uprising, taifeh terminology, concepts, expectations and process came into prominence in the village.

Because I conducted anthropological field research in Iran for 18 months during the 1978–1979 Revolution, I was able to study firsthand the transformations, events and cultural influences that led residents of Aliabad to become participants in the Revolution and in a local uprising nine months after the Revolution. Anthropological participant observation entails living in a community in close interaction with residents. The anthropologist participates in ongoing social life as much as possible. One observes action while listening to discussion of views and interpretations. Usually anthropologists work with regular people rather than with elites.

When studying a revolution, the motivations, interpretations and courses of action of grassroots people become of great interest; without masses of individuals interrelating with organizers, a revolution would not be possible. Researchers who focus on national and international politics or who interview only political elites may overlook the great significance of individual decision making and the influences on those decisions. Fieldwork entailing frequent contact with the same people over a long period allows concentration on the individuals who make up those masses. One can watch and listen as individuals come up against authority and power, and collect case stories of how they respond, along with interpretations of why. Surrounded by ongoing action in a community setting, it is easier to see connections and mergers between areas that otherwise might be thought of as distinct.

When living in a village and trying to grasp as much as possible about the total lives of persons, it is not simple to separate political activities out from the rest of life. One begins to see the political aspects of many types of behavior and relationships, and the connections between revolutionary action and other facets of life. I began to see how previously existing local political culture channeled national revolutionary action.

Through fieldwork, I was able to gather oral history about village conflicts and to observe taifeh-keshi culture in action when, during the period of relative anarchy before and after the Revolution, the village again saw local violent confrontations between kinship-based factions. I heard people talk about the two sides in the revolutionary conflict much as they would have talked about the two sides in a local conflict over the position of kadkhoda. I saw the stages of change in power in Aliabad during the revolutionary period follow the progressive stages characteristic of taifeh-keshi in the history of village strife. In fact, the process of the Revolution at the national level also fit into such a schedule of stages. Without the benefit of conducting anthropological fieldwork in an Iranian community, it probably would have been impossible to perceive the persistent influence of taifeh culture in people's local and national political understandings and activities.

Taifeh

Aliabad people used the term *taifeh* in many different contexts; the meaning was fluid. The most general meaning was any group with a common identity and interests. The clergy, for example, were considered a taifeh, as were policemen, the armed forces, and literacy, health and reconstruction and development corps. These groups wore the same clothing, were under the leadership of one person and had interests in common, villagers pointed out.

As an American, I was assumed to belong to the taifeh of Americans. Once, when a son of Haidar Amini was behaving abruptly with me, obviously suspecting me of working against the interests of Iran, probably with the CIA, his step-grandmother, Seyyid Ayyub's wife, Ezzat, asked him in an undertone, "Don't you like their taifeh?" The word *taifeh* always carried the connotation of an interest group and therefore of a group to one degree or another in competition with other groups, whether overtly or not.

A second meaning of *taifeh* was a faction or side in overt political competition or conflict with an opponent. People spoke about the struggle between Moaviyeh and Imam Husein in Shia history in terms of the taifeh of Moaviyeh and the taifeh of Imam Husein.[12] They discussed other conflicts in Shia history in similar fashion. The political activities of the Soviet Union and the United States were analyzed using references to typical taifeh strategy of Aliabad.

Within Aliabad itself the bipolar political factionalism was always spoken of in terms of conflict between two taifeh. People often said, "There are two taifeh in Aliabad," and went on to name them.[13] Often the conflict was seen as occurring between the upper and lower neighborhoods, especially before the 1962 land reform, or the two taifeh would be called by the names of their respective kadkhodas. After land reform, when the Askaris took over ownership of most village land, villagers talked in terms of the landlord taifeh and the peasant taifeh.[14]

People used the term *taifeh* to refer to any kinship group, large or small. It could refer to an extended family, consisting perhaps of a father and his sons and sons-in-law, or a group of several smaller kinship groups connected through either father or mother, or more likely both, as well as in-law relations and marriage ties. The term *taifeh* might be used to refer to a coalition of taifeh. During the land reform struggle, the peasant taifeh was actually composed of quite a few kinship groups.

Taifeh never meant simply a kinship category, a group of people connected merely by kinship ties, but always included the implication of interaction and association. If someone quarreled with his relatives and no longer associated with them, he was not included in the taifeh. Persons who moved away and no longer involved themselves with Aliabad relatives, associates and events were not considered taifeh members. On the other hand, work and political associates, as well as dependents such as wife and children, poor relatives, and people who worked for a taifeh head or member, were included in the taifeh.

While kinship always played a role in taifeh alignments, in the larger groupings close kinship ties naturally did not directly connect all of the members; a number of smaller, tighter groups with more direct kinship connections together formed a larger taifeh, but association or common identity and interest were relevant for both small and large taifeh groupings.

The term *taifeh-keshi* meant mobilizing a taifeh for action in political competition or conflict. It could refer to the drawing together of a taifeh for actual political struggle, generally over property—such as land, water, gardens and orchards—or political position or status, or for protection or revenge. The term could also mean keeping up kin and associational ties through active social interaction, hospitality, providing assistance of various types to others and maintaining control over some type of needed resource with the intent of maintaining a large group of supporters.

Taifeh were dynamic—they changed in composition as people joined or left, and in intensity as events transpired and people's level of passion and commitment heated up or dropped off. In 1978–1979, Aliabad people did not think of kinship as separate from politics. The denotation of *taifeh* as kinship groups, associational groups, and groups to which obligations of support and assistance were owed added pressure for unity of action and loyalty in political competition and conflict.

In contrast to societies in which people see factions as outside formal political process, disruptive and somehow inappropriate, Aliabad people did not see taifeh as outside the main culturally acceptable political process. They viewed taifeh-keshi not as irregular political activity but as *the* way to engage in politics. They used taifeh terminology and a taifeh narrative to talk about all types of interaction and alliances. *Taifeh* was a key metaphor, the lens through which they viewed the world, current and past, both their local world and political relations and events outside the village, up to the level of international politics. Through oral history, participant observation during conflict, interviewing, accounts of conflicts, and social interaction and conversations, I pieced together information about Aliabad taifeh-keshi culture and the process of changeover of power typical in Aliabad before governmental centralization and the 1960s land reform.

Taifeh-Keshi Political Process

Political process seemed to be carried out in eight stages. These stages also seemed to represent Aliabad people's expectations of political process and its results.[15]

1. *People work to develop useful ties.* Political effort continues, whether or not it is a period of outright confrontation. People think about

what type of ties are advisable, with whom, and at what level. They attempt to create, strengthen, curtail or eliminate ties according to their perceived usefulness. They live politically.

2. *A contender gathers resources.* A potential leader gains wealth and status and begins to build up a following. He mobilizes relatives, makes alliances through marriage, and tries to pull in supporters using a variety of strategies and connections.

3. *Clashes occur between the contender and the incumbent.* A series of clashes takes place between the upcoming political leader and his group and the incumbent and his group. Everyone follows the degree of success of the two parties.

4. *The incumbent performs an outrageous act.* The incumbent headman or someone in his group performs an outrageous act that becomes the last straw, the signal for all-out attack by the upcoming group and the rationalization for many previously acquiescent followers of the incumbent to shift to the other side.

5. *The opposition, outraged, grows in numbers and resolve.* The opposing leader and group are outraged to the extent that they are willing to do anything to get rid of the incumbent and his cohorts. They are no longer concerned about their own safety. Even people who heretofore have half-heartedly accepted the incumbent headman's leadership, although less firmly attached to him, become enraged at the incumbent's behavior. A large number of people simultaneously decide that obviously they cannot tolerate this evil leader and his faction, and they shift sides. The judgment about which act is outrageous and intolerable is actually influenced by calculation of trends in power balance.

6. *A final confrontation demonstrates the victory of the contender.* A battle or confrontation occurs that establishes the now overwhelming power and support for the contender—the new incumbent. His predecessor is routed from his position and from the area, or an act of aggression may occur and the *sangar* (fortification or entrenchment, the gathering or failure to gather of the respective sides) that follows indicates the respective levels of support and thus the relative political standing of the two leaders and their followers. The old incumbent may flee, along with his closest supporters. His property is taken and his skillfully constructed political faction is shattered. His

followers are prevented from taking unified political action. Control over ritual and public space is a means to demonstrate control, unity and victory, as well as the powerlessness of the formerly powerful incumbent and his following.

7. *The village is reunited under the new leader.* Others rush to join the side of the newly victorious leader. Supporters of the former leader attempt to attach themselves to the new order by mobilizing diverse ties. The village community comes together again under the new regime. Dissenters are quieted. Eventually, even the closest support-ers of the ousted leader will hold their peace and recognize the new leader, even if they are dissembling their actual displeasure. They may verbalize or act out rituals of deference to the victorious political contender. At some point, peacemakers may travel to the settlement where the old incumbent and his staunch allies are hiding out, if they had fled, and persuade them to return and join the community.

8. *People live politically, whether or not they are aware of it.* People are politically active in everyday life, in large, formal settings and in small, informal ways, creating, maintaining, strengthening, cur-tailing, eliminating, and putting on hold ties through networking, exchange and social interaction. They gather and disseminate infor-mation, participate in rituals of power and try to persuade others of their own viewpoint and the strength of their own leader and group.

Taifeh-Keshi:
A Cultural Model for Political Process

This book traces the processes of change in Aliabad from the early de-cades of the 20th century until December 1979, ten months after the Iranian Revolution, and then the changes apparent during 2003 and 2008. During the period before the Revolution, Aliabad had changed from a social unit where most residents were largely restricted politically to the community, to a settlement whose inhabitants could be involved as individuals in national politics. Earlier on, people had moved between villages, traders had traveled lesser and greater distances and some people at various levels of political and economic power had maintained connections with others outside the village setting. Before land reform in 1962, however, villagers were largely dependent on local-level politicians, kadkhodas and taifeh heads for access to a livelihood and protection. They were forced, therefore, into political support of such figures and were not free political agents. There was not much of an alternative to political acquiescence to a powerful figure, other than leaving to take up a similar relationship elsewhere.

My research suggests that economic transformation was a primary prerequisite for the emergence of villagers from the brutally repressive village political environment of the 1950s, 1960s and 1970s into eventual participation in the revolutionary struggle. While I see economic and political changes as pivotal in leading to the Revolution, I find such influences to be inadequate for explaining the course of the revolutionary movement.[16] Political culture must also be examined, as must how people's understandings, words and actions play out in the dynamics between political and economic transformation and aspects of political culture.

Political cultures—the models or paradigms in people's heads about how to understand and channel political action—are created through practice, through what people do.[17] Such a process might be compared with the way people make a path by walking along a certain course. Certain factors influence the course along which people walk from one location to another. After they have walked a certain way for some time, a path begins to be visible. The existence of the path then begins to influence the way people get from the one location to the other.

The approach taken in this book is that a people's ethos, worldview, values, expectations and behavior complexes regarding politics rise out of and are a reasonable response to real conditions as they see them, much the way understandable reasons influence the path people take—and therefore make—through a certain area. These values, expectations and behavior complexes then influence evaluations and channel ongoing events. Together they can be called *processual paradigms*—cultural models for behavior common in a society that serve to channel and order behavior regarding current situations and events, resulting in a typical process. Also, ongoing events are interpreted in the light of the existing processual paradigms.

Aspects of culture—in this case the processual paradigm of taifeh-keshi—are reproduced through practice,[18] my fieldwork in Aliabad showed. In Aliabad, people reproduced taifeh-keshi culture through acting it out; telling stories of past conflicts; staging performances such as weddings, religious rituals and "entrenchments"; socializing children;[19] conveying attitudes in informal chatting, commentary and admonishment; discussing several levels of political activity; and the structures, relationships and processes in other areas of life similar to those found in political life. I take the approach that people will continue to be guided in interpreting reality and in behavior by a specific ethos, worldview and processual paradigm—here the taifeh ethos and the processual paradigm of taifeh-keshi—until repeated experience persuades them of the greater usefulness of an alternative ethos and worldview.[20]

The processual paradigm of taifeh-keshi[21] is a cultural paradigm or model that served to influence interpretations and channel behavior related to political events so as to produce the typical process and stages of factional conflict. In Aliabad, people followed the taifeh-keshi processual paradigm according to whether or not it fit their circumstances,[22] and in pre–land reform Aliabad, as well as during the 1962 land reform conflict, it did.

An advantage of using participant observation to gather material about the enactment of cultural schema or processual paradigms is that one can also elicit commentary on why or why not and under what circumstances people follow a particular political paradigm. In the pages that follow, I show how people's connection with the taifeh-keshi processual paradigm changed with changing conditions. Many people were conscious of the changes, as well as conscious of the reasons for their own behavior and of the attempts of some to manipulate the paradigm for their own advantage. In the taifeh-keshi worldview, insecurity is rampant, a protector is required and political power is unreliable. People must work, therefore, to develop compelling ties with some degree of diversity, to enable them to mobilize alternative ties to shift to a new power holder when necessary. Because of the potential for modification in political power and political alliances, all social acts are the object of scrutiny and analysis as to their possible political portent. Social interaction becomes a chief means of demonstrating or modifying alliances and is thus the topic of careful observation and thoughtful discussion. Contenders struggle against each other for power and resources. A number of skirmishes generally culminate in a final confrontation. The winner takes all, and the loser is vanquished and his property and position are taken. Since he loses control, then, of resources, such as land and the means of protection, he is of little use to followers, who are left in the lurch. Thus, followers and dependents must be prepared to mobilize connections and shift to the side of the up-and-coming leader at just the right moment. People tend to change sides in a group, with a particular incident or confrontation signaling and explaining the move. There is no such thing as loyal opposition; everyone must adhere to the victorious leader and his outlook, or at the very least keep silent. After the shift in power, most people eventually become connected with the new politician. They feel forced to dissemble any private dissatisfaction in the interests of well-being of self and family, as well as access to resources and community membership, now monopolized by the new political personnel.

Taifeh-Keshi and the Iranian Revolution

A number of authors have pointed to the significance of Shia religious symbolism, rituals, organizations, leaders, and beliefs in providing structure and motivation for the Iranian Revolution. I have worked with this topic as well.[23] In this book, however, I focus my investigation on the local, secular political culture and paradigm of taifeh-keshi. A primary finding, to my surprise, was that most Aliabad villagers applied this same processual paradigm, which they had used in dealing with local factional politics, to the revolutionary struggle at the national level, for political conceptualization and decision making.

When I first came to this conclusion, I felt rather abashed, and indeed was criticized for paying attention to old-fashioned and outdated concepts, and for failing to recognize the dramatic revolutionary change that had taken place. Since then, other scholars have suggested the existence of some continuities in the revolutionary period and in post-Revolution Iranian government and society.[24] Another anthropologist, Agnes Loeffler, found traditional Iranian ideas and practices still in operation, in spite of Western influence, in the field of medicine in Iran.[25] Several other anthropological works have been published that demonstrate the resilience of cultural paradigms through periods of economic, political and social transformation.[26] The "basic structure of a culture" can remain relatively stable over time.[27]

During the course of the Iranian Revolution, most Aliabad villagers turned to Shia slogans, rhetoric, imagery, gatherings, religious leaders and rituals only *after* they had decided to support the revolutionary forces.[28] It was the political processual paradigm of taifeh-keshi with its related political symbols and culture, rather than a Shia framework, that motivated most villagers into action and channeled their behavior during the revolutionary period, as well as during the following uprising against Seyyid Ibn Ali Askari, the largest Aliabad landowner.

Before the empowerment of the Iranian government in the 1950s and 1960s using oil revenues to develop infrastructure and agents of force, and before land reform in the early 1960s, the Qavam landlords of Aliabad had allowed taifeh to fight over power and position in the village. The Qavams would then ratify the leader of the winning taifeh as their village kadkhoda in charge of the distribution of agricultural land, irrigation and collection of the landlord's share of the produce. A sensible policy for the Qavams, this process recruited the strongest taifeh leaders as the family's village representatives. The process also deflected dissatisfaction away from the landlord and toward the Qavams' local representatives. The system allowed for flexibility; when other men gained power in terms of resources and supporters, they could challenge incumbents and struggle to take over leadership in Aliabad. For villagers, the taifeh-keshi system meant they had a recourse; when enough people became dissatisfied enough with the kadkhoda—because of too much injustice, brutality and extraction of produce, and too little assistance—they could do something about it. They could throw support to another contender for office, and hopefully bring in another, more responsive kadkhoda. Local political power—the most significant influence on villagers' lives—depended on gathering the largest and strongest group of local supporters, and was therefore to a large degree subject to local influence.

The primary condition on which the operation of taifeh-keshi political process rests is a weak central government. Before the Iranian government gained the means, in the 1950s and 1960s, to rule directly in rural areas, then also during the chaotic period of the 1978–1979 Revolution and for some months afterward, the central government could not directly control the population and politics in many parts of the country, including Aliabad.

The central government's direct rule in the countryside that developed during the 1950s, 1960s and 1970s was based on its increased revenues. In 1951, the Iranian *Majles* (parliament) voted to nationalize Iranian oil and elected the leader of the effort, Mohammad Mosaddeq, as prime minister. The Anglo-Persian Oil Company—which later became the British Petroleum Company—had developed the southern Iranian oil fields after their discovery in 1908. The formal agreement for the oil concession, negotiated in 1901, had provided Persia[29] with only 16% of the profits, and Persia actually received less than this prior to the 1950s. Persian oil workers at the Abadan refinery, the largest in the world for half a century, lived under terrible conditions and received very low wages.[30]

After the vote to nationalize Iranian oil, the British persuaded the United States to join them to reverse this situation. The British and the

American CIA engineered a coup to get rid of Prime Minister Mosaddeq and bring Mohammad Reza Shah Pahlavi, who had left the country, back into power.[31] However, public pressure prevented them from reinstating the original agreement. While the British Anglo-Iranian Oil Company did get 40% of the shares in the newly formed National Iranian Oil Company, Iran was to receive 50% of the profits. Some of this increase in Iranian proceeds was put to use for dramatic infrastructure development and modernization projects, such as in education and health. Although modernization and access to its benefits were inequitable, oil money made better lives possible for many Iranians. Development could be seen in all areas of life—except the political.

In the political arena, democratization did not occur. Government was top-down, and citizens could not influence political structure and process. Rather, the government used force to maintain its power when persuasion was not enough. Assisted by the United States, which became very influential in Iran after the coup that put Mohammad Reza Shah back in power in 1953, Iran's government under the Shah also used the oil money to develop its military and other agents of internal political control: police, gendarmes and the notorious SAVAK. These oil profits therefore continued to serve the interests of England and the United States, who wanted a pro-American government in power to provide a base for their military and political influence in the Middle East.

Although development occurred more slowly in rural areas than in cities, and less among the lower classes than among the more advantaged, the government's modernization projects had an effect in Aliabad too. By the late 1970s, children were attending school in Aliabad. A few students went to high school in Shiraz, capital of the southwestern Iranian province of Fars. People could visit the health office in the village or see doctors in Shiraz. Many men had found jobs outside the village, made available by oil revenues directly or indirectly. People had electricity and natural gas and often piped cold water into their courtyards.

Along with improvements in living standards, however, villagers experienced the dark side of this oil-enabled development. The central government, by using the gendarmes stationed nearby, could enforce its rule in Aliabad directly. After several violent struggles to improve the situation in their village, people realized they could no longer influence local politics. In fact, local politics was no longer controlled locally. Resentment and dissatisfaction against the local political elite continued to build up, but people could do nothing about it; they were no match for the armed gendarmes. In any dispute, the de facto village boss and main government representative, Seyyid Yaqub Askari, could call on the gendarmes to stop any resistance.

By the time the revolutionary movement swelled in 1977 and 1978, a majority of Aliabad villagers were very dissatisfied with their local political elite—and they had realized that this dissatisfaction could be blamed on the national government, which backed this local political structure with its agents of force. They could not try to improve conditions for themselves through taifeh-keshi activity at the local level because the gendarmes would violently punish anyone who attempted to complain or resist the power of the Askaris and their associates. Instead, villagers applied their local taifeh-keshi political culture and locally learned political process to the national conflict between the Shah's forces and the revolutionary movement—the level they now realized determined conditions in Aliabad. Without any other political education or experience in a different kind of political system, most Aliabad villagers had only their own taifeh-keshi political culture to call on to understand the national revolutionary movement, make decisions regarding their potential participation, and channel their post-Revolution political action.

1

Historical Aliabad

BY NOW, Shiraz and Aliabad have both expanded so that they all but meet. In 1978, though, Aliabad was half an hour by bus, some 35 kilometers, from the outskirts of Shiraz. The city of Shiraz had been built up a ways out on the road leading to Aliabad, with lovely residential areas and then walled-in gardens and orchards as one traveled toward Qasr el-Dasht on the outskirts of the city. Buses loading up to go to Aliabad and other settlements in the same direction waited near the Qasr el-Dasht square until they were filled with passengers. People could do some last-minute shopping for fresh fruit and vegetables at the outdoor shops near the square, as well as for other items in nearby stores. When the bus was finally out of the city, the scenery turned plain, with dry stony ground between ranges of hills lining either side of the highway. The skyscrapers of the Hossainabad housing project just outside Shiraz, where several Aliabadis had found construction work, caught one's attention. Even in 1978, traffic was heavy, in part because of the presence of several factories between Shiraz and Aliabad. Large trucks sped along, bringing gravel to the city from the two gravel pits on Aliabad land. Moving further up the valley, one saw high rocky crags in the distance. The bus stopped at several factories to let off workers, who walked the rest of the distance off the main road to their work sites. The village of Qodratabad lay on the left, with its gendarmerie station not far off the paved highway, and then only two kilometers further on was Aliabad.

Aliabad

Aliabad is located in a valley that not many decades ago was populated by villages of riyat (sharecroppers). The province of Fars produced wheat, barley, rice, cotton, sugar beets, fruit, dates, legumes and vegetables. By 1870, opium had become an important crop, although its cultivation was banned in 1955. Grape varieties from the region were famous and included those used to produce Shiraz, Syrah and Sirah wines. As is much of Iran, Fars is arid and hot in the summer. Although dryland agriculture was also practiced in Aliabad and other villages in the area, irrigated land of course produced much more. Water sources were valuable and often the subject of contention. Before land reform in the 1960s, most of the area was under the control of the absentee Qavam family landlords. Cultivation was carried out by means of animal and human power, with produce divided between landlord and peasants. The riyat and their families in Aliabad and the other villages in the region lived in what would be seen by middle-class Western eyes as severe poverty.[1] Modern roads and transportation, education and health facilities, plumbing, electricity, and natural gas for heating and cook- ing came to Aliabad only in the 1950s and 1960s, although this was sooner than in many other Iranian villages. Animal products were also significant in the regional economy, both for villagers and even more so for nomadic tribal groups, who shepherded their flocks up and down mountain slopes depending on the season. People of Aliabad and other villages in the area interacted with the various tribal groups making their home in Fars prov- ince, such as Qashqai and Lurs, as trading partners, political allies or victims of bandits preying on itinerant traders walking between villages, or even of large tribal groups taking over control of the village before political central- ization in the 1950s and 1960s.

When I approached Aliabad, a village of about 3,000 people, for the first time in 1978, I could see several rows of new houses and their court- yards, with construction still proceeding on new additions, to the right of the highway. On the left stood the high-walled, square-shaped old village with a tower rising up at each of its four corners. The bus stopped near the entrance to the old village, where quite a few men and boys generally sat enjoying the sun and the opportunity to catch up on village affairs and news from Shiraz. A few vehicles in various stages of repair and several shops, such as a "coffee house,"[2] welding shop, motor repair shop and bread bakery, as well as an old, rundown shrine, were just outside the vil- lage gate. Further on, just past the village wall, another small residential area had been built some seven or eight years earlier. The village cemetery and the little building for washing bodies before burial lay to its left. On the right side of the highway, just past the large residential area with its rows of recently built homes, were several government buildings: health center, post office and school. Beyond these and further away from the highway lay the main shrine of the village, Seyyid Seraj,[3] with a little road providing access and surrounded by another, smaller cemetery.

Anyone entering the village gate would first go through a passageway lined on either side by four or five rooms, each with a corrugated metal door pulled down and padlocked. Prior to land reform, these rooms were used to store the grain produced in the village before it was transported to the landlord in Shiraz, and to keep seed for the following year. The rooms were also used as a prison for recalcitrant peasants. Just inside the passageway, large Pepsi and Coca-Cola signs marked two or three minimal grocery shops edging the large, open area. Here men often gathered to sit in the sun and talk. The mosque courtyard lay just to the right of this square. Leading off this open area were several little alleyways. The main one formed a

FIGURE 2. Men and boys hanging out in the large open area just inside the entrance to the walled village of Aliabad. The sunshade of Haj Khodabakhsh's shop (see Chapter 5) is on the left, and the entrance to Kurosh Amini's courtyard (see Chapters 4 and 5) is to the right of the village entrance. Photo from 1978–1979.

circle around the village. Subsidiary alleys branched off from the main alley to give access to all homes. A small ditch for disposing of waste water ran through the center of each alley. Walking through the alleyways, one could catch glimpses through courtyard doors of activity within, such as women washing dishes or clothes at the courtyard water spigot.

Although the "new village" homes across the highway were built of fine-looking fired brick, homes in the old village were constructed of sun-dried mudbrick plastered with mud. The color of the mud-covered buildings together with the dusty, plain appearance of the alleyways gave a drab look to the interior of the village. I remember watching dirt and scraps of paper tossed up by wind gusts and feeling rather dismayed at the thought of living there for a year and a half.

Several Aliabad residents told me the history of the settlement. It had been decimated by the Mongol invasion in the 13th century. Over time, people—many from the surrounding areas—immigrated in and out. According to local historians, at some points it contained some 8,000 households. For the last 200 years, people told me, Aliabad had been a large village and an important political, market, cultural and religious center. Persons trained in religion and religious law who had long ago emigrated from Bahrain to Aliabad had directed the mosque and Qoranic school. Aliabad, along with most other villages in the Shiraz area, became the tax farm of the Qavam family of Shiraz, though not without some resistance, villagers told me.

Later, many tax farmers—the government tax-collectors of agricultural areas—took over as their own private property the villages from which they were supposed to collect tax revenue for the government.[4] In Aliabad too, the head of the Qavam family was able to take ownership by force. Stories have been passed down of men tied up and beaten or taken to Shiraz and put in chains in the Qavam effort to gain possession of the village. In Aliabad, this process apparently took place 100 years or more before my 1978–1979 fieldwork.

Informants talked about the great power of the Qavams and how for some hundred and fifty years the current head of the Qavam family had controlled the regions of Darab[5] and Fasa and acted as the "shah" of the region from Shiraz to Bandar Abbas. They owned at least 50 villages similar to Aliabad, people reported. According to one informant, there had been three "shahs" in the region: Qavam, Qashqai and Shaikh.[6]

Reza Shah—the father of Mohammad Reza Shah Pahlavi—who ruled Iran from 1925 to 1941, wanted to cut back the power of such regional political figures and bring the country under centralized political control. In the 1930s, Reza Shah abolished the office of mayor of Shiraz, held by Ibrahim Khan Qavam, who had controlled Aliabad. Ibrahim and his family were exiled to Tehran for a time,[7] as was the head of the Qashqai tribespeople, Solat ed-Doleh Qashqai. One complaint against Ibrahim Qavam was that he acted like an independent power and cooperated too closely with the English. Later, though, he regained the favor of the central government, which was concerned about Qashqai power in Fars. Ibrahim Qavam was appointed governor-general of Fars in 1943 and provided with rifles to distribute among the Khamseh tribesmen.[8] At some point, Aliabad was given over to Khanum Khorshid Kolah Qavam, sister of Ibrahim Qavam and daughter of Habibollah Qavam ol-Molk.

The villagers of the next village, Darab, could relate even more vivid tales about the period several decades after the Qavams took over ownership of Aliabad, when Nazem ol-Molk, Khanum Khorshid Kolah's husband at the time, came with a retinue and tented outside Darab. Nazem ol-Molk wanted to forcefully take over ownership of his tax farm. The struggle continued for some time in Darab, with members of the Qavam family, Nazem ol-Molk and his wife, Khanum Khorshid Kolah, attempting to use internal factionalism and gaining the support of a poorer group who owned no land or orchards to obtain control of Darab. The members of this minority faction were willing to cooperate with the Qavam outsiders in the struggle against the dominant faction. They hoped thereby to serve their own interests through taking over as the socioeconomic and political village elite. Sometime between 1935 and 1938, a number of Darab villagers were killed, and Khanum Khorshid Kolah was able to appoint a kadkhoda and a bailiff and enforce the giving of one-sixth of dryland crops and one quarter of irrigated crops to her as landlord. But the matter was not settled conclusively, and for another 30 years or so the conflict continued, with eruptions of violence every few years.

After Nazem ol-Molk died, Khanum Khorshid Kolah married Asadollah Khan Arab Shaibani—"Arab"—who had been the Qavams' bailiff for Aliabad.[9] The Qavams owned the large building in Aliabad that housed the government kindergarten in 1978–1979. When Khanum Khorshid Kolah came to Aliabad for a visit accompanied by a retinue of some thirty horsemen, she stayed in that building. Seyyid Ibn Ali Askari, who became the largest landowner in Aliabad after land reform, later bought this building from the Qavams. Seyyid Ibn Ali lived there with his family until the hostility of other villagers during the 1962 land reform conflict forced him to move to Shiraz. Khanum Khorshid Kolah also owned the house and court-yard that in 1978–1979 was home to Seyyid Ibn Ali's brother, Seyyid Yaqub Askari. Together the two brothers controlled village affairs, with Seyyid Ibn Ali residing in Shiraz, before the Iranian Revolution of February 1979.

Before the 1950s and 1960s, half or more of the working force of Aliabad, at least 200 men, engaged primarily in agriculture. Another 200 villagers worked primarily in trade. Others filled the specialties required by the local population, such as carpenter, shepherd, bath attendant, bar-ber, blacksmith, guard of the vineyards, guard of the fields and religious specialist. Ten or more men were shoemakers, sewing the tough, hand-made shoes with crocheted cotton uppers and leather—later rubber tire—soles worn by villagers and especially valued by migrating tribespeople because of their durability. Only some ten men practiced migrant labor, journeying to Abadan to work for extended periods in the oil industry. Women were not expected to work outside the domestic environment but kept busy in their own courtyards. Agricultural families kept animals, and women took responsibility for them in the courtyard, feeding chickens and milking goats, sheep and cows, as well as preparing milk products and preserving other foods. Widows were often forced to work to support themselves and their children and might go out to camps of migrating tribespeople to trade.

Khanum Khorshid Kolah continued to be the owner of Aliabad until land reform in 1962. Ibrahim Qavam died in 1969.[10] His two sons, Ali and Mohammad Reza, and his daughters lived in Tehran in 1978. Khanum Khorshid Kolah died in the early 1970s. Her husband Arab Shaibani, who had also served as her agent, died at about the same time. Although the former landlords of Aliabad were no longer in the picture when I came in late summer 1978, their ownership of Aliabad and the taifeh-keshi political system in operation during their time were recent enough that oral history interviews could shed light on them.

Political anthropology had become one of my main interests before I went to Aliabad for field research. To study political anthropology, which typically deals with local politics and the connections between national and local politics, I should talk with men, I assumed. I owe it to the revo-lutionary turmoil and to periods when, with few exceptions, men would not talk with me—a suspect American in their midst—that I was forced to start asking women about their activities and observing their interactions with others, and began to realize the unique roles women played in politics. I questioned them about engagements, weddings, cooking and distributing food in the name of holy figures, mourning ceremonies, women's visits and gifts when a daughter became pregnant and then gave birth, and women's many other formal and informal visits and exchanges. Through observation and asking questions, I became aware of women's lively socializing and networking, which helped keep political alliances active, and of the close relationships between women and their families of origin— which could provide men with more political clout to protect people and resources, as well as alternative alliances in case men deemed it best to shift allegiance to another coalition of taifeh. Then, when taifeh-keshi emerged again during the revolutionary upheaval, I was better prepared to understand the parts of both men and women. Men's and boys' public actions of violence were more visible and dramatic—and resulted in outrage and extensive discussion. Women's part in politics was less apparent but went on as part of everyday social life before, during and after eruptions. Without being sensitized to the political aspects of women's lives, I might well have overlooked a crucial part of taifeh-keshi politics in village history—political relations through women and women's political work—and then in the Revolution and the post-Revolution local uprising.[11]

Bilateral Kinship and Political Alternatives in Aliabad Taifeh-Keshi

Much of the flexibility of taifeh and the ability of men to shift from one taifeh to another to best serve their own and their families' interests was based on the bilateral kinship system: in Aliabad as elsewhere in Iran,[12] children are considered equally related to their mother's and father's families. The nuclear family is primary, and a woman is considered to be a member of her husband's household rather than her father's. Beyond the nuclear family, almost equal importance is placed on ties through both men and women, rather than only on patrilateral (through the father) kinship.

In Aliabad, matrilateral (through the mother) and affinal (in-law) ties held weight: in-laws were called relatives. Wedding celebrations were held at the home of the bride as well as at the home of the groom, indicating the significance of the bride's family in social and political alliances.

In form (or rather lack of fixed form), the Aliabad taifeh system resembled the kinship system commonly found in other Iranian communities, urban as well as rural, which is characterized by indefinite boundaries, alternative ties, leadership yet interaction among members, flexibility and fluctuation. Ties with new allies could be cemented and turned into moral ties through intermarriage. Indeed, the taifeh system was largely based on the kinship system.

In form, the Iranian kinship system resembles kindreds, or networks of people tied together by a variety of kin, marriage and associational ties rather than bounded, corporate lineages. The system is fluid, enabling people to activate, mobilize and modify relationships as they see fit, therefore allowing individuals choice and alternatives in political alliance.[13]

Although both the taifeh system and the kinship system were largely based on actual bilateral and affinal (in-law) kin relationships, people could be brought into the taifeh through other means. Kinship relations could be initiated through marriage. In addition to kinship ties, there was also an almost institutionalized intimacy in ties of personal friendship.[14] Kinship-like relationships could be formed through close friendship, fictive kinship, intense social interaction or the institution of partnership. Partnership, physical proximity, previous association, assistance rendered and common identification, such as sharing seyyid identity and defending justice, could be used to align people with one's group and add moral imperative to political alliance, or to recruit for political alliance. Under conditions where a personal relationship was seen as the only means to obtain protection, justice, and important resources or political support and allegiance, every effort was spent on utilizing moral relationships for transactional ends and imbuing transactional relationships with moral tones.[15]

Interaction, sentiment and proximity were more important in a relationship than actual degree of kinship. Kinship relationships might be cut off by terminating association. They did not carry fixed rights and obligations, beyond the pressure on parents to get their children married off to appropriate spouses.[16]

Lack of kinship boundaries and the extensive reach of bilateral kinship networks were related to the great importance placed on relationships through women and ties with in-laws. Kinship was calculated along lines of association rather than actual kinship relationships. Included in kinship groups were friends, associates and in-laws. Other researchers have also noted the flexibility of the Iranian kinship system and the possibility of diluting or magnifying the significance of ties and providing a multitude of ties and alternatives among which to choose.

The bilateral Iranian kinship system of reckoning kinship through both male and female lines offered a variety of potential ties to a person who wanted to shift affiliation to another faction. Because of the emphasis on bilateral kin and in-laws, political relations through women were of great significance. Aliabad women, through extensive social interaction, handled much of the work of maintaining ties with extended kin and keeping open the possibility of mobilizing alternative kin ties in case shifting alliance became desirable.

The Politics of Visiting

A crucial characteristic of a taifeh, one that informants invariably mentioned, was the extensive social interaction (*raft-o-amad*—going and coming, visiting) among members.[17] Taifeh members formed a social as well as a political group. As one informant succinctly put it, "A taifeh means a group of ten or twenty people who sit together [implying they spend their time together, visiting in each other's homes]. In playing and in fighting, they are together. If a fight comes, they help each other."

The amount of interaction and the related attitude of obligation between people affected political behavior. People frequently referred to the importance of social interaction for relationships in comments such as "Neighbors are better than anything, even better than father and mother."

The intensity of social interaction and consequent feelings of empathy, generalized obligation and warmth affected relationships among families and relatives as much as or more than actual biological connection. One woman described kinship gradations as follows:

Qom [relatives, kin] means having good raft-o-amad and being concerned. Like the Askaris. If Seyyid Ibn Ali is unhappy, they are unhappy. *Ham famil* [being related] means just saying hello and how are you in the alleyways of the village, but not having raft-o-amad. *Famil vabasteh* [distant relatives] are even further away. Like Seyyid Jafar and the others. Their hearts don't burn for Seyyid Ibn Ali.

In defining gradations of kin, this woman used interaction, warmth and degree of concern rather than the criteria of biological kinship. A kinship relationship, through father, mother or an in-law, did carry implications for political behavior. However, a mere kinship tie was insufficient for political support, according to villagers; social interaction and reciprocity were perceived as also necessary to encourage loyalty and helpfulness.[18]

A kinship relationship and social intimacy together formed an important pressure on political activity.

Just as in the case of kinship relations, acquired intimacy with an unrelated person also brought with it restrictions on political behavior. Friendships, business associations and special favors carried implications for political activity, especially if social interaction was a part of the relationship. Seyyid Enayat Askari, father of a girl working at the carpet workshop in Aliabad, said he felt unable to help organize a strike at the workshop because he was friends with the workshop supervisor and his wife, Rana, was friendly with the supervisor's wife.[19]

Because villagers assumed that raft-o-amad was an indication of political influence and alliance, they were sensitive to obligations of social interaction and to lapses or changes in social interaction. Attendance at or failure to attend social functions as well as informal visiting indicated the current state of relationships. People watched visiting closely and discussed it at length. Political figures and others were acutely aware of who came to see them and who did not, who attended their rituals and gatherings and who did not. Intense social interaction did not guarantee support. Alliances changed over time and with the subject of contention, but heavy social interaction increased the likelihood, commitment and duration of support. People looked at social interaction as a strategy for maintaining, modifying, and gaining political relations.

Recruitment to Taifeh

In addition to increasing social interaction, recruitment to taifeh for the purpose of building strength for possible political conflict or mobilizing for fighting was similar to the means of recruitment to political alliances mentioned by Reinhold Loeffler for the Boir Ahmad, a tribal group not many hours away from Aliabad, "force, co-optation, ingratiation, marriage ties, dependency relationships, and the demonstration to the others of one's own political assets."[20]

One means of recruiting support for one's own taifeh and diminishing support for the opposing taifeh was to practice psychological warfare. One such strategy was a show of strength and force in numbers during occasions such as weddings, funerals and other gatherings. Especially dramatic were the noisy processions, complete with women singing wedding ditties, chanting wedding couplets and shouting and ululating while bringing the bride from her family home to the groom's family home on the wedding night. Such a display of strength and solidarity was especially ostentatious when the bride was from another village. I observed one such wedding in summer 1979. The groom's party made special efforts to cause an uproar when going through the alleyways of their own village, Aliabad, at the outset of the trip, when entering the bride's village some hours away and leaving it later, and then when arriving back at the groom's village. Honking vehicle horns accompanied their singing and sometimes the beating of drums. Just before reaching the bride's village and once again before entering the groom's village, vehicles in the front of the procession paused until all had arrived, in order to enter the village en masse for the greatest effect possible.

Another strategy of psychological warfare entailed committing acts of violence against members of the opposing taifeh, especially its leaders, or attempting to persuade others that violence had been committed. At least one leader of a taifeh had been killed within the memory of village informants. The life of yet another had been threatened. Less drastically, a person could fail to demonstrate the expected tokens of acquiescence or respect to a political leader. These steps would be taken in hopes of demonstrating that a faction was unable to protect its members, retaliate or provoke the fear necessary to elicit demonstrations of respect.

People were anxious to get revenge. Unless they took action following violence against one of them, members of a taifeh feared, other people would suspect they were weak and take further advantage of them. In fear of losing status and prestige, persons who felt slighted by an inadequate show of respect complained. To recruit and keep taifeh members, leaders had to get revenge and enforce shows of respect.

To recruit or to encourage long-term loyalty, people attempted to imbue relationships with a moral overtone, thus arousing feelings of duty, obligation and loyalty, and discouraging protests, complaints and oppositional political activity.[21] Political leaders in Aliabad attempted to elicit political loyalty in their followers by pointing out kinship and in-law relationships, mutual identity as seyyids, mutual adherence to Shia neighborhood relationships, former loyalties, and obligation because of assistance or favors rendered. They attempted to build up feelings of unity and closeness through sponsoring and mutual participation in ritual. They attempted to gain legitimacy and thereby political deference through donations given for the martyred Shia imams. Other recruitment strategies included force, intimidation, violent confrontation, maintaining control over means to a living, and the "politics of hospitality."[22]

Rituals of Deference:
Accepting Hospitality to Demonstrate Loyalty

In a central means of recruiting and maintaining support, taifeh leaders received followers in their homes, extending to them hospitality of tea, smoking, food and religious entertainment.[23] People commented, "One must spend money and give to the people so they will be supporters."[24]

High attendance at weddings and other occasions, such as return of a pilgrim from Mecca, demonstrated political and economic strength.[25] When the son of Mashd Musa Saedi was married in summer 1979,[26] attendance was high; even many people from Shiraz and associates from other villages came to show their respect. Esmat Ajami, an in-law of Mashd Musa, remarked to me,

Mashd Musa is one of the *bozorgha* [most influential men] of the village. He's a member of the village council. He goes to everyone else's weddings. Now it's his turn and everyone went to his. One courtyard was for men, one for women, one for the cooking and one for all of the people from Konfiruz.

People went even without invitation. No women were invited, but if a husband or brother got invited, the women went too, to show respect.

When my relatives get married, everyone in the village goes, not just their own relatives, because they are the big people of the village.

Beyond attendance at weddings and the extravagance and length of the celebration, the amount of money received as gifts indicated prestige and political and economic strength. A main topic of conversation after a wedding concerned the amount of gift money received and how it compared with the gift money of other weddings of the season and of previous years. Detailed discussion and analysis centered on the food served, its amount and quality, eating arrangements and other aspects of wedding parties.

In addition to the demonstration of prestige and political and economic strength that indicated the advisability of continuing to be or becoming a supporter of a person, hospitality facilitated recruitment and maintenance of political support by providing needed material support. Some people were to a degree dependent upon the assistance received through hospitality and gifts of food or other materials. They thus contin-

ued to support the provider of this assistance through need for its continuation. Others might not be particularly dependent upon the hospitality
received but would be dependent upon the political leader for access to
means to a living, for protection, or for other types of assistance. For these
people, acceptance of hospitality was symbolic of dependence, subservience, respect and loyalty. Acceptance of hospitality in hopes of receiving
access to valued resources or protection, or just through needing the assistance of that hospitality, incurred debts and obligations to support the
leader in political struggle and to speak well of the leader in public. In
Aliabad, accepting unreciprocated hospitality symbolized accepting the
obligation of uncritical loyalty as well as political support.[27]

A political leader could tell if someone would support him in political struggle through raft-o-amad, by what a person said about him in public and by behavior toward him, whether or not it was respectful, pleasant,
warm and concerned, according to informants. Since people who accepted
hospitality from a political leader were expected to support him politically,
only persons who needed such hospitality or were in other ways dependent
upon the leader would consent to receiving unreciprocated hospitality.

The acceptance of hospitality, visiting at the home of a political
leader and engaging in social interaction with a political leader symbolized political support because these activities implied that the relationship
between leader and follower was a personal, moral one rather than a purely
business or political one. Friendship and emotional and social closeness
were assumed to be involved, or at least there was the pretense that they
were involved.

Of course hospitality was not only a tactic for gaining and maintaining political support but also a culturally valued activity. Decisions
and actions can stem from complex motivation. Political leaders may have
desired political influence and economic well-being, but they also sought
prestige, the respect of their fellow men and the fulfillment of family and
kinship obligations and culturally valued criteria for behavior. Followers
could also have mixed attitudes toward the leaders on whom they were dependent. They might deeply resent arbitrary and brutal actions by the patron and their own positions of subservience but would admire the ability
of their patron to practice hospitality, sponsor religious rituals and instill
fear and deference in others.[28]

The intertwining of respect for providing culturally valued hospitality and sponsorship of religious rituals with power and economic

domination encouraged an attitude of generalized reciprocity and obligation, including the extension of political loyalty.[29] Social interaction and sharing in events of happiness and sadness, eating together, talking together and expressing concern and interest in one another's problems and daily lives all served to create feelings of closeness, unity and mutual concern, or at least the semblance of such. The more social interaction occurred, the more close, dear and warm the relationship was assumed to be, and the greater was the obligation to assist during times of political conflict. Also, if one got help from someone, one was obliged to interact with them and share in their joys and sorrows. As one villager pointed out, "If someone helps us [and one might also say if one hopes that someone will help us], we must share in their sorrow and their joy."[30] All of these obligations would be a good reason to avoid accepting assistance if at all possible. But during the Qavam period, Aliabad villagers did not see it as possible.

Villagers accepted hospitality to fill empty stomachs, but also to fulfill requirements of demonstrating allegiance. The main ritual of fealty occurred on the Iranian New Year, or *Noruz,* March 21. In Aliabad, political and economic realities had required sharecroppers and others who needed support from those of higher status—for protection and access to means of livelihood—to make Noruz visits as an indication of dependence and political loyalty. During the Qavam period, peasants were required to attend the New Year's celebration at the home of the kadkhoda as a token of political loyalty, dependence and subservience. Even in 1978–1979, the Noruz rituals of deference still stood out in many people's minds, as the following quotes from quite a few individuals show:

My father, Mohammad Khan, was kadkhoda. It was the time of guns and horses. He had 10 to 20 servants. The whole area was under him. At Noruz he had maybe 100 *man* [about 300 kilos] of rice cooked.[31] People came here and ate. People brought eggs, lump sugar and lambs for the kadkhoda. (A son of Mohammad Khan Darvishi, deceased former kadkhoda)

They would cook 20 or 30 *man* of rice for Noruz. The night before Noruz, they didn't go to sleep at all. They just cooked—seven or eight huge kettles of rice. They had lots of servants. Men came in groups to eat at the kadkhoda's house. Four days before Noruz, the bathhouse manager cooked 400 eggs, dyed them different colors and brought them to the kadkhoda. People brought him money too. (A daughter of Mohammad Khan Darvishi)

At Noruz, people cooked from one to ten *man* of sweet bread. The kadkhoda made a lot, because he had to give some to everybody. In the morning, all of the men got together—especially all the sharecroppers and agricultural workers. It was a requirement for them. If other people didn't go, it wasn't so important. But the kadkhoda was the peasants' superior. They had to go so if they had some problems or business with him later, he would remember and help them. A 100 or 200 men, enough to fill two or three rooms, ate at the kadkhoda's house. Women didn't go unless they were relatives. They gave out sweet bread to take home to the kids.

First people went to the kadkhoda's house. Then they took the kadkhoda to Seyyid Yaqub's house. Then they took Seyyid Yaqub and all went to Seyyid Ayyub's house, for example. (Esmat Ajami, relative of Mulla Jamshid Ajami, a deceased kadkhoda)

Everybody in Aliabad came to our house on Noruz. We put on a huge meal, fruit, *sharbat* [drinks made from fruit syrups] and so on. People came, ate, offered their congratulations and then left. (Rezvan, wife of Seyyid Yaqub)

Women and Their Families of Origin

The political importance of relationships through women is related to the strategy and the perceived political effectiveness of hospitality and raft-o-amad. Much of the work of social interaction and the politics of hospitality was left to women, who generally wished to spend much of this time and effort maintaining connections with their own families.

Although after marriage a woman was considered a member of her husband's household, not her father's, women normally retained a close relationship with their own family of origin. They continued to interact with their own family on a regular basis and had feelings of empathy and concern for them. Women were far more active socially than men, keeping up ties with relatives through frequent visiting and reciprocity, women asserted. Women of course preferred their own families, so the relationship of a nuclear family with the wife's relatives could be closer than the relationship with the husband's relatives. Since political alliance was related to intensity of social interaction and feelings of warmth, closeness and obligation, it is easy to see why relationships through mother or wife were important for politics. Women gave reasons such as the following for why a family interacted socially more with the mother's relatives:

When someone is kinder than other people, it is natural that you have more raft-o-amad with them. We see more of a mother's brother than a father's brother, because the mother's brother is more empathetic and concerned about us. A mother's brother asks about his sister's children, but a father's brother doesn't ask about his brother's children. A father's brother isn't kind. He's cold and indifferent.

A person likes his mother's family more than his father's family because they are kinder to him. So of course he has more raft-o-amad with them. He doesn't have much raft-o-amad with his father's family. Women do more raft-o-amad. So when a sister goes to see her brother, he feels obligated to return the visit. Men don't visit as often, but when they do, they feel obligated to visit sisters because sisters have come to see them. And we see sisters more often than brothers. Brothers don't have much to do with each other.

Women hold relatives together. And the relatives of the mother help more than the relatives of the father.

Another woman gave this explanation for closer relations with the mother's kin:

There is more social interaction with closer relatives. We have more to do with the mother's brother and the mother's sister and the mother's mother than with the father's sister because we are closer relatives with them. We are closer to the relatives of our mother. We go to see the mother's brother, who lives closer. Seyyid Rahim lives just at the gateway of the village. We go to his house and he comes to ours more often than the other mother's brothers. Another reason we go there more often is because our mother's mother lives with him, so we go to see her, and also because we have fought with the other mother's brothers. The wives of the other mother's brothers are bad, so we don't go to see them.

Our mother's relatives are dearer than our father's relatives, so we like them more.[32]

As a female I was expected to spend time with women and I felt more comfortable interacting with women. Especially right after the Revolution, when men became hesitant to spend time with the Americans, I was thrown into women's company. I could see for myself many reasons why women were closer to their own relatives and why these ties held great political significance, not all of which were articulated by villagers.

Brothers felt some pressure to take responsibility for their sisters. As this included responsibility for their modesty, it could sometimes cause trouble. But in the absence of parents, a brother should provide the required set of household equipment for his sister to get married. Although according to Islamic law daughters should receive an inheritance from the father equal to half of a brother's, this did not happen. Sons received all of the inheritance from their fathers, because supposedly a brother would care for his sister if her husband died. In any case, sisters and brothers often felt attached to each other. Adult sisters frequently did favors for their brothers or prepared food for them, I noticed.[33] Such attachments meant that a wife might be able to pull her brother in to assist her husband's taifeh, or a brother might be able to bring his sister's husband's taifeh in to support his.

Daughters were often very attached to their mothers. From an early age, girls' activities were much more restricted than boys' and they were expected to be at home much more than boys. Even in 1978, when girls were able to go to school for a few years, their school attendance generally came to an end at about puberty, and then they stayed home. Girls were expected to help their mothers,[34] and worked with them on various tasks throughout the day or performed them under the mother's direction. Girls learned their work from their mothers.

In 1978–1979, girls were generally married at about age 14, 15 or 16—and in earlier years even sooner than that—when they were still children in some ways and wanted to be close to their mothers. Interaction between a mother and a married daughter was accepted by custom and did not cause adverse comment or gossip. One 18-year-old woman who had been married four years went to her mother's courtyard every day, taking her wash or other work, and spent the day there, returning home only to cook dinner before her husband came from Shiraz after work. It was customary for a daughter to visit for a week or two at her natal home shortly after the wedding. Such visits were made in all cases of which I am aware during my fieldwork. Outside the constant companionship of other women in the courtyard—due to proximity—the most intense social interaction was often between mother and daughter.[35]

Women in Aliabad all did the same kind of work. Female relatives could help each other by exchanging services or working together cooperatively on a task. Women sometimes turned to their mothers or other female relatives for assistance in child care. One woman admitted that an important reason she had more to do with the people in her own natal family's courtyard than with her husband's relatives was the assistance she could get there in caring for her children. "It's close," she said, "and there are quite a few girls there who can help me with the children."

Much of the interaction involved in maintaining social relationships was related to cooking and distribution of food, such as stews and soups of various kinds. Women, of course, did the cooking, with women relatives often gathering to help a person make a stew. The girls of the family, sometimes with help from the women, distributed bowls of stew to various households of relatives. (Sometimes boys helped too.) Most often, at those households women rather than men were present to receive the stew. Many of the life-cycle events celebrated with gatherings, distribution of food and gifts concerned women rather than men and were thus occasions for women's social interaction, especially among female relatives. Because they generally felt closer to their own relatives than to their husband's relatives, women spent a disproportionate amount of their socializing time interacting with their own family of origin and relatives, if they could manage to do so given their responsibilities and the necessity of their husband's permission.

Political Alliances Through Women

Because of the importance of social interaction in political relations and the close relationships women usually had with their own kin, in-laws could be important political allies. Marriage was a common strategy for reinforcing political and economic ties. Such marriage alliances were generally the result of decisions and associations of men. Marriage alliances provided men alternatives and choices in deciding which faction or leader to follow. Relations through marriage provided a valid excuse for joining another faction or refraining from support or political activity. But such marriages could also exert severe pressure on a man to follow one political course or another. A wife and in-laws could be effective political agents.

Two or three decades before my fieldwork, sons-in-law and fathers-in-law had special obligations to each other. A son-in-law especially was required to serve his father-in-law and assist him in any way requested. In the words of one informant,

Before, the bride's father could order the groom to do anything: to bring him charcoal in winter, harvest wheat, provide him with flour. Whatever fruit the groom had, he had to give to his fiancée's father. He had to give him a lot so he could distribute it to the whole family. When there wasn't any fruit in season, he had to give his father-in-law bread. Now it isn't like that anymore.

In the past, the father-in-law had to invite the son-in-law and give him sweets and nuts and do something in return. Then, whatever work the fiancée's father had, he was required to call for the groom, who was required to do it, because he wanted to marry his daughter.

The groom was his father-in-law's servant.[36]

Pressure on a groom generally declined once he had actually married and gotten the bride home with him. By 1978, with hierarchies loosening up, no one would have characterized the relationship of a son-in-law to a father-in-law as being that of a servant. Still, one could discern pressure to assist a father-in-law. Social pressure and fear of damaging one's own reputation discouraged men from complaining about their fathers-in-law, taking them to court or fighting against them in political factionalism. This was the case with Haidar Amini, who did not take action against his father-in-law in spite of being cheated by him. "All of his livelihood was in the hands of Seyyid Ayyub," his sons explained. Long ago, Seyyid Ayyub had procured a government trading monopoly for Haidar and was important to his economic situation in other ways. As Seyyid Ayyub was then probably among the most powerful persons in Aliabad, Haidar was hesitant to antagonize him by complaining about ill treatment. As marriages were generally contracted with political or economic associates, the norms for behavior between son-in-law and father-in-law served in practice to reinforce such political and economic associations; a son-in-law might also feel obligated to a father-in-law because of political or economic dependence, as well as social pressure.

In contrast, an appropriate marriage might be contracted between families belonging to different factions. Finding an attractive, pleasant, responsible and well-off spouse for one's children constituted a serious responsibility and duty for parents. A young person from a family belonging to an opposing faction might be the best choice for a son or daughter. A tie with another faction could prove to be politically advantageous, a choice in case of conflict and a graceful and acceptable reason for changing sides or getting out of supporting one's own faction. A man could blame it on his wife's father.

A couple of decades before my fieldwork there had been some cooperation among male relatives in agriculture or trading. Even then men had very often worked alone or with a partner who was not a close relative. Even such cooperation as had existed became less frequent as more men became employed outside these two economic sectors. Interaction among male relatives declined. In explaining the decreasing importance and cohesiveness of the family taifeh of male relatives, men frequently cited the changing occupational structure.

Even interaction between fathers and sons declined. Several decades earlier, boys learned to make their livelihoods in trading and agriculture from their fathers. In 1978 this was becoming far less so. In 1978–1979, boys went to school or otherwise prepared for work outside the village rather than agriculture or trading. Most boys expected to earn their living in the urban labor market, where fathers' instruction would be of little use. Women, however, continued their social interaction with one another.

The social expectation that women should stay close to home meant women, concerned about earning the reputation of being immodest gadabouts, limited their social interaction to women of their own or neighboring courtyards and close relatives outside their own immediate neighborhood. Women generally interacted most frequently with other women in their own courtyard, who often were their husbands' relatives. They carried on much of their household work outside their own rooms. They washed clothes and dishes and prepared food near the single courtyard water spigot shared by the families living in the courtyard. During their working hours and while relaxing in the sun, knitting, crocheting cotton uppers for handmade shoes or eating fruit in season, women enjoyed the companionship of other women in their own or neighboring courtyards.

Women were ashamed to go elsewhere, to go to a courtyard they had not previously visited or where no close relative lived. Daily social interaction of women, then, tended to be restricted to fewer people—neighbors and relatives—than social interaction of men. Men interacted with more people, but on a less frequent and less intimate basis.[37]

Women were commonly believed to be more sympathetic and concerned about others and their misfortunes. It was assumed that women would respond to the needs of others with emotional and material help and other forms of assistance more readily than men. Women were expected to be more willing to assist kin and even to respond to misfortunes of nonrelated persons. In cases of tragedy, more women rushed to the involved courtyard and stayed longer. For example, when a young man of the village, Kurosh Amini, suffered a life-threatening knife wound in a local conflict two months before the final day of the Revolution, more women than men were present in his courtyard, weeping and screaming to express their support and sorrow.

Women had more opportunity than men to socialize with others in Aliabad because, with few exceptions, they were not employed outside the home. Elite women and women whose male family members were traders or worked in Shiraz were especially freer from economically related responsibilities than women whose male family members were riyat. Traders' wives didn't have to help with the animals or process animal products. Even peasant women assisted in the care of animals only while the animals were in the courtyard. Elite women especially were able to engage in the intensive round of social obligations required to keep up social relationships and maintain political alliances. As one woman said,

Women have more time for social interaction than men do. They are relatively idle. Women have much more social interaction and many more social obligations. Women go to mourning gatherings much more and sit longer. Men do less of that. For weddings, women go to help a week or so before the wedding. Men do some cooking to help at the weddings of relatives, but less than women.

Women do the cooking and distributing of food on different occasions, and women go to help with the cooking, tea and smoking pipes when there is a death. Women make noodle soup on the third day after someone goes on a trip. Like yesterday, Mohammad's mother made noodle soup for her husband's departure for Mecca. On Thursday afternoons women go to the cemetery. Men don't go so much. On holy days and anniversaries of the deaths of imams or relatives, women go to the graveyard, but men don't go.

In 1978–1979, most men worked outside the village for much of the day in nearby factories or Shiraz. They became friends with their workmates. They could interact with other village men, sitting in the sun near the village gateway or roaming around within the village walls or in the surrounding countryside.

Women attended religious feasts of close relatives only, whereas men of any social standing attended feasts of most other village men. Unrelated men were invited to the meals that followed the return of a haji from Mecca, but only related women attended. Differences between men's and women's social interaction became apparent during weddings. Explaining why only her husband was attending a certain village wedding, a friend stated, "Women go to the weddings of relatives only, but men also go to the weddings of friends. Men become friends with each other out in the village alleyways."

Women were so much more socially active in the village than men that people commented, "Women hold the family together. The reputation of a family depends on its women—because women know each other." While the great majority of men worked outside the village, whether in agriculture, trading, factories, or construction or in Shiraz, women stayed in the village, engaged in social interaction with relatives and other female associates—the interaction so crucial to political alliance.

Women's Political Work

Women did most of the work of kinship,[38] the hospitality and raft-o-amad so central to political process, and performed other crucial tasks in the kinship-based taifeh-keshi political system as well. Through their networks and groups, women played central roles in information gathering, communicating, connecting and persuading, to protect their families and relatives' interests and well-being, promote justice and maintain taifeh and community harmony. Assumed to be more sympathetic than men, women carried out the emotional work of community-level factionalism. In case of strife within the village or threat or injury to a taifeh member, women reacted in distress. They rushed to the courtyard of the person affected or to their taifeh head, weeping and wailing, screaming, beating their chests, perhaps tearing their hair out, scratching their cheeks and moaning or shouting out the injustice, the terribleness of the crime, the dearness and uprightness of the person affected and angrily criticizing those responsible. They tried to find out the details about the conflict, shared their knowledge and comforted the female members of the immediate family and other female relatives of the injured person. In general, women hoped for peace, as conflict could potentially result in injury to their menfolk, but they also supported the interests of their taifeh and attempted to promote their faction's reputation, cohesion and interpretation of the incident.

During tense moments of factional conflict, men ceased interacting with those on the opposite side of the conflict even if they were relatives or in-laws. Mourning ceremonies for men were generally cancelled during periods of political conflict, especially if they involved men from both sides of the dispute. Villagers assumed that only men were political actors. While in the presence of women from the opposite faction during fights, women told me, they avoided talking about the controversy or claimed to be unconcerned. "What do the fights of men have to do with us women?" they would comment, or "We aren't on one side or the other," "What good does it do to fight," or "We're all relatives, so why should we fight?"[39] Women could disclaim involvement in current tense political conflict and therefore maintain contact and interaction with women, relatives or otherwise, belonging to the opposite faction and then later facilitate mending of relations.

People obtained and maintained membership in a kinship-based faction through repetitive social interaction with the faction head's family and other faction members. Men were away pursuing economic activities and not available for such time-consuming social interaction. It was left to women to manage the complicated, intensive rounds of social interaction needed to demonstrate and strengthen political alliances. Maintaining the necessary political position in village political conflict and competition was the work of a two-person team.[40] The wife kept up the sociopolitical connections so the husband could take his place in the strategy and support meetings of the kinship-based factions and the acknowledged public political roles of violent confrontation.

Women were in charge of the day-to-day care of their families, of both physical and emotional needs, and of the maintenance of the family's position in the network of sociopolitical relations. Women felt very heavily the responsibility to care for and protect their family members. The emotional bonds between them and other family members were usually profound. Their feelings of self-esteem, as well as their reputation, rested primarily on how well they were able to care for and protect their family and relatives.

Since a woman's own welfare rested primarily on the welfare of her husband and family, and on their satisfaction with her care and devotion, she was all the more encouraged to devote herself to the task of caring for her family. Women had nowhere to turn for meeting their own needs and for support except to their husbands and families. To work for her own interests, a woman had almost no option but to work for the benefit of her family. Such efforts would hopefully improve the situation of her family and her position within the family, bringing benefits to herself.

It was through their networks that women were able to participate both in local politics and later in the 1978–1979 revolutionary marches and demonstrations. They did not have opportunity for social interaction outside these boundaries, as men did when they went to work or spent their leisure time away from home. Occupied with work inside the home, with their tasks of caring for house, husband and children, women were restricted to courtyards, neighborhoods and homes of close female relatives. Any trip outside this confined area had to be in the company of a male relative or one or more women from her neighborhood or kinship network, to ensure propriety. Their neighborhood and kinship networks constituted women's main social outlets.

Especially given the typical hierarchical relationship between husband and wife, the devotion and attention the husband should give to his parents, and the relative segregation of the activities and tasks of the sexes, it was with her female neighbors and kin that a woman generally found companionship and the emotional gratification of caring and intimate social interaction—as well as cooperation on domestic needs and work projects. During the day, while men were gone for agriculture, trading or other work, courtyards and neighborhoods became the province of women, who were free to interact without the interruption of husbands seeking their services. Women developed easy-going relationships—sometimes disrupted by disagreements of course—as they chatted while washing clothes and dishes around a water spigot shared by the several families in a courtyard, visited the village public bath together or helped each other with household tasks.

Women maintained their connections with neighbors and relatives for their own emotional gratification and aims as well as for the benefit of their families. Such networks, as well as women's informal communication styles and work in general, were crucial in the pre–land reform taifeh-keshi political process and in its reemergence during the 1978–1979 Revolution and the local conflict between Seyyid Ibn Ali Askari's faction and the peasant faction some months after the Revolution.[41]

Taifeh Composition

The taifeh system in Aliabad consisted of a network of ties and potential ties, most along kinship lines, including patrilateral (through the father's side), matrilateral—the crucial ties through women—and in-law ties. This network and the political work of strengthening ties, much of it accomplished by women through visiting and hospitality, allowed for the expanding and shifting nature of taifeh as people worked for their own interests.

In the network were several unbounded clusters or groupings with more intense interaction within the cluster than with the rest of the network. Each cluster centered on a leader who exerted firm control over others during his period in power. The degree of power he could exert over an individual varied according to the degree of that person's perceived dependence on the taifeh head. The edges of clusters were indefinite and moved in and out to encompass fewer or more people, became more and less distinct, and widened and narrowed to include more or fewer subsidiary clusters depending on conditions and the political process. Relationships among followers were also important. Realignment of clusters and movement of individuals from one group, degree of support, leader or taifeh to another was common.

A taifeh's core[42] was made up of a group of close male relatives. A large number of sons, brothers, nephews and other kin was especially useful in factional struggle. A taifeh could be composed of relatives from either or both the mother's and father's sides, neighbors, dependents, economic associates, persons whom the taifeh head or a member had assisted, "friends of friends," "enemies of enemies," and in-laws. In-laws, literally "those grafted on" (*paivandkar*), were always mentioned as members of one's taifeh. One informant commented, "If someone becomes your son-in-law, even if you had nothing to do with him before, he becomes your relative."

During the ownership of Aliabad by the Qavams, a kadkhoda's dependents included all of the *rish-sefid* ("white beards," heads of organized groups of riyat) under him, and the riyat under each rish-sefid.[43] Carpenters; herders; field, orchard and gate guards; and other persons hired by each kadkhoda to assist in the agricultural process were also members of the kadkhoda's taifeh. Other dependents, also taifeh members, included servants, armed horsemen, grooms, poor relatives supported to any degree by the head of the taifeh, and other persons attached more personally to him. After land reform, dependents and associates of the Askaris and therefore members of their taifeh included employees and persons earning their living through Askari intervention, such as opium smugglers, those working at the gravel plant, persons farming Askari land and otherwise working for them, and persons holding their positions through Askari mediation, such as those on village governmental bodies.

A taifeh could expand as a conflict escalated or continued in time, with more and more people joining in on each side. At such times, alliances through women, matrilateral and in-law ties, became particularly significant. If the conflict proved to be critical and continued unabated, one taifeh after another might be pulled into the fray, often because of connections through women. An in-law of someone in the taifeh might become involved and then pull in his entire taifeh, including persons related to his taifeh through marriage who would in turn pull in their own taifeh. The process might continue until most villagers were involved, pulled into one side or another through kinship and marriage relationships or other types of association.

In such cases of mobilizing for conflict, the principle of "friend of friend" and "enemy of enemy" become relevant. As one villager explained, "Each person has two friends: one is his friend and the other is the friend of his friend. The enemy of an enemy also becomes a friend."

Another person said, "Relatives are supporters and so are those people who are bad with one's enemies. Like if someone becomes bad with Seyyid Yaqub, for this reason he will go and support the person who is against Seyyid Yaqub."

The category of "friends of friends" and "enemies of enemies" points to the fact that a taifeh was by no means a bounded group, either in its purely kinship meaning or in its political meaning. No corporate or bounded kinship groups comparable to the more bounded patrilineal groups made famous in anthropological analyses existed in Aliabad.[44] The size and composition of an Aliabad political taifeh could vary over time and from conflict to conflict, depending on the reasons for the dispute, its severity and significance, and the point at which peace was made. Leaders and followers attempted to imbue transactional relations with moral qualities in order to strengthen bonds.[45] Support and loyalty for the leader and affiliation to a taifeh could be measured by degree rather than definite membership or nonmembership. Not all members were willing to struggle to the same extent, to expend the same amount of time, energy and resources in the conflict. The firmest supporters seemed to be those who profited most or felt in greatest need of the alliance, which often included closest relatives. Time, effort and resources spent to support a leader and taifeh evolved over time.

A choice often existed for a person as to which side of the conflict he would join. Connections on both sides of a conflict brought an advantage; one could hope for protection from a relative or associate on the winning side, in case one's own side lost the struggle. Also, a connection on both sides provided one with the rationalization as well as the means to shift sides should it be deemed wise to do so. Since both sides wanted more support, they would accept a turncoat. A brother-in-law or father-in-law might go to someone currently on the other side and explain why that person and his side were in the wrong, why the in-law's side was in the right and why the person should change sides. Such a relative might also be the one to bring the person to a gathering of his side and announce that this person had now seen the light and wanted to help them.

A taifeh might split if two persons within the taifeh both wished to become its head. The most outstanding example of this in recent village history was the split between two brothers and their supporters several decades before my fieldwork. Mohammad Khan Darvishi pushed his brother Mulla Hamzeh Rajabi out of the position of kadkhoda, taking all of his

FIGURE 3. The courtyard of a formerly powerful kadkhoda who died a poor man after losing his position. Photo from 1978–1979.

possessions and property and causing his utter ruin, as was usual when a newcomer took over the position from an incumbent. Mulla Rajabi and his close supporters had to flee. Persuaded by peacemakers, they eventually returned to the village, but bitterness and rancor between the two groups continued even to 1978–1979, although both groups had long since lost political power. The two brothers and the two groups of relatives even took different last names.

Taifeh Hierarchical Structure

A taifeh was always assumed to have a strong, powerful leader whose orders were carried out by everyone. The head of one's taifeh might be father, father's brother, mother's brother, a relative of either father or mother, or an unrelated superior. This person controlled access to valued and needed resources. He was well-off and powerful, as many people indicated in their conversations with me[46]:

A taifeh is when a family, a number of persons, gathers around one big person.

The head of a taifeh has more power, so people gather around him. He becomes head of the taifeh by himself with his own power; he makes himself head.

The other people must show respect to the head of their taifeh.

Without such a strong, well-off person around whom to gather, a taifeh, in the sense of a group prepared for political action, would not develop. Poor and powerless persons did not join with relatives to try to mobilize a political taifeh, informants agreed. A small, weak taifeh would be helpless against a strong taifeh headed by a rich and powerful person. In any conflict, the larger taifeh would always win. "If there were 100 people in one taifeh and 20 in another, the larger one would always be stronger and win, so there would be no use to form a taifeh against them."[47]

A taifeh head's followers generally depended on him or felt dependent in some way, such as for protection, resources or assistance or even hope of future assistance. Under the landlord, the kadkhoda and his peasants depended on their own fighting strength to protect access to their means of livelihood—agricultural land and other resources such as water and protection from other villagers.[48]

Members depended on their taifeh heads and other members for assistance at weddings and mourning ceremonies and in obtaining a bride.

Older, more important members of a family or taifeh acted as judges or guarantors of contracts; other people would trust only taifeh heads. They were needed to sign documents such as marriage contracts and peace agreements. A peace agreement could not be made without the *bozorgha*, the seniors of the taifeh.

Even in 1978–1979, taifeh ties were activated for formal visits to ask for a bride and for weddings and mourning ceremonies. The more persons who accompanied the family of the prospective groom to the bride's home to ask for her hand, the more the family would be respected. At weddings and funerals, the presence of a large, unified group gave prestige to the family as well as providing practical help. A large number of people attending a wedding ceremony, with each family giving a gift of money to the bride's or groom's family, provided important financial assistance. If a young man or his father did not have enough money for a wedding, he borrowed money. If enough people attended the celebration, he might gain back more than enough to repay the loan. Such was the case of a young Askari orphan whose wedding took place in summer 1979. Although not well-off himself, he was able to pay back his wedding expenses and even received some extra cash above the amount of his debt to his mother's brother, because he belonged to a large, united taifeh, the Askari taifeh. Its members were willing to help him out, thereby adding to the prestige of the whole taifeh.

A large crowd at a wedding brought prestige and status to the hosts of wedding festivities. A large, noisily supportive taifeh, dancing, singing, clapping and otherwise making efforts to ensure the festivity of the occasion, demonstrated strength and support. A taifeh should be crowded. A taifeh should have strength in numbers to give prestige, offer mutual protection of people and property and enable control over resources. For many reasons, it was judicious for villagers to remain on good terms with the head and other members of their taifeh and, until the 1960s land reform, it was verging on suicidal to neglect relations with the head of one's taifeh.

A large taifeh, in the sense of a coalition, was often formed of a number of stronger kinship groups in the village. In some cases, stronger taifeh called a truce or cooperated closely with other strong taifeh to center their attention on the acquisition of resources belonging to smaller and weaker taifeh or persons who did not belong to a taifeh. Sometimes the relatives of a person quarreling with a powerful person in the village, realizing the futility of struggling against someone from a stronger taifeh, failed to back this unfortunate villager. One informant made the following comment:

Seyyid Ibn Ali and Seyyid Yaqub had power and could do anything they wanted against the poor and weak, and they did. They took land from the poor and weak, not from the strong. During land reform, they took land from the poor and weak, who had no ability to speak up and complain. The ones they took land from couldn't do anything to stop them. The only thing they could do was go to a stronger person and ask, "Why did they take my land?" But all of the strong people were on the side of Seyyid Ibn Ali.

Seyyid Yaqub helped the powerful people so they could all eat together and steal from the people together. People with taifeh were those who had power; they had guns and men. Taifeh were not for rights but for stealing.

Indeed, in Aliabad there were marriage relationships among the most powerful taifeh throughout recent village history, attesting to political alliances and cooperation among them.

The agricultural hierarchy basically replicated the internal structure of taifeh. It was due to a man's powerful taifeh that he would be able to gain the position of kadkhoda—the top position of the village and agricultural system and the landlord's local representative—in the first place.

Aliabad's bailiff worked as intermediary between the kadkhodas and the landlord, Khanum Khorshid Kolah, often represented by her husband, Arab Shaibani. A main function of the bailiff was to stay in a village for about six months to supervise the harvest and make sure there was no cheating against the landlord's share of the crop. Often the bailiff working in a village was a native of another village. Thus a person from Darab was the bailiff in Aliabad one year, and Mulla Jamshid Ajami, who later became a kadkhoda in Aliabad, worked as bailiff for the Qavams in the regions of Fasa and Darab. The landlord of Aliabad also kept in contact with the village by visiting it or through visits by the kadkhodas to her home in Shiraz.

In contrast to the usual practice of sending a bailiff into a village from the outside, in about 1947, Arab Shaibani appointed Seyyid Yaqub Askari bailiff. At about the same time, he appointed Mulla Jamshid Ajami kadkhoda of the lower neighborhood and Mulla Ismail Moradi kadkhoda of the upper neighborhood. As was always the case for a kadkhoda, each one of these persons was a *taifeh-dar*, the head of a strong, political taifeh. Each kadkhoda reportedly commanded some 100 armed horsemen.

Each kadkhoda was head of a taifeh in the sense of a coalition of taifeh, as well as head of the taifeh of his own kinsmen. Each year, the kadkhodas redistributed agricultural land to the *herateh*[49] (the organized groups of sharecroppers under them), collected and transported the landlord's share of the crop, and kept order in the village and the surrounding area.

Internal taifeh structure followed hierarchical lines, with heads at several levels. The largest taifeh of the village, a kadkhoda and his following, included several different smaller taifeh as well as other people tied to the kadkhoda in various other ways. Before land reform, the heads of the smaller kinship groups within each kadkhoda's taifeh were at the next level below the kadkhoda. They were often the same as the rish-sefid, the heads of herateh. The rish-sefid redistributed the agricultural land allocated to them by the kadkhoda to the sharecroppers in their groups and thereby controlled access to their sharecroppers' means of livelihood.[50] Of course plots of agricultural land could not be entirely equal. Those on better terms with their kadkhoda and rish-sefid had a better chance at working the preferable areas.

Like kadkhodas, rish-sefid were maintained in their positions of relative economic advantage and power by the political support of their taifeh members and the peasants under them. Because of their position of political strength, people readily deferred to their wishes. The rish-sefid conveyed the wishes of the landlord from the kadkhodas to the riyat under them. In order to decide which herateh would receive irrigation water first, the rish-sefid drew numbers. The position of rish-sefid, like the position of sharecropper, might be inherited from one's father.

In contrast to some herateh elsewhere in Iran, the members of a herateh in Aliabad did not conduct agriculture cooperatively, at least in the memory of informants. Rather, the rish-sefid assigned land to each holder of an agricultural share who then worked it separately. The only cooperation was based on agreements between individuals. Persons might agree to exchange labor and assistance on a short-term basis or agree to become partners and work together over a longer period.

Usually riyat worked their land with the assistance of sons. Peasant fathers controlled access to sons' means of livelihood. Young men who went into trading also depended on fathers to help them get started. Sons of both riyat and traders needed their fathers for getting work, for the means and process of getting a bride and for a room in the family courtyard for themselves and their bride. The father-son relationship was authoritarian, with little opportunity for sons' dissent or self-expression, just as were relationships between superiors and underlings at all levels of taifeh structure. The taifeh political system as well as the agricultural hierarchy that paralleled it offered little opportunity for individual political expression—other than shifting allegiance to a different taifeh and taifeh head, who would hopefully be successful in future conflicts over resources.

THROUGH ORAL HISTORY, anthropological fieldwork and consultation with several gifted Aliabad political analysts, I was able to gain some understanding about how the taifeh-keshi political system worked, including the activities of both women and men. I could see how the bilateral kinship system—counting kinship through the mother equally with kinship through the father—provided alternative ties that men could mobilize when they wanted to shift alliance from one taifeh and taifeh-dar or kadkhoda to another to best serve their perceived interests. A wife's close ties and frequent interaction with her own family of origin and relatives provided her husband and his male relatives with the means and rationalization to shift sides in a conflict or to recruit more men to their own taifeh, depending partly on their assessment of the balance of power between taifeh and kadkhodas. Men came to the fore during times of actual conflict, to plan strategy, protect one another and engage in combat. Women carried out most of the work of hospitality, raft-o-amad and reciprocity, which maintained the unity and strength of taifeh and of kinship and associational networks. They performed verbal and emotional political work and expressed support through physical presence during times of conflict. Men's participation in taifeh-keshi was suppressed between 1964 and late 1978, but women's social interaction patterns continued. In spite of a gap of some 14 years in the practice of taifeh-keshi in Aliabad, clearly taifeh-keshi culture continued to be the dominant political culture among most of the Aliabad population. During the chaos of the revolutionary period in late 1978 and afterward, taifeh-keshi political culture, behavior and stages of conflict were activated in Aliabad once again. The next chapter addresses how changing conditions in Iran, and therefore in Aliabad, stifled taifeh-keshi between 1964 and 1978—until the chaos of the revolutionary period.

2

Political Repression
The Mosaddeq Era

WHEN MOHAMMAD REZA SHAH PAHLAVI was made monarch by the British and Americans in 1941,[1] he was young and ineffective, but he began to rule more firmly after World War II. From the 1940s on, Mohammad Reza Shah continued his father Reza Shah Pahlavi's work of consolidating central government power and gaining direct control over the country, speeding up his efforts in the 1960s and 1970s. Oil revenues and American clout and military assistance provided the means to centralize political power, using policemen, armed forces, secret police (SAVAK), gendarmes (rural police) and other agents of force and persuasion.[2] The Shah did away with regional "shahs" such as tribal leaders and large landlords and powerful urban political figures. Government policy changed from indirect rule—playing powerful rivals against each other and basically allowing populations to choose their own local rulers—to using central government power to enforce the reign of local government representatives.

Three struggles in recent history forced realization of political change on Aliabadis: the 1953 clash over Prime Minister Mosaddeq, the peasant strike in the same period and the land reform conflict in 1962 and afterward. During the course of these conflicts, village residents became aware of new restrictions on political action. By the end of the third confrontation, people realized it was no longer possible to swing support from an unpopular and unsatisfactory village head to a contender. No longer could villagers bring local political hierarchy into a rough approximation of the balance of support, size and strength of taifeh through contests between these local kinship-based factions. Rather, people had to tolerate village administrators—who were also central government representatives. The ability of these administrators to use outside force and persuasion thoroughly intimidated villagers. Only rarely did villagers attempt small acts of resistance against the local central government representatives. The three events' disastrous results for villagers, frequent and brutal gendarme incursions into the village and monopolization by a small group of the new rural government institutions enabled the local political elite, the Askaris and their associates, to rule with impunity.

The Clash over Prime Minister Mosaddeq and the Tudeh Party

The clash over Prime Minister Mohammad Mosaddeq (1951–1953) was closely associated nationally—and in Aliabad—with conflict over the *hezb-e tudeh* (Party of the Masses), the Iranian communist party, formed in 1941. Tudeh founders wanted to attract a broad spectrum of support from socialists, communists, radicals, democrats, patriots, constitutionalists and progressives. They were highly successful and by 1945–1946 had gained much influence, especially among urban wage and salary earners. The party pressured the Anglo-Iranian Oil Company and the government for better working conditions. Although the Shah tried to clamp down on the Tudeh in 1949, even outlawing the party, the Tudeh had introduced such ideas as mass participation in politics, responsibility of the state toward citizens, class conflict and nationalization of Iranian oil away from British ownership.[3]

Village Support for the Tudeh and Mosaddeq

In 1946, during the Soviet occupation of Azerbaijan,[4] Tudeh representatives came to Aliabad.[5] Proclaiming the formation of a new political party by the government, they tried to mobilize support for the Tudeh Party. They set up an office and began sharing their views with villagers: it wasn't right that one person had two houses while another person had none, that one person owned 100 animals while another had none. People should be independent and have no landlord and no kadkhoda and no one telling them what to do, they said. People shouldn't have to give up a share of wheat to a landlord or a kadkhoda.

The Tudeh party was actually not established by government de-gree, Seyyid Yaqub Askari, the main Aliabad representative of Khanum Khorshid Kolah Qavam, Aliabad's landlord until the early 1960s, soon realized. The party was not for the good of the people, in Seyyid Yaqub's estimation, but rather worked against public interests. Seyyid Yaqub and his supporters informed the Tudeh representatives they were not wanted in Aliabad, Seyyid Yaqub told me. The Tudeh activists then went to the neighboring village of Darab, where within a short time their recruiting efforts were successful.

Emboldened by the Tudeh message, the decline in central government control during that time, and probably the hope that Tudeh forces would be successful at the national level, Darab villagers cut off Aliabad's water for two years. In spite of several attempts by Aliabadis to clear out obstructions and regain their water, they were not able to and their crops suffered.

Darab possessed a good water supply but little level land. Aliabad was surrounded by good level land but lacked water for irrigation. In order to use both Darab's water supply and Aliabad's level land, the Qavams, landlords of both villages, had earlier decided to bring Darab's water by ditch and *qanat* (underground water tunnel) to irrigate Aliabad crops. During times of instability, the Darabis filled the qanat and ditches with rocks and kept the water for irrigating their own orchards and vineyards.

During the early 1950s, national politics became tumultuous. Many Iranians resented the heavy British political influence and the control of oil by the British Anglo-Iranian Oil Company (later called British Petro-leum), which took most of the profits, leaving Iran with little. The British had used Persian oil to fuel their standard of living, World War I, and World War II while Iranians lived in poverty.

In 1949, a coalition of diverse groups, the National Front, was founded by Dr. Mohammad Mosaddeq and others to work through the Iranian Parliament to resist control by foreign powers, promote free elec-tions and defend rights of Iranian citizens. In March 1951, due to efforts by the National Front movement, the Iranian Parliament voted to nationalize Iranian oil. Mosaddeq, a main leader of the National Front, nationaliza-tion and anti-British intervention, was elected prime minister on April 28, 1951, by the Iranian Parliament. On May 1, he began steps to move ahead with nationalization of Iranian oil, bringing about a worldwide oil crisis. Mosaddeq also attempted to cut back on the power of the Shah, even arguing that under the constitution he could take over control of the military from the Shah and appoint the war minister and other ministers himself. The Shah resisted and Mosaddeq responded by calling for public support. The power struggle between Prime Minister Mosaddeq and the Shah continued through 1953.[6]

The following chant, which surfaced after nationalization of oil and evacuation of many British from Iran, is an example of political chants popular during the period. Sheikh Rahim Kazemi recited it for me:

> *sab, miri landan, jun-e ma?* yes, yes, yes.
> *dar miri az maidan-e ma?* yes, yes, yes.
> *sab, digeh iran nemiai?* no, no, no.
> *jang-e musalman nemiai?* no, no, no.
> *sab, murashes montazereh.*
> *sab, murashes raft kai bereh.*
> *hala kai rafti, rafti.*

> Saheb, so you're leaving for London? Yes, yes, yes.
> So you're fleeing our battlefield? Yes, yes, yes.
> Saheb, aren't you coming back to Iran? No, no, no.
> Aren't you ready to fight the Muslims? No, no, no.
> Saheb, the Murashes [a British evacuation battle ship][7] is waiting.
> Saheb, the Murashes is leaving, so hurry.
> Now that you're going, you're gone for good.

Enabled by the national success of the oil nationalization movement and Prime Minister Mosaddeq, support for the Tudeh party and the National Front grew in Aliabad, in spite of Seyyid Yaqub Askari's opposition. The Kazemi and Rajabi families took leadership roles. Shaikh Karim Kazemi, the leading religious leader in the village, and his two sons, Shaikh Rahim and Shaikh Abbas, along with Mansur Rajabi, Mulla Hamzeh Rajabi and Haj Ali Hemmat Hashemi, became the six main Tudeh leaders in the village. They persuaded many others to join them. Several people were forced into becoming Tudeh faction members, some villagers reported. According to their accounts, Tudeh affiliates closed and locked the gate to the village so that people could not come or go unless they agreed to join the Tudeh faction. At the height of Tudeh strength in the village, apparently only close relatives of Seyyid Yaqub and his neighbors, in-laws and other dependents, such as his carpenter, held out against the Tudeh faction. For the month or so during Tudeh faction supremacy in the village, Tudeh supporters met at the Kazemi home in the evenings to show their solidarity and strength and to plan strategy, as was usual during village factional struggle. Tudeh leaders came from Shiraz to Shaikh Karim's home and gave speeches in the mosque, people told me, arguing for abolition of landlords and kadkhodas and for ownership of land by sharecroppers. Shaikh Karim spoke in the mosque against the government and against Seyyid Ibn Ali Askari, wealthy brother of Seyyid Yaqub, just as—one informant pointed out—the visiting mulla from Qom and the local mulla spoke out against the government in the mosque during the 1978–1979 Revolution a quarter of a century later.

Soon much of the village supported Prime Minister Mosaddeq, who was struggling against both the British and the monarchy. People traveled into Shiraz to demonstrate in favor of Mosaddeq and shout chants promoting him and the Qashqai *khans* (tribal chiefs), who also favored Mosaddeq. One village observer commented, "All the world became Tudeh."

During that period, discussion in Aliabad was often political. Everyone knew the latest news and all that was happening in various parts of the country. The newspapers "printed everything," informants recalled. Shaikh Rahim collected all of that period's newspapers, but later destroyed them, fearing reprisal if government officials learned about his stash. Children marched through village alleys shouting pro-Mosaddeq chants and clapping their hands in rhythm.

The National Front party and the Tudeh (initially, anyway) supported Mosaddeq, with frequent resort to strikes and mass demonstrations against the Shah's government. Prime Minister Mosaddeq continued to push toward a democratic and constitutional government. By July 1953, some of his associates were even talking about getting rid of the monarchy and replacing it with a democratic republic. Intimidated by the swing of national resistance against him, the Shah fled the country on August 16. In response, Tudeh crowds and other Mosaddeq supporters flooded the streets, occupying government buildings, destroying statues of royalty and demanding a republic.[8]

In Aliabad, Seyyid Yaqub's son Hemayat brought a note from a Tudeh official in Shiraz warning him that if he did not present himself before this official within 24 hours, he would have only himself to blame for the consequences. Seyyid Yaqub consulted with Mulla Jamshid Ajami, then kadkhoda. They both should acquiesce, Mulla Jamshid advised, and become Tudeh members along with their followers. Seyyid Yaqub, however, decided to fight against the Tudeh instead.

Pro-Shah Forces Rally

One night, Seyyid Yaqub told me, he called relatives and supporters to his home, armed them with the 14 rifles provided to him to keep order in Aliabad and gave them instructions. They attacked the homes of Tudeh leaders, who were sleeping or talking on their roofs. They tore up their books. In a rage, Seyyid Yaqub himself pulled Shaikh Karim's turban down to his shoulders—a great insult. They beat Tudeh leaders and smeared their faces with grease and lampblack. The Tudeh leaders were forced to walk barefoot through village alleyways to the rooms lining the village gate passageway, where they were locked up until morning. Haj Manuchehr Zamani, who later became kadkhoda, was stopped on his way to the mosque and told to come to Seyyid Yaqub's home. When he refused, retorting that he wanted to go and pray, he was beaten and locked up with the others in the gate passageway rooms.

Seyyid Yaqub took his supporters into Shiraz to demonstrate against the Tudeh. People at the side of the road gave fruit drinks and sweets to the pro-Shah Aliabadis, along with the other demonstrators, Seyyid Yaqub told me, a customary indication of support. According to Seyyid Yaqub, on this very day the Tudeh party disintegrated in other towns of Fars. "It all started in Aliabad," Seyyid Yaqub said, seeming to take credit for leading the fight against the Tudeh in the whole region.

Because the nationalization movement threatened their control of Iranian oil, the British had tried to get US President Harry Truman to cooperate with them and get rid of Prime Minister Mosaddeq. Truman would not agree. When Eisenhower became president of the United States, though, the British were able to persuade him to intervene in Iran. The British and the American CIA, directed by Kermit Roosevelt, in cooperation with Mohammad Reza Shah, staged a coup on August 19, 1953.[9] Unfortunately, the American ambassador, perhaps worried that Tudeh activists with their red flags meant a victory for communists, persuaded Mosaddeq to get the demonstrators off the streets the day after the Shah fled, and the crowds erupted on August 17. Because of this directive, Tudeh personnel did not support Mosaddeq against the coup two days later.[10] Prime Minister Mosaddeq was ousted.

The Shah returned and regained his throne. After that, the Shah and Iran were even more under American influence.[11]

Aliabad was able to regain its water from Darab. Through the intervention of Khanum Khorshid Kolah, Aliabad's landowner, the army was brought in. Some 400 soldiers surrounded Darab. Aliabadis were involved in the struggle as well. A young man from Aliabad, the father of Kurosh Amini (see Chapters 4 and 5), was killed during the conflict. When resistance was squelched, about 40 men from Darab were put in prison. Darab was placed under martial law. Some 100 armed soldiers stood guard while cleaners and diggers from the village of Gomsheh cleared the underground water channel. It took about four months, villagers told me, before water finally flowed to Aliabad again.

Dissension Subdued

After the coup, hundreds of Mosaddeq supporters were arrested, and about 60 military officers were shot. The Shah persecuted Tudeh members. About 3,000 were arrested. Lower-level members were released upon signing recantations, but 31 leaders were executed and about 11 were tortured to death. Fifty-two were able to get death sentences changed to life in prison. Ninety-two others received sentences of life in prison, and seven of them were still in prison until the 1979 Revolution.[12]

In Aliabad, when Mosaddeq was removed, Seyyid Yaqub brutally punished pro-Mosaddeq villagers. He accused local Mosaddeq supporters of being Tudeh members and was able to punish them severely on this account. At least 18 Aliabadis were put in prison in Shiraz for about four months, people told me. With their leaders apprehended and beaten, the rest of the population grew quiet.

In actuality, most villagers were confused about the difference between being a Tudeh Party member (considered to be a more damning accusation as it was the Iranian communist party) and being a Mosaddeq supporter, several people told me. Only the leaders were more sophisticated in this regard. A member of the Rajabi family protested, "We weren't Tudehi; we were Mosaddeqi."

Local resistance to the Shah's regime was squelched, and Askari rule was reinforced. Several persons reportedly died from shock or from beatings they received in retribution for their support of the Tudeh or the Mosaddeq faction in Aliabad. Seyyid Ibn Ali Askari reportedly gave 60,000 *toman* (about $8,000 then) and 7,000 *man* of grain (one *man* is approximately three kilos) to the gendarmes who stayed in the village for 41 days to intimidate pro-Mosaddeq people. Shaikh Rahim was exiled to Shiraz for eight or nine years, where he taught school before returning to teach again in Aliabad. Several Mosaddeq supporters moved to Shiraz and never came back to live in the village. A member of the Rajabi taifeh told me, "We were mashed to a pulp during the Mosaddeq crisis—we learned caution."

After the fall of Mosaddeq, pro-Shah groups shouted their own political slogans and couplets. The following chant was often heard:

> *setareh mah nemisheh.*
> A star can't become the moon.
>
> *Mosaddeq shah nemisheh.*
> Mosaddeq can't become shah.

Commenting on those who deserted Mosaddeq to join the faction supporting Seyyid Ibn Ali and Seyyid Yaqub, some villagers said things like "Well, Seyyid Ibn Ali gave him his daughter" and "Seyyid Ibn Ali's rice is coated with more animal fat and is longer grained," indicating that these people had changed sides for their own advantage or because of in-law relations.

Similarly, most village people, several villagers told me, who supported the Tudeh Party and Mosaddeq did so in hopes of material and political advantage. They would share in the spoils, they thought, if Mosaddeq became Shah.

After the removal of Mosaddeq, Haj Manuchehr deserted the pro-Tudeh, pro-Mosaddeq dissidents. He didn't really know why he had supported Mosaddeq and been a Tudeh Party member, he said. When commenting on his desertion, others cynically suggested that the Askaris had bought him off by offering him the important position of kadkhoda. My friend Esmat Ajami described the retreat of the majority of villagers from the Tudeh and Mosaddeq:

At first my husband's father was very much on Mosaddeq's side. Haj Manuchehr, who's now on Seyyid Ibn Ali's side, and Haj Shir Ali Shaikhi and many others were all for Mosaddeq. But many people, when they saw the US and England helping the Shah so that he was victorious, went to the Shah's side. When Mosaddeq lost, when there was a coup, and all of his supporters were put in jail, people became afraid. Before, they said, "Death to the Shah. Long live Mosaddeq" (*marg bar shah, durud bar Mosaddeq*). Then they said the opposite.

One can note several characteristics of taifeh-keshi political process expressed in the Mosaddeq struggle in Aliabad. Many people looked to whichever side appeared to be winning, and then shifted to that side, or shifted after it achieved victory. Both when Mosaddeq supporters held the upper hand in Aliabad and when pro-Shah forces took over again after the CIA coup, the successful group used force to maintain and strengthen its position. Pro-Mosaddeq villagers used force to gain support, and the Shah's people used force to punish pro-Mosaddeq villagers after the ouster of Mosaddeq. The group in power believed they should monopolize power, force others to join their side and punish those who did not. In Aliabad, local politics around the Mosaddeq struggle demonstrated that among many people tolerance for opposition remained low. There was no room for an openly opposing stance.

The British and American CIA-supported coup against the democratically elected prime minister became a crucial defeat to forces for democracy in Iran. It caused many Iranians heartbreak. A dear friend's uncle in Tehran committed suicide, surely not the only case of such bitter despair. Mosaddeq died on March 5, 1967. Visiting in Tehran shortly after then, I heard middle-class people hesitantly bringing up the story of Mosaddeq and the coup, which had destroyed hope for many Iranians. In the 1970s, up to and including the revolutionary period (and even today), many Iranians, young and old, idolized Mohammad Mosaddeq and felt deeply betrayed by the United States in particular, for its role in the coup. (The British were already distrusted.) Iranians had hoped the United States would support their democracy.

While the principal Aliabad pro-Mosaddeq leaders—Sheikh Karim Kazemi and his family and colleagues—did not desert to Seyyid Ibn Ali and Seyyid Yaqub's side, they realized the wisdom of keeping their views to themselves. Although forced into acquiescence, the pro-Tudeh and pro-Mosaddeq leaders in Aliabad did not forget their opposition to the Shah. When opportunity presented itself once again to join forces against the regime—in the form of the Iranian Revolution of 1978–1979—they did.

The Peasant Strike

The 1950s peasant strike in Aliabad was significant because of its effects on the 1962 land reform and on the decline of the taifeh-keshi political system. I heard different dates for the time frame of the strike. Some said it took place after the Mosaddeq period. People may have feared connecting their strike activities with the Mosaddeq era or the Tudeh for political reasons. According to several informants, the strike took place in

1952–1953, which would overlap with the Mosaddeq and Tudeh period. The relative condition of peasants was better at that time, they explained. They felt more empowered to strike. This seems more likely as Shaikh Rahim Kazemi took a leading role. Because Shaikh Rahim was exiled after the return of the Shah to power, he would have been available for participation only before Mosaddeq's overthrow. In addition to Shaikh Rahim and other political activists, the main strike leaders were *rish-sefid*.

The peasants went on strike because they felt their share of crops was insufficient. The landlord was receiving one-fifth of dryland crops and two-thirds of irrigated crops. Although they continued to work unirrigated land, for one year the riyat refused to cultivate their shares of irrigated land under the current sharecropping arrangement. Arab Shaibani, Khanum Khorshid Kolah's agent (and husband), and Seyyid Yaqub, her main local representative, worked together to proceed with cultivation. They brought the landlord's tractor for plowing. To carry out other agricultural tasks— sowing, building the graded irrigation compartments, opening and closing the squares of land for watering, and hand reaping with a sickle—the two men were forced to find labor. Mulla Faht Ali Saedi, the "landlord's kadkhoda" or overseer at the time of my fieldwork, rounded up some 50 people from Aliabad—workers, landless villagers (khoshneshin) and even a few sharecroppers to perform agricultural labor. The harvest was a poor one. During the year, Seyyid Yaqub's taifeh protected him against aggression threatened by the peasant faction.

At the end of the year, neither the landlord nor many riyat were willing to relent. Yet, pessimistic about attaining their goals and fearful of punishment, some sharecroppers decided to end their strike. Although none of the strikers was put in prison, the riyat were punished. The landlord's representatives reduced the number of agricultural shares (*gaw*),[13] dividing the previous 100 shares into only 40, meaning fewer men had access to this sharecropping opportunity. All previous sharecropping agreements were declared null and void. The landlord did not offer agricultural rights to strike leaders among the rish-sefid and riyat, who did not want to resume sharecropping agreements anyway. By the end of the strike, some former sharecroppers had found jobs elsewhere, mainly in Shiraz. Some had even moved into the city and preferred to continue earning a salary or wages rather than return to work for Seyyid Yaqub. Others, too stubborn and resentful of the landlord and her representatives, abandoned their traditional agricultural rights. Only a minority of the riyat relented and took back their rights to agricultural land. These included most of the riyat who had worked for the landlord as agricultural laborers during the strike period. Sharecropping rights (*riyati*) became available to others for the asking.

Because Aliabad peasants had not refrained from farming their dryland during the strike, access to unirrigated land was unaffected by the strike. The riyat did not lose rights to their dryland fields, but some former riyat did abandon their dryland fields because they had begun working elsewhere. Beginning with the peasant strike and then throughout the 1960s and 1970s, less and less dryland was cultivated as more men found work elsewhere. It wasn't worth it to the former riyat to hire others to cultivate their dryland fields.

As described earlier, Aliabad usually had two kadkhodas, one for the upper neighborhood and one for the lower neighborhood. The landlord appointed as kadkhodas those who had in effect been chosen by the majority of peasants under them through the taifeh-keshi political process. After the strike, though, the landlord entrusted her Aliabad land to only one kadkhoda instead of the customary two, and she chose him on her own. Haj Manuchehr Zamani was considered "the landlord's kadkhoda" and not "the people's kadkhoda." Haj Manuchehr became responsible for all 40 shares (reduced from the original hundred). The two former kadkhodas—Mulla Jamshid Ajami and Mulla Ismail Moradi—as well as all rish-sefid had been involved in the strike and had supported peasant demands for a greater share of the crops. In the view of many villagers, their stance in the conflict was an important reason why these two khodhodas lost their positions.

Not only in Aliabad did peasants resist landlords at this time. In the region of Mukri Kurdistan in northwest Iran, around Mahabad and Bokan, Amir Hassanpour writes, peasants rose up against the landlords in 1952 and 1953. They protested repression and the many fees and payments—beyond the one-fifth share of crops—they were forced to give landlords. Kurdish peasants refused to hand over payments or perform extra labor, forced some landlords to flee and formed councils to run villages. They were encouraged into this resistance by the 20% law passed under Prime Minister Mosaddeq: 20% of the share of agricultural production paid to landlords was to be used for peasants' benefit.[14] Possibly the same 20% law also encouraged Aliabad peasants and their rish-sefid to strike. The uprisings in Mukri Kurdistan were eventually brutally squelched, with some activists killed and some peasant families evicted from their villages.[15]

In Aliabad, the strike itself did not bring an increased share of the crop to cultivators. A year after the strike, however, wanting to change the division of irrigated crops to one half each for landlord and cultivator, the new rish-sefid of the newly apportioned 40 shares traveled into Shiraz to see the landlord. They brought a petition signed by each new sharecropper. Afraid of another strike, the landlord agreed to the proposal. The landlord's share of irrigated crops was reduced from two-thirds to one-half and her share of dryland crops from one-fifth to one-eighth.

The Land Reform Conflict

Land reform was initiated in Iran in 1962 and originally limited each landlord to ownership of one village only. The rest were to be sold to the state, which would immediately sell it to the sharecroppers currently working the fields. Later revisions permitted landlords to transfer villages to relatives and to keep agribusinesses and farms that had been mechanized. The Cold War–era Kennedy administration was pressuring the Shah toward reforms. Apparently the Americans thought land reform might help avoid leftist rural discontent and uprisings, such as those taking place in some Latin American and Asian countries. The Shah himself wanted to cut back on the power of the large landowners and extend central government control to villages.[16]

Pre–Land Reform Land Sale

Aliabad's landlord in the early 1960s, Khanum Khorshid Kolah Qavam, received advance warning of impending land reform, villagers told me, because of family ties between the Qavams and the Shah. Ali Qavam, son of Ibrahim Qavam, Khanum Khorshid Kolah's brother, had been married to Ashraf, sister of Mohammad Reza Shah Pahlavi. When the Qavams learned of the planned land redistribution through this connection, they moved quickly to protect their interests. They sold land from many if not all of their villages before the 1962 implementation of land reform in Fars. In Aliabad, Khanum Khorshid Kolah sold three *dang*,[17] or half of the village, to Seyyid Ibn Ali Askari and his supporters, I was told in 1978–1979.

Villagers gave two reasons for this sale: Khanum Khorshid Kolah didn't like Aliabad people because of the peasant strike, and she could get a better price by selling land before land reform. Money received by landlords for land distributed through land reform was calculated on the basis of taxes paid on land before 1962.[18] Powerful landlords who managed to pay low taxes on their land would not receive as much compensation for this land. Khanum Khorshid Kolah was one such case, according to Aliabad peasants. She received 600,000 toman (about $80,000 at that time), at 7.575 toman to the US dollar, or about 1 *rial* (one-tenth of a toman) a square meter, for the three dang sold before land reform, and 300,000 toman (about $40,000), or about half a rial a square meter, for land sold under land reform.[19]

Seyyid Ibn Ali Askari bought two of the three dang that Khanum Khorshid Kola sold before land reform for 400,000 toman (then about $52,800), people told me in 1978–1979. A highly successful opium smuggler, he was the richest man in Aliabad. His brother, Seyyid Yaqub Askari, who had served as Khanum Khorshid Kolah's main local representative for 30 years, bought the next largest share of land for 64,000 tomans (about $8,500). Haj Manuchehr, kadkhoda for the 40 shares, was also a large buyer. Other new small owners (*khordeh-malek*) were mainly traders and shopkeepers, people who had a little capital. Many new owners had some knowledge of agriculture. Only four or five possessed no sharecropping rights (riyati) whatsoever, but none were truly peasants; they had taken over riyati after the strike and all had some other work or occupation in addition to their riyati. Peasants, of course, did not have money to buy land.

Not until my summer 2008 visit did I learn that in actuality Seyyid Ibn Ali Askari had initially bought the entire three dang, or half of the village, from Khanum Khorshid Kolah. As he owned only half a village then, under land reform terms he would not be required to hand over that land to the cultivators during land reform. It was only later, realizing he would need village support, that he sold about a third of it to the other small owners. Because he didn't want to face peasant fury by himself, Seyyid Ibn Ali somehow managed to make it appear that not only he but also the whole group of about 24 small owners had initially bought the land. That way he could share with other owners the blame for the small land area left to divide among the sharecroppers. His full responsibility in originally buying half of the village had become commonly known eventually. Because of this pre–land reform purchase, only half of Aliabad irrigated land was available for distribution during land reform,[20] which the sharecroppers did not find out until the actual implementation of land reform in 1962.

Peasant Anger

One day in mid or late 1962, a loudspeaker from the mosque announced registration for division of land.[21] Villagers were directed to come
to the mosque immediately. There, land reform officials asked people how
much land they controlled. The area of land received under land reform
was to be based on their answers. Land was calculated in amount of seed,
with 23 to 25 *man* of seed representing 1 hectare (about two and a half acres)
of irrigated land and 15 *man* of seed representing 1 hectare of dryland.

Afraid that land reform officials wanted to find out the size of their
shares of land to take it from them, some men reported controlling less
land than was actually the case. Others lost land because they were not in
Aliabad but in Shiraz or trading in other villages on the few days allowed
for registering land claims. In a few cases, one brother claimed as his own
the entire area of land he actually shared with another brother. Addition-
ally, Seyyid Ibn Ali and Seyyid Yaqub influenced officials into favoring
their friends in land division, to the detriment of others who enjoyed less
cordial relations with the Askari brothers, some villagers charged. Seyyid
Yaqub even created and reported to land reform officials a herateh for
himself and some close supporters, I learned during my 2005–2006 visit.
That way they could present themselves as men possessing sharecropping
rights to agricultural land so they would be eligible to receive land in the
distribution.

When land reform officials returned to the village for actual land
distribution, Seyyid Ibn Ali came forward to announce the earlier purchase
of three dang of village land. He presented documents to prove it. When
the sharecroppers heard this, they were outraged. Seyyid Ibn Ali had acted
without right, they protested. They, the sharecroppers, should own the
land. The government was giving the land to the riyat, and they refused
to hand it over to Seyyid Ibn Ali. Furious because only three dang rather
than the full six dang were to be divided among them, sharecroppers who
held riyati at the time of land reform joined in resistance with former peasants who had lost access to land during the 1950s strike against Khanum
Khorshid Kolah.

Those who had taken over riyati after the peasant strike were mainly
Seyyid Yaqub's relatives and supporters, landless villagers and traders. During land reform, these individuals were to receive land because it was to
go to those who currently possessed riyati.[22] Former sharecroppers whose
rights had been taken away after the strike lost out and did not receive any

land from land reform. These former peasants were bitter that the strike had caused them to lose the opportunity to receive land.

As they had neither won the struggle nor gained anything, many peasants now regretted their participation in the strike. The winners, they pointed out, were those who took over the 40 shares of sharecropping rights. These people were the ones who received land from land reform, they told me in 1978–1979, who now owned urban-style houses and apricot orchards across from the highway and sold their land for 250 toman (about $33 at 7.575 toman to US dollar in 1978–1979) a square meter. To their great anger, they—the real peasants—hadn't received land, while people who weren't even agriculturalists had. People were also angry about the reduction in number of shares after the strike, with village land divided into only 40 shares instead of the former 100, resulting in a decrease in the number of people who could make their living from agriculture.

Land above the road running between the highway and the local shrine, Seyyid Seraj, was to go to the 24 small landowners. Seyyid Ibn Ali and other small owners would control the most valuable land; water flowed first to this area above the village. The land below this line, further away from water sources and therefore less productive and valuable, was to be divided among the sharecroppers with current rights to agricultural land.

Seyyid Ibn Ali, with the help of the head of the gendarmerie station in Qodratabad, attempted to round up sharecroppers and persuade them to sign documents signifying agreement to the land division. The peasants refused to sign. Then Seyyid Ibn Ali mobilized his relatives and close supporters to attack and beat up recalcitrant sharecroppers. Several were badly wounded. At least one lost consciousness. After several incidents of violence against the peasants, they began to rally their forces and put up a determined resistance.

Seyyid Ibn Ali's Strategy with the Small Landowners

Seyyid Ibn Ali had wanted support in the struggle against the share-croppers, which he suspected would ensue at the time of land reform. That is why he allowed others to buy some of the land from him, some villagers suggested. If so, he analyzed the situation correctly: all of those who bought land from Seyyid Ibn Ali were or became supporters of the Askari brothers and cooperated with them in the violent conflict against the rest of the village. Through providing a self-interested reason to 23 other people and

their sons and close supporters to join him in fighting to protect his purchased land, Seyyid Ibn Ali succeeded in mobilizing a large group of villagers to join his own close relatives and supporters in the land reform battle.

If they had not bought shares of land before land reform, admitted
Seyyid Ibn Ali's relatives who also possessed riyati, they would not have
fought on Seyyid Ibn Ali's side. Those relatives of Seyyid Ibn Ali who had
possessed a share of riyati before land reform and did not purchase any of
the khordeh-malek land bought by Seyyid Ibn Ali from Khanum Khor-
shed Kolah before land reform did not support him in the struggle over
land that followed the attempted implementation of land reform. Some 10
to 15 persons, either seyyids or more distant relatives, fell into this category.

Ongoing Land Reform Conflict

The two neighborhoods of the village—the upper neighborhood,
where most of the peasants and those not related to the Askaris lived, and
the lower neighborhood, where most of the Askari relatives lived—were
cast against each other. Seyyids and *mirzais* (the term Aliabad villagers
used for offspring of a female seyyid) were pitted against non-seyyids.

Conflict between the two sides continued for two or three years.
Assuming they would not gain access to their purchased land due to violent opposition, a group of small owners who had bought some land from
Seyyid Ibn Ali decided to ask for their money back. The peasant side appeared to be winning, they concluded. Therefore they chose to fight on
the peasant side, hoping to increase the area of land they would receive as
riyat under land reform. These men, including at least one member of the
Rezai taifeh, a large and unified peasant taifeh, were among those who later
fought most bitterly against Seyyid Ibn Ali and his supporters.

At one time, both sides traveled to Shiraz to complain to authorities
and attempt to evoke support for their cause. The peasants' side talked
with officials of the court system, and Seyyid Ibn Ali and his followers
sought assistance from Khanum Khorshid Kolah, their former landlord.
On the return trip, the peasant faction leader, Haj Baqer Rezai, lost his hat
to the wind. He leaned out from the back of the pickup to retrieve it, fell
out and was killed. The Rezais blamed Seyyid Ibn Ali for his death. "Since
the death of Haj Baqer," one villager told me, "there has always been bad
feeling between the Rezai taifeh and Seyyid Yaqub's taifeh." The Rezais
became important leaders in the land reform struggle.

As the struggle continued, peasants went into Askari vineyards and orchards and picked fruit for themselves. The peasant faction leaders took their animals into alfalfa fields belonging to Askaris to feed. Then, at night, Seyyid Yaqub's boys sprayed the alfalfa with poison. The feeding animals died, and so did animals of people who took home bunches of poisoned alfalfa.

One day, the peasant faction gathered and attacked the homes of Haj Manuchehr, Seyyid Ibn Ali and Seyyid Yaqub, breaking windows. The three men escaped to Shiraz and were gone for a month, some people said. Others reported a six-month absence from Aliabad.

After at least a year of "war," the "peasant" taifeh succeeded in routing the taifeh of Seyyid Ibn Ali, now the largest owner of Aliabad land. Some 50 men who supported Seyyid Ibn Ali were no match for the 500 who fought bitterly against the Askari taifeh, now called the landlord's taifeh. Those of Seyyid Ibn Ali's taifeh who remained behind in Aliabad were afraid to stir out of their homes.

As with the peasant strike, the revolt of Aliabad villagers against the inequities of land reform was not unique. In the area of Maragheh, in the northwest province of Azerbaijan, a landowners' bulletin printed 21 cases of violence against landlords or their property in March 1962 alone.[23]

Seyyid Ibn Ali Returns

Seyyid Ibn Ali used his period of absence from the village to rally support from influential political figures. He even traveled to Tehran to see Ibrahim Qavam, head of the powerful Qavam family and Khanum Khorshid Kolah's brother. According to a secondhand report, the meeting went as follows:

Qavam was wearing a white European suit.
Seyyid Ibn Ali said, "I'm Seyyid Ibn Ali."
Qavam asked, "The same Seyyid Ibn Ali who bought my land in Aliabad?"
Seyyid Ibn Ali said, "Yes."
Qavam said, "Congratulations."
Seyyid Ibn Ali said, "Don't congratulate me. They're giving me a hard time. You have to help me."
Qavam said, "If I pay my gardener to trim and train my trees in a certain way but he can't do it and I have to do it myself, I'm wasting my money, aren't I?"

But eventually Qavam, Princess Ashraf Pahlavi (Ibrahim Qavam's former daughter-in-law) and Prime Minister Asadollah Alam (Qavam's son-in-law) helped Seyyid Ibn Ali. Seyyid Ibn Ali even obtained a letter from the Shah, villagers told me. According to one story, if Seyyid Ibn Ali would gather in one place all those peasants who were giving him trouble, Gholam Reza, the Shah's brother, would have these peasants bombed or shot. Seyyid Ibn Ali turned down this offer. Since everyone in Aliabad knew each other, he reportedly concluded, such an action would cause more trouble than it would solve.

In 1963 or 1964, Seyyid Ibn Ali and his closest supporters triumphantly re-entered the village armed with a government order giving him permission to take over his purchased land and ordering imprisonment of dissenting peasants. Seyyid Ibn Ali was accompanied by several truckloads of armed gendarmes and soldiers and a number of armed irregulars (some said 50, others reported 150), Lurs[24] from Delli. Instructed by Seyyid Ibn Ali, Seyyid Yaqub and Ali Reza Amini on which men to attack, the gendarmes and irregulars fell upon the peasants.

Although initially the peasant faction put up resistance, they were badly outnumbered. Three days of severe violence followed. Men and boys hid in terror. Women did not dare venture outside their homes. All those seized were tortured and beaten, held a few days within the village or at the nearby gendarmerie station and then taken to prison in Shiraz. Young boys were hung upside down and beaten on the bare soles of their feet for a day or more, until they revealed the whereabouts of older brothers and fathers.

It was harvest time. The intruders seized the grain at the threshing floor. Men held in village gate storage rooms or in Seyyid Yaqub's home were not given food or water "but only blows," as one victim commented. Mothers and sisters were not allowed to bring food to them.

For two months there was martial law; no male over 15 was allowed out of his home. If a male ventured out into a village alleyway and was discovered, he was taken and beaten. Seyyid Muslem, Seyyid Yaqub's son, searched each home one by one and pulled men out to be taken and beaten. Men hid on roofs, in hay and in large containers for wheat and feed. Some of them were found and beaten with clubs and rifle butts. Some men escaped from the village to Shiraz or elsewhere to avoid gendarmes and irregulars. One man stayed with friends in Darab for ten days. Another escaped to Shiraz by hiding in a car trunk. Several went to the Dushmanziari area, where they had friends. One person fled to the village of Ab Pardeh. Ali Reza Amini, the Askari brothers' father's sister's son, went after him, but Ab Pardeh residents refused to hand him over. He stayed there for twelve years before returning to Aliabad. One young man was tied to a tree and beaten with a thick stick from his head down to his feet and then from his feet up to his head for 24 hours. He was never able to work again.

Four or five persons reportedly died as a result of beatings. I questioned Majid Jafari, whose family had been leaders in the battle, about his father, who died, others informed me, during the land reform conflict. At first Majid gave vague, noncommittal answers; he was married to a relative of Seyyid Ibn Ali and he had made his peace with the Askari taifeh. Finally, he said,

I can't tell you. I suffered so much at the hands of Seyyid Ibn Ali, but now I want to forget it. It's all in the past. I spent 25 nights sitting up with my father. You know how uncomfortable we are when we can't sleep for one night? I didn't sleep for 25 nights. The lights were turned out—they had some rest, but I didn't.

My father was broken because he realized he had accomplished nothing. He died from the knowledge that he had gotten nowhere. My brother was beaten up so much that his liver ruptured. Then my mother was so distraught over my brother's death that she went blind and also has been bedridden all these years. They gave me so many blows that I still can't sit or walk straight.

Our taifeh was the biggest and most important in the village. No one else could compare with us. But during land reform we were ruined. Before, I was as big and strong as five men put together. Now, because of torture and mental anguish, I'm just one weak man.

Those arrested during land reform were forced to pay a 500 toman fine (about $66 at the time).[25] At least 27 people were imprisoned for 40 days. After 40 days, those who presented their house deed as a guarantee for good behavior were released. Court officials retained the deeds for six months. If any of the peasants had caused trouble during that time, the government would have seized their homes. At least one person was kept in Karim Khan Zand prison in Shiraz for three months. Following their release, some men moved to villages in the outlying Konfiruz or Beyza areas or to Shiraz, as others had already done, in order to avoid further retribution from Seyyid Ibn Ali.

With help from the Qodratabad gendarmerie station head, Seyyid Ibn Ali was then able to take over any Aliabad land he wanted without interference from peasants. He took over areas close to water sources and next to irrigation ditches, the paths of water.

Seyyid Ibn Ali's village relatives served as his bodyguards. Speaking in 1979, one of his relatives, Seyyid Kazem Askari, recalled,

Wherever he went, day or night, a group of us accompanied him so the peasant faction wouldn't kill him. Several times a group of the dissidents attacked us with clubs and shovels. They wounded several people, and they had to go to the hospital. Whenever there was a confrontation, Seyyid Ibn Ali immediately sent for gendarmes from Qodratabad. They would come to his aid right away. Even now, if Seyyid Ibn Ali weren't always surrounded by people, members of the peasant faction would attack him.

Seyyid Ibn Ali was not always the winner in conflicts over land, even with the support of the other small owners and outside agents of force; people with stronger political connections could defeat him. After the suppression of the 1962–1963 conflict, Seyyid Ibn Ali sold a colonel 200 hectares of land below the village that actually should have gone to riyati holders under land reform. He again attempted to mobilize small owners to assist him in protecting his interests. The colonel built a gravel factory and then began extracting gravel beyond his purchased land, taking over more than 400 hectares, according to villagers, instead of the 200 he had bought from Seyyid Ibn Ali. Sixty of these extra 200 hectares should have fallen to the share of other small owners, Seyyid Ibn Ali pointed out to them. He urged them to assist him in protecting their land from the colonel. Several sons of small owners camped on the unpurchased 200 hectares to prevent extraction of gravel there. But the colonel's connections with government offices proved to be more effective than Seyyid Ibn Ali's; the colonel obtained a court order allowing him access to the unpurchased land.

Results of Land Reform

Land reform left the majority of villagers with bitter resentment and deep fury toward both the Askaris and the central government. They resented the central government's continuing support of the Askaris, the central government's local representatives.

While land reform brought positive results to some other villages in the region, it did not improve conditions for most Aliabad peasants.[26] Only three dang, the less valuable half of the total village land of six dang— actually less than this—had been distributed, because of land sale to the

Askaris and other khordeh-malek and then Seyyid Ibn Ali's continuing takeover of more and more land. One villager commented, "The Qavams stole the land in the first place—so how can they sell it?"

A smaller landowner, Seyyid Ibn Ali, who eventually took over per-haps two-thirds of village land—the most valuable areas, closest to water sources—replaced the large landowner, Khanum Khorshid Kolah. Since his land claims were supported by the central government, now more powerful than ever, Seyyid Ibn Ali in effect controlled the village. Con-versely, since Seyyid Ibn Ali, his brother Seyyid Yaqub and their associates served as government representatives in the village, their firm control over the village and their cooperation with the government ensured central gov-ernment domination at the local level.

Indeed, following land reform, the small owners and government representatives—Seyyid Ibn Ali, Seyyid Yaqub and their associates—exerted even more control over villagers than the original landlord had. As described earlier, before, if too many peasants became dissatisfied with the landlord's representatives—the kadkhodas—they could throw support to a new candidate. Because of her relative lack of power and control, Khanum Khorshid Kolah generally ratified villagers' choice for kadkhoda rather than attempting to impose her own choice on the village. After land reform, however, if there was dissatisfaction with the rule and policies of Seyyid Yaqub and other government representatives, villagers had no ef-fective route of appeal. Seyyid Yaqub's brother Seyyid Ibn Ali and the local gendarmes always supported Seyyid Yaqub. Seyyid Yaqub had only to call for the gendarmes to quiet dissent.[27]

The small landowners, like the peasants, had no recourse against the power of Seyyid Ibn Ali, who did not always respect their rights or keep his promises to them. They had bought their land in the form of shares rather than specific pieces of land. They planned to divide the land into plots later, according to number of shares purchased. The khordeh-malek were to receive half of the dryland as well as half of the irrigated land. They planned to use the irrigated land to plant orchards.

Their purchase included half of the grapes harvested by those holding traditional rights to vineyard plots surrounding the village. The 24 small owners were to divide their half of the grapes among themselves, accord-ing to their purchased shares. But Seyyid Ibn Ali appropriated most of the small landowners' share, villagers told me. He stationed one of his representatives at each vineyard entrance to extract the portion from each person. About eight years before my 1978–1979 fieldwork, he fixed an assessment on each plot, to be paid to him each year.

Later, a law was passed forbidding landlords to take shares of fruit. Then the entire harvest of grapes was kept by persons with traditional rights to specific plots, and they in effect became full owners. These people did not, however, possess ownership documents. Even in 1978–1979, Seyyid Ibn Ali Askari had not given up hope of getting some vineyard area: a case concerning vineyard ownership was pending in Shiraz courts.

In Aliabad, the land reform process resulted in less land available for agriculture and, therefore, a drop in agricultural productivity. Added to the population explosion at the time, this meant a drastic increase in number of village men not able to support themselves and their families through agriculture. Of course those villagers who had gained ownership of land through either land reform or purchase became well-off when real estate prices skyrocketed in 2001 and later, due to the suburbanization of Aliabad and real estate inflation.

After land reform, when men were no longer working irrigated fields and therefore had to turn to jobs outside of Aliabad to support their families, their involvement with their traditionally held dryland plots also declined. Large areas of village dryland were simply abandoned after land reform. Their owners, lacking labor, capital or both either could not cultivate them or chose not to, judging it not worth their while.

Those receiving land felt it was their right to receive all of the village land and not merely the half left after the sale to Seyyid Ibn Ali Askari. Villagers who had lost the opportunity to gain land from land reform because they had abandoned their sharecropping agreements during the peasant strike felt cheated. Those who had bought land from Seyyid Ibn Ali and then, fearing failure of their attempt to establish control over their land, took their money back were bitter about the lost opportunity to gain land. These people, especially the Rezais, continued to be the main opponents of the Askaris and came to the fore in any conflict with them. According to other villagers, before land reform the Rezais had no quarrel with the Askaris. They fought with Seyyid Yaqub and his taifeh at every opportunity only after land reform.

Even the khordeh-malek eventually became alienated from the Askaris and angry at the government; Seyyid Ibn Ali failed to give them their fair share of land or profits when he sold land to outsiders. The khordeh-malek, like other villagers, blamed government officials for cooperating with Seyyid

Ibn Ali in his encroachment on their land. They took him to court several times after situations where he failed to give them their due. However, the court always ruled in his favor because of bribes and friendly relations between Seyyid Ibn Ali and court personnel, villagers told me.

The land reform conflict was the major trauma in the lives of quite a few villagers; they never really recovered from the sense of loss and despair from their defeat and injuries to themselves and family members. Villagers were bitterly indignant about physical violence and affronts to their dignity suffered at the hands of Askari and government agents during the land reform conflict. The majority of villagers were left disillusioned with land reform and outraged by Askari and government agents' actions.

Even Seyyid Yaqub, the most powerful person in the village and main representative of the national government, frequently talked critically about land reform. According to Seyyid Yaqub, land reform was bad and did nothing for peasants. They didn't get enough land, he told me. Land reform cut land up into tiny, inefficient, scattered pieces. Peasants were left without assistance for obtaining water and repairing underground irrigation channels. Before, the absentee landlord, Khanum Khorshid Kolah, had helped finance the heavy expenses of annually cleaning out and repairing the underground water channels in Aliabad. Now no one was organizing and funding this. Land reform should have divided peasants into work groups similar to pre–land reform agricultural groups, the herateh, Seyyid Yaqub felt, each with its own head and under overall direction of one boss. Peasants, according to Seyyid Yaqub, need a boss. The government should have provided loans and assistance for obtaining water and other agricultural necessities. Land reform was good only for former large landlords: "They are better off now; they don't have to worry about peasants stealing their crops."

In fact, Seyyid Yaqub appears to have been correct in his implication that large landlords had not suffered severely from losing agricultural land. Owning agricultural land was becoming less financially rewarding than investing capital in construction, trading or business.[28] In Aliabad, the landlord's share of crops had decreased at least three times during the decades before land reform. Production was diminishing. The number of men engaged in sharecropping had been cut at least three times. In addition, the price of wheat was dropping. Profits to Khanum Khorshid Kolah from her Aliabad land were declining.

Even after Seyyid Ibn Ali bought Aliabad land and then took over more, his profits from agriculture were relatively insignificant. The land he purchased and expropriated was of greater importance to solidifying connections with political figures through gifts or reduced sales to them and through land sales to provide him with capital for investments elsewhere.

The apparatus of force available to the Askaris as local representatives of the central government left villagers cowed and intimidated. Brutal repression of dissent against unfair distribution of land left villagers terrified of the gendarmes. Their apprehension and fear were exacerbated by the gendarmes' frequent appearances in the village; their obviously cordial relations with the Askaris, at whose homes they were regularly and warmly received; and their immediate and savage descent on the village in cases of trouble or any threat against Askari control or interests.

Villagers had only two options, it became apparent: they could retreat from their stance of dissent or at the very least silently submit to Askari administration, or they could move away from Aliabad to Shiraz or somewhere else. The best way to advance materially and politically in Aliabad was to ally with the Askaris, villagers saw. Struggling against them would bring no hope of gain. Some villagers chose to join the Askaris. Askari control was irreversible, the heads of most dissenting taifehs decided. They joined forces with the Askaris and the central government to administer village affairs and share the economic and political rewards. Once again, as before land reform, when a new taifeh and taifeh-dar won the power struggle—and after the defeat of Mosaddeq—supporters of the vanquished side had to either leave or remain silent, or if they wished to benefit from the current regime, they had to shift to the victorious side, which now monopolized power and resources.

Direct Government Control in Villages

After land reform, the central government set up a number of rural government institutions. A kadkhoda, deputized for administrational and bureaucratic tasks, was now the intermediary between the central government and a village population. A five-member village council was to be elected and responsible for collecting a tax of 2% from each family for improvement projects. Rural cooperatives, under the direction of a manager and a local executive council of three members, were set up to provide credit and sell some staples for reasonable prices. The rural courts were to settle disputes. Further, personnel from other branches of the Shah's "White Revolution" (or "Shah-People Revolution") development program—Literacy Corps, Health

Corps, and Reconstruction and Development Corps—reached many villages. Through these bodies, the central government entered directly into village affairs.[29]

In Aliabad, the Askaris and their supporters monopolized opportunities to become post–land reform village officials. Seyyid Yaqub, who served as his brother Seyyid Ibn Ali's local agent, controlled all government organizations and offices established after land reform. Seyyid Ibn Ali thereby enjoyed ultimate control of the local governmental structure. As one villager commented, "Seyyid Ibn Ali has his hand in all government offices. Seyyid Ibn Ali controls all government business in Aliabad."

Cooptation of Influential Taifeh

As indicated earlier, during the land reform struggle in Aliabad, the battle was organized along taifeh-based lines. The Saedis were perhaps the largest taifeh and because of this did not lose any of their members during the land reform fights. Because they suffered nothing worse than imprisonment, their members were not as beaten down by land reform trauma as some other villagers. Although the peasant side ultimately lost this conflict, leaders of more powerful taifeh, such as the Saedis, were able to use their strength to advantage after land reform. Their taifeh strength made three taifeh heads attractive for Askari cooptation. The Saedis, Rezais and Jehangiris—three of the larger taifeh—were able to gain positions in village government bodies, and therefore economic and political benefits. The Askaris and the government bought off appointees to government organizations to keep them from engaging in further rebellious activity, dissenting villagers felt. One critic said,

The government felt if they could get the most important person of each taifeh, they could control the whole village. Like Hamid [the kadkhoda] and Mashd Musa [Saedi]. [The government] put them on the village council to buy them off. If the government could get the taifeh head, they thought, they could get the whole taifeh through control by its kinship group leader.

Government officials from Shiraz, in cooperation with Seyyid Yaqub, chose heads of powerful taifeh to serve as village council members, rural representatives to the government, after land reform. Haj Khodadad Saedi, perhaps the most important opposition leader during land reform, was chosen as president of the village council. Hamid Jehangiri, who was also kadkhoda; Rahmatollah Saedi, head of a branch of the Saedi taifeh; Majid Jafari, who lost his father and brother during the land reform struggle; and Evaz Jehangiri, head of yet another influential peasant taifeh, were the four other council representatives. When Haj Khodadad Saedi died, his nephew and successor to head of the Saedi taifeh, Mashd Musa Saedi, took his place as president. According to Rahmatollah Saedi,

Mashd Musa Saedi was chosen to be president of the riyat by the government because he is literate, because the people wanted him and because he has a big taifeh—he is influential.[30] His relatives have shops in Shiraz. He has more relatives than anyone else, so the Saedis aren't afraid of anyone. His cousins live in Shiraz, and they are all hajis.[31]

Seyyid Yaqub appointed members to the various other local government organizations established after land reform as well. All appointees were or became Askari supporters and cooperated closely with Seyyid Yaqub and the government.

During my 1978–1979 fieldwork in Aliabad, members of government organizations continued to be influential and wealthy villagers. According to one villager, "Whoever has power and money becomes a member of the village council." Mashd Musa Saedi and Hamid Jehangiri, members of active and influential taifeh against the Askaris during the land reform conflict, were still important members of the village council and other village organizations. Hamid Jehangiri was still kadkhoda. Another member of the village council belonged to the Rezai taifeh, also active against the Askaris during land reform. Ali Reza, right-hand man to Seyyid Yaqub, and an important member of the Amini taifeh, was also a member, as was Fazlollah Rezai, son of the Rezai taifeh head, who was taking over from his father as taifeh head during my 1978–1979 stay in Aliabad.

The most powerful villagers tended to monopolize government offices. Several held more than one office. According to informants, the following five men were the most powerful villagers before the 1979 Revolution: Seyyid Ibn Ali Askari, Seyyid Yaqub Askari, Mashd Musa Saedi, Hamid Jehangiri and Ali Reza Amini. When the central government established rural institutions after land reform, Seyyid Yaqub ran the village council and the Rural House of Justice, some villagers said, although Mashd Musa was president of the council and, some said, of the House of Justice. Mashd Musa was also president of the village cooperative. His nephew operated the cooperative store. Ali Reza Amini, the Askari brothers' father's sister's son and their close supporter, served as treasurer of both the village council and the House of Justice and had been kadkhoda for a period. Hamid Jehangiri was both kadkhoda and an important member of the village council. Earlier, Seyyid Asadollah Askari, Seyyid Yaqub's brother, and Seyyid Ibn Ali had been members of the village council. Other than a member of the Rezai family and two peasants closely associated with the Askaris, people did not mention any other villagers as belonging to these village organizations. Other Askari relatives and supporters might attend meetings, even though not formally members of the organizations.[32]

In addition to controlling local government organizations and offices, Askaris monopolized contacts with government officials.[33] They monopolized access to the nearby gendarmerie station. They supervised government employees who came into the village. Three Literacy Corps young women lived in Seyyid Yaqub's courtyard during their village stay. A Literacy Corps man whose tour of duty ended shortly before my arrival lived in the kindergarten building owned by Seyyid Ibn Ali. Askaris tried to monopolize his social interaction, he said.

When my family and I were brought to Aliabad by the head of the nearby Qodratabad gendarmerie station, who was responsible for us, he took us first to Mashd Musa Saedi's home. When I said I needed to live within the old village walls rather than in the "New Village" across the highway, they placed us in Seyyid Yaqub's home. In the following months, through various subterfuges and cautionings, Seyyid Yaqub and his wife attempted to restrict my interaction with persons outside their own social group. "You'll get fleas from those dirty courtyards full of animals." "Watch out for him—he's a communist" (about Shaikh Rahim Kazemi, who had been a Mosaddeq supporter).

Just as in earlier conflict between taifeh over the position of kadkhoda and control over land, after land reform, those attached to the current administration gained the most influential positions and access to resources. A significant element of earlier factionalism continued: to the victor went all, and to be pragmatic, one should transfer support to the current power structure.

Dissatisfaction with Rural Government Organizations

The great majority of villagers were dissatisfied with local government organizations and the local officials of these organizations. They did not help villagers, people complained, but were only out for their own advantage. They cooperated with each other for their mutual benefit. They used for themselves resources and funds from higher levels of government and contributed by villagers to provide assistance to other villagers. This dissatisfaction and strong suspicion of local government officials' corruption added to villagers' resentment of the local political elite—and of the central regime as well—for failing to provide needed services and for allowing local officers to embezzle and steal funds and supplies.

The kadkhoda received 3% of all crops. He provided no services in return, some people complained, and called this payment a bribe. During my first stay in Aliabad, in 1978–1979, dissatisfaction with the kadkhoda was widespread. Several attempts had been made to remove him from office, including gathering signatures for a petition against him.[34] A common observation about the kadkhoda was, "He takes our wheat but doesn't do any work for people."

Another 2% of the harvest was relegated for village development funds. Landholders had to hand this money over to the village council. Council members took these funds for themselves, villagers complained, and did not use them to benefit the village as a whole. After the 1979 Iranian Revolution, people circulated a sheet of paper listing funds reportedly stolen by various village council members during the previous 15 years.

Most complaints, however, were reserved for the cooperative, probably because expectations had been raised that the cooperative would provide villagers with much-needed resources, such as loans and supplies. These expectations had not been fulfilled. The cooperative store usually had few staples, villagers complained. One time when I checked, rice, lentils, yellow split peas and most other commonly used foodstuffs were not available. Rice was not available even at cooperative stores in Shiraz, the operator was telling prospective customers, although from another source I heard this was not true. Members of the village council took cement provided for sale at the cooperative. "The rest of us have to buy it on the black market," other villagers complained.

The cooperative store was useless, most villagers concluded, and seldom attempted to shop there. In contrast to many other areas where cooperative stores had been opened, in Aliabad, local shopkeepers' businesses did not suffer after the establishment of the cooperative store—an indication of its lack of utility in Aliabad.[35]

The cooperative was apparently broken into in fall 1978 and all its goods, such as shortening and oil, were stolen. The store manager, it was widely believed, had actually stolen the supplies, taken the proceeds for himself and then blamed it on thieves. Villagers demanded a new manager for the store. After two months, a new manager still had not been found because, according to village administration, the salary was too low.

Villagers were dissatisfied with the cooperative's loan services. Credit was inadequate and for too short a period, and villagers charged it was extended to officers and their friends rather than to the intended recipients.

The Aliabad Rural House of Justice was apparently without function. I never heard of meetings of the organization, nor were any local dispute cases brought before the body. Conflicts were taken to the nearby gendarmerie station, brought before the Shiraz court system or settled through violent confrontation or traditional forms of mediation—usually by a respected seyyid. Although related to the Askari brothers, these mediators were not involved in village administration.

Decline of Taifeh-Keshi Political Significance

The Askari monopoly over government resources and means of force and the growing effectiveness of central government control influenced the role of kinship-based factionalism, the taifeh-keshi system, in local political process after land reform. The Askaris and their associates—with gendarmerie assistance—controlled villagers even more firmly than the large Qavam landlord had earlier. In contrast to kadkhodas of previous periods, the Askaris didn't need village popular support to stay in power. In contrast to kadkhodas before land reform, they did not maintain their positions of political eminence and control over village resources by redistributing agricultural land and material resources to gain local people's support. Rather, backed by powerful central government force, they took land away from villagers in order to develop connections with government officials and to sell it for investments in other economic areas.

The land reform struggle was the last time taifeh organization was utilized in local violent confrontation until just before the Iranian Revolution of 1979. After land reform, taifeh-keshi became largely irrelevant to politics. Those individuals who had been most powerful before land reform became the post–land reform political and economic elite. Central government agencies and the main government representatives at the local level, the Askari brothers, chose the others in their administration because of their economic and political strength, just as Khanum

Khorshid Kolah had done through the taifeh-keshi process before land reform. Then, however, with support from central government agencies and the gendarmes based in Qodratabad, these individuals were able to hold on to their power, no matter how dissatisfied villagers were with their administration.

Taifeh-keshi became frozen in place. The central government, which took over ultimate political control of the village from the landlord, could enforce the indefinite tenure of its chosen representatives, the Askaris and their allies. Hence, less effort was spent maintaining taifeh cohesion. Seyyid Yaqub, the most powerful man living in Aliabad after land reform, felt no great need to prop himself up through sponsoring rituals,[36] redistributing food and other goods and socializing with villagers. Askari brothers' social interaction with other villagers declined. In the past, villagers commented, Seyyid Yaqub constantly had large numbers of guests, both villagers and his allies from throughout the area. In the late 1970s, however, Seyyid Yaqub's main guests were gendarmes from the nearby station and his top political allies within the village, most of them his cousins the opium smugglers.

FIGURE 4. Dancing at a wedding celebration of a large kinship group, summer 1979. As it is after the Revolution, some of the women are wearing chadors for better modesty in an open area where nonrelated males could see them.

The Askari brothers did not need extensive local political support, because other villagers could not compete for office by building up a local support group. Askari resources were now used to build up contacts with power centers outside the village.

Membership in a large, cohesive and strong taifeh still gave one prestige and status and generally resulted in being treated with respect within the village. This was important during weddings and other ceremonies and for a satisfying social existence. Villagers did not speak carelessly of or belittle members of large taifeh, nor would they thoughtlessly get into fights with them. Members of kinship groups usually avoided acting disrespectfully toward their own taifeh heads.

In addition to providing the important gifts of money at weddings, taifeh members accomplished most of the tremendous amount of work necessary for a wedding. The formal visit to the bride's home to ask for her; negotiation over material and financial arrangements; lending money for marriage expenses; purchasing, preparing and cooking food as well as serving it at the wedding; lending dishes and pots and other items; providing space for the celebration; hosting; preparing the bridal chamber; dancing, singing and otherwise celebrating at the wedding; cleaning up and returning borrowed items after the celebrations and visiting the bride and groom in the bridal chamber during the days following the wedding were some of the tasks of taifeh members. "The more people go on behalf of the groom and his family to ask for a bride, the more the bride's family will respect them," a villager told me. A successful wedding would not have been possible without cooperation from one's relatives and friends. Gatherings for mourning required assistance from one's taifeh too.

One's taifeh, however, was no longer intrinsic to survival and making a living. In 1978–1979, one villager described changes in taifeh as follows:

Taifeh were important when governments had no power, like at the first part of the Shah's father's regime, when there was no order. Only in the last ten years—actually less—has there been any order. Taifeh are important when the government is weak. Then there was a government, but it didn't have enough strength to punish someone who harmed someone else if that person complained. So two taifeh fought. Whoever lost, lost and couldn't complain. After one, two or five years, the losing taifeh might get stronger. Taifeh were never peaceful. They always tyrannized. Whoever had strength tyrannized over others, until the other side became stronger. Then it [the newly successful taifeh] would tyrannize over the other side.

Now it's not like that. Now, instead of fighting, people go to court to testify.

It's always good to have a taifeh, always nice to be surrounded by members of your taifeh. But now taifeh aren't the same as they were before. Each person is a taifeh for himself.

The Askaris were the most powerful taifeh, villagers agreed, emphasizing their wealth and government connections:

The Askaris had the strongest taifeh—they put Tudeh people in prison.

The Askaris have the most important taifeh. Seyyid Yaqub and Seyyid Ibn Ali have a big family and lots of wealth. No one has as much money as Seyyid Yaqub and Seyyid Ibn Ali.

Before the [1979] Revolution, the Askari taifeh was the most important. They had money and good relations with the court, SAVAK and gendarmes. They came to Seyyid Yaqub's house, and he gave them opium and liquor. The Askaris could do anything they wanted. They just had to make a phone call. People were very afraid of them. They had powerful connections.

The Askaris are the largest taifeh. All of the seyyids are Askaris. They all belong to the same family. Next largest is the Hashemi taifeh. They have 40 or 50 families. Then comes the Saedi taifeh. Since Mashd Musa Saedi is president [of the village council], no one dares bother a Saedi. The Jehangiri taifeh is also big.

Connections with the government had became more politically effective than a large taifeh of strong fighting men, and the Askaris enjoyed the most effective connections with the government. One villager listed Seyyid Ibn Ali's contacts with Shiraz political figures: Land Reform Office engineer, advisor to the governor, head of the Fars Province Office of Education, Office of Cooperatives president, Fars *Rastakhiz* ["Resurgence," the one party of the government's one party system] deputy, an important SAVAK official, and a person expected to become mayor of Shiraz. Another villager told me,

Seyyid Ibn Ali has connections with SAVAK. Seyyid Yaqub has good connections with powerful people—like the gendarmes who took you to Seyyid Yaqub's house when you first came. Now, why didn't they take you to the house of some poor person who would tell you the truth about Seyyid Ibn Ali stealing land and those things? Because Seyyid Ibn Ali and Seyyid Yaqub are in good with the gendarmerie.

Instead of courting villagers' loyalty with hospitality, Seyyid Ibn Ali and Seyyid Yaqub used the strategy of hospitality to create obligations for assistance and a friendly relationship with gendarmes and outside officials. A villager commented,

Seyyid Yaqub would have the gendarmerie colonel to his home and would bring him an opium pipe, liquor and food. Then, if the peasants fought against him, Seyyid Yaqub would have contacts and could have the peasant thrown down the stairs. Whoever came from the city, Seyyid Yaqub and the other Askari brothers would introduce themselves, take them home and give them tea and food—they entertained them.

Taifeh membership was considered useful when a taifeh head was connected with the government. Members of the Saedi and Askari taifeh, for example, took care not to offend their heads, not only out of general respect but also because they might need those heads' political power at some point. Taifeh sentiment was most apparent among the Askari political supporters and relatives. Otherwise, the political impact of taifeh organization was considered to be negligible. Villager after villager commented on the decline of taifeh-keshi political significance:

A taifeh was 20 or so people—uncles and so on—who were united. If a problem occurred or something happened to one of them, the other 19 would then help. I don't think taifeh are necessary or helpful anymore.

There used to be a lot of repression in those days. People had a lot of fear, not like now. From ancient times until now, the upper part of the village and the lower part have been fighting with each other. But from the time of land reform—about 15 years ago—until now, there hasn't been fighting. Now everyone is the same.

A taifeh is a family—several people who are related. A number of relatives are in the same taifeh and cooperate with each other. A son-in-law who before had nothing to do with one is also part of the family. If—God forbid—there is fighting between taifeh, it is important to have a lot of people in your taifeh. Before, there was a lot of fighting. Now there are a lot of taifeh but not much fighting. Now people go to school. They're literate and they understand more, so they don't get so aggressive.

Taifeh don't really exist anymore.

These days, taifeh [as kin groups and networks] are mainly for weddings and funerals.

As described before, during earlier taifeh factional conflict, people gathered together at the home of faction heads and might even stay there—for protection, planning, demonstrating support and announcing their strength to the opposition—in a process called *sangar* (entrenchment or fortification). Indicative of the declining prominence of taifeh factionalism in political process during the period between the end of the land reform struggles and the Revolution is the lack, to my knowledge, of even one case of sangar during that time.

Well-off people in the village now used government positions and government force and did not need to rely on mobilizing local taifeh power. Also, other economic opportunities had become available. Seyyid Kazem Askari, a poverty-struck son of the formerly powerful Seyyid Ayyub and a gifted analyst, described the changes in how well-off people could pursue their own interests in the late 1970s:

In those days, power was based on able-bodied men, supporters and the hanging to-gether of a few families. A person had to have wealth to give bread to the people. Then they would gather around him and support him and have confidence in him so that he would be an important person.

Today it isn't like that. Today, people put money in the bank.

Before, whoever was powerful would give food, clothes and so on to his relatives who weren't so well-off, so when the wealthy person needed help, they would help him out, and no one would be able to do anything against him. They would stick together. They were his supporters. This was a taifeh, like Mulla Mohammad Khan's taifeh or Haj Suleiman's taifeh.

The big person helped the little people so that when he had a conflict, they would gather around him. He would have social interaction with them.

At that time, those who were kadkhodas and ran things used up whatever they earned; they had guests. They didn't use it to buy land; they didn't see any value in buying land.

In those days, wealth was sheep, grain, horses or four carpets. When these things weren't looked after, they died or were destroyed, not like money in the bank, which earns interest. So their situation would decline. All of the wealth of the kadkhodas would be divided among their children.

In those days, people who ran things had supporters and power and a crowded house: five or six sons, a lot of nephews. In those days, people gave respect to a person with a lot of supporters. Today, it's capital.

Before, if someone lost his money or position, his children would become poor. If someone died or lost influence, someone else would take over his position. When another person took over the position of kadkhoda, the previous kadkhoda would see bad times.

Now it isn't like that. Seyyid Ibn Ali and his family will stay in their advantaged position. His sons will study and become professionals. He'll use his money to send his sons to the university and will give them a good profession, land and so on.

By the 1960s and 1970s, advantaged individuals, who under the Qavams might have been candidates competing for the position of kadkhoda, had means other than using their money to pull together a powerful taifeh to hold on to their positions and wealth; they had banks, capital investment, education and land valued as real estate.

FOR 15 YEARS (1964–1979), the Askaris, backed by the Qodratabad gendarmes two kilometers away, enforced loyalty to themselves and to the central government in Aliabad. With the frequent intervention of the gendarmes and higher-up government officials on behalf of the Askaris, villagers began to turn their attention and blame toward the central government, which was backing Askari corruption and brutality, as the cause of their local difficulties.

3

Economic Transformation and Political Space

AFTER THE THIRD STRUGGLE AGAINST THE ASKARIS, the local political elite, villagers learned that they could no longer swing support to a contender for village boss who might be more responsive. The Askaris doubled as agents of the central government. They took over the village political structure used by the Qavams and strengthened it with the powerful means of coercion now available. The Askaris had long experience in administering the village. They shared close kinship, neighborhood and social ties with other villagers and were in a position to know about villagers' attitudes and activities and to manipulate social, economic and political factors. With the added power of access to government bureaucracy and force, Askari control over dependent villagers was complete. The brutally repressive post–land reform political system prevented dependent residents from protesting against the local elite or the central government. During the same period, however, economic transformation freed most villagers from the grasp of the Askari-controlled political system by opening up new job opportunities outside of Aliabad.

The oil boom economy in Iran provided means to develop industry, government work and services. The central government used oil revenues on large industries, military expenditures and consumer durables. From 1963 to the late 1970s, the Iranian economy experienced a very high growth rate. The gross national product increased from the equivalent of $200 to $1000, although, because of government politics, benefits were largely enjoyed by Iranians at higher political and economic levels. In spite of a great deal of corruption, emphasis on large enterprises rather than small crafts and workshops, dependence on imports and foreign personnel and increase in income disparities, most Iranians did benefit to some extent. Living standards for most Iranians improved, at least somewhat, although the poverty level of many had been so low that improvements were not always impressive.[1]

In the 1960s and 1970s, land reform and development of transportation brought about a drastic reduction in the number of Aliabad men involved in agriculture and traditional trade. Further, the population explosion meant many more young men in need of work. In spite of development shortcomings, because of economic growth in Iran, most Aliabad men could turn to construction, industry, services and small businesses, most often outside the village. These economic changes allowed them to escape the Askaris' economic, social and political domination for the larger world's relative freedom. Under cover of urban environment anonymity in Shiraz, such men were able to join the resistance movement against the Shah's government as it grew during the late 1970s.

The Post-Land Reform Economic Elite

In many Iranian villages, land reform substituted an indigenous ruling elite for absentee landlord control. Before land reform, local landlord representatives enjoyed political and economic advantage, an advantage they often used during land reform to continue their political and economic domination. Former kadkhodas, bailiffs and rish-sefid often received more land from land reform than village sharecroppers received, either aboveboard or through underhanded means. These elites' ownership of more land, along with other economic resources, control over local government offices, access to government agents of force and monopoly over other government resources and sanctions sustained their economic and political supremacy locally.[2]

In Aliabad too, formally advantaged men took over post–land reform economic and political power. Political and economic stratification in Aliabad became more extreme.[3] In addition to the Askaris, politically powerful persons in Aliabad included the Amini brothers—the sons of the Askari brothers' father's sister. They had worked as servants for Seyyid Ayyub Askari after their father died when they were young. As adults they became associates of the Askari brothers and cooperated with them in opium trading and administration of village affairs. As they did not come from a peasant family but had been khoshneshin, they received land under land reform only through Askari intervention, then bought some additional land from Seyyid Ibn Ali Askari. The financial resources that allowed them to purchase land during the 1960s land reform resulted mainly from opium smuggling, although they also traded in other products. Even as small landowners, their increasing economic prosperity during the 1970s came mainly from opium smuggling.

Some taifeh heads who had possessed sharecropping rights just before land reform—all but one of whom were also heavily involved in trading—decided to accommodate to Askari administration, in spite of the land reform violence. They became successful members of the post–land reform elite due to their cooperation with the Askaris, membership in various local government bodies and trading activities. One even owned a shop in Shiraz. They also enjoyed ownership of a disproportionate share of village land.

Several persons who had been relatively prosperous before the early 1950s strike did not join the local post–land reform upper socioeconomic group. At least three men who were rish-sefid and taifeh heads before the strike refused to go back and work for the landlord after the strike. They lost their positions and land rights. All three had been active in agriculture only and not in trading.

Peasants without direct access to irrigated land of course lacked the resources necessary to join the post–land reform village elite or upper classes: capital, education, assistance from the Askaris and connections with influential outsiders. Former peasants and their sons got jobs elsewhere or became agricultural, vineyard and mudbrick construction and repair day laborers. They became members of the proletariat.

The Significance of Capital for Maintaining Elite Position

At no time during recent Aliabad history has land for the production of crops been the most important route to economic self-improvement for villagers. Rather, land or control over land has been acquired for investment or as a means to political power. Before land reform, the village elite had initially gained their positions through successful trading and Qavam approval, rather than through agriculture. Likewise, the post–land reform elite enjoyed advantaged positions acquired through trading and business activities and connections with government officials more than through agricultural profits. Even Seyyid Ibn Ali, who controlled more than half the village land, derived more profit from his businesses, investments and land speculation than from agriculture.

Successful traders, in opium or other goods, had possessed the capital to buy some of the land Seyyid Ibn Ali had purchased from Khanum Khorshid Kolah before land reform. They could then sell the land as a means of collecting more capital. If they worked the land rather than selling it, most hired other villagers to perform agricultural labor. Successful traders employed their surplus funds for investment. Several chose to send their sons to high school, teachers' training and university, which at that time enabled their entry into better economic situations.

Trading and the manipulation of capital provided greater benefit than raising crops for internal consumption. Capital allowed people to be flexible, to adjust to changes in the general economy by moving from one area of endeavor into another currently more rewarding enterprise. Prosperous traders increased their profits not only through trading activities but through lending capital to other traders. In the 1960s and 1970s, real estate, land speculation, capital investment, construction and business gained economic significance. Villagers with access to capital—the opium smugglers and other successful traders—were the ones who could convert to these activities.

Not only were trading and the capital accumulated through trading the most important route to economic success, but they also led to the development of useful ties to persons in authority, such as the landlord and important political and governmental figures. Through trading, pre–land reform village politicians attracted the attention of the landlord and her Shiraz agents and gained the financial ability required for ascension to the position of kadkhoda. Through economic success originating from trading activities and through their positions as mediators between the village and outside authority—then the landlord—kadkhodas enjoyed control over virtually all villagers. Through administration of agricultural land, they exerted authority over those who derived their livelihood from agriculture. Kadkhodas controlled those who earned their income from trading, through their ability to extend or deny protection and relative security for trading operations—extremely important due to insecurity in the countryside at that time. In the post–land reform situation in the 1960s and 1970s, intermediaries between the village and the outside authority—then the central government—gained their positions originally through trading and access to capital.

The Askaris had been traders and it was through their trading activities and the attendant capital accumulation that they gained their first contacts with government officials—through their *shobeh* (concessions to sell government-controlled goods) activities and then Seyyid Ibn Ali's smuggling activities—and their connections with the Qavams and their political contacts, such as Asadollah Alam and the Pahlavis. Their capital and connections allowed them to acquire land in the village and further solidify ties with government officials, either directly through selling the land to them at a reduced price or giving it to them outright, or indirectly through bribes, the money for which was obtained through land sales.

Decline of the Agriculture Sector

During the 1960s and 1970s, the number of men in Aliabad making their living from agriculture declined dramatically, and agricultural production decreased sharply. The 1952–1953 pre–land reform strike had left many peasants dispossessed of land rights, which were taken over by more prosperous persons, many of them traders. The number of riyat dropped after the 1950s peasant strike, when the landlord reduced agricultural shares from 100 to 40. Most men taking over the riyati at that time were not primarily agriculturalists but traders.[4] Instead of farming their riyati themselves, they made sharecropping arrangements with other village men, hired men to cultivate it or leased it, requesting a fixed amount of the produce. With land reform and subsequent conditions in the village, the number of full-time cultivators decreased even further for several reasons.

Shortage of Agricultural Land

Land reform cut back even more the land available to local cultivators. More and more land left the hands of peasants and went to traders and Askari-affiliated men or was sold by Seyyid Ibn Ali to outsiders. Rights to land were concentrated in the hands of fewer villagers.

Particularly detrimental for former peasants was the loss of irrigated agricultural land. Men who had previously supported themselves and their families through sharecropping suffered a drastic reduction in the amount of grain they could produce.

Before the strike, rish-sefid often controlled two gaw (eight hectares) of irrigated land while other herateh members generally controlled one gaw (four hectares) or a half of a gaw (two hectares) of irrigated land. Sometimes a father and son or two or more brothers held a share of land cooperatively. All peasants controlled larger areas of dry land. But not even the more fortunate Aliabad men who had kept or taken over riyati after the peasant strike and received land under land reform acquired irrigated land they could use to raise grain.

The land received under land reform by holders of riyati was rarely enough to support a family.[5] Among the 200 or more peasants with traditional rights to dry land, the average amount of dry land received by a person or a small group of brothers was about two hectares, with another two hectares held in fallow for the following year. The average yield of each hectare was 150 *man* (about 450 kilos). The great majority of households practicing agriculture would derive little more wheat from their land than what they needed for their own bread.[6]

As far as I know, only one person received enough land from land reform to almost entirely support himself and his family. He was the only one who did not resort to another line of work or supplement his income by working as a sharecropper or agricultural laborer for Seyyid Ibn Ali or another of the larger landowners.

The land received was usually much smaller than the areas sharecroppers had cultivated before land redistribution. One observer summed up the loss in land:

Before land reform, most of the land in Aliabad was under cultivation, and we gave a bit to the landlord. After land reform, agriculture declined. A family who before had farmed 30 hectares got two to five hectares from land reform. So only old men who can't go to work in factories work their land.

After land reform, for a period of only two years, Seyyid Ibn Ali allowed the riyat who were to receive land under land reform to cultivate wheat in a section of irrigated land above Seyyid Seraj. He then took it over for himself. The former sharecroppers were left with only the area across the highway behind the new residential area and the school and other government buildings, which they planted with apricot and apple trees.

Among the 24 small owners, as far as I know, only Seyyid Ibn Ali used any of his purchased and seized irrigated land to raise grain. He built three wells and operated a pump for irrigation. He brought in a tractor for plowing. He hired peasants to do the other hand labor of cultivating two large areas of irrigated wheatland every year. Seyyid Ibn Ali and Seyyid Yaqub hired peasants to cultivate dryland grain too.

Those who had bought land from Seyyid Ibn Ali, the khordeh-malek, received land in three different areas. They were given a small area just above the village, which became a residential area; several khordeh-malek built courtyards and homes there for themselves. On the other side of the highway from the village, they were given strips of land behind the government buildings and below the road to Seyyid Seraj that actually was supposed to fall to the lot of the sharecroppers. The ground here was stony and too far away from water sources for irrigating. It was used to construct homes. Third, Seyyid Ibn Ali allotted strips of irrigated land above the village to the khordeh-malek. Since irrigation water there was insufficient for wheat, the other 23 khordeh-malek utilized these strips to plant apricot trees and sometimes grapevines in their walled-in gardens. They and any former sharecroppers with sufficient land from land reform often exported fruit as a cash crop to the Gulf States. Cultivation of crops for the internal market lost economic significance after land reform. Considerable areas of village land, including all irrigated land acquired by the riyat and owned by the khordeh-malek (other than Seyyid Ibn Ali), were converted from grain production to fruit production, "because it is more profitable," as one small owner explained.

Irrigated land produces much more than dry land. One hectare of irrigated land generally yielded 1,500 *man* (about 4,500 kilos) of wheat from 25 *man* (75 kilos) of seed, peasants told me in 1978 and 1979, but one dryland hectare yielded only 150 *man* (450 kilos) of wheat from 15 *man* (45 kilos) of seed. Irrigated land produced about 2,000 *man* (6,000 kilos) of barley from 20 *man* (60 kilos) of seed, but dryland produced only 170 or 180 *man* (510 or 540 kilos) of barley from 13 to 14 *man* (39 to 42 kilos) of seed. Before land reform, sharecroppers had been allowed to keep one-half of their irrigated land crops. The loss of more than half of their irrigated grain fields and lack of sufficient land area or water to raise grain on what they did receive dramatically reduced the grain self-sufficiency of Aliabad villagers.

Without access to irrigated land, villagers could not raise summer crops such as chickpeas, mung beans, tomatoes or other vegetables. No longer self-sufficient, villagers were forced to buy these staples from village shopkeepers or on trips to Shiraz. Food prices in the village rose. Mung beans, for example, had been cheap locally, about two toman a *man,* but when people no longer grew it themselves, the price suddenly rose to 20 or 22 toman a *man*.

In addition to losing all irrigated land for grain and other agricultural products, agriculturalists lost more than half of their dryland during land reform. In pre–land reform days, dryland had been less closely supervised by the landlord and her local representatives; it was of less interest to her. Access to dryland plots had been based on tradition; they were passed from father to son or in other person-to-person ways, with minimal interference from the landlord or kadkhoda. Men who had gone on strike in 1952–1953 and then refused to return to work under Seyyid Yaqub lost their agricultural rights to irrigated land. However, they had not refused to work their drylands. Therefore these men had been able to go on cultivating their traditionally held drylands to provide at least enough wheat for the family bread. It was only during land reform that, for distribution purposes, holders of dryland were organized into herateh. When the khordeh-malek purchased half of the dryland and Seyyid Ibn Ali seized even more of it, those who had been working their traditionally held dryland lost much of it too.

Loss of this dryland was detrimental to villagers for two main reasons. Persons holding traditional rights to dryland had used it to grow grain for their own family bread, selling any excess. With the loss of several plots of dryland, many people were forced to buy some or all of the grain needed by their families. Since the large, flat, round homemade bread was then the mainstay of diets—the more so for less well-off families—this was troubling. A second reason the loss of dryland seriously cut village families' grain production was that before land reform only one-seventh of dryland crops was given to the landlord; their loss of dryland during land reform meant grain loss mainly to the cultivators.

Much valuable village agricultural land was taken out of cultivation. Seyyid Ibn Ali sold land to be used for setting up factories, gravel pits and a dairy, and to officials from Shiraz, such as the head of the court system and the head of the city police. Other villagers saw that their land could be more profitable through selling it than through agriculture. Both peasants and khordeh-malek sold land to other villagers and sometimes to outsiders. The post–1971 oil boom economy in Iran, which brought urban job opportunities, negatively affected agriculture in Aliabad in another way in addition to taking away labor: many villagers earned enough money from their city jobs to buy plots of land in Aliabad and build urban-style homes. Several villagers made impressive real estate profits. Land speculation was rampant. Buyers rarely used the land for agriculture but held on to it as an investment, sold it to others or used it to build a house and courtyard. Prime wheat-producing land, both above the village and across the highway, was transformed into residential areas. The former area had been built up seven or eight years before my fieldwork. The latter area was under construction in the two years preceding fieldwork, with active building going on during my stay.

Shortage of Water

In addition to shrinking agricultural land, another reason for the declining place of agriculture in the village economy was lack of water. Before land reform, all village water resources, except that used to irrigate the vineyard areas below and behind the village, were used to irrigate agricultural land. At that time, the water rotation schedule was ten days long. Water was reserved for the peasants of one kadkhoda for five days and nights, and for the other kadkhoda's peasants the next five days and nights. Each of the ten herateh enjoyed 24 hours of water every ten days.

Since land reform, the total volume of irrigation water had decreased. During my fieldwork, men with irrigation rights received water only every 22 days. The peasants who received land under land reform were allowed ten days, with one day for each of the ten herateh. This water was used to irrigate the orchard areas behind the new residential area across the highway from the village. Water flow was low. Often it would not reach trees at the lower slope of the ditches in the time allotted for an individual orchard before the owner had to dam up the ditch coming into his orchard and turn the water over to the owner of the adjacent orchard.

Ten days were allotted to the khordeh-malek—Seyyid Ibn Ali, Seyyid Yaqub and the other 22. They used them to irrigate their orchards above the village. During the other two days, the water flowed into Seyyid Ibn Ali's large orchard behind the village. Except for Seyyid Ibn Ali's irrigated wheat fields, all village water was used for orchards instead of grain, legumes or vegetables.

Seyyid Ibn Ali took more than his share of Aliabad's water resources. Seven or eight years before fieldwork, he even attempted to take over the water for villagers' household needs to irrigate his large orchard behind the village. This stream, called Khanum Zhireh's water (*Ab-e Khanum Zhireh*), was from a spring in the hills behind the village. It ran in an underground channel (*qanat*) and then in a pipe through Seyyid Ibn Ali's orchard and the vineyard area behind the village before coming into the village. Seyyid Ibn Ali had opened the section of pipe going through his orchard and was using the water to irrigate his fruit trees. Irate villagers, including his supporters—even his nephew Seyyid Muslem Askari—went into the orchard and smashed the pipe. They constructed a new pipe outside Seyyid Ibn Ali's orchard. Then Seyyid Ibn Ali built a pipe four or five kilometers long to bring water from two other village resources, Seyyid Hashemi Spring and Mashd Mirzali Spring, to his orchards. He also built a pipe to bring overflow water from the pool storing water behind the village.

Yet another attempt by Seyyid Ibn Ali to take over village water failed. A stream, Sar Cheshmeh, which brought water from the hills behind the village, flowed down to the village through a stretch of trees after emerging from its qanat. Before land reform, it had been used to irrigate some four hectares of summer crops. In 1978–1979, some village women washed their clothes in the stream and then hung them to dry on the stones of the cemetery next to it. According to a village informant,

At one point, Seyyid Ibn Ali tried to get a loan to build a little channel to bring water from the public stream flowing down past the village where women wash clothes now. He wanted to direct the water to his own orchard. But the bank officials said other people must testify that it was his water. Otherwise, he wouldn't get the loan. Someone came out to the edifice [used for the kindergarten in 1978–1979]. Some peasants told this person that the water belonged to the whole village. And this person was very good—Seyyid Ibn Ali didn't get the loan to divert village water to his orchard.

Seyyid Ibn Ali also tried to divert village water into another orchard he now owned that originally belonged to Khanum Khorshid Kolah Qavam, just beyond the wall of the village. Villagers found out about it and pulled out the pipe.

After land reform, qanats conveying water from springs or watersheds in the hills to the village fell into disrepair. Before land reform, the landlord paid half of the large expense of repairing qanats yearly and raised the other half from peasants. After land reform, it was difficult to raise funds for qanat maintenance. The two springs taken over by Seyyid Ibn Ali each had about five of the necessary holes about 30 meters apart to allow access from the surface down into the qanat. Ab-e Qavamabad, one of the two sources for the stream flowing past the trees, and the village stream, Sar Cheshmeh, together flowed through about 800,000 meters of qanat.

The most important water supply of the village, called both Ab-e Deh and Ab-e Cheshm-e Shabshotori, came from the nearby village of Darab. It provided four or five times as much water as the second most important source, Ab-e Qavamabad, and sometimes even ten times as much. One kilometer of this waterway coursed through a qanat; the other seven kilometers flowed in an open ditch. When the qanat fell into disrepair, less water reached the village.

Ditches fell into disrepair too. Villagers themselves had cleaned out the ditches prior to land reform. No special training or knowledge was needed for this work, as was required for cleaning and repairing underground qanats. However, in the 1960s and 1970s, when more men worked outside of the village and few persons were interested in agriculture, villagers no longer cooperated on the ditches. Stones and roots obstructed water flow. One villager commented,

In three or four kilometers, twenty inches of water turns into two inches. For the last six years, water from the mountains hasn't reached our land. The ditches haven't been repaired in six years. The ditches are ruined—we've abandoned them.

The important water coming from Darab, Ab-e Deh, was just a trickle because of disrepair along the seven-kilometer waterway. The water was wasted, seeping into the ground. If the same amount of water leaving Darab would arrive at Aliabad land, people said, it would be good, but all too much water was absorbed into the soil between the two villages. In years past, people reported, some 400 men got together and went out to work on the ditch coming from Darab, but for some years they had not done this.

Because fewer people were interested in keeping water flowing at its highest levels, outsiders were able to use the water with little reaction from villagers. Some years earlier, Darabis planted vineyards near the irrigation ditch and a few fruit trees too. They dammed the main ditch and opened their own little dams leading to subsidiary ditches to irrigate their fruit only on Fridays. But then they planted more vineyards and orchards near the irrigation stream and more and more often dammed up the stream to divert the water for their fruit. The water resource was valuable, they were beginning to realize. They could produce fruit as a cash crop to sell to dealers for export to the Arab Persian Gulf States. The Darabis also wanted the water for their homes that were springing up in the new residential area outside the old village.

By November 1978, Darabis were keeping their subsidiary water courses open all the time, residents of Aliabad complained. The Darabis were diverting water that according to long-standing tradition should have gone to Aliabad. If all the people in Aliabad would get together and take action, the peasants felt, they could get their water back from Darab. Peasants made complaints such as the following:

Everyone goes about his own business. People work in factories and companies. No one does agriculture any more. Only a few old men who don't have any other opportunities are forced to continue in agriculture. The others don't care so much about the water, so they don't fight for it.

Migrating Qashqai put stones in the ditch coming from Darab to flood an area for their flocks. Community action to rectify this was minimal. Rather, one person from each herateh generally walked up the ditch toward Darab laboriously removing rocks just before his herateh's turn to irrigate.

Coming from Darab, Ab-e Deh flowed through two walled-in orchards, and Ab-e Qavamabad flowed through five orchards, all belonging to people from Shiraz. The orchard owners were using the water, Aliabad people suspected, but no attempts were made at surveillance or rerouting the water outside the walled orchards. In addition to these orchards, Seyyid Ibn Ali had sold other sections of land in the same area to Shirazis. Villagers feared the new owners would also build walled-in orchards around the waterway and use the water without right.

A far larger percentage of villagers than those who wanted water for irrigation joined together to maintain access to water for household use. Household water was important for all villagers, but only the agriculturalists were interested in protecting irrigation water. Because they were a small group, the agriculturalists failed to maintain a good water supply.

Because most men worked as wage laborers or earned salaries in the city, they did not have the time or interest to clean and repair waterways. They did not care to protect irrigation sources or join conflicts over water rights. They felt no compunction to contribute money to improve the irrigation water supply.

Lack of water continually frustrated the agriculturalists. When I first talked with them, many assumed I was a government worker coming to look into agriculturalists' problems. The peasants—and even more so their sons—were cynical. They said, "Plenty of people like you have come to ask questions and write things down, but nothing ever happens," or "You could fill a hundred notebooks like that one and it wouldn't do any good. Some people are like stones. They just don't listen."

In spite of such bitter pessimism, peasants could not resist discussing their need for water, just in case there might be hope for assistance. The most important thing the government could do for peasants was to help them improve their water supply, they told me. Without water, they felt, the land was worthless. Return on the effort and expense of dryland agriculture was inadequate. For several months, peasants reacted negatively to local attempts to mobilize them into a local revolution against Seyyid Ibn Ali after the February 1979 Revolution because dryland was so lacking in value. "We already have more land than we can use," peasants would say. "What would we do with more land?"

Lack of Capital and Credit

Another factor that lowered Aliabad's agricultural production and cut down the number of men following agricultural pursuits was inadequate capital and credit. Credit from the agricultural cooperative was completely inadequate. Villagers were to put in 1,000 toman (about $132) and then should have been able to take out 3,000 toman (about $396) in a loan. But sometimes cooperative officials told villagers that insufficient funds were available and therefore not everyone could obtain a loan. According to informants, officials gave loans to their friends and took out large loans of perhaps 20,000 toman (about $2,640) themselves to use in trading, such as buying animals. Then those persons who wanted loans for agricultural purposes couldn't obtain them. To other villagers, officials extended loans of only 1,000 or 1,800 instead of 3,000 toman.

Interest on loans was 6%, taken out when a loan was granted. But in one loan booklet I examined, 80 toman rather than 60 toman was withheld as interest on a 1,000 toman loan. Another 5% was withheld, supposedly as a deposit for the borrower, to add to the capital controlled by the local cooperative branch, although as one borrower commented, "We have no idea where this 5% goes."

Villagers complained about the loans: too few loans were available, they were too small and the loan period was too short. "If I want to plant an orchard, do some farming or improve my property, how can I do it with my loan when I have to pay it back in nine months? It isn't useful to me," one villager said.

Those who used loans for agriculture were never sure their crops would be ready for harvest before their loans fell due. In 1978, the harvest was late. Villagers who had borrowed from the cooperative were forced to seek funds elsewhere to repay cooperative loans. The kadkhoda provided many of these villagers with loans at a high rate of interest, he told me, so they could repay their cooperative loans.

If credit had been more readily available, agriculturalists might have used it to improve their water supply for irrigation and multiply their agricultural production. Two attempts were made to get credit for developing Aliabad's irrigation water system, but both failed.

In one attempt, villagers had hoped to asphalt the ditch bringing Ab-e Deh water from Darab. They planned to raise money from the villagers who used that water. In addition, they wanted to obtain an interest-free loan from the Shiraz Office of Water for about 40% of the cost. However, there was a disagreement between the khoshneshin, who owned the larger proportion of vineyard area below and behind the village, and the former sharecroppers, who owned the apple and apricot orchards behind the residential area on the other side of the highway from the walled-in village. The khoshneshin wanted to give a larger share of the money, with the stipulation that the vineyard area should then be watered as often as the orchard area. The peasants refused to agree to this suggestion, saying that the vineyard area required much more water than the orchards. First, it was larger than the orchard area. Second, the irrigation system in the vineyard area entailed depressed areas surrounded with ridges to hold the water in. Each depressed area was entirely filled with water before the dam to the next depressed area, slightly lower in elevation, was opened, allowing it to be filled with water in turn. The orchard area, in contrast, was irrigated using ditches. This ditch system, with the trees planted in or next to the ditch, required only that water run down the length of the ditch. Because the peasants would not agree to their demand, the khoshneshin refused to sign the required letter asking the Office of Water for a loan. The project did not proceed.

Then the former sharecroppers hoped to obtain a loan to dig a deep well for irrigating their orchard area. Government officials came and discussed the plans with the villagers. Since the sharecroppers had never formally signed the documents agreeing to the division of land under land reform, the government agents pointed out, all of the sharecroppers were legally still partners in ownership of the land. Therefore, in order to receive a loan, every single person who had received land from land reform needed to sign the loan application. The peasants protested: some of the original recipients had died, some shares had been divided among several children, and not all owners were living in the area—it really was impossible to have all owners sign the application. The government officials did not relent. The peasants blamed government administration for their failure to obtain a loan enabling them to dig a deep well.

Peasants and small owners did not even have the capital or credit to get full benefit from the current production of their land. Out of all owners of former sharecroppers' orchards, only one family could afford to sell their apples and apricots when ripe. Because of insufficient money for living expenses, the other families leased their gardens to Seyyid Muslem early in the season, at tremendous loss.

Shortage of Labor

Because of competition from other areas of employment, labor for agriculture was lacking. In 1978–1979, plentiful job opportunities were available in factories, construction and other areas of work, and they paid more than agriculture. Most men in Aliabad chose nonagricultural work. Competition from the city for labor tended to drive up wages for agricultural labor until it was 60 toman a day in 1978 and 70 toman in 1979. Because agricultural labor became so expensive, only those persons with access to capital could afford to pay others to work their land. Most landowners could not pay wages; they restricted cultivation of their land to an area they could farm with their sons or other relatives or through cooperative agreements. Large areas of land were left fallow. Only peasants who were still vigorous and had several sons who were willing to assist them in their spare time—and most sons were not—could cultivate larger areas of their dry land. One trader who was also a former sharecropper with three sons and at least one other relative to assist him cultivated 12 hectares of dry land in 1978. However, this case was exceptional.

Lack of Profit for Grain Production

Another reason for the decline of agriculture was the government's policy of keeping the price for domestic wheat artificially low. Because at the same time labor expenses for cultivating grain continued to climb, profits fell. Motivation to continue agriculture dropped.

By fall 1978, agriculturalists were complaining that the expense of raising wheat was greater than the return. It cost 610 toman to cultivate one hectare of wheat, not including funds to transport the wheat and straw back to the village and elsewhere. Wheat sold for 4 toman a *man,* or as much as 4.5 toman for very high quality wheat. The value of the wheat raised on one hectare of land, with an average production of 150 *man* of wheat a dryland hectare, was therefore 600 toman. One hectare generally produced 100 *man* of straw, valued at 2 toman a man, equaling 200 toman worth of straw per hectare. The total value of produce from one hectare of land was about 800 toman, if the straw was sold, whereas the expenses amounted to more than 610 toman, not including the cost of transportation. Some years, due to a poor harvest, the income was less.

An unskilled laborer earned an average of 1,500 toman every month working in a factory, with a yearly income of 18,000 toman, generally supplemented with a New Year's bonus of a month's pay. The laborer did not need capital or credit before he started, nor did he fear failure; wage labor did not carry the risk of a poor crop. It is no wonder that agriculturalists turned to wage labor.

One father and son cultivated four hectares of wheat in 1978 and, by performing most of the labor themselves, were able to cut their expenses to 1,500 toman. The yield for the four hectares was 600 *man* (about 1,800 kilos) of wheat. As buying 600 *man* of wheat would have cost them 2,400 toman, at four toman a *man* (about three kilos), they saved 900 toman by raising the wheat themselves rather than buying wheat for bread at market. The 600 *man* of wheat covered the needs of their two nuclear families for flour,[7] and even provided a small surplus they could sell. That savings of 900 toman required their own contributions of almost a month of agricultural workdays each, much less than an unskilled laborer earned—1,500 toman a month. Wheat raised for family consumption was therefore cultivated either by older men whose labor could not be used elsewhere or by young men using time not taken by their other jobs or their studies. Cultivating his dryland was not a reason to keep a capable man away from earning wages in the city. As one villager stated, "Now there are fewer people to work on the land. All of the people of the village have gone to work in the city. Only the old and weak have remained in the village."

Because agriculture brought in less money and most men worked outside of Aliabad, not many people were interested in agricultural resources.

The response of most people working outside the village to the political agitators aiming to taking over Seyyid Ibn Ali's land in the aftermath of the 1979 Revolution was slow. Agricultural land did not hold much value for them. Haidar Amini's son Hushang commented on the post-Revolution anti–Seyyid Ibn Ali agitators' initial lack of success:

Mohammad Ali has gotten into being a worker and so he is getting away from being involved in the village and village affairs—that's what has happened to almost everyone. If you've done any research on *dero* [harvesting with a sickle], you've seen that almost the only people doing dero are old men—everyone else has gotten involved in factory work and things like that. That's why the people don't get together and take back their land. Their interests are elsewhere.

All of these problems drastically affected the occupational structure. An opportunistic sample of 392 village adults,[8] including more than half the men in Aliabad, then a village of about 3,000 people, showed a striking drop in reliance on agriculture. Before land reform, about half of Aliabad families had survived through agriculture, along with animal husbandry and vineyards, but in 1978–1979, out of 392 adults, only 61 practiced agriculture or animal husbandry or worked in vineyards or orchards, and only 38 of these counted themselves as agriculturalists working their own land. This actually overemphasizes agriculture. As far as I know, only one person supported himself largely from farming his own land. The other 37 farmed insufficient dryland and did not produce much more than grain for the family bread. They supplemented this with sharecropping, agricultural day labor, trading or other jobs, or they were semiretired and partially supported by sons working outside the village. Others were underemployed. The 13 men in the sample who did not own land but were agricultural workers included some also employed as day or construction workers. Seyyid Ibn Ali employed two men from the 61 people as his tractor driver and his overseer. Five men busied themselves in orchards or vineyards, although most could not make a living this way but got help from or were supported by a son. Three of the 61 derived their income primarily through animal husbandry. Two of these herded other villagers' animals. A widow whose husband had been a trader kept animals, including cows, in her courtyard but also received help from two adult sons living in the courtyard. This sharp decline in cultivation and animal husbandry is startling.

Nonrevolutionary Poor Peasants
and Small Landowners

Those persons who did continue to depend on agricultural work in Aliabad and other jobs controlled by the Askaris generally did not feel able to join the 1978–1979 anti-Shah movement. While many Aliabadis with outside connections embraced revolutionary attitudes during 1978 and 1979, poor former sharecroppers did not join the revolutionary movement.[9] They depended on Seyyid Yaqub Askari and his wealthier, Shiraz-based brother, Seyyid Ibn Ali, for agricultural work and other small jobs. They had to tailor their political attitudes and activities accordingly. Also, peasants had struggled against the Askaris before, in the peasant strike and in the land reform conflict, and had been beaten down. They weren't ready to join a resistance movement again.

Other Aliabad villagers commented on the peasants' lack of participation. Mohammad Amini observed, "The peasants were the worst [regarding lack of participation], yet they're the ones who need the Revolution the most, their positions are so bad."

In addition to the irrigated land owned by his brother Seyyid Yaqub and his other close political supporters, Seyyid Ibn Ali controlled about four-fifths of all irrigated land and virtually all agricultural work on irrigated wheatland. Except for one employee who drove a tractor for the two plowings before planting, unmechanized human labor handled all other tasks. Seyyid Ibn Ali hired older, illiterate agriculturalists to sow wheat by hand. These men also used specialized tools to construct the complicated irrigation system and then irrigated the wheat during the growth period. Each inlet and outlet for each channel and compartment had to be opened and then closed with a shovel as the water gradually flowed down the slope of the land, filling one compartment and then the next in many parallel rows. Because the irrigation system left the terrain too bumpy to harvest with a combine, Seyyid Ibn Ali also hired the older agriculturalists, who no longer had access to irrigated wheatland to farm for themselves, to harvest with hand sickles. These older, illiterate peasants, with little experience outside the village, relied on income received from agricultural work for Seyyid Ibn Ali—crucial in poorer peasants' yearly budgets.

In addition to controlling land, the Askari brothers controlled capital—which also helped ensure their monopoly over local jobs. Seyyid Muslem, Seyyid Yaqub's son, was able to lease all but one of the apricot and apple orchards belonging to small owners early in the season. As picking season approached, Seyyid Muslem hired help to pick and pack fruit from these leased orchards. The Askaris also required labor to prune, irrigate, pick and pack grapes from their extensive vineyards. The older, illiterate peasants wanted this work.

Through their ownership of other village enterprises—such as the bread bakery and a carpet factory that employed 20 to 30 girls from poorer village families—the Askari brothers controlled other village jobs as well. The Askaris hired villagers to perform domestic labor. Seyyid Yaqub's courtyard was the largest in the village and he had his mudbrick rooms repaired and improved often. Such tasks as adding another layer of mud and straw to the roof before fall rains provided much-needed cash to those chosen for this work. Although Seyyid Yaqub entertained far fewer guests than he had in the past, his wife sometimes brought in villagers, usually women, to help with household tasks. Realizing the significance of these jobs to their livelihoods, not one of the 20-some poorer peasants or poorer khoshneshin was willing to jeopardize his good standing with Seyyid Yakab by defying his wishes and participating in the resistance movement.

Just as in the past villagers had maintained ties with the current kadkhoda, post–land reform peasants and small landowners felt forced into maintaining good relations with the Askaris. Before land reform, the peasants depended on Khanum Khorshid Kolah to protect their agricultural land and their access to the irrigation water coming from Darab. They felt helpless without ties to political superiors and, ultimately, the landlord. After land reform, agriculturalists, from bitter experience, considered themselves to be without recourse other than their political superiors. Just as Khorshid Kolah Khanum had regained their water rights from Darab during the Mosaddeq period, peasants felt they had no hope other than Seyyid Ibn Ali to regain their water rights when Darabis took their water during the chaotic period of the 1978–1979 Revolution. Even Majid Jafari, the one man in the village who depended on farming his own land to support himself and his family, who had suffered greatly under Seyyid Ibn Ali during land reform, was unwilling to join the growing movement against him during October and November of 1979. He felt he had to remain loyal. Without Seyyid Ibn Ali's intervention, he feared, Aliabad would not be able to regain its water rights from Darab. "We are helpless," he said. "We can't do anything without Seyyid Ibn Ali. He has power." In spite of mistreatment by Askaris, peasants and small landowners felt their only option was to tolerate the Askari administration.[10]

Local political elites had maintained a degree of independence from Khanum Khorshid Kolah Qavam through their influence over local political factions. Both of the kadkhodas, for example, had supported the peasants in their strike for an increased share of the crop. After land reform, the local political elite became more and more dismissive of local opinion, even encroaching outrageously on local resources belonging to others. Increasingly they maintained their tenure in office against the will of the majority of villagers. They retained no independent power base within the village. Instead, they depended on connections with government offices and access to government means of coercion to maintain themselves in office. Therefore, they could be trusted to be loyal advocates of the current Pahlavi regime.

After land reform, Askaris were able to continue their earlier political and social relationships with villagers engaged in agriculture. Local central government representatives' control over cultivators after land reform was even greater than the landlord's control before land reform. Before land reform, dissatisfied peasants could mobilize taifeh and try to get a new kadkhoda. After land reform, villagers realized they could not do this. Cultivators were afraid of the Askaris because of their ties with government offices and their easy access to the gendarmes' brutal repression.

In 1978–1979, Aliabad peasants seemed to live in a different world from the defiant, fired-up, commuting young revolutionaries and were impervious to their wild enthusiasm. The peasants took a detached, patiently cynical, what-relevance-does-it-have-for-us attitude. They tended to look at the struggle as contention between two politicians for headship of the country, like a struggle between two taifeh and their heads over the position of kadkhoda—but a struggle with little relevance for their own lives—and nothing more. One peasant commented, "What difference does it make to us? One shah goes and another comes."

After Ayatollah Khomeini's arrival in February 1979, another old peasant stated, "I have lived through four shahs—including the present one" (referring to Ayatollah Khomeini).

Petty Itinerant Trading Declines

In the 1960s and 1970s, demand for traders and shopkeepers in outlying areas declined. Before, petty traders walked or rode on horses, donkeys or mules and eked out a precarious living with low levels of inventory. The oil boom and development brought roads and highways where only rough paths existed previously. People could take the bus into Shiraz and do their own shopping. With better transportation to Beyza, Konfiruz and other out-lying areas, profits from petty trading and small shops declined. Now dealers could earn enough only by handling a much larger quantity of goods, which required a pickup and more capital. Those with such resources could do relatively well; those without them faced hardships. Fewer Aliabad men could make a living from taking goods to rural areas. Some men used their capital from trading to move into more lucrative areas of investment, such as real estate and city enterprises, but not many men could.

Before pacification of the countryside, so that travelers could feel safe from robbers and roving tribesmen, and before development of modern transportation in the 1960s and 1970s, about half of Aliabad men earned their livelihoods through petty itinerant trading or shopkeeping. In my 1978–1979 opportunistic sample of 392 Aliabad adults, only 49 worked in traditional areas of trading and shopkeeping. Eight had small grocery shops in Aliabad, and one person assisted in a shop. Two men had butcher shops in Aliabad. Two other people sold cloth. Four men bought and sold animals. Nineteen men were traders or shopkeepers in outlying areas while maintaining families in Aliabad, something many more men did in earlier years.[11] Thirteen people bought and sold opium. Again, for a village that only a couple of decades earlier had provided the traders and shopkeepers for a large rural area west of Shiraz, this was a dramatic decline.

Economic Alternatives

In the 1960s and 1970s, relatively few Aliabad men could support themselves through agriculture, petty itinerant trading or operating shops in other villages. Dramatic population growth had added to the surplus of rural labor resulting from decline in agriculture and trading. At the same time, due to oil boom revenues, other areas of employment and investment were opening up. Village men were drawn into construction, factories, companies, government employment and operating new types of shops and businesses, both in Aliabad and, even more, in nearby Shiraz.[12]

In contrast to the many Aliabad men leaving agriculture, the number of people employed in constructing factories, construction support, constructing buildings, and other industries was increasing rapidly—an astounding 113 out of the 1978–1979 sample of 392! Twenty-eight worked with a local construction company, and villagers estimated it actually employed some 100 villagers and another 100 men from outside of Ali-abad. Another 15 men fell into the categories of worker, wage laborer and construction worker and were employed by construction companies in Shiraz, the Hossainabad construction company or the local construction company, or in various other unskilled labor jobs. Ten people were employed at local businesses having to do with construction, such as welding, electrical wiring, interior plastering and selling metal window and door frames. The Hossainabad construction company, located on the way to Shiraz, employed another four villagers in positions higher than unskilled labor. Three men worked at the cement factory in Shiraz. Twenty-three men in the sample worked at the German cable company between Aliabad and Shiraz. Three were employed at Eshtad Motor, the Iranian machinery factory built on village land bought from Seyyid Ibn Ali. Three men worked at the Senai-ye Namazi, an armaments factory close to Aliabad. Sixteen men worked at various other companies. Eight villagers, a son-in-law of Seyyid Asadollah Askari (Seyyid Ibn Ali and Seyyid Yaqub's brother) and seven poor relatives and village associates of the Askaris, worked at the gravel pit on village land sold by Seyyid Ibn Ali, who was also a partner. All of the men who worked in construction, factories or companies, except for the gravel pit employees and any men doing day labor for the Askaris, of course, were exempt from Askari economic control.

Another impressive 81 of the 1978–1979 sample of 392 adults held government positions. Several of these remained under Askari influence. Two kindergarten teachers—Askari relatives—and three other kindergarten workers—a cook and two janitors—felt they owed their positions to Seyyid Ibn Ali. He had donated his former village home to be used as the government kindergarten. Eight men had gained government positions through Askari intervention: Seyyid Yaqub, who headed many village government offices; the kadkhoda; head of the agricultural cooperative; head of the cooperative store; drug dispenser and driver at the local health center; and two poor relatives whom Seyyid Asadollah, who was in charge of this installation, hired as night guards at the local natural gas regulator. The two post office employees had probably gained their positions independent of Askari influence. Five men worked for the Office of Malaria Control, going out to villages to spray insecticide. The first to be hired was Seyyid Mostafa Askari, the son of the brother of the Askari brothers' father, which might have been through Askari intervention or at least information. He then pulled in other friends and relatives. Eight men taught grade or high school, which was outside Askari control. Other men got their government positions in Shiraz or elsewhere without Askari intervention. Ten villagers were city police. Two others worked at the Shiraz police office. Six men worked for government banks in Shiraz. Two men acted as prison guards in Shiraz. Five men out of the sample were in the army and three in the air force. According to villagers, some 100 young men were doing their required military service at the time, although that figure may be a little high. (I did not include this estimate of 100 in military service in the sample.) Thirteen men worked for the Offices of Water and Electricity in Shiraz, and 12 more worked for various other government offices in Shiraz. Of the 81 government employees, then, only about 14 had gained their positions through the Askari brothers.

In the few years before my fieldwork, 41 of the 392 villagers in the sample had succeeded in raising enough capital to establish a new type of shop in Aliabad, open a shop in Shiraz or start a small business—another dramatic economic change. The capital was generally accumulated from trading activities or from selling land owned in the village, land obtained under land reform or purchased from Seyyid Ibn Ali, who had bought it from the Qavams before land reform. Eight traders and shopkeepers had moved their shops to Shiraz, where they sold general merchandise, and two villagers assisted in traditional shop settings in Shiraz. Ten men had opened shops offering new types of goods or services in Aliabad: shops selling pastry, sandwiches, household equipment and rugs; a "coffee shop" offering ice cream, yogurt and soda; and a vehicle and motor repair shop. Three villagers had become successful entrepreneurs in real estate, land speculation and other middleman dealings, although one of them is included with the opium smugglers as that work was more profitable for him. Four men had bought taxis and operated them in Shiraz. Four men had opened chicken and egg shops in Shiraz. Four others worked as assistants in new types of stores or shops in Shiraz, selling such items as radios and tape recorders and pastry. Seyyid Ibn Ali employed two men in his farm machinery store. Three other villagers had opened *chelokababis*—traditional restaurants—in Shiraz. Four villagers worked in or owned business enterprises in Aliabad. Seyyid Asadollah owned the gasoline station in Aliabad, and another villager worked for him there. Seyyid Ibn Ali and Seyyid Yaqub had invested in a rug workshop in Aliabad and hired a man from Yazd to operate it. Another villager had bought a knitting machine and knit sweaters and slacks at home to sell to Shiraz shops. All of these men—except those working at Seyyid Ibn Ali's Shiraz farm machinery shop, Seyyid Asadollah's gasoline station and the Askari brothers' carpet workshop in Aliabad—worked outside the Askari brothers' sphere of influence and therefore outside their political control as well.

In 1978–1979, 17 of the 392 adults in my convenience sample worked in service areas, some of them independent, at least to a degree, from the Askaris. Two men were religious specialists, chanting from the Qoran and other religious sources for special occasions, such as the return of pilgrims from Mecca, and reciting religious stories. Two people, a man and his wife, worked as public bathhouse attendants. Two women served as informally trained midwives. One man ran the mill to grind grain. Three baked bread. One ran the bakery owned by Seyyid Yaqub, and another villager assisted him. A widow earned much of her meager livelihood by helping other women bake bread in their homes. Five people were employed as tailors or seamstresses: two men worked at the shirt shop and the coat and slacks tailoring shop in Aliabad, and a young widow supported herself and her two sons by sewing simple clothing for other villagers. The young widow's brother had opened a tailor shop in Shiraz and taken on another villager as his assistant. Two other men worked in services in Shiraz, showing the trend toward getting away from the village. One man was the driver for a Shiraz doctor. Another man worked in a Shiraz hotel.

Under land reform, persons who performed services needed by villagers, such as carpenter, blacksmith, bathhouse attendant, armed horsemen and miller, were paid by kadkhodas out of the village harvest. In 1978–1979, however, people who worked in Shiraz or received payment for their services from villagers other than the Askaris could stay away from Askari political pressure.

The category of unemployed and retired[13] persons in the sample of 392 villagers tells much about the village employment structure in the recent past and sheds light on economic transformation. Ten men were retired and four were semiretired traders or shopkeepers. Eight men were retired peasants. Along with the semiretired peasants discussed earlier who put themselves in the agricultural category, this category shows the preponderance of agriculture and trading and shopkeeping in Aliabad up until the 1970s. Only four retired persons had worked outside of agriculture or trade. Two retired teachers alone represented government employees, showing how recent the upsurge in government employment was. One person was a retired oil worker and one the retired accountant of the landlord's representative and therefore part of the agricultural system. Not one person had retired from construction, a factory, a company or one of the new shops or small businesses, again showing how new such work was for Aliabadis. Four men who had just returned from their military service were unemployed. Although a number of Aliabad men had until recently been shoemakers, this occupation had declined so precipitously that no one I knew about had retired from it. When I came to Aliabad in fall 1978, three men were shoemakers. When I left in December 1979, no one still worked in this craft.

Loosened Ties of Dependency

Only two or three decades earlier, virtually all men in Aliabad—with the exception of the few who traveled south to the Abadan oil fields—had been economically dependent on the landlord's village representatives. On the eve of the 1979 Revolution, though, some 290 people, about three-fourths of the sample of 392 adults, worked outside the village bosses' sphere of influence. One hundred and fifteen worked in factories, companies and construction outside Askari influence. Government positions resulted in freeing some 67 men out of the 392 adults in the sample from economic dependence on the Askaris.[14] Thirty-seven men had opened new types of shops or small businesses in Aliabad or Shiraz. Five worked in the service sector in Shiraz, away from the Askaris. Several others—such as a midwife, a seamstress and religious story reciters—did not depend on the Askaris but earned fees from other villagers. The 30 retired or unemployed men were of course not economically dependent on the village bosses.

Even among people involved in agriculture and traditional shopkeeping and trade, Askari domination had declined. Of the 49 people in more traditional shops and trading, probably only the 13 opium smugglers felt dependent on the Askaris for mediation should they run into legal problems. Because of this, I did not count them as economically independent from the Askaris. Because of pacification of the countryside, though, the other 36 traditional traders and shopkeepers operated outside Askari control. The few remaining itinerant traders and shopkeepers in outlying rural areas and the shopkeepers in Aliabad had gained political independence from the Askaris. Before centralization of the government and pacification of the countryside in the 1950s and 1960s, traders depended on Aliabad kadkhodas to provide the security necessary to carry on their work. Traders on good terms with the powerful Aliabad kadkhodas could expect armed horsemen in the kadkhoda's service or even the kadkhoda's own horse—a sign to marauders to stay away—to accompany them on trips to outlying areas. If a trader didn't show up when expected, or if his goods were taken, the kadkhoda could send men out on horseback for a search. When the central government gained strength in the 1950s and 1960s and the number of rural police grew, traders didn't need the protection of the kadkhoda anymore and didn't feel obliged to seek the Aliabad political elite's favor.

I am not including the 61 people involved in agricultural pursuits among those freed from Askari economic and political domination. Many of them, though, did not bring in much income from their farming work and were partially or largely supported by sons, did some trading or worked elsewhere.

Economic Transformation
and Decline in Taifeh-Keshi

Another reason for the decline of taifeh-keshi in the late 1960s and 1970s, in addition to the inability of other taifeh to compete with the government-backed Askaris, was that villagers' economic interests now lay outside the village and therefore outside the control of Askaris and their taifeh heads as well. Economic changes eliminated villagers' need to form alliances with village political leaders to obtain access to agricultural land. Few villagers continued working in the agricultural sector. In any case, Seyyid Ibn Ali and Seyyid Yaqub owned most of the irrigated land, and it would not have been possible, given their gendarmerie backing, to fight them for it.

Most villagers' livelihood now came from jobs outside the village. Networking with other villagers might be useful to obtain positions, and a large kinship group was good for weddings and gave some status. But membership in a large taifeh full of men ready to battle over access to agricultural land and good standing with a kadkhoda who would send his armed horsemen after thieves were irrelevant.

Several villagers' comments in 1978–1979 connected the decline of taifeh-keshi with the economic transformation from agriculture—and fighting over access to agricultural land—to outside jobs:

In those days, there wasn't enough of anything. People were always fighting over things to make a living. Everyone had shares of irrigated wheatland, and they fought over the borders. People fought over land, orchards and vineyards. Now people have enough to eat.

Before, the fighting was over land and position, like kadkhoda. Now everybody is a worker or a government employee. Now everyone is equal.

Before people went to the city, they had strong ties with their taifeh. Now they have occupational ties.

Toward the end of the 1970s, some 90% of village men were deriving most of their income from sources outside the village. The village was no longer a unit, with political leaders monopolizing villagers' access to economic, social and ritual resources. For men working outside the village, village heads—Seyyid Yaqub, heads of their taifeh and their taifeh in general—did not hold economic significance.

Political Space

Aliabadis who needed work in Aliabad were susceptible to Askari influence. At the time of the Revolution, Aliabad cultivators, forced into acquiescence to the central government and to the local political elite through the power the Askaris held over them, lacked the political and economic independence to turn to revolutionary ideology, take part in political action against the government or participate in revolutionary marches.

However, in the 1960s, and even more in the 1970s, economic transformation provided most villagers with alternative sources of income, allowing them to escape from the firm political grip of Askari bosses. Developments in education and literacy, communication, transportation, services and business and rising standards of living brought more ideas, contacts and interaction with the larger society. These developments and the new employment opportunities outside the village and Askari control provided villagers with new political space.[15]

Aliabad men who worked as itinerant traders or small shopkeepers in outlying rural areas no longer felt constrained to maintain good relations with the Askaris. Most village traders had very little to do with them. Even those fortunate few who could do well as shopkeepers in Aliabad didn't need to keep up good raft-o-amad relations with the Askaris. Only two were on relatively good terms with them: the shopkeeper next to Seyyid Yaqub's courtyard door, from whom his wife purchased what she needed, and Haj Khodabakhsh, an Askari political ally who was married to the sister of Ali Reza and Mashd Yusef Amini, the sons of Seyyid Yaqub's father's sister. In the 1960s and 1970s, shopkeepers were increasingly influenced by their bazar and trading associates in Shiraz rather than by the village political elite. Freedom from Askari constraint was later demonstrated by many village shopkeepers' and traders' support for the revolutionary movement, against the wishes of the Askaris.

Although not economically dependent on the Askaris, villagers could not directly oppose them—because of the gendarmes. Although a growing majority of villagers were against Askari rule, they were unable to bring about political change at the local level. By the late 1970s, however, the great majority of village men were in regular contact with city people and knowledgeable about national politics. Realizing that the Askaris were held in power by higher-level government officials, these commuters aimed their dissatisfaction with local political elites, inequitable distribution of resources and their own conditions at the national government.

The Askaris were the central government representatives in Aliabad and in charge of enforcing loyalty to the Pahlavi regime. Ironically, then, government-fostered economic development and government employment freed many village men from economic and therefore also political control by the village arm of the central government. Maintenance of Askari domination by the heavy-handed gendarmes made villagers even angrier at the central government.[16] Their new political space in Shiraz, away from the Askaris and the Qodratabad gendarmes, enabled many Aliabad men to finally vent their anger and take political action against the central government—which had kept the Askaris in local power—in the anti-Shah movement. They became a receptive audience to their fellows in Shiraz who were resisting the Shah's regime.

4

Recruitment to Revolution

IN CONTRAST TO ONLY A DECADE OR TWO EARLIER, when the Aliabad economic and political system kept many villagers in its grasp, by 1978, villagers had gained better access to Shiraz and, at least through mass media, to other parts of Iran. Newspapers and radio in Iran, under government control, broadcast the government line. During the several years of the growth of the anti-Shah uprising, however, foreign radio stations (such as the BBC Persian language service) became popular sources of trusted news about the anti-Shah movement and the government attempts to stop it. Many channels brought revolutionary communication back to Aliabad. With the bus trip into Shiraz taking only a half-hour, many villagers could go to the city and bring back what they heard and saw. Village students attending outside schools and rural-urban migrants and commuters who traveled daily to Shiraz for work or education brought back news of the developing resistance forces as well as ideologies supporting revolution. Leading up to the final fall of the Shah's government on February 11, 1979, fliers, tapes and frequent speeches in Shiraz mosques and shrines[1] provided information and perspectives. These and three religious specialists in Aliabad and visitors from mosques and the Religious School of Zahra for females in Shiraz often propagated the newly developed Shia revolutionary ideology.[2]

Yet all of these sources of revolutionary news and views, in addition to the new political space outside the village to which some Aliabad men now had access, did not in themselves provide enough motivation to urge the Aliabad population into supporting the movement. Then, beginning in summer 1978, some younger Aliabad students, migrants, commuters and

religiously inclined people witnessed government forces injuring and killing demonstrators in Shiraz. People who saw these brutal attacks became so
angry and shocked that they didn't care about their own welfare anymore,
they reported, and were ready to risk their safety by becoming activists.
Horrified, they became committed to the revolutionary admonition that
they must struggle against injustice. Next, two events of government brutality, which took place right in Aliabad, served to so infuriate the local
population that the majority of villagers swung abruptly from either supporting the Shah's regime or staying neutral to passionately joining the
resistance movement.

Commuters as Revolutionary Activists

Religious specialists made the newly developed Shia revolutionary ideology available to a large sector of the Iranian population, including many
Aliabad villagers. More important, Aliabad commuters and migrants, who
were not Islamic specialists, became the most significant culture brokers—
people who move between groups carrying new ideas and practices—bringing actual change in attitudes and behaviors to Aliabad. Home village culture
brokers were all the more persuasive because of kin, neighbor and fellow villager bonds.[3] Because of their preexisting personal relations, villagers could
trust them.[4]

Commuters usually came back to the village after work every day.
Migrant families often returned to Aliabad on Thursdays to spend Friday,
their day off, with relatives. Young men got together, and families commonly visited relatives in the evening. Aliabad young men spent time with
other resistance-minded men at their place of education or work and in
the village. Women and girls related to the commuters and, informed by
them, joined neighbors and relatives to discuss politics. They could easily
run to a neighbor's or relative's home for a quick chat during the day.[5]
Information, ideas, perspectives and emotional discussions about the dis-
sident movement became a part of busy village social life.

In effect, these commuters gathered information about the process
of the revolutionary movement and resistance perspectives from their daytime contacts, then in the evening, back in Aliabad, disseminated the information and discussed the issues. Commuters included construction and
factory workers, taxi drivers, service workers, shopkeepers and assistants
and government employees. Students were also a conduit of information

and ideas. Ten to fifteen young men from the village attended high school in Shiraz along with six to eight young women. Some of these students, especially the young women, who because of modesty expectations could not take the bus by themselves, lived in the homes of their Shiraz relatives, but most males returned to the village daily. Other villagers attended the teachers' training college in Shiraz. A few studied in universities. At least one young village man went to Tehran University for education in fall 1978 but returned to Aliabad because of anti-Shah university strikes. At the university, he had associated with leftist classmates and adopted their leftist anti-Shah ideology.

Many of these young students took the side of the revolutionary forces. Most of them eventually participated in the anti-Shah resistance movement within the Shia political framework—irrespective of their motivations, religious beliefs, levels of religiosity and the events that prompted them to get involved—because the government prevented other forms of political activity.[6]

The three struggles against the Askari regime in recent Aliabad history, followed by ongoing gendarmerie punishment of any villager who complained about the Askaris, had left the majority of villagers resentful about the local political situation. Then, as the oil boom economy expanded and more men worked outside of Aliabad, villagers became aware of others living under better conditions or even in opulence. Their inability to get opportunities enjoyed by others made villagers all the more dissatisfied and frustrated. They began to condemn the government for failure to respond to the needs of rural people. Kurosh Amini's cousin Mohsein Saedi concluded an interview with a diatribe against the Shah's regime, in words similar to those used by other young revolutionaries with independent economic bases outside of Aliabad:

We have nothing in this country. We see that others are rich and have seven- or eight-story homes, and we live in tents. It takes us one or two months to get something done in government offices, and the other side has good connections and is able to ruin us. If they attack us and fight us and we go to court, the court does nothing because they are in cahoots with them.

In some villages there aren't any bathhouses. There aren't any toilets. Women have to go naked and bathe themselves in streams in the winter. If they are sick, they die on the way to the hospital. If they have to give birth, they die on the way to Shiraz. Right now in villages like Dehbid [up the valley from Aliabad], they don't have a bathhouse or clinic, no piped water, no electricity. Animals have a better life than they do. No bathhouse even to purify themselves.[7] They live in tents and broken-down ruins of houses. No mosque. No toilet. To go to the bathroom, they have to go out behind the village.

In contrast to their parents, the young commuters had gone to school, at least for a few years. They had been exposed to the better and more modern standard of living enjoyed by many in Shiraz, and would have liked to enter this world themselves. These young Aliabad men saw others getting opportunities for higher education. Young commuters frequently mentioned how disappointed they became when they were not able to gain admittance to a university. Kurosh Amini, a leading young revolutionary whose stabbing by a pro-Shah policeman turned Aliabad against the Shah's regime, and Seyyid Mostafa Askari, whose recorded description of his experiences in the 1978 Tasua and Ashura processions is in the next chapter, had both wanted to go to the university but were unable to pass the entrance exam. During a conversation I had with Mohammad Amini in July 1979, this young activist talked at length about his bitter disappointment at not being able to attend university, a disappointment that surely increased his dissatisfaction with the government. Four times he had taken the entrance exams, failing each time. Because he had gone to an agricultural high school, he had not been able to take chemistry and physics and was not prepared in these subjects. Acceptance into a B.S. program in agriculture should be based on experience, knowledge and interest in agriculture, Mohammad felt. Others with mediocre grades had been accepted. With his good grades, he believed, he should have been admitted. After four years of trying, Mohammad gave up and sat for the easier teachers' training entrance exam. Those villagers who supported the revolutionary movement often complained about inequality and perceived injustice in the distribution of opportunities—for education and jobs—under the Shah's regime.

Young commuters who became active in demonstrations usually did not have families to support. To participate, then, they did not risk the community censure of those who did not think of their families. They did not have positions or property to lose as the older generation did. Older men remembered the disastrous results when they had tried to struggle against authorities in the past, such as in the peasant strike, the Mosaddeq period and the land reform conflict. They judged it best to avoid political involvement. Their sons knew about these conflicts, and it added to their revolutionary fervor. But as they had not actually experienced the crushing defeats of previous struggles, they were not as intimidated and cautious as older villagers.

With the economic boom and modernization of the 1960s and 1970s, barriers between the Aliabad economic and political system and the outside world were breaking down. Although Seyyid Yaqub Askari could oversee people's activities within the village, he could not monitor what they did outside of Aliabad. The Aliabad political elite could no longer control the interaction of most villagers with outsiders. Families relying on outside jobs did not feel the need to display deference any more. Some boys, Seyyid Yaqub Askari complained to me, did not even greet him in the village alleyways.

A striking characteristic of the culture brokers who mediated between Aliabad and the outside world in the late 1970s was their large number, due to both population explosion and decline of agriculture and traditional trading at the same time as outside opportunities were expanding. Because of dramatic economic growth, younger, more modern migrants and commuters lived in almost a different world from that of older, illiterate peasants back in the village—a world in which they enjoyed new political opportunities.[8]

In my interview with central young activist Kurosh Amini after his stabbing had transformed village opinion into fervent support for the revolutionary movement, he talked about the generational differences and how exposure to the city had influenced young men in the nearby village of Darab too.

In Darab [which took over Aliabad water during the Tudeh period], those who are out in society more and go into Shiraz are for Khomeini. But the old men who haven't studied and don't go into the city much aren't. There is a difference between those whose level of thinking is lower—who are illiterate and haven't seen much of the situation—and those whose level of thinking is higher. Before, it was like this in Aliabad too—a division between the old and the young.

Ironically, the Shah government's modernization program raised expectations of young commuters through exposure to others' advantages, as well as providing them with contacts and information and the economic and political maneuverability to question that same government's legitimacy and power.

Government Brutality in Shiraz

Because Shiraz, like other large cities, was a main center for antigovernment demonstrations, commuters and migrants had access to resistance attitudes and actions, which they could then pass on to Aliabad relatives and friends. Activists demonstrated and marched in Shiraz in memorial processions for "martyrs," those killed during demonstrations. These processions started as early as February 18, 1978, with other memorial processions on March 29, 1978, May 10, 1978, June 5, 1978, July 22, 1978, and on.[9]

Through their exposure to urban social interaction, relative freedom from village authority figures, new educational and financial opportunities often closed to them, information about political and economic conditions in the country and alternative ideologies, some young Aliabad commuters became attracted to the resistance movement. Typically their process of involvement was gradual until they became personally involved in a situation where they or others were brutally attacked by government personnel. Several of these young people described experiences in Shiraz that affected their attitudes toward the anti-Shah movement and their subsequent actions.

Confrontation with Police at the Teachers' College

Although Mohammad Amini was the son of Mashd Yusef Amini, one of Seyyid Yaqub's staunchest supporters, and related to the Askari brothers through his father's mother, he became one of the leading young anti-Shah organizers in the village. In political attitude, he was a liberal democrat with some socialist leanings. Mohammad was friends with several young men attending the seminary in Shiraz; he could accept reframed Shia Islam as long as it taught the attitudes in which he believed. He was also influenced by his classmates at the teachers' training college in Shiraz.

Mohammad began his revolutionary involvement cautiously, performing small, relatively harmless acts of subversion such as serving as lookout while someone else tacked up leaflets. During this process, he took part in three incidents in Shiraz that resulted in violence to protesters. During each, his anger and resolve increased.

At my request, Mohammad Amini wrote an essay describing his involvement in an incident at his teachers' college in Shiraz.

It was the 15th of *Khordad* [June 5, 1978]. We had exams that day. I got up at 6:00 and set out for the teachers' college. As I got out of the taxi across the street from the college, I noticed that slogans had been written on the walls and gate the night before. They'd already been painted over. Something still showed through, so I could make out the words: "Death to the Shah" and "Hail to Khomeini." I was shocked. This was the first time I had seen such slogans anywhere. I went in through the college gate.

Inside too the walls were covered with slogans. "Something's going to happen today," I thought to myself. I opened up my book and began to study. Other students came in, one by one. Since we all had exams, they got busy studying right away. It was almost 7:00. Some of the students were talking with each other: "It's the 15th of Khordad. Everyone's taking a holiday. All the shops are closed. We should be closed too."

I didn't know anything about the 15th of Khordad or what had happened on that day.[10] I started studying again. At 8:00 a woman announced over the loudspeaker that students should go and sit down in the exam room. At that moment, everyone started shouting—all the students, men and women together. A few minutes later she repeated the announcement to go and sit for the exam. This time the students shouted even louder. The dean of the college then told us over the loudspeaker that if we didn't go and take the exam, we'd get into serious trouble. Again the students began to shout. But some, about 40 or 50, mainly girls, went to the examination hall.

A group rushed into the examination hall and threatened the students there. They even slapped a few students. After that, all the students gathered together in the college yard. The dean and the teachers locked the hall door and the gate to their parking lot. They went inside and watched us mockingly from behind their office windows.

A group of students called out, "Unity!" Then a second and a third group shouted the same. The moment I heard the call "Unity!" my whole body trembled. I don't know if it was from fear or happiness. Everyone watching shouted: "Be united! Unity! Unity! Unity! We've got to go to Shah-e Cheragh Shrine and join the people! They're waiting for us!"

Suddenly someone said, "The police have surrounded the college!"

My brief arrest several months earlier flashed through my mind; fear seized me. I stepped aside from the crowd. But as I was drawing away, I heard some students shouting, "Don't be afraid! Stay together. Unity! Unity! Unity!"

My fear left me and I rejoined the other students. We were about 200 or 300. We headed for the college gate. The police were waiting for us, armed with plastic shields, police sticks and guns. One student spoke up: "If we go out like this, we'll be badly beaten. We have to go back and get the rest of the students."

We went back and started shouting slogans such as, "Sisters, brothers, join us! Unity! Hail to Khomeini! Death to the Shah! Death to America!"

We gradually grew in numbers, although some of the students, mostly girls, continued to study. They thought they wouldn't be bothered if the police rushed into the college. But they wouldn't have been safe since the police wouldn't stop to think about who were "troublemakers" and who not. The college had only one entrance, so we were trapped. But some of the more apprehensive students fled over the college's rear wall. We were now about 500 to 600 men and women. We went on shouting slogans. Some girls in European dress appeared to be frightened and motioned for us to stop, saying slogans weren't worth anything. But girls who wore headscarves, chadors and other religious and modest dress shouted slogans with great force.

I had never seen such a scene before. I felt like crying. Tears filled my eyes, although I didn't know why. Every time we shouted slogans, more people would join us. We tried to get all of the students on our side, but from behind their windows the teachers told them not to join us. This made some students angry; they threw rocks at the windows. One group even went into the parking lot and attacked the teachers' cars. Most students were intensely charged up, in a frenzied state. Suddenly, someone shouted for us to go into the street. We headed toward the gate. Everyone picked up a rock.

We had gone only a few steps when police started to come toward us. But we weren't afraid. We continued to push forward. The police took up positions and then attacked us. We fought them with our rocks. A violent struggle broke out, but we weren't an equal match for them. We were forced to retreat. When we went back into the college yard, I noticed the dean was watching from his window and laughing. At that very moment, a student threw a rock at him. The window shattered.

As I was watching this, I suddenly became aware that police had completely surrounded the college walls. They blocked all exits. The police then rushed into the yard. Each one grabbed a student and beat him. I didn't know where to turn. I joined the women students, hoping to lose myself among them. But one big, fat policeman had seen me from a ways off and lunged toward me. Several girls from my class surrounded me and said, "He didn't do anything."

But the policeman didn't listen. He hit my head several times with his police stick. An officer saw me and said to the policeman, "Beat up that bearded son of a bitch!"

Several other policemen joined the assault on me. I kept weaving in and out, trying to avoid blows. I was ready to give anything to find a hole for escape.

Suddenly I saw a policeman I thought I knew—Gholam, from my village. But no matter how much I tried to call out to him, my mouth wouldn't open. All at once he recognized me. He jumped several meters, and fell upon me. He warded off everyone who tried to strike me."Don't hit him, I know him." But policemen didn't listen and hit me anyway.

Since I felt I had been saved, I didn't feel sorry for myself. I felt sorry for other students. I saw one girl whose clothes were torn up wandering about in a state of shock and shame. I saw another girl fall unconscious after being struck on the head by a police stick. One boy had lost his shirt. You could see welts from a police stick on his back. Gholam, God bless you, you've saved my life.

Slowly, Gholam brought me halfway up to the college gate. He really wanted to take me outside but of course he couldn't. "Go," he said. I didn't hear anything else.

Later he told me he'd said to go outside and ask for Husein, another policeman from Aliabad. As we parted, every policeman I ran into struck me with his stick. A policeman hit me hard above my right eye. It was swelling up. It seemed as if the police purposely struck us on the face, maybe so that later they could recognize people who escaped, to take them to prison.

Somehow I managed to reach the college gate. Near the gate was a cloakroom where women left their chadors when they came into the college. There my luck turned bad. Some policemen grabbed me and ordered me into the cloakroom. I pleaded with them, to no avail.

As I was shoved into the room, I realized that comparatively I hadn't suffered much. The room was full of men and girls in far worse shape than I was. Some were missing clothes. Blood was flowing from the temples and heads of others. Many were crying and trembling. There were a lot of us in that room. There wasn't any air. Every several minutes someone opened the door to let in fresh air so we wouldn't suffocate. We stayed there about half an hour.

Suddenly the door opened. We could see a prisoner transport police van waiting outside the gate. The cops fell on us and, hitting us all the while, ordered us into the van. The policeman who was hitting me yelled, "Goddammit, get into the wagon."

His voice sounded familiar. I realized he was from Aliabad but I couldn't remember his name and he didn't know me. No matter how much I tried to think of his name, it wouldn't come to me. Just as I was climbing into the wagon I whispered the name of our village, Aliabad. Upon hearing it, he grabbed me, pulled me several paces away and then let go of me and said, "Get out of here fast."

As I watched the students being taken away, tears welled up in my eyes. I started to cry. I shouted at people who had gathered around: "Aren't they your brothers? You must help them! Don't let them be taken away."

Then the cops attacked the people. They scattered. Feeling distraught, I turned into the street. I recognized several students wandering about aimlessly. We all joined together, about 20 of us.

We walked along the street and threatened every shop that was open, since it was a public holiday and everyone must close. One of the students shouted, "Pull down your shutters," to a man standing inside his shop with the door half open. He pulled down the shutters from the inside.

As we walked in the street, a police car drew up. Cops jumped out and started after us. We all fled. I ran down an alley, looked back, and saw two cops running after me. I rushed on to a turn in the alley. A woman was walking toward me. "Lady," I asked, "Is there any trouble up ahead?"

"Yes," she replied. "Police are searching for students' places and are arresting them." Since most students came from outside the city, they tended to rent rooms in the college neighborhood.

"What'll I do?" I asked her.

She stood beside a telephone pole, opened her chador and said, "Stand behind me, under my chador." And she bravely hid me under her chador until the cops had passed by.

I thanked her and went to check on my friends. I rang and rang, but no one opened the door. Everyone thought it was the police.

"It's Mohammad. Open the door!" I shouted.

They let me in. A lot of students had crowded into the room. Fortunately, they had escaped. Everyone was describing his own experience. They asked me, "How did you get away?" I told them what had happened to me. They were amazed at my good luck.[11]

Mohammad described his feelings and attitudes during this experience—not understanding, shock, fear, a sense of unity that helped him forget fear, pity and sympathy for other victims, distress that the police could beat up students—their "brothers"—empathy with the young woman's shame, gratitude to fellow villagers who helped him, gratitude to the woman who bravely hid him under her chador, anger, distress, crying and relief when he met up with other classmates in a student's room. This experience, and his emotional reactions, became transformative, bringing about a change in his sense of self, political attitudes and behavior; it became an "identity-altering experience."[12] He entered into more revolutionary activities, such as putting up posters, networking, organizing, distributing leaflets and speaking out. The eventual result of such incidents was Mohammad's position as an anti-Shah leader in Aliabad. Mohammad addressed his fellow villagers in the mosque several times during the height of revolutionary activity.

When I talked with him in July 1979, some five months after the culmination of the Revolution, Mohammad thought back on the revolutionary process and his participation in it. His experiences with police and SAVAK, the feared secret police, radicalized him, he said, and made him more determined in his anti-Shah stance. The experiences of Mohammad and other commuters with the repression and brutality of SAVAK, police and soldiers in Shiraz made them disagree with arguments that the Shah's regime should stay in place because it provided security.

Older Peoples' Fear of Retaliation and Insecurity

Some people worried about the possibility of a tribal uprising such as had happened several times earlier in village history, resulting in loss and hardship for many villagers. Those who supported the Revolution looked with critical eyes at this attitude. In early January of 1979, one villager told me,

Some of the older people are afraid that tribes will again rise up like they did 35 years ago and come and pillage and steal. Like Seyyid Yaqub where you live. He is worried about his possessions so he sells everything—his children and his self-respect—for the sake of his possessions.

Seyyid Enayat Askari, a son of Seyyid Yaqub's sister but a firm supporter of the Revolution and Ayatollah Khomeini, in late December of 1978 dismissed the security argument:

In the past, when we went out trading, we had to go in groups and take armed guards. Now people who remember those times say the Shah has brought peace and order. They support him for fear that if he goes, law and order will go too. But they are wrong. The Shah hasn't done all that well. Iran has a history 2,500 years long. The US is only about 200 years old, and they are far ahead of us.

There is peace and order all over the world now. Robbers and highwaymen just can't operate anymore. In those days, maybe two people were killed every year. Now thousands are killed every year [by government agents and armed forces]. It was *better* then.

After the Revolution, in July 1979, Mohammad talked with me about the antigovernment current before the Revolution, including generational differences in attitude:

The most important factor holding people away from the Revolution in Aliabad was fear of insecurity. Those over 45 were afraid. They remembered what it was like before the Shah's time: no security, the village surrounded by thieves. Thieves tried to take things when villagers went out to trade. They were afraid that if the Shah left, things would return to those conditions. They thought the Shah was the only one who could manage the country. Even some hajis didn't support the Revolution at first because they were afraid of insecurity. I and others like myself even thought that at first.

It takes a long time to build up the country. It can't be done overnight; give the Shah a chance, I thought. But then I realized he's not good for the country in any way.

At the forefront of the Revolution were university students and other students who have run into the regime's repressive measures. They saw SAVAK take their classmates off, so they knew what the government was like. What do villagers know compared with university students? The religious, the young and the educated influenced others and brought them toward the Revolution.

According to Mohammad Amini, those who received land from land reform were afraid they would lose it if the Shah was overturned, or perhaps the former large landlords would take over again:

At first villagers weren't for the Revolution. The peasants thought that if the Shah went, the landlords would take over their land again. When the landlords were here, they repressed peasants in so many ways. Peasants were afraid of a return to those conditions, so they didn't support the Revolution.

In families where the fathers were Shah supporters, young commuters' revolutionary activities resulted in serious family conflicts. The relationship between Mohammad Amini and his father was ruptured for a number of weeks. His experiences and contacts at the Shiraz seminary and teachers' training college led Mohammad to political conclusions different from those of his father, a firm supporter of his cousins, the Askari brothers, and a trader and opium smuggler who likely hoped that, should he run into legal trouble with the government, Seyyid Ibn Ali would come to his rescue.[13]

Massacre at the New Mosque in Shiraz, August 10, 1978

Behnam Amini is a son of Haidar Amini, son-in-law of Seyyid Ayyub Askari—the brother of Seyyid Yaqub and Seyyid Ibn Ali Askari's father. Although a close business relationship had existed between Haidar and Seyyid Ayyub in the past, contact between them was minimal at the time of my fieldwork. Haidar felt his father-in-law had taken unfair advantage of him. He felt no compunction to support the Askaris, his in-laws. Although his wife and children continued to visit Seyyid Ayyub's home often, even they were not at all close to Seyyid Ayyub's brother's sons, Seyyid Yaqub and Seyyid Ibn Ali Askari and their families.

Haidar and his family didn't supported Seyyid Yaqub, Seyyid Ibn Ali or the Pahlavi Shah's government. Haidar preferred to take neither side in the Shah-Khomeini conflict and was critical of both. All of his sons, including one attending university in the United States favored the resistance movement. Later, though, they were quick to find fault with the policies of the Islamic Republic government.

Haidar's son Behnam, a young man who still lived at his father's home with his wife and baby, commuted to work at the government Office of Electricity in Shiraz and went to adult school to earn his high school degree. With his other married brother, he was cautious about actually participating in dangerous political activity. The massacre at the New Mosque in Shiraz on August 10, 1978, solidified his opposition to the Pahlavi Shah's government:

My wife's sister's husband works at a dry cleaner near the New Mosque. My school is near there too. That day, I went to the dry cleaner after class. Four trucks full of policemen were in the square in front of the mosque.

The people starting demonstrating and shouting slogans. The police went into the mosque and attacked them. To stop the police, some people went up on the roof of the mosque, overlooking the square, and started throwing stones down on the police. These police didn't have guns. They just had police sticks. People took their sticks and were pleased when the police fled—they thought they were victorious. Everyone gathered in the square and the mosque.

FIGURE 5. Behnam Amini holding his young daughter and the author's daughter at a family outing in his father's apricot orchard, spring 1979.

But in a quarter of an hour a large group of police arrived, and a whole troop of soldiers came with a lot of weapons—guns and tear gas. The people scattered. They ran into alleyways. Some sought refuge in the mosque. People on the mosque roof started throwing stones again, but this time the soldiers had guns. They starting shooting into the air and setting off tear gas to frighten people. Since people on the roof kept throwing stones, the Shiraz chief of police gave the order to shoot at them.

Women and children out in the street starting shouting "Allah o akbar" (God is great). They were crying too. Some people on the roof were wounded. Others were forced to go down into the mosque. The soldiers poured into the mosque. They burned motorcycles in the mosque courtyard. They dragged people who were trying to escape outside. "We didn't do anything," they kept saying, but the police put handcuffs on them and threw them into the trucks anyway. I saw this with my own eyes.

The chief of police gave orders to shoot into the mosque because one of the stones thrown from the roof hit him on the head and made him furious. They shot people who were trying to escape from the roof, and they fell down into the alleyway. People were running every which way. They arrested a lot of people. The tear gas hurt women and children. Five or six people from Aliabad were there that day. One of them got beaten up outside of the mosque and was arrested.

On that day, I felt like striking back. I was in a safe place. It was too bad I didn't have a gun so I could shoot at the soldiers, or if not a gun, even just a slingshot so I could fight back. I felt I couldn't rest until the fall of the Shah and government responsible for these things.

Three days later, Ayatollah Mahallati announced a day of public mourning because 89 people had been killed. For the day of mourning too, a lot of soldiers stayed in the square so there wouldn't be another demonstration.

Behnam Amini's witnessing of the New Mosque massacre, his personal contact with an act of government brutality, brought emotional distress and exacerbated his disdain for the Shah's regime; it became for him "an identity-altering experience."[14]

A Shiraz March During Martial Law

Roqayeh Askari is the daughter of Fatimeh Askari, sister of Seyyid Yaqub and Seyyid Ibn Ali. Although in her mid-20s, Roqayeh was not married. She was free to stay with relatives in the city. Her older sister and family lived in Shiraz. During these visits, she enjoyed daily outings for religious meetings that her female relatives attended, such as *rozehs*—recitations of martyrdom stories—and gatherings to study the Qoran. As a seyyid (descendant of the Prophet Mohammad) and member of a trading family, she was duly modest. When taking part in marches, she covered herself with a black chador, like the great majority of women, and marched with her female relatives in groups separate from the men.[15] Like the rest of her family and seyyid social group, Roqayeh was an outspoken and fervent defender of the anti-Shah movement and of Ayatollah Khomeini. Her experience at a Shiraz march before martial law was lifted reinforced her position:

We started out from Shah-e Cheragh and headed straight for Zand Intersection. We hadn't yet reached Setad Square. The leader said to sit down, someone wanted to give a speech. The leader told us not to bother soldiers or the Shah statue. We shouted slogans to soldiers. Some soldiers held pictures of Khomeini and kissed them. The women sat down.

Suddenly there were bullets and tear gas. Two people were killed and one wounded. One person was unconscious for an hour because of the gas.

The boys said the women should leave. We all went into courtyards in a street near Setad Square. There were about 12 courtyards on the street, and maybe 50 women crowded into each one. People gave us tea and warm water. They gave us sliced potatoes and told us to put them around our eyes and mouths. They burned things in the courtyard—smoke helps get rid of the gas. Men told us to say our final prayers.

After we came into the courtyard and the owner locked the door, someone starting pounding on the door and shouting, "Open up! Open up!"

We screamed. We thought it was soldiers coming to get us but it was the friend of someone who had been killed. He had taken the body to the hospital. The owner of the house got him some clothes so he could take off his bloody ones. He finally fell unconscious from the trauma.

Three or four men in the courtyard had been at the front of the demonstration. The tear gas had made them faint. People fed them warm sugar water.

The soldiers set the Ariana Theater on fire and then said the people did it. Boys told us not to come out of the courtyard, that the soldiers were burning the theater.

We were in the courtyard from noon until 4:00 in the afternoon. There was tear gas all the time. The men kept shouting slogans. Some of them set fire to a pile of tires in the middle of the street so that army vehicles couldn't get to us.

Finally some ambulances from the hospital came and took the women home. People who knew their own blood type went and gave blood for the wounded.

Roqayeh shared her experiences and her anger and disgust with pro-Shah forces because of this experience with her relatives and their neighbors in

Shiraz and her social circle in Aliabad. She became one of the most vociferous females against the Shah's government and in favor of the revolutionary movement among seyyid women of the lower neighborhood.

The Habib Mosque Massacre in Shiraz, November 20, 1978

Jafar Askari, like his sister Roqayeh, was pro-Khomeini. He was 23 in 1978. Jafar had completed several years of high school before going into the army. He worked in a Shiraz company and lived there with his married brother, making frequent visits to Aliabad. Jafar was present during the Habib Mosque massacre. This is what he described for me:

The night before, at the Friday Mosque they had announced there would be a meeting after the speech at Habib Mosque. I went to the mosque at 9:00. When I got there, the speech had already started. It was one of the clergy. The army had surrounded the mosque. There were tanks there too. As I was going in, an officer came and told an *akhund* [cleric], "Go tell him to end his speech."

The akhund replied, "I won't. Go yourself."

The officer got angry and started cursing the akhund. The akhund got angry and hit the officer on the head with an umbrella, telling him to stop insulting religion. The akhund was *very* unhappy. A fight started.

The officer ordered the soldiers to fire. They opened up the gate to the mosque and soldiers went in and fired at the people. Then helicopters came. The helicopters fired down on the people in the courtyard from above, and the army shot at them from the ground. After a while, they stopped shooting and set off tear gas—that American tear gas that Jimmy Carter sent. People ran out of the mosque, and soldiers fired on them some more. They killed about 60 people.

Women were screaming and shouting in the mosque. Someone told me one woman was crying because her son had been killed. An old woman told her, "Don't cry for your son. Be happy instead. I've lost four children."

All I was thinking was I was about to be killed. Every bullet fired might be aimed at me. I was horribly upset.

People were gathering up religious fliers, Qorans and mosque rugs so they wouldn't be burned. They seemed to be more concerned about this than saving themselves. People tried to gather the bodies of those killed as soon as possible so soldiers wouldn't get them. They took them out and tried to find their families so they could take them to the cemetery. The bodies the soldiers got they dumped all together in one grave. Now there is a little plaque at this grave saying that 36 martyrs are buried here.

The army came because they knew there was going to be a speech against the regime. The soldiers cut off the loudspeaker so people couldn't tape the speech. I saw how important speeches are and what criminals the family of the sultan are. After this, a lot more people came over to the side of Khomeini and the *mellat* [the people].

After this experience, Jafar became all the more involved in revolutionary activities. On December 7, 1978, he joined the procession traveling to the town of Ardakan, up the valley from Aliabad, and because of this, became a central figure in the stone throwing that resulted in the swing of support in Aliabad toward the side of the revolutionary forces.

Through their association with religious and educational circles, some young commuters and migrants from Aliabad had been attracted by revolutionary ideology. After encounters with SAVAK, police and soldiers, and personal exposure to regime-perpetrated violence such as they described for me, some commuters became committed activists. They joined in more demonstrations in Shiraz. They talked to their friends and family in the village. They painted the words *Imam Khomeini's Village* on the arch of the covered passageway leading into the village. They prepared the way for the majority of villagers to become partisans of the revolutionary movement when government violence struck in Aliabad.

Government Brutality in Aliabad

Even after some commuters encountered government violence in Shiraz, the great majority of villagers still remained uninvolved. It was only two incidents of violence in Aliabad itself that thoroughly disgusted and infuriated most villagers and motivated them to rise up against the authorities. Conflicts right in the village and harming fellow villagers brought about the precipitous tilt in Aliabadi popular opinion to the side of the resistance. The stone throwing and the stabbing of Kurosh outraged villagers to the point that they were no longer afraid to defy Seyyid Yaqub or to demonstrate within the village walls and shout *marg bar shah* (Death to the Shah).

By early December 1978, a small group in Aliabad supported the revolutionary movement and Khomeini. These people included those who had opposed the Shah's government and the central government's Aliabad representative, Seyyid Yaqub Askari, for a long time, such as the educators who had supported Mosaddeq. Some of the seyyids and traders, influenced by religious ideology and their contacts with the Shiraz bazar, spoke in favor of Khomeini, and so did some commuters work-ing or going to school in Shiraz. Another small group opposed Khomeini and the revolutionary movement. Seyyid Yaqub and other village admin-istrators and policemen were in this group. But most villagers remained "middle-of-the-roaders."

By remaining outside of the conflict, people hoped, they would not suffer, no matter which side ultimately won. Most people were afraid of Seyyid Yaqub. They were afraid he would bring in the gendarmes from the Qodratabad station. It was the month of Moharram, the Shia Mus-lim month of mourning for the 680 CE martyrs of Karbala. Concerned that mosque gatherings to commemorate the death of Imam Husein, chief martyr of the Shia, and his followers might turn political, gendarmes were stationed by the mosque in the evenings and whenever a speaker came from Shiraz.

The Stone Throwing

On December 7, 1978, I was going over to the home of my friend Rana, Seyyid Enayat Askari's wife. Her sister-in-law, Roqayeh Askari, called to me from a neighbor's roof where she was sitting and asked me to come up on the roof with her.[16] I was in the neighbor's home and about to start up the stairway when Roqayeh came running down, crying and screaming and striking herself on the cheek. She ran out the door and toward her own courtyard.

A university student from Ardakan, a town up the road, had been martyred at the Habib Mosque massacre. On this day, his supporters planned to commemorate his death. A number of clergy and some semi-nary students and other students had hired some minibuses and were plan-ning to go to the commemorative gathering. Roqayeh knew her brother Jafar was among these mourners.

From the roof, Roqayeh saw the convoy of vehicles coming from Shiraz, and behind them, in fast pursuit, trucks of soldiers. Then she saw helicopters coming after the convoy of mourners. The buses of demonstra-tors shouted "marg bar shah" as they approached Aliabad. Seyyid Muslem Askari, who with his father, Seyyid Yaqub (both Shah supporters), spent a lot of time standing around near the front entrance of the village, was there as the first vehicle drove by. He told boys to throw stones at the minibuses. When Seyyid Yaqub arrived, he ordered boys, Aliabadis who worked as policemen, and soldiers home on leave to shout *javid shah* (Hail to the Shah or Long live the Shah) and throw stones at the vehicle windows. They broke windows, but the buses managed to get past. In the next three villages, the demonstrators met with a similar reception. In the fourth, Yusefabad, villagers brought out rifles and shot at them.

With the addition of gendarmes and armed forces, coming toward them from settlements further up the valley, this was too much. The mourners were forced to turn back. Now they were caught in between; Aliabad villagers, soldiers and gendarmes attacked them with stones and clubs. As they tried to get past Aliabad again on their way back to Shiraz, these people beat them up badly. Aliabad women watched in horror from roofs, screaming and crying and tearing out their hair as people beat up demonstrators right in front of them.

An older son of Seyyid Yaqub (by his previous wife) who was religious and, with his wife, supported Khomeini took some of the more seriously injured into his home to wash their wounds. When his wife returned from a visit to Shiraz, she told me later, she found blood all over.

The attackers killed a two-year-old child in his mother's arms, villagers told me. Apparently at least three other people were injured, including a woman whose eye was struck by flying glass. The stone-throwers and club wielders damaged the minibuses badly, and gendarmes confiscated the battered vehicles. Government forces arrested many of the demonstrators.

Gendarmes came to Seyyid Yaqub's courtyard to congratulate him for his part in preventing the mourners from reaching Ardakan and to thank him for his services. But they couldn't resist badgering him about his orders to attack mourners, clerics and religious students, asking him in a joking manner, "It can't be true that you're a seyyid! You must be a Bahai!" (a great insult in the village).[17]

At first Seyyid Yaqub delighted in his apparent victory. He reported,

The gendarmes wanted to give me a medal, but I said it wasn't necessary. They gathered the important people of the village together and told them to make the young people stop demonstrating: "This is our territory—we don't want any problems here." [Only about 12 men could be persuaded to come and give their signatures to indicate they were willing to help stop further demonstrations. Seyyid Yaqub sent for Haidar Amini, for example, but he didn't come, suspecting that Seyyid Yaqub wanted people to sign to show their support of the government.] From the loudspeaker gendarmes called, "Long live the people of Aliabad who helped stop the buses of demonstrators from going to Ardakan and helped the army."

They're going to talk about it on television.

I was at the gate of the village. I told everyone either to go inside or to shout *javid shah* and throw stones. You can't believe how many kids from Aliabad were out there shouting *javid shah*.

The kids threw stones, and the soldiers battered the buses until some of them were a wreck. All the people shouted *javid shah*, and the soldiers danced.

The Shah's not going to go, he doesn't have to go. He has the support of the Americans.

They don't understand this. The people who don't understand this are donkeys. We have a list of 15 people who belong to the opposition.[18]

Response to the Stone Throwing

Seyyid Yaqub's mood of jubilation didn't last long. Dramatic repercussions started shortly after. People saw mourning and praying for a deceased fellow Muslim to be a religious and cultural obligation. Seyyid Yaqub's family and pious seyyid relatives were furious with him. The next day, several of his sons came to his courtyard. For a while one could hear loud, angry shouting. One son said to him, "You're a Muslim, a seyyid. How could you do this? Sixty thousand villages in Iran and this has to happen in Aliabad. Well, I'm not from Aliabad." (He was living in Shiraz at the time.)

Seyyid Yaqub's sons sat around reviling him. Seyyid Muslem even refused the milk sent over to his home by his mother the next morning. (As he had assisted his father in the stone-throwing incident, this seemed an obvious political ploy on his part.) At one point, Seyyid Yaqub's grand-niece screamed at him in his own courtyard, while he maintained a sheepish silence. He was afraid to go outside his courtyard. He tried to get the mosque, now a center for revolutionary activities, closed down. He wanted to pay some gendarmes to come and live in his courtyard for a period, but they wouldn't come. People put up crude pictures of Seyyid Yaqub on the door of the mosque and in some village shops. His wife, daughter and female relatives berated him for his part in encouraging violence against mourners. Only his cousins the smugglers backed him. They came to the courtyard singly or in twos to demonstrate their support. No women came.

Villagers were so incensed by his action that Seyyid Yaqub did not dare leave his courtyard for two weeks. People could be heard commenting, "Seyyid Yaqub's turned Bahai." Everyone in Aliabad could speak of nothing else. "Children shouldn't do that—throw stones at mourners." "The demonstrators shouldn't have said things against the Shah." "The Shah isn't a Muslim."

The next day, Ayatollah Dastgheib, one of the two most important religious leaders in Shiraz, spoke of the incident from his pulpit. He talked about the people of Aliabad who used to be so religious and now have thrown stones at clergy and religious students. Then he wept. Revolutionary activists put up pictures of Seyyid Yaqub in Shiraz mosques so people would recognize him and refuse to wait on him in Shiraz shops. Village activists provided names of Aliabad Shah supporters to Shiraz clergy. Several villagers went to Ayatollah Dastgheib in Shiraz. Only a few people from Aliabad supported the Shah, they assured him. Most were followers of Ayatollah Khomeini.

During the Shiraz Tasua and Ashura marches shortly afterward, commemorated as the eve and anniversary of the 680 CE martyrdom of Imam Husein and his followers, organizers prevented Aliabadis from carrying a large sign with the village name on it. Still sore about the stone throwing and wanting to show who was in change now, the organizers tore the sign away from them. Aliabadis were forced to march mixed in with other groups rather than in a group by themselves.

After the stone throwing, Seyyid Yaqub was thoroughly intimidated. He thought of escaping to Bandar Abbas, along the Persian Gulf, where a pro-Shah son lived. When he couldn't reach this son by phone, he went to stay with his daughter who lived on the other side of Shiraz with her husband and taught school in a village. Even his daughter and wife chastised Seyyid Yaqub for his actions and urged him to stay out of trouble in the future. For the next few days, rumors spread about Khomeini supporters coming from Shiraz to confront those responsible for the stone throwing. Other members of the village council—Hamid Jehangiri, Mashd Musa Saedi and Hashem Rezai—had assisted Seyyid Yaqub in directing the stone throwing. These leaders left for Shiraz, villagers told me, to escape potential violence on Ashura, which was expected to turn political. People warned me not to visit the homes of these political leaders, for fear I might be present during a potential attack by revolutionary activists.

Seyyid Yaqub started saying his prayers more often. He mumbled "marg bar Shah" and "durud bar Khomeini" (Hail to Khomeini or Long live Khomeini). He put up a large photo of Ayatollah Khomeini in his home. Meanwhile, in Shiraz, Seyyid Yaqub's brother Seyyid Ibn Ali Askari was busy visiting clerics and giving them gifts. After the Revolution, when an important cleric from Shiraz came to speak in Aliabad, Seyyid Yaqub, in the company of his supporters, went to the mosque to apologize publicly for his behavior in the stone-throwing incident.

From this date on, gendarmes no longer came to Aliabad. A little later, higher authorities removed them from the nearby station in Qodrata-bad. Authorities feared that people might take over the station, and then weapons would fall into the hands of revolutionaries, villagers suggested.

Aliabad residents could not tolerate the stone throwing. They were outraged because it showed disrespect to the dead. Mourning and joining in prayers for fellow Muslim dead constituted a religious duty. People attended mourning ceremonies for other villagers without invitation. In the village, etiquette required even worst enemies to join in mourning and prayers for each other's deceased family members. When Seyyid Yaqub's feeble-minded old aunt who lived in a room in his courtyard died, even his greatest adversary, Shaikh Rahim Kazemi, came to the mourning ceremony. Preventing mourners from attending the commemoration for the young Ardakan martyr was behavior no decent Muslim could abide.

Villagers were also horrified at the disrespectful treatment of clergy and religious students. Villagers might sometimes make fun of akhunds and display some cynicism about their character, but throwing stones at religious figures was going too far.

Several villagers had joined the convoy of mourners attacked at Seyyid Yaqub's prompting, including his own sister's son, Jafar. Seyyid Yaqub immediately lost all support from his own relatives. Harm or potential harm to a relative turned people against Seyyid Yaqub and his side of the conflict. Personal relationships became a significant factor in switching sides.

The Stone Throwing and Taifeh-Keshi

Crushed by the brutal retaliation of the Askaris, who were backed by central government force, Aliabad people had not felt able to test their strength through taifeh-keshi since the hushing of the resistance to the unjust implementation of land reform in 1964, some 14 years earlier. The local response to the stone throwing showed that villagers were beginning to see some possibility of again joining together in resistance to the Askaris and central government forces.

The stone-throwing incident exemplified many characteristics of traditional taifeh-keshi over the position of kadkhoda and political power in

Aliabad. As in past conflicts, both sides made efforts to rally others to support them. People became outraged at the callous and unjust use of power. They became concerned about the helpless victims, and they expressed their anger.

People talked endlessly about the stone throwing and the pepetrators' bad behavior. They tried to communicate their perspectives to others.

Similar to the losers in taifeh-keshi conflicts in Aliabad history, those who instigated the stone throwing, even the leaders of the formerly powerful Askari faction, fled for a time in fear of violent retribution. Those who won the conflict took over political power, while those who lost had no more say. As in taifeh-keshi battles in village history, leaders of the faction formerly in power felt forced to apologize. When Sajedi, an important cleric from Shiraz, came to speak at the Aliabad mosque a few weeks after the stone throwing, Seyyid Yaqub went to apologize publicly. He and his relatives and supporters listened quietly with downcast eyes to Sajedi's harsh reprimand. According to villagers, Seyyid Yaqub and Mashd Musa Saedi planned to visit an ayatollah in Shiraz to apologize for their mistake and announce their change of allegiance. In the city, Seyyid Ibn Ali was already busy forming connections with members of the incoming regime.

After the stone throwing, people analyzed the relative strength of the two sides and modified their behavior accordingly. Those on the side of the revolutionary forces felt enabled to take action against the Shah's supporters. They got so angry at the perpetrators and clearly were so unworried about potential repercussions that they tried to insult and punish them, including even broadcasting names and photos in Shiraz. Because of the stone throwing in Aliabad, and their observations about people's reactions, many people began to support the pro-Khomeini, pro-Revolution side of the conflict.

The stone throwing became the turning point of the resistance movement in Aliabad. The insurrection against the Shah's government and its local representatives had begun.

The Stabbing of Kurosh

Kurosh Amini had finished high school and worked elsewhere for a period. Then he returned to live in Aliabad while working at a nearby factory. He was well liked and respected and a main revolutionary leader among the young men. Kurosh seemed to be invested in the religious meaning of the uprising. Yet it was the attack against him, the son of a village hero, rather than any dissemination of revolutionary Shia ideology by Kurosh, that prompted the sudden surge of village sentiment against the Shah and for the Revolution.

Kurosh and his friends were incensed by the December 7, 1978, stone-throwing incident. They decided to hold a protest demonstration the next evening, December 8, two days before Tasua.

Kurosh Amini Tells His Story

By Tuesday, January 23, 1979, six weeks after he was stabbed, Kurosh was still walking cautiously because of the knife wound in his side. He described for me the December 8, 1978, demonstration against the stone throwing the evening before and its repercussions:

It was Friday, two days before Tasua. In the morning I was with some friends and suggested to them that we practice for the chest-beating to be held on Tasua and Ashura [the 9th and 10th of the month of Moharram]. Especially during the first ten days of Moharram, men observed the martyrdom of Imam Husein and his followers with ritual chest beating, called *sineh-zani*, or beating the back with chains, called *zanjir-zani*, while chanting mourning couplets in unison.] Some of them said a group is against us and want to pick a fight. We don't need to have anything to do with them, I said. All we wanted was to do the traditional chest-beating and mourning. No matter what, I said, we wanted to do sineh-zani that night, so we should get slogans ready. We wanted to find out who's for us and who's against us. At that point, we really didn't know who wanted to beat us up.

So that evening at 7:00, a large group of us—about 100—went to the mosque. We started with religious slogans. One of us put the tape recorder on. We started sineh-zani and did it for about 10 minutes. There were two lines of people facing each other, and I was between the lines directing the sineh-zani. Then the opposition, about 30 or 40, came into the mosque and joined the sineh-zani, mixing in with the rest of us. We knew they were against us and came to make trouble. We had to get out of the mosque so they wouldn't fight in God's House. It is pretty small, and it would be a sin. You shouldn't swear inside the mosque; it's a place of worship.

Our group went outside to the open space, the square in front of the mosque. I said to the others, "Guys, let's go around the village once or twice so our friends who haven't come out yet will hear us and join us." We started out. In the mosque, we had been shouting only religious slogans. Outside, we shouted both religious slogans and anti-Shah and anti-regime slogans. We started shouting anti-Shah slogans when we got to the kindergarten [about a fourth of the way around the alleyway circling inside the village]. When we got back in front of the mosque, we went back to the religious slogans. All the while, we were doing sineh-zani and were in two rows facing each other. I was in the middle. We didn't use the Ashura *noheh* [couplets mourning Imam Husein's martyrdom], but just religious and anti-Shah slogans.

The other side came out of the mosque. We went into the passageway at the gate of the village. It echoes there, so our chanting sounded louder. Then I realized we'd better not stay there. If gendarmes came, we'd be trapped between gendarmes on one side of the passageway and the pro-Shah group opposing us on the other. One opposition group had gone to Qodratabad at 7:00 when we went inside the mosque. We weren't afraid of the opposition. So I suggested we go back into the mosque. The opposition came back in too and mixed in with us. They started shouting anti-Shah slogans, so we did too. At that, they started to fight with us.

When we had gone into the mosque, some of the opposition had stayed outside. They were holding clubs and knives. I ran and closed the mosque door so those outside wouldn't be able to come in. I recognized only two of them inside the mosque. One of them said, "We've already informed the gendarmes. Wait here in the mosque till they come and arrest you."

I said, "Whoever comes, we won't come out of the mosque. We're not afraid of anyone." I told them fighting wasn't allowed inside the mosque. We kicked them out and closed the door. We stayed in the mosque shouting slogans and doing sineh-zani. When the others saw we weren't afraid, they went out and hid behind the wall of the mosque so that when we went out we wouldn't see them and they could attack us. [It was dark; the electricity was off for several hours every evening because of the anti-Shah strike by employees of the Shiraz Office of Electricity.]

Later we looked out and didn't see anyone so we came out. I was the last to come out of the mosque because I had to lock the door for the night. I saw some of the opposition beating someone up. As I ran toward them, someone came from behind and stabbed me by the left shoulder and then tried to stab me in the left thigh. I grabbed his hand to stop him. Then someone else hit me on the right arm with a club and I had to let go. The first person then stabbed me twice in the lower left side. Another person was thrashing my neck with a chain. I fell unconscious.

They had pushed me into that broken-down open water tank in the open square by the mosque while they assaulted me. I recognized the person knifing me; he was a policeman.

Three or four others were hurt the same night. Mohsein, my mother's brother's son, went and asked the policeman, "Did you stab Kurosh?"

"Yes," he retorted, "and I'll get you too." And he stabbed Mohsein in the left arm.

I was losing a lot of blood. I didn't know what was going on. Some people lifted me up and took me home. After my friends brought me home, there was more fighting, mainly with clubs and chains.

My relatives all gathered and realized they had to take me into Shiraz. My relatives, Hushang and Mostafa and my uncles, got a car belonging to a middle-of-the-roader, someone in the army. He drove us to the gendarmerie station in Qodratabad. They knew I was against the regime. The gendarmes said army personnel weren't allowed to come into Shiraz now, and a private citizen should take me. So we had to go back to Aliabad. I was in bad condition, not far from death. We got another car and driver. This time we didn't check in with the gendarme station. They stopped us at Qasr el-Dasht, but when the officer saw me, he said to take me to the hospital. We had to stop at five check points before we got to the hospital. [It was after the martial law curfew.] We left Aliabad at 8:30, and it was midnight by the time we got to Nemazi Hospital. They examined me, took six X-rays, and wheeled me into the operating room. I was in surgery from midnight until 6:00 in the morning.

They kept me in the hospital for a week. Every day, 50 or 60 people would come during the visiting hours from 2:00 to 4:00 in the afternoon. Someone was with me all the time—Hushang, Mostafa, Behnam or one of my uncles. We didn't even know some of the people who came to see me. A lot of people who live in Shiraz came. People even came from Ardakan.

From the day I was wounded, the head of the gendarmerie station hasn't come out. Yesterday noon, when I was coming back from getting a shot at the hospital, I saw that the gendarmes were leaving their station in Qodratabad. They took everything with them. They're gone.

The result of this is now Aliabad people realize that those on the other side are all like this. People were very, very unhappy that I was knifed. They were terribly angry at the people who did this, and they joined our side.

We wanted to go and complain at the gendarmerie station, but they didn't accept our complaint. They said that the people of Aliabad must solve their own problems. Whoever is killed is killed. They said this because an anti-Shah person had been stabbed. But we weren't willing to take revenge ourselves. So we went to the court. But there's a strike at the court now [in support of the uprising], so we have to wait until the strike is over.

Because of this incident, the middle-of-the-roaders came to our side.

Another influence was Ashura [the day of huge revolutionary marches all over the country, which basically marked the end of the Shah's regime]. They have faith now and are with the *mellat*. They'll support the struggle as long as it lasts.

Kurosh Amini ended his interview with me by condemning the Shah's government representative in Aliabad, Seyyid Yaqub Askari, and his brother Seyyid Ibn Ali Askari: "Seyyid Yaqub used to control everything in Aliabad. He was like the dictator and shah of Aliabad. Seyyid Yaqub and Seyyid Ibn Ali stole the land of Aliabad people."

Other pro-Revolution Aliabadis complained often about the Askaris in their conversations, using similar terms. Clearly Kurosh and the others placed the local Askari faction and its supporters together with the Shah's government and rose up against both simultaneously.

Mohsein Saedi's Story

Kurosh's cousin, Mohsein Saedi, had worked in Shiraz. Later he purchased a knitting machine and sold knit pants and sweaters for men, women and children to Shiraz shops. He lived with his wife and young child in his father's home in Aliabad. Mohsein told me about his experiences on December 7 and 8 and then about how people had switched sides after these pivotal events.

The day after the stone throwing, a bunch of us had a demonstration. We shouted slogans and did chest beating. All of the *mojahedin* [holy war soldiers or warriors for religion—in other words, the anti-Shah, pro-Khomeini men] went around in the alleyways inside the village walls. Then Mehdi, Kurosh's brother-in-law, and some of his relatives attacked us. They fell upon us with chains and knives.

Three of us were wounded and three or four others were hurt. Mehdi stabbed me in the arm. I had to have stitches. Kurosh was in the hospital for a week. Five or six other people had to go to the hospital.

When we got out, we had more demonstrations protesting the beating up of mojahedin. We kept shouting slogans and marching around the village. More and more people came over to our side. People who had moved into Shiraz started coming back to Aliabad and shouting slogans in the village with other Aliabad people.

The same afternoon Kurosh was wounded we had gone and listened to Dastgheib. We read religious leaflets. We believe in freedom and rights for the people. We want an Islamic government.[19]

Mehdi's cousin Fazlollah Rezai and Fazlollah's whole family were for the Revolution. But Mehdi's father and another uncle were against the Revolution, so they all fought with each other. The two brothers were afraid that if the Shah goes, the piped water, electricity and piped natural gas will go too. But we explained that no, God gives all this and God gives freedom. God and the Qoran give us freedom.

Now they've made up. They've all joined the side of the people. Mehdi and his father and uncle have come and shouted slogans. They've said they made a mistake and have given speeches supporting the people.

The Story Behind the Stabbing of Kurosh

Kurosh did not mention this nor did he give the name of his assailant, but it was Kurosh's brother-in-law. Mehdi had married Kurosh's sister Goltaj a couple of years earlier, when she was 14. Mehdi found fault with her. Several times he sent her back to her father's home, then later sent for her again. The last time, he sent a female relative to fetch her back. Kurosh refused to hand her over, asking that Mehdi himself come along with several of his male relatives, to show they took the situation seriously, to discuss the matter. Mehdi was not willing to do this. He was furious and bore a bitter grudge against Kurosh for not sending his wife back to him when he wanted her. Mehdi's mother kept Goltaj's little daughter. Reports of her mistreatment further offended Kurosh and his family. The situation continued at an impasse until the revolutionary movement came to the village.

Mehdi felt the political conflict offered him an excellent opportunity to get revenge on Kurosh, even to kill him, according to villagers. Mehdi was Haj Khodabakhsh's sister's son. Haj Khodabakhsh's wife was the sister of Mashd Yusef and Ali Reza Amini, who were Seyyid Yaqub's closest allies. Mehdi was thus well connected with the Shah's government power structure in the village and therefore with the Shah's government officials and forces outside of Aliabad as well. As Kurosh was a key revolutionary organizer, Mehdi felt he could bring him to harm while appearing to be merely defending the Shah and his government from revolutionary threat.

Many villagers resented those Aliabadis like Mehdi who were policemen, saying they were arrogant and thought they could do anything they wanted. Villagers believed Mehdi thought the following: "I can strike him down under the cover of revolutionary conflict. The Shah's on his throne, and the government supports me."

Reaction to the Stabbing of Kurosh

When Kurosh was knifed, practically the whole population of Aliabad was outraged.[20] After taking Kurosh to his own home, his group of supporters, in a fury, went back out into the village alleyways and shouted "marg bar shah, " hitherto not heard within the village walls. In the words of one young man, "After Kurosh was stabbed, we all poured out and screamed 'marg bar shah' without fear."[21]

Villagers were incensed beyond the point of toleration by the knifing of Kurosh, for several reasons. Kurosh's father had been killed, or "martyred," as villagers said, several decades earlier in the struggle to get Aliabad water back from Darab during the chaos of the 1950s Mosaddeq-Shah conflict. The memory of Kurosh's father was enshrined in village history. As one villager explained,

It was Kurosh's father who was killed in the fight with Darab over water. They hid the body. We couldn't find it for four months. When it was finally found, there were worms in the knife hole. Kurosh was still in his mother's stomach at the time, or maybe he was a year old. To have such a past and then to have to go through this—

Partly because he had been orphaned in this way, Kurosh was a village favorite. Also, he was educated and considered to be a good person. Further, villagers could see that Mehdi and his supporters, most of them policemen, had taken blatant advantage of their positions and connections to get revenge on a personal matter. The message of the older antigovernment leaders and the young commuters was brought home to the whole village community: Shah supporters are corrupt and care nothing for the people. They use their positions for their own interests.[22]

In his interview with me, Kurosh analyzed the effect of his stabbing on the political stances of Aliabad people:

At that time, the middle-of-the-roaders were the largest group. They thought they wouldn't have any problems no matter which side won. But because of this situation, they came over to the side of Khomeini. Before, they didn't know about this regime. Now they know more about it. Mohammad [Amini, who recounted his experience of violence at the Shiraz teachers' training college] has been giving speeches. Now they know that this regime is dirty.

Kurosh's enemies and village pro-government forces in general were intimidated. When Kurosh returned home from the hospital, some 70 people went to his home to apologize and ask forgiveness.

Haj Khodabakhsh's two sons, Mehdi's sister's husband and Reza Amini, a son of Mashd Yusef, had joined Mehdi in his attack on Kurosh and his friends. Mashd Yusef pledged to prevent his own sons and his sister's sons—Haj Khodabakhsh's boys—from getting involved should further conflict develop in this family problem.

When Kurosh returned home from the hospital, everyone came to his courtyard to see him except his assailant, Mehdi—even Mashd Yusef, Ali Reza and Haj Khodabakhsh. They were afraid, other villagers pointed out. They were afraid people wouldn't let them stay in the village, they would be put in prison, they would be beaten up. The tables had turned. Public sentiment and the village balance of power had reversed. The gendarmes and Seyyid Yaqub and his assistants had lost control.

Meaningful, Relevant and Imperative

The stone throwing in Aliabad initiated a chain of events and a precipitous upswing in revolutionary activities.[23] Kurosh's cousin Mohsein Saedi's story recounts how the next afternoon after the stone throwing he and others went into Shiraz to listen to the pro-Khomeini, pro-Revolution cleric Ayatollah Dastgheib, and they began reading revolutionary leaflets and supporting an Islamic government.

During his January 23, 1979, interview with me, Kurosh also reported the following:

At the stone throwing, the same policeman who knifed me threw stones, and others did too. I was in the city that day. It was to protest the stone throwing that my friends and I held the demonstration the next night, and I got stabbed. When Sajedi came and spoke in the Aliabad mosque, he also told them they shouldn't have done this. The day of the stone throwing wakened the mellat. It raised their consciousness.[24]

When the other people wounded during the attack against Kurosh were released from the hospital (including Mohsein), they held more demonstrations in Aliabad, "shouting slogans and marching around the village," Kurosh's cousin Mohsein said. More and more people came over to their side, Mohsein reported; people from Aliabad who had moved to Shiraz even came back to demonstrate with them.

The evening following the stabbing, December 9, 1978, and the eve of Tasua, a large group did zanjir zani while shouting "marg bar shah" and other anti-Shah slogans in rhythm with the chain blows hitting their backs, until 12:00 or 1:00 at night. On Tasua and Ashura, December 10 and 11, several hundred villagers marched in the processions in Shiraz and then returned in a long convoy of vehicles with horns blowing and thunderous shouting of anti-government slogans. They convened in the mosque and then marched around the village lanes, accompanying their zanjir-zani with defiant, victorious, jubilant shouting of "marg bar shah" and other antiregime slogans.

As this sequence of events clearly shows, instead of Aliabadis being motivated by Shia ideology to rise up against the Shah's government, it was the stone throwing and stabbing of Kurosh that brought about Aliabadis' sudden shift in views and actions toward the revolutionary movement.

The various ideologies of resistance were available before. Many channels of communication had exposed villagers to the modified Shia ideology of revolution.[25] However, until the resistance movement made sense— when it became meaningful, relevant and imperative because of the violent incidents in Aliabad involving villagers—the majority of Aliabadis felt no compulsion to act, to participate in the revolutionary movement. The majority of villagers became outraged and willing to support the anti-Shah movement publicly only when Shah supporters harmed a relative, a fellow villager. Only after these outrageous events of violence in Aliabad did Mohsein and the majority of other villagers turn to supporting the Shia clerics and an Islamic government—the political framework available to contest the Shah's regime.

The Stabbing of Kurosh and Taifeh-Keshi

The resistance movement against the Shah's government also became meaningful, relevant and imperative because it fit into villagers' taifeh-keshi political culture. The Shah-Khomeini conflict could be interpreted using villagers' taifeh-keshi political processual paradigm, discussed in the Introduction, and villagers could effectively use that paradigm to guide their reactions and decision making regarding the national revolutionary process.

My interview with Kurosh showed the influence of taifeh-keshi attitudes and process, the taifeh proccessual paradigm:[26]

People gave loyalty to the Shah's regime because of access to means of livelihood.

Shah supporters were joined by fathers and brothers.

Relatives gathered when a kinsman was injured.

Harm to a taifeh member provoked political activity.

Conflict between taifeh developed during the sineh-zani of Moharram.

An attitude of outrage mobilized political action.

Villagers relied on physical prowess and numbers of taifeh members rather than on government and formal means of social control.

Government personnel provided no assistance if one wasn't on the right side.

Many people showed support through physical presence.

Villagers established a sangar (fortification or entrenchment for the purposes of protection and show of force) both at the hospital and in Kurosh's courtyard.

The assailant came to beg forgiveness and make up.

People expected the Islamic Republic, when established, to punish the opposition. (Pro-movement people provided a list of names to the Shiraz clergy for this purpose, just as Seyyid Yaqub had provided the gendarmes in Qodratabad with a list of people opposing the Shah's regime.)

The incident demonstrated the strength of support for the opposition.

The losing side joined the winning side out of fear and after concluding that the winning side was continuing to make progress.

Middle-of-the-roaders joined the opposition after outrageous events.

People expected that even Seyyid Yaqub's staunchest supporters would "gradually come over to our side."

The newly victorious faction was willing to accept members from the losing side without question.

The resisting faction used the concept of justice to turn people away from the previously dominant faction and to explain their own attitudes.

Main figures of the losing side fled.

Supporters held high expectations of the new regime.

Leaders of the resistance expressed a desire for "unity" and "consensus."

The losing side was intimidated into "unity" through the use of force.

The losing side cooperated and showed support by joining in demonstrations because they realized the former opposition was now stronger.

"Unity" was restored.

People who supported the resistance complainted about the tyranny, corruption and injustice of previous village and national leaders and held idealized expectations of conditions under the new regime.

My conversation with Kurosh's cousin Mohsein about the knifing of Kurosh also exemplified many aspects of attitudes and behavior connected with taifeh-keshi, such as the following:

Sticking together of male relatives

Political alliance of people related through women

Harm to a kinsman provoking mobilization of the taifeh

Reliance on physical prowess and numbers of taifeh members rather than on government

Physical violence in confrontation

Loyalty to the Shah because of assistance received (piped water, electricity and piped natural gas)

Crowds and demonstrations

Rapid shifting of more people to the opposition after the stone throwing and stabbing of Kurosh

Complaints about the government's failure to provide for the people

Complaints of receiving no benefits from this government, of not having good connections like people on the other side did and receiving no assistance from government offices

Complaints about the lack of humanity and the terrible behavior of incumbent forces

An incident of outrageous behavior that infuriates people and instigates and provides the rationale for uprising and conflict

Leaders and followers from the previously dominant faction visiting, apologizing, admitting to having made a mistake, and shouting slogans and giving speeches to show they support the people

Restored (forced) unity under the newly dominant faction

Declarations of allegiance to the new regime and no possibility of independent, alternative opinions

Comparison of these two accounts of the stabbing of Kurosh with Hushang Amini's account in the Introduction of the taifeh-keshi process that occurred when the taifeh of Hushang's father, Haidar Amini, ousted Mulla Jamshid from the position of kadkhoda shows many points of similarity. The striking parallels can be taken as an indication that taifeh ethos and worldview and the taifeh-keshi processual paradigm still molded political perceptions, values and expectations and channeled political behavior, even when the arena of conflict included national politics. In discussing further how taifeh-keshi culture permeated the process of involvement of the majority of Aliabad villagers in the revolutionary movement, I focus on four main areas: (1) the size and strength of Kurosh's taifeh—which, as in the past, made them feel able to fight; (2) how taifeh-keshi perceptions channeled emotions; (3) how looking at the revival of the institution of sangar further documents the resurgence of taifeh-keshi process in villagers' participation in the national-level revolutionary movement; and finally (4) how people carefully observed the balance of power to decide which side they should support, feared retaliation and shifted to the side they calculated was winning, and how losers lost all political power, had to flee, were punished and had to apologize and join the winning side—or to put it briefly: losers lose all, winners take all, and no room is available for open political discussion or legitimate opposition.

Kurosh's Taifeh

Kurosh belonged to a large and influential taifeh. His close relatives— his father's brothers (his father's family included seven male siblings) and their offspring—alone numbered 60 or 70. One uncle, his future father-in-law, Haidar Amini, had been taifeh head and long an influential and respected leader in the village, though he had never accepted the position of kadkhoda. Haidar had seven sons as well. Two had married, and their wives were from other large, influential kinship groups. Kurosh was related to other large, influential taifeh as well, including relatives of the Askari brothers: his father's brother Haidar was married to the daughter of Seyyid Ayyub Askari. Because of the bilateral kinship system, including ties through both male and female lines and with in-laws, almost all villagers could trace kin ties with Kurosh and felt personally affronted when this son of a village martyr was attacked. Almost any villager who discerned the shift in power in terms of number of supporters and strength of conviction away from the pro-Shah side and toward the pro-resistance side could use kinship ties to Kurosh, in addition to village values, to explain their outrage and facilitate their abrupt move over to the resistance.

Channeling Emotional Expression

Emotions and attitudes played a significant part in pulling Aliabadis into the anti-Shah movement. Events of government brutality in which villagers were personally involved left them feeling so outraged and furious that they no longer cared about their own safety and well-being, they reported. The Persian phrase *az khod gozashteh* (beyond caring about one's own person, going beyond oneself)[27] describes this attitude and action orientation.

Emotions aroused by acts of government brutality turned people away from the government, ratified the resistance movement's condemnation of the Shah's regime and made people so determined that they were ready to support the uprising no matter what the cost to themselves. Yet the response of "az khod gozashteh" appeared to come after a period of careful observation of political conditions and several tests of political strength. Both Kurosh and his cousin Mohsein talked about how Shah supporters saw they were badly outnumbered and therefore shifted sides. People apparently allowed themselves to act on their outrage because they judged the emerging resistance forces to be becoming the majority. They calculated the relative strength of the two sides, then channeled their emotions according to their political analyses.[28]

Villagers were exquisitely aware of the surge of sentiment related to the brutal attack against Kurosh, and of its political implications. The outpouring of horror, rage and grief occurred in a community setting, where people were all related to each other, knew each other well, knew village history and knew how others would react to events. Villagers could see they were in a large and fired-up company. The emotions of shock and outrage from the stabbing of Kurosh, the realization that most villagers would have similar reactions and observations of the huge, angry crowds expressing emotions and protesting this violence made new political actions possible for Aliabad villagers. It seems likely that Kurosh's supporters were able to rise up against the village's Shah supporters, pouring out and screaming "marg bar shah" without fear, because of the size of Kurosh's taifeh and their observations of the relative strength of their own side, recognition of how angry this violence made many other villagers, perceptions of the gendarmes' recent growing caution, knowledge of the population's anger at Seyyid Yaqub because of the previous day's stone-throwing event, understanding that the injury to Kurosh would further strengthen their own position because villagers became outraged about the stabbing of a village martyr's son, and realization of the common motivating emotion of outrage and other villagers' reactions.

The old regime's brutal violence and people's outraged sense of justice provided an occasion and a good rationale for suddenly and safely deserting the old regime and joining the emergent movement along with the village majority. As people came together, they could see the size of the crowd and people's postures and gestures, hear the outbursts and sense people's sentiments and level of anger—and feel all the more free to express horror and outrage themselves. As they were all together, they could watch others' responses and move with them in that response. Large groups of people could declare their switch simultaneously, decreasing the chances of punishment against any one of them.

Reemergence of Sangar

Sangar had not taken place in Aliabad since 1964. Because of the ever-present threat of gendarmes coming in to "settle" community conflicts for the Askaris, the Askaris had no need to practice sangar or taifeh-keshi. For opposing factions, it had been useless to do so. The erosion of central government political control and the shifting balance of power in Aliabad during late fall 1978 and afterward could be followed by focusing on sangar and was also further influenced by sangar. By observing who held a sangar and who did not and noting relative size and strength of the competing sangar, villagers could see for themselves the degree of support retained by the Askaris in Aliabad and, by extension, by the Shah's regime. Villagers made political decisions influenced by this perception, and many shifted over to the side of the revolutionary forces.

After his brother-in-law Mehdi stabbed Kurosh, crowds of neighbors, relatives and friends streamed into Kurosh's family courtyard to show their outrage and support in the first sangar held since 1964, as far as I know. Women screamed and lamented, beating their chests and spewing out their anger and grief. Kurosh was taken to the hospital later that night, his relatives getting him past the gendarmerie blockade in Qodratabad only with difficulty. His courtyard in the village continued to be the scene of activity.

During Kurosh's hospital stay as well, many people—according to reports, some 30 to 60 a day—came to show support for Kurosh, concern about his welfare and condemnation of his brother-in-law—a progovernment policeman. Kurosh's taifeh made sure a close relative was with him at all times. Even some people from Ardakan, the destination of the convoy of vehicles attacked in Aliabad, came to the hospital. The commotion and crowds—holding, in effect, a sangar at the hospital—presented an overwhelming visual indication of the strength in numbers of Kurosh's supporters and, by extension, of the anti-Shah forces. People knew about the surging antigovernment movement throughout Iran and realized that outside backing for village government personnel was weakening. The message came across clear. Realizing the flood of village sentiment against him, even Kurosh's assailant came to the hospital.

When Kurosh was released from the hospital after a week, the sangar continued at his home. Behnam Amini and Haidar Amini's other sons were among those most attentive to Kurosh. Kurosh was the son of Haidar Amini's brother and was close friends and associates of his cousins, Haidar's sons. He was engaged to Haidar's only daughter. He married her a few months later.

Those present in Kurosh's courtyard included even members of the Askari taifeh, because Haidar Amini was the son-in-law of Seyyid Ayyub Askari, who was the brother of Seyyid Ibn Ali and Seyyid Yaqub Askari's father. Haidar's wife and sons were frequent visitors in Seyyid Ayyub's home. Seyyid Yaqub's son Seyyid Mostafa Askari and the womenfolk of Seyyid Ayyub's household, his wife and daughter—the latter a good friend of one of Haidar's young sons—were among those most grieved and incensed by the injury to Kurosh.

Self-Interests, Fear of Revenge and Forced Unity Under the New Power Regime

Another striking parallel with early taifeh-keshi conflict over the position of kadkhoda and control of Aliabad agriculture was affiliation decision making based on self-interest, as well as the perception that others made decisions based on their own interests rather than on ideology. People expected others to analyze the strength of the two sides and join the side they felt would win. They were forced to come over to the winning side. They would be punished for their previous affiliation unless they could successfully apologize and ask forgiveness for the past. (However,

Kurosh did say that he and his supporters were not willing to take revenge on his attackers themselves, so they complained to the gendarmes.) Then they should stifle any personal feelings of allegiance to former authorities. Opposition was not allowed.

Kurosh reported some of this in his interview with me. His interview showed heavy influence from taifeh-keshi political culture, in spite of the fact that some of his words implied religious motivation:

The people on the other side were mainly policemen and their brothers and fathers. They are afraid that if this regime falls, they'll lose their jobs. That's why they're on the other side. And then their fathers and brothers support them.

. . . Most of those who are against the mellat are from the third class, uninformed and uneducated. And government representatives and landlords, those in positions of authority, have gotten used to this government. People from the upper classes and government employees had raft-o-amad with the representatives of the regime. For 50 years they cooperated with this regime in stealing from the people. They're afraid the people will want revenge. This is mainly why they're against the Revolution. But if the Islamic government is a good one, this won't happen.

. . . Some of the other side left and didn't come back for a week. Others were afraid to go outside their homes.

. . . The person who stabbed me came to see me [in the hospital], but I didn't recognize him because I was still in bad shape—a suction tube in my nose and an IV in my arm. He came to beg forgiveness and make up.

. . . I didn't go to Dastgheib. A group came and got notes from me and then went to Dastgheib. They gave him names of the opposition so that when the Islamic government is established, they'll be punished.

From this situation the opposition learned they weren't very strong. They came over to our side. They saw our side was larger and the Pahlavi Shah's regime is repressive.

. . . I wouldn't want to see the people of Aliabad separating into two groups and fighting. Now people here support the mellat. This struggle is for the people.

Because we were afraid of a split into two groups, some of my friends went after the attackers to beat them up. There were really only eight of them. In fear they announced that they aren't against us, they agree with us, they're united with us and hold the same attitudes as we do. So now we aren't afraid of a split into two groups anymore. We let them go and aren't angry at them anymore. Now they come and demonstrate with us and cooperate with us.

They saw our side was larger and we were making progress while the other side wasn't making any progress. So they came over to our side. And now they've experienced Tasua and Ashura and the 40th [the 40th day after the anniversary of Imam

Husein's martyrdom, when again huge marches were held throughout the country]. After this referendum, a great number of people came back to Aliabad and frightened those who were against the people. They saw that the supporters of the people were a much larger group, so they announced their support by coming to demonstrations. They told us they were on our side and want to cooperate with us and demonstrate with us. So now Aliabad has become one. Even Seyyid Yaqub can't do anything. His group is very small and will gradually come over to our side. I don't want to see two groups in Iran either. If there are two leaders, maybe they will divide Iran between themselves.

For the majority of villagers, it was only after the acts of government brutality against the convoy of mourners and then the stabbing of Kurosh that they became revolutionary activists. Rather than Shia ideology and symbols motivating villagers' revolutionary activities, the majority accepted the Shia revolutionary framework *after* they had decided to join the side of the revolutionary forces, based on taifeh-keshi culture, analysis, and expectations of political dynamics and political leaders. The events of government brutality, the stone throwing and the stabbing of Kurosh, transgressed against local values and sentiments. People responded with outrage, an emotional response influenced by taifeh-keshi culture and analysis and that further influenced taifeh-keshi political dynamics. People used the taifeh-keshi paradigm to analyze their observations of social interaction and political dynamics during these events, resulting in the dramatic shift in balance of power—just as earlier in village history people were motivated to shift sides after an outrageous act by an incumbent kadkhoda or member of his taifeh and after analysis of how others responded and the trends in balance of power. The newly emergent set of personnel would then take over political power, and everyone would unite under the new leader—now Ayatollah Khomeini. The new political leader, like the old one—the Shah and the ousted kadkhodas in Aliabad's past—would monopolize political power. No opposition to him would be possible.

LATER, A YOUNG VILLAGER, a brother-in-law of Mohsein Saedi, was killed (martyred, in villagers' words) when he participated in Shiraz revolutionary activities. Many villagers attended the various mourning ceremonies for him in Aliabad and Shiraz, where he had been living at the time of his death. All the more, his death motivated Aliabad people to support the resistance movement.

5

The Final Months

AFTER THE TWO VIOLENT EVENTS IN ALIABAD, more villagers joined in revolutionary activities. People who supported the anti-Shah movement talked about demonstrations, words and actions of dissenting figures, incidents of violence, reasons for dissatisfaction and government forces' aggression. They listened to foreign radio broadcasts, especially the twice-a-day BBC Persian service. In emotional exchanges, villagers gathered and passed on information and opinions. Those who went to school or worked in Shiraz continued to interact with fellow students or work colleagues, getting revolutionary information and perspectives and being influenced through these connections. More villagers visited with their anti-Shah relatives in Shiraz and attended discussion groups and gatherings to listen to speeches and sermons in Shiraz mosques and shrines. They learned and joined in shouting revolutionary slogans and couplets and used and distributed movement leaflets and tapes. Some sprayed anti-Shah and pro-movement graffiti on walls and buildings in Shiraz and, finally, even on the walls around the village entrance gate. They took part in demonstrations and marches in Shiraz and eventually even in Aliabad. Aliabad men who worked in the bazaar or government departments in Shiraz joined in the strikes, which became a crucial revolutionary weapon.

Given the social segregation of the sexes, as a woman I spent much of my time with women and formed most of my closest friendships with women. Whether sitting in village compounds talking about the Revolution or listening to revolutionary tapes, sitting in on revolutionary speeches in the village mosque, watching scenes of verbal confrontation or—later—

walking in demonstrations and processions in Aliabad and Shiraz, I did so with Aliabad women and girls. Much of this chapter, therefore, focuses on women's participation in the revolutionary conflict.[1]

Aliabad Women in the Revolution

Aliabad women did not work outside the village and had more restricted lives than men. Fewer women than men became active in the Revolution, but the revolutionary activities of those who did showed striking similarities to men's. Their opinions about the Revolution did too. Observing or hearing about injustice, despicable behavior or violence committed by government agents against other Iranians created similar emotions and attitudes in both men and women. During fall and winter of 1978–1979— the period of massive, nationwide demonstrations—more and more village men and women became persuaded that a revolution was necessary, particularly because of the horror, rage and frustration they experienced when witnessing or hearing about government violence against fellow Iranians.

Although the stone throwing and stabbing of Kurosh had increased the disdain of both male and female villagers for the local representatives of the Shah's government, and for the government as well, that did not translate into revolutionary participation by everyone. I focus here on those Aliabad women who actively supported the anti-Shah movement, but such women were in the minority.

Commuters into Shiraz or to nearby factories, mainly sons of former peasants and traders and shopkeepers, formed the largest group of male Aliabad revolutionary activists. Many of them participated in protest marches in Shiraz and Aliabad. Their wives too were incensed and highly offended. Some, as a result, became politicized during the fall and winter months of 1978. However, not many wives or daughters of former peasants or their sons actually traveled to Shiraz to participate in demonstrations, though some of them eventually joined the nightly demonstrations in Aliabad initiated by the seyyid women in early January 1979.

In Aliabad, two main groups of women, paralleling two of the men's groups, joined the revolutionary movement. One group of women was principally from the upper neighborhood—on the side of the village going up the valley away from Shiraz—and the other from the lower neighborhood—closer to Shiraz. The upper neighborhood women included female relatives of educators, traders, religious figures and factory workers. Most of these were relatives of men long opposed to the Askaris and their supporters. Some were related to men, such as Shaikh Rahim Kazemi, who had suffered after the 1953 coup against Prime Minister Mosaddeq because of supporting him. Other members of the upper-neighborhood faction were wives, sisters and daughters of a few peasants, most firm in their anti-Askari stance, who had lost land after the strike or during land reform to the Askari family.

Initially, daughters of the upper neighborhood schoolteachers and wives and daughters of the lower neighborhood seyyid shopkeepers and traders showed the most commitment to the anti-Shah movement. Eight to ten young unmarried women from the upper neighborhood were the first Aliabad females to become involved in the Revolution. They were attending high school in Shiraz, staying with relatives there during the week as commuting in by bus would not be proper for young females. These young women were influenced by their Aliabad fathers and brothers and Shiraz relatives, as well as by fellow students in Shiraz. They began participating in Shiraz demonstrations even before the December 1978 Tasua and Ashura demonstrations. As high school students in the city, they were accustomed to public life. They planned careers for themselves, though whether such plans would become reality was questionable. Probably they would have participated in revolutionary demonstrations even if they hadn't been given a religious connotation. They did not require the legitimization of a religious framework for activity outside the home.

The largest group of female activists was made up of 20 to 30 seyyid women from the lower neighborhood and several of their neighbors. These women were influenced by their husbands and fathers, who were shopkeepers in Shiraz and traders connected with the Shiraz bazaar and thus felt more affiliation with a religious movement. Their sons and brothers also worked in Shiraz. Some—such as Jafar, the young man who described the Habib Mosque massacre in the previous chapter and was in the convoy of mourners going to Ardakan—were early proponents of Ayatollah Khomeini and the Revolution. Before the Revolution, my family and I lived in the lower neighborhood, in Seyyid Yaqub Askari's courtyard, and it was among these lower neighborhood females that I spent most of my time. I participated in revolutionary demonstrations with them.

The major topic of conversation for the lower neighborhood activist women during winter 1978–1979 was the process of the Revolution. Women sat with men during political discussions even when male visitors were present. When male relatives and associates or customers of husbands, brothers or sons came by, women quizzed them on recent occurrences, even in the absence of household men. Mothers and sisters questioned boys coming home from school for the latest news. The brother of the young widow Esmat worked as a tailor in Shiraz and belonged to a group of men there who studied the Qoran and engaged in religious and political discussion. Everything she knew she had learned from her brother, Esmat declared.

Village women did not work outside the home, with a few exceptions. Women could find time to travel into Shiraz frequently and keep informed about developments through discussions with relatives there. A few attended home-based religious gatherings with Shiraz female relatives. Several of these women packed a lunch and took their children in to virtually every procession after January 7, 1979.

When I asked women what women did in the Revolution, they invariably replied that women did the same things as men. In contrast to regularized political activity, which would include public roles and require relatively long work hours, education, and permission to work outside the home, earn money and interact with men, significant revolutionary efforts included activities that even rural women from socially conservative families could do.

Like men, women held a variety of ideologies and opinions regarding the struggle. For women and men alike, interpersonal relations and membership in specific taifeh, groups and socioeconomic categories influenced whether they were pro-Shah or pro-Khomeini or kept out of the controversy.

Wives of the political elite, a total of five or six families, were of course firmly against the revolutionary movement. Rezvan, wife of Seyyid Yaqub Askari, in outspoken fashion berated those who took part in the uprising. She admonished mothers whose sons were involved to stop them. The wives of Seyyid Yaqub's cousins (his father's sister's sons and his closest supporters in Aliabad) shared Mrs. Askari's position on the political confrontation. One of them, Mohammad Amini's mother, continuously fought with him over his involvement. Although they toned down immediately following the events of February 11, 1979, in deference to the political majority, it was not long before these women's actual sentiments came out again in carefully selected company. Only a few months after the Revolution, several of these women described Ayatollah Khomeini to me in off-color fashion. These women and their husbands had good reason to be pro-Shah. They owed their power and prominence to their support for the monarchy and their efforts to encourage loyalty to the regime and prevent dissension.

Dependents of the Askari family were also staunchly pro-Shah. Women who worked for the Askaris reflected a pro-Shah position in their discussions. The kindergarten cook, whose position was controlled by the Askaris, was such an example.

Some of the poorer peasants, including those who had lost their irrigated agricultural land during the strike or during the land reform process, prepared the irrigation system, managed the regular irrigation and hand-harvested wheat for Seyyid Ibn Ali and Seyyid Yaqub and worked their vineyards for wages. They could not afford Askari disapproval. The poor peasants, both women and men, remained cynical toward participation in the political struggle. They considered revolutionary activity to be peripheral to their lives.[2] Their cynicism did not lessen when the struggle was couched in religious terms. They were convinced that the best action was no action; risking their lives in support of the Revolution would be fruitless. Shortly before Ayatollah Khomeini's arrival in Tehran from Paris on February 1, 1979, I heard a peasant remark to his mother, "Khomeini's supposed to come soon."

"So?" his mother replied, "What's he bringing with him?"

Three Narrations of Tasua and Ashura Processions

The most important days of the Shia calendar, Tasua and Ashura— the 9th and 10th days of Moharram—mark the eve and the day of the martyrdom of the most important Shia figure, Imam Husein, and some 70 other men in his band on the plains of Karbala in 680 CE. On these days, practicing Shia mourn for the martyrs. They remember the courage of the womenfolk taken into captivity in Damascus, the seat of the Caliph Yazid, whose forces had killed Imam Husein and his male followers. Shia men and boys in less modernized and westernized circles have traditionally practiced self-flagellation[3] to show their regret at not being present with Imam Husein and their readiness to undergo harm for his sake.[4] The days of mourning frequently turn political, and on December 10 and 11, 1978, the Shia mourning processions became the most compelling rituals of resistance against the Pahlavi government.[5]

The government had at first declared Tasua and Ashura processions to be illegal. When it became clear that the processions would take place anyway, this ruling was rescinded. But the government attempted to cover the political meaning and pretend the processions were typical mourning for Imam Husein by cutting the sound of the marchers' chanting—revolutionary slogans rather than traditional mourning couplets—out of TV reports. But TV audiences could tell what they were saying anyway. "They were raising their fists in the air, not beating their chests in mourning," a friend crowed.

Many village men went into Shiraz to join the pivotal Tasua and Ashura marches of December 1978, which turned the tide of the revolutionary movement. In the following paragraphs, several people describe their experiences in these processions and the effect on their attitudes and outlooks.[6]

Seyyid Mostafa Askari—Agnostic, Cynic, Maverick

Since finishing high school, Seyyid Mostafa Askari had been working several years for the Office of Malaria Control. Although much of the time he was away from Aliabad traveling to other villages for his work, he maintained a small room in the courtyard of his father (Seyyid Ayyub Askari) and returned whenever possible to spend a few days with family and friends. Mostafa loved music and the visual arts. He seemed to enjoy his role as a maverick and social critic. He was not interested in religion and considered himself somewhat of an agnostic. Although he was a son of Seyyid Yaqub's father's brother, he complained about the government. He was disillusioned with society under the Shah, but pessimistic about the possibility of change. He didn't have much respect for Iranians and distrusted their ability to cooperate to bring about improvements.

Mostafa had been spending time at the hospital bedside of Kurosh, the husband-to-be of his half-sister's daughter, along with many other relatives, to protect Kurosh and to show support. He had intended to be only an observer at the Tasua and Ashura marches, but he got caught up in the excitement and atmosphere of unity and brotherhood, as he recounted in his taped interview with me:

On Tasua, I went to Shah-e Cheragh [the main shrine in Shiraz]. People were sitting in the square in front of Shah-e Cheragh chanting slogans. Someone was giving a speech. I was with Hushang [son of Haidar Amini and Mostafa's half-sister, a daughter of Seyyid Ayyub by his earlier wife]. We decided to go and watch the people instead of staying there and shouting slogans. We walked to Ahmadi Street. It was really crowded. We joined in chanting slogans. People were carrying pictures of Dr. Sanjabi,[7] of Mosaddeq and a lot of Ali Shariati, and signs on which slogans were written: "Get lost, America." "Leave, Americans." Another said, "America, the Soviet Union, Israel and Great Britain are enemies of the Iranian people." Some demonstrators carried a sign on which they had drawn a picture of the hammer and sickle, the communist symbol, and then crossed it out in red to show that they weren't communists.

We went as far as Ahmadi Intersection and then turned back. The people were all going toward the New Mosque. We gathered inside, and Mr. Mesbahi [a cleric] spoke over the loudspeaker from the pulpit. "We're going to march, and no one can stop us. We're not going to bother anyone. We just want to chant slogans. Maybe today fliers [from the Shah's regime] will be scattered from helicopter by the army. Don't read *any*. If someone gives you a flier today, don't read it."

He talked for a while longer. The people gave *salavat* [set prayer responses], and then we all came out of the mosque. Another group came from the Friday Mosque. The two groups united and started the march. I looked around and saw that people completely filled Godarabun or Lotf Ali Khan Zand Street.

A space of about two meters separated groups. People marched in groups so that the pressure of the crowds wouldn't be too great. After they marched a ways, people sat down. If a group sat down suddenly, they might be crushed by the people coming up from behind if there hadn't been space between the two groups. But this way, after the first group sat down, there was still room for the next group when they sat down. We sat and rested every kilometer or so. By the time I reached Godarabun Street, I had seen two or three people from Aliabad.

I was with Hushang. We weren't with any group. I hadn't planned on coming to take part in the demonstration. I had just planned to come and *watch*. I hadn't slept the night before because I had been at the hospital [with Kurosh]. The night before that [the night Kurosh was knifed], I hadn't gotten any sleep either. Because I hadn't slept for two nights, I planned to go home to sleep that day. I was going to watch the crowds a bit and then go home to bed. I just wanted to see what was going on. But when I came and saw so many people, I suddenly decided to join in.

We walked on. We saw Shaikh Rahim [Kazemi] and his sons, all of them. His daughters were marching with the women, they said. After that, we marched with the Kazemis, with Shaikh Rahim and his sons.

We came to Shiraz Hospital at Valiahd Square. Someone I didn't know, a city person, tapped me on the shoulder and handed me a piece of paper. On it was written, "The men who beat up the people on their way to Ardakan that day in Aliabad are Seyyid Yaqub, Ali Reza Amini, Mashd Musa Saedi, Hamid Jahangiri—the kadkhoda—and their sons." There were some other names too.

When we got to Zand Avenue, we saw Seyyid Muslem [Seyyid Yaqub Askari's son]. We walked on and saw some people from Yusefabad. They had joined the demonstration too. We asked them, "What are you doing here?"

"Our reputation has been ruined too," they answered. "We're in the same position you're in." They hadn't thrown stones just as we hadn't thrown stones.

We marched on. Until this point, we still hadn't shouted "Death to the Shah," only religious slogans like "There is no God but God" and things like that. Here, though, the revolutionary slogans started. At Valiahd Square—Shiraz University— people distributed xeroxed sheets of paper on which a lot of chants and slogans were written. Mr. Mahallati [an ayatollah and one of the two most important religious leaders in Shiraz at the time][8] had provided them. Some people didn't want to take them. They said, "They told us at the mosque not to take any fliers, so we don't want them." The people distributing them said, "No, don't worry about that. Take them and read them."

We came to the city police station. There weren't any policemen in front of the station, not even one. There is a precinct station right next to the main police station. Only one old policeman was standing in front of the precinct station—an old man, and he didn't have any weapons. He had nothing. He didn't even have a police stick. He looked afraid of the crowds, but people didn't bother him.

When we came to Zand Avenue, the leaders told us to do our noon prayers. They told us to pick a leaf from a tree to use as a prayer stone[9] because we didn't have any with us. Some people pointed out that we couldn't do the ritual washing necessary for noontime prayers. So some people talked to Mr. Mahallati about this, and he suggested doing the *hajat*[10] prayer, which doesn't require ritual washing. People picked leaves from the trees along Zand Avenue. Some picked a bunch and handed them on to others. Everyone stood still and did his prayers. It wasn't possible to do prayers together as it was so crowded, so we all prayed individually.[11]

No policemen directed the marchers or kept order. Some people wore armbands with *marshal* written on them. These people stood in front of the movie theaters, for example, so no one would damage them. University and high school students, government employees—people who had been in demonstrations before and were experienced—acted as the marshals. Not people like me. I hadn't been in a demonstration before. This was my first one. I had seen a lot in Tehran, but I hadn't even watched one before in Shiraz. I was afraid. The truth is I was afraid. It's different from going to a demonstration in Washington. In your Washington there aren't machine guns. Here there are machine guns! Mr. Mahallati had said in the mosque, "Young men, please, I beg of you, don't expose yourselves needlessly to machine gun fire. Whenever there is shooting, don't go toward it. Don't go and get killed. Run away. Run away. Whenever you see that conditions aren't good to demonstrate, don't demonstrate. The government wants to kill you. If you go and get killed, what good does it do? Don't go and get killed."

It depends on the situation. You have to anticipate what will happen. You have to use intelligence. When the soldiers have orders to shoot and you are empty-handed, it's stupidity to say, "Go and face the machine guns." When you have a machine gun in your hands, that is the time to go and confront the machine guns. So they said, "Don't go in front of the machine guns." They had said this on other days too. On this day, though, there weren't any machine guns. There were none at all.

We reached Zand Intersection. Whenever we marched past a hospital, we didn't shout slogans—nothing—we stayed very quiet. We even tried to breathe quietly. When we reached Shiraz Hospital, a group of hospital employees went up to the fifth floor and shouted slogans out of the window using a huge loudspeaker. But we didn't shout slogans back, because we were in front of a hospital.

Helicopters didn't drop fliers after all. A helicopter flew over once and then went away.

Some people who were standing on the sidewalks watching joined us and some didn't. The further we marched, the larger the number of demonstrators became.

Along the route, people passed out cold water and fruit drinks. For instance, if a person's house was close to the demonstration route, he would bring out a container of cold water or fruit drink and give it to the demonstrators. Some people were standing next to maybe 20 glasses and a large container of water. Both men and women did this. They handed out bread, water, halva, charcoal-broiled meat, cheese—that sort of thing. And a lot of cookies. As they gave people something to eat or drink, they might say, "We salute our *mojahedin* brothers," or something like that.

Anyone who happened to have anything at home they could give out did so because they were happy. If marchers asked them, "Could you give me a drink of water?" they would give them fruit juice instead. They were so happy.

Someone asked, "Could you get me a drink of water?"

The person on the sidewalk then asked him, "Do you just want water? How about some bread, food or something else? If you want anything else, I'll get it for you."

"No, I just want water," the marcher replied.

But the other person got him an orange. It was like this. The people all wanted to help.

We came to Khayyam Street, the Christian hospital. Here too we didn't chant slogans. Then we came to Lotf Ali Khan Street and to Mushir Intersection.

The Jews also gave slogans, it is interesting to note. The Jews' homes are in this area, from Mushir Intersection to Ahmadi Intersection. They came out of their homes—men and women. They didn't join us but stood at the side of the street, on the sidewalk, and chanted slogans from there. I'm not sure why they did this. Maybe they thought people would damage their homes. Or maybe they just wanted to. Maybe they were dissatisfied too. Amazingly, all of the Jews wore black that day. I recognized a lot of the Jews and knew they were Jews, but they were wearing black, probably to show they were with the people. Either they were afraid or they really wanted to join. I didn't talk with them, so I don't know.[12]

We returned to Mushir Intersection and then again to Shah-e Cheragh. So our route was a circle. At Shah-e Cheragh, Mr. Mesbahi again started giving a speech. He talked about the day, that our demonstration was a good one, but that he hoped the next day—Ashura—would be even more impressive, that even *more* people would come.

That night we went to Valiasr Mosque on Daryush Street. Everyone went to that mosque. People gave a lot of speeches. People filled the mosque. The hotel next door didn't take any guests that night but emptied all of their rooms for the women. They set aside the mosque balcony and terrace for women to sit and listen to the speeches.

The men occupied the mosque and the mosque courtyard. Even Daryush Street was filled with people. Men sat in the street. It was really crowded. They didn't allow any traffic through. They set up four loudspeakers at Mushir Intersection and four more at Zand Intersection and four in Daryush Street. The only vehicles in Daryush Street were two ambulances. They had come on their own. No one bothered them. The drivers and attendants had put up pictures of Ayatollah Khomeini all around the ambulances.

Mr. Mahallati spoke for a long time. He said he'd gotten a phone call from Tehran telling him that the demonstrators there had extended from Foziyeh or Shahnaz Square to Shahryad, about 12 kilometers. Bearing this in mind, he hoped that the demonstration in Shiraz the following day would be far more impressive.

In order to provide for the comfort of the women, they were to gather at the New Mosque the next morning, and the men at Shah-e Cheragh and the Friday Mosque. This way, men and women wouldn't intermingle, and women wouldn't get bothered or lost.

We didn't stay around to listen anymore. We were so hungry that Hushang and I went with Mr. Kazemi and the others to his home to eat. So this was Tasua.

When we arrived the next day [Ashura], it was like it had been the day before, but so many more people came—three times as many people. You couldn't really say what the difference was in the people who hadn't come on Tasua but came on Ashura. They were from different classes and different groups. All sorts of people came. On the second day, a lot of government employees came, from all of the different departments. The head of my own office was there. All of the heads of the Health Department were there. The heads of tribal groups came; Bahmanbegi [a prominent Qashqai tribal educator] marched with the mullas. The head of Nemazi Hospital was there. All of these people marched in the front, in the same group with the mullas.

The second day, I wasn't with Hushang. I was by myself. Later I found out some people from Aliabad were there. I ran into some tribesmen I knew and started talking with them, and then I marched with them. That day I saw a lot of soldiers in civilian clothes. I don't know why they came. They shouted slogans.

We reached the square in front of the police station. Mr. Rahbani gave a long speech. People had made a pulpit out of flowers. I didn't hear what he said because I was so far away. Then we started marching again. That day we went by way of Daryush Street. We went by the Paramount Movie Theater and then to Qasr el-Dasht Street. When we got there, the people from Aliabad and Qasr el-Dasht went home. We went on.

Later the army stopped us. There were foot soldiers and armored vehicles and the Air Force Brigade—most of the Shiraz armed forces had gathered together. They stopped the people and then later let them go. They said they made a mistake and asked us to forgive them. The people went on and made a circle around the armed forces and chanted slogans. The soldiers were all standing behind the fence and listening—officers, enlisted men, noncommissioned officers—they were all standing and listening. They didn't join in shouting slogans, but they waved at the people. They were afraid, after all.

Suddenly, about 30 truckloads of soldiers came out of the regiment headquarters and made a ring to protect it from attack. Mr. Dastgheib spoke to the armed forces: "Come and unite with us. Stop supporting this government. If you stay, someday we'll get machine guns. Someday we'll obtain weapons and fight with you. We're warning you. If you don't come over to our side, someday you'll regret it." He talked for a long time.

As we marched along, people said that the names of the streets had been changed. For example, Daryush Street was renamed Dr. Ali Shariati Street. Qavam Boulevard became Khomeini Boulevard. At first they were going to change the name of Zand Avenue to Khomeini. But at night in the mosque, they said because Karim Khan Zand had been a good person, and people had liked him, the name of this street shouldn't be changed. This was the only street whose name didn't change.

We went on and reached Kazerun Gateway. On this day, we marched a longer distance. People had started out marching from Shah-e Cheragh at 8:00 that morning, and at 4:30 in the afternoon, they were back at Shah-e Cheragh. There were some other differences between the first and second days. The second day, the speeches were better. The first day, they hadn't really made speeches. The feelings of the people were more intense on the second day. On the second day, some people marched who I never thought would have come—for example, the heads of government offices. They all came. They all chanted slogans. Maybe the first day they had been afraid. There was a possibility that there would be shooting. But when they realized it was all right, they came on the second day. That evening, I didn't go to the mosque. At night I didn't go back to Aliabad at all. I went to the hospital.

Joining in the December 1978 Tasua and Ashura marches had a transformative effect on Mostafa. Before, he had taken a dismissive attitude toward the Iranian population, believing them to be self-centered, undeserving and incapable of cooperation—and certainly incapable of getting rid of a bad ruler. From his experiences on Tasua and Ashura, he developed a new respect for Iranians and new confidence in their innate goodness and capabilities. In his interview, he talked about his changed ideas:

I've done some thinking about these two days, and I've come to some conclusions. If these people have a good leader, they're a good people. If a truly nationalistic government would come into existence and not be hard on these people, they would be a good people. This was very important for me. After what I saw that day, I no longer believe the accusations attributing destructive acts and terrorism to these people.

And then the unity and cooperation I had always thought would never happen! The marchers had a very good attitude toward each other. On Tasua, my nose suddenly started bleeding, and then everyone wanted to help me. One person gave me a handkerchief. Another gave me a Kleenex. Someone asked, "What happened?"

Another said, "Let's get an ambulance."

"Hey, it's just a nosebleed," I said. "I'm all right."

People gathered around me. Finally they realized it was nothing serious.

This is the way it was. Everyone wanted to help everyone else. If there was an old man, people would make sure there was enough room left around him so that he could walk without being shoved. People carried little children so they wouldn't get tired.

This behavior was out of the ordinary. I had never seen anything like it before. There were so many people, but there wasn't any fighting whatsoever. Nothing. If a problem developed between two people, if a person accidently stepped on someone else's foot and the two started to argue, others would come and say, "No, no, we shouldn't fight today. Today we should get along with each other."

They didn't mean just for that day. What they meant was from that day on we must be brothers to each other. We shouldn't make each other unhappy. People said this to each other. The unity and cooperation among the people on that day was amazing.

Mostafa also talked about the contrasts between the 1978 Tasua and Ashura and the Moharram commemorations and processions of earlier years. They had been purely traditional religious rituals, and not all that significant, he felt. They had also been an opportunity for people to fight about pre-existing quarrels and demonstrate power over others. That year, however, the Tasua and Ashura marches carried a new and deeper meaning; they conveyed a new kind of attitude of people toward one another, a new kind of social and political existence:

Other years, if there were ongoing conflicts between persons or groups, these differences came to the fore on Tasua and Ashura. On these days, people are usually excited and tense. Let's say that from a certain street or neighborhood there are 20 or 30 people who are together. On Tasua and Ashura, these groups sort of feel they have power. They feel that if they get into a fight, all of their friends and neighbors are right with them and will help them. Most of the time when fights start, it's for this reason. If they had quarreled in the past, on these days it would get worse because everyone was present. People weren't alone. The fights were between groups. The fights got really bad until the police came to stop them.

Other Tasuas and Ashuras weren't like this year. They didn't have a political meaning like they did this year. Other years, Tasua and Ashura were just traditional mourning. Men just went out into the streets without their shirts and beat themselves. I went several times. I watched, but I didn't do sineh-zani. The role of the women was just to watch, and when someone chanted a martyrdom story, the women wept. They stood at the side of the street and cried. They didn't participate directly in the mourning or chest-beating.

But this year, when the procession had a deeper meaning, and all of the women joined, it differed from other occasions. This year, women marched in the streets many times. Whenever there was a speech in the mosque, women came and listened. And on Tasua and Ashura this year, women marched as well as men.

This year was different. This year it was political activity.

Pulled in by the high spirits of the crowds, their attitudes of consideration and cooperation—unusual behavior toward strangers—and their determination and belief in their power to overturn the Shah, Mostafa stayed on. For Mostafa, and surely for millions of other Iranians as well, the marches marked a radical transformation in outlook. Mostafa gained new respect for Iranians and began to believe in the possibility of them working together to make a better society—if they could have a good leader. After he joined the Tasua and Ashura marches, Mostafa became an advocate of the revolutionary movement—that is, until after the Revolution, when Islamic Republic officials spoke out against alcohol, music, movies, opium and dancing.

Soheila—A Woman from a Shiraz Clerical Family

This book is about Aliabad and the people who live there, as well as about some who had moved from Aliabad into Shiraz, but their Shiraz contacts had great influence on Aliabadis. I became acquainted with a Shiraz woman from a clerical family whose male relatives frequently gave speeches where Aliabad men, and later women, were in the audience. Born into an important religious family, Soheila experienced overt gender pressures, made more obvious for her than for Aliabad females by her education and exposure to modern and Western influences. (She had gone with her doctor husband for his American education and knew English well.) She would have liked to have a larger world for herself. Soheila complained about restrictive requirements for women in Iran, which Aliabad females did not do openly in 1978–1979 as far as I know. Soheila experienced the opposing pulls of her responsibility to her family and her responsibility to oppose the Shah's regime. Her father even told her she should not go to demonstrations, that it was more important to fulfill her duties as a mother. Although she was from Shiraz, not Aliabad, I include her narrative about her participation in the Ashura march because of her articulate description of the emotions this experience aroused in her, her enmity toward the Pahlavi Shah, and her determination to struggle against him.

Before, I was ashamed of myself because I didn't do political activity. I was raising my children. I had no choice. I rationalized: I'll raise my family to fight. I always told them all about the Shah so that they wouldn't have respect for the Shah. One day, [my daughter] Laleh's teacher asked, "Who doesn't like the Shah?"

Only Laleh raised her hand. The teacher asked her why.

Laleh answered, "Because he gets good people and puts them in prison."

The teacher wrote me a long letter saying, "You shouldn't teach your child this." On this one day, I felt I was doing some small thing.

I didn't do anything special in the Revolution other than the same thing other women like myself did. I went to all of the marches, went on the roof with my children to shout "Allah o akbar," gave awareness to my children and passed on revolutionary fliers. All of my aunts are high school teachers. I explained to them how important their responsibilities are, that they shouldn't go to school but should keep the strikes—

strikes broke the back of the government. Whatever Khomeini said to do, I did. I listened to all of the speeches. The most important thing for me as a mother is to make my children aware.

When I went to the Ashura march, I didn't know if soldiers would be shooting at us or not, or perhaps we might be bombed from the air. But I didn't care. I had given up on my own life. My heart felt no fear. My heart was filled with hate. I put all the hate in my voice. Hearing the great sound of "Allah o akbar" made me weep. I was full of hate for the Shah. It was only three months after the 17th of Shahrivar [Black Friday, day of the massacre in Zhaleh Square in Tehran]. When I thought of myself, I was a drop in the sea. I felt smaller and smaller. Sometimes I felt lost among all of those voices. I was very proud of my nationality. On this day, I felt so proud. Before, I had been ashamed that I didn't take part in political resistance. But on this day, I was so happy I could take part.

On Zand Avenue, a woman was standing on a balcony all dressed in black, as were all of us. She was holding her child and probably couldn't join us, but she was shouting "Death to the Shah" with such force that the balcony was shaking.

Soheila had been prevented from doing resistance work and living a more active public and self-developmental life by her early arranged marriage and then her role as mother. Although from a clerical family, and accepting the injunction to struggle against tyranny that was common among many Shia at the time, her main focus seemed to be resistance to the Shah. With all her strength, she shouted out her hatred of the Shah, still erupting after the massacre of fellow Iranians three months earlier in Tehran's Zhaleh Square. She didn't think about her own life and safety anymore, she reported. She was *az khod gozashteh,* beyond caring about herself. She felt the power of being surrounded by a huge ocean of others joined in hatred of the Shah's regime. Joining in the Ashura demonstration gave Soheila the opportunity to express her beliefs and emotions openly, engage in a powerful, public anti-Shah activity and feel at one with millions of other Iranians.

Mohammad Amini—Leading Young Village Activist

On Ashura, I went with Rezvan, Seyyid Yaqub's wife, over to the home of Rezvan's son, Seyyid Muslem Askari, and his wife, Mina Amini. Their house was in the "New Village," right next to the highway; it afforded a good view and a place to wait and watch for the crowds of men returning from the Ashura procession in Shiraz.

Shortly after the pickups of men returned from Shiraz, Mohammad Amini came into his sister's home, excited and inspired and with a hoarse voice. Although he was a son of Mashd Yusef, a strong supporter of Seyyid Yaqub and a son of Seyyid Yaqub Askari's father's sister, Mohammad was a leading young activist in Aliabad. His mother frequently berated him for his revolutionary involvement.

About 500 people from Aliabad had gone to the demonstration, Mohammad told us. Of those, maybe 300 were people from the village and some 200 were people who had moved to Shiraz. Mohammad was attending teachers' training in Shiraz. He had shared with me the story of how he became involved in the revolutionary movement through his fellow students (see Chapter 4). At his sister's home across the highway, he now told me about the Ashura march in Shiraz:

All of us from Aliabad went in a group with our sign—"Aliabad, marg bar shah"—but the Shiraz people were still so angry at us [because of the stone throwing] that they tore up our sign. We had to march in several different groups instead of all together.

We went to Qasr el-Dasht and marched from there to Shah-e Cheragh and then to Valiasr Square. Even more people came than the day before. More women came. Maybe half of the people were women. And there were lots of children. Groups of girls walked in the march, the first group of girls older and then getting younger and younger. Even four-year-old girls were marching. We were all like one person. Usually during Ashura, old quarrels come to the fore, but it wasn't like that this time. Everyone got along so well. People gave out sandwiches. They came with maybe 100 sheets of flat bread and tossed it out to mothers for their children. People handed out fruit drinks, water, cookies. Everyone was hungry, but we all shared. If I got a piece of bread, I gave half of it to someone else.

There were so many black chadors. The women shouted, "We salute our moja-hedin brothers." The men shouted back, "We salute our mojahedin sisters."

And everyone cried.

There weren't any soldiers or police around. The demonstrators themselves managed traffic. The traffic controllers wore armbands. All was very peaceful.

The people shouldn't weep for Hosein this Ashura, the religious leaders told us. After all, Imam Hosein didn't weep when he went into battle. This should be a happy occasion. There shouldn't be any fighting, no violence to selves, no chest-beating. All should be peace. It should be the opposite of other Ashuras. Everyone was excited and crying. We felt so united.

Mohammad also talked about the sharing and the sense of being one large community rather than thousands of strangers. He was struck with the outpouring of emotion, the delight people felt in themselves, in each other and in their amazing accomplishment—this huge demonstration of united opposition to the Shah's government.

Everyone I interviewed about the marches spoke in glowing terms about the joy, pride and confidence, about what a tremendous experience it was to have been with such an endless mass of unified people all shouting in terrible anger, "Down with the Shah." Their pride and confidence in themselves, in the anti-Shah movement and in the Iranian nation had expanded.

They had pride and confidence in themselves because they felt they had withstood the test. They had conquered fear and, knowing what the results might be, had decided to participate in the illegal march. Participants gained a feeling of personal power and confidence through the overwhelming feeling of unity present during these marches. The great mass of people spoke in one voice and had one goal, they sensed. Other marchers became like brothers and sisters and close friends. They were one large family all connected with ties of support and concern for each other. Behavior of people toward each other differed radically from behavior usually shown to strangers on the street. The mutual support and cooperation helped participants to look at fellow Iranians and the Iranian nation with new love and respect. If such a huge crowd could act with the courage, self-restraint and cooperation needed for this demonstration, they were displaying the characteristics necessary to persevere in the struggle against the Shah until he was brought down from his throne. The Iranian nation was capable of doing what it wanted, what it felt should be done, and of fulfilling its own needs rather than depending on others, they began to believe. In these three narrations, people reported how the huge numbers of marchers, the sense of unity, pride and joy, and the judgment that success was actually possible strengthened their determination.

Bringing It Back to Aliabad

Before Ashura, revolutionary activists at the village level had begun openly declaring their opposition to the Shah's regime. As activists publicized plans for the oppositional Ashura marches in Shiraz, Seyyid Yaqub did all he could to discourage villagers from going into Shiraz to take part.

But the majority of village men and a few village women took buses, pick-ups, cars and trucks into Shiraz. Comparatively, the rather insignificant traditional Ashura mourning procession held within the village made a poor showing. Only 30 to 40 men took part. Half of them, the younger and more vigorous, practiced sineh-zani, and the older, less physically fit men tapped their heads in a token of sorrow for the death of Imam Hosain. This little parade was obviously the feeble result of Seyyid Yaqub's efforts to restrict Ashura to a purely religious connotation; directing the small group of mourners were two of Seyyid Yaqub's cohort.

Almost 200 men from Aliabad marched in the Shiraz Tasua and Ashura demonstrations along with maybe 200 Aliabad men who had moved into Shiraz, some estimated. Most women did not go into the Shiraz marches but, rather, waited on rooftops and in front of the village gates for the men.

Topping off this exciting and emotion-filled day was the trium-phant return of the marchers from Shiraz in a long convoy of vehicles, horns blasting. Pickups full of exuberant men holding large pictures of Ayatollah Khomeini and men in other vehicles drove into the village. They all returned together, crowded into the backs of trucks, shouting out antigovernment slogans and "marg bar shah" from hoarse throats with great spirit and joy.

Only one young woman returned with the 200 men; she was a high school student and the daughter of an important revolutionary leader from the upper neighborhood. Other high school girls marched in those demonstrations but did not return to the village that evening, instead stay-ing in Shiraz with relatives.

The men piled out, joining a group of mainly younger boys already assembled. They all set off for the mosque, chanting slogans in loud voices. Those who lived in Shiraz were going to come out to Aliabad at 4:00 to join in sineh-zani at the mosque.

The group of about 400 men, both village residents and villagers who had moved to Shiraz, convened at the mosque and then marched around the alleyway inside the village walls several times, their hands beating their chests in time to thunderous, defiant, victorious, jubilant shouting of "Death to the Shah" and other antiregime slogans.

Those who had participated obviously were filled with joy and ex-hilaration. Some men who had just returned from the march gathered in a neighborhood shop in the lower neighborhood next to Seyyid Yaqub's entryway. They congratulated each other and shook hands, proud and elated. They poked fun at a young fellow who hadn't joined in the march. But they were in such a state of good humor that their warmth seemed to extend to all—except the Shah and his supporters, of course—and they couldn't be too serious in their ridicule.[13]

The demonstrators intimidated Kurosh's enemies and village pro-government people. After participating in the mass processions on Tasua and Ashura, Aliabad men became regular and confident participants in Shiraz revolutionary marches and demonstrations.

Women Initiate Nightly Demonstrations in Aliabad

Women were the ones who initiated nightly anti-Shah demonstrations in Aliabad.[14] They had felt it was not appropriate for them to take part in the demonstrations as they should not appear before men in public displays. But then suddenly in early January 1979, this attitude shifted.

My family and I had been invited to Shiraz on a Friday evening and stayed the night. We arrived back in Aliabad on Saturday morning, January 6, 1979. That morning, Rana, sister-in-law of Jafar and Roqayeh and leader of the seyyid women, slipped into Seyyid Yaqub's courtyard. (I was still in the unfortunate position of living in the courtyard of the leading pro-Shah figure in Aliabad, currently the target of other villagers' fury.) The women had shouted revolutionary slogans the night before, she told me. She was pleased, excited and very proud of herself. "Too bad you weren't there," she said. The women were going to protest again that evening, she told me, and I should come over to her house at 7:00 without telling anyone from Seyyid Yaqub's household where I was going.

A short while later, Akhtar, another seyyid woman who was a staunch supporter of Ayatollah Khomeini, sneaked into the Askari courtyard and upstairs to my room. With great delight and pride, Akhtar repeated the story of the women's activity the night before. Ayatollah Khomeini, who was still in France, had declared Friday, January 5, to be a day of mourning for the many persons martyred during the recent month of Moharram in the clashes between the military and police and demonstrators. Honoring his request, Aliabad men demonstrated in Shiraz that Friday. Some boys and men also marched and chanted slogans in the alleyways of Aliabad itself.

On the afternoon of that day, a group of seyyid women had been sitting outside in the little dead-end alley where their homes were located, chatting and crocheting the cotton uppers for shoes handmade in the village. They began to discuss the demonstrations in the cities and the day of mourning. Laila, a young wife with a small baby, said, "We should shout slogans too!"

Rana, the leader of this social group, replied, "In the village it's improper. In the city it's okay, but in the village it's bad."

Laila insisted, "No, it's not improper. Are the women in Shiraz any better than we are?"

Aktar added, 'If we had any courage, we'd go too."

So the women agreed to hold their own demonstration after dark, at about 7:00. When the time came, some of the women were having second thoughts, but a few resolute ones gathered the group together. By evening, Rana had forgotten about it, and anyway her legs hurt. Aktar went into Rana's home and asked, "Aren't you coming? All the women are outside."

So she went out. They shouted their slogans as they walked a little way up their own little alley. The women were nervous, but they were also pleased, excited and very proud of themselves, Akhtar told me.

That evening, I eagerly waited for 7:00 and then rushed over to Rana's. She and her family were hurriedly eating dinner. We went just outside her courtyard door and one of the young teenage boys from the neighborhood began to shout slogans. The women gradually gathered, all joining in the chants. The teenage boy then led the people up the alleyway. Others joined the marchers as they proceeded. When we were opposite the door of the young widow Esmat, known for her piety and modesty, she peeked out the door. Rana, also known for her religiosity, was in the group, Esmat observed, and ran to get her chador. She came out to join us. We walked on and chanted, going somewhat further up the alley than the women had done the night before.

Each night after that, the women found courage to venture further through the village. When a few men heard their voices, they came out too and joined them in chanting religious and revolutionary slogans. The demonstrations became larger, with both women and men joining in. Their chanting began to follow a pattern: the group of boys and a few men marched in front and shouted the first phrase in a revolutionary couplet. The group of women and girls walking behind responded with the second phrase. The demonstrators gave special attention to shouting slogans whenever we passed the courtyards of known Shah supporters. Finally they were making an entire circuit around the alleyways inside the village walls two or three times an evening. The demonstrations grew in complexity, becoming more organized and less spontaneous. Routes were planned out. Teenage boys assembled the nightly group by shouting slogans. To make sure no one fell, young boys with flashlights were stationed at each of the rough parts of the alleys where gaping, water-filled holes might cause the marchers difficulties. A few women threw salt down on us from their roofs or burned rue in charcoal braziers to show their approval of our demonstration and wish us good luck.

The women were happy, spirited and self-confident. After the first evening of chanting, they began to feel anything was possible. Quickly forgetting their former reticence, they delighted in their mastery of resistance through demonstrating and chanting. They took on an almost blasé air about their involvement.

The first demonstration was initiated and planned by women themselves, without the suggestion or encouragement of men. It was held immediately outside the courtyard gates of the group of women who planned it. At first, the women demonstrated under darkness; the Office of Electricity workers in Shiraz were on strike and turned off the power at about 7:00 for several hours every evening in sympathy with the revolutionary forces. Darkness and their own blind alleyway traditionally constituted an appropriate time and space for women's emergence from their own courtyards.

Although women initiated the regular nightly demonstrations, when men saw no ill result they began to join in, younger teenage boys at first. Soon after, the marches were taken over and administrated by men, with women as followers. I remember no complaints from women about this usurpation. They did not insist on women's leadership or even equal participation, but rather were intent on voicing their complaints about the Shah's government.

Protesting in regular nightly demonstrations in the village was a new form of activity for the village women. Imitating the political protests they knew women in Shiraz were performing, the group of Aliabad women initiated these forms in their own arena of activity.

In a number of ways, the nightly marches initiated by women and directed at national politics showed continuity with women's roles in local political activity. Their motivation was in large part a concern about justice and people's freedom from harm, as well as distress that government forces had disrupted the village. Men and older boys were afraid of being reported to the rural police if they demonstrated in the village, but no one would think about taking a village woman in for questioning. Relatively confident they would not be harmed, women were more able than men to initiate regular village demonstrations. Apparently liminal, weak and outside the political arena, and not counted as true political actors, women were actually able to take steps and play political roles that men felt they could not at that point.

More Rituals of Revolution in Shiraz

After demonstrating in their own alleyway under the cover of night, the seyyid women were ready to take their protest beyond the village. Two days of mourning were declared for Sunday and Monday, January 7 and 8, 1979. On both days, about 25 of the lower neighborhood women went into Shiraz to march in the huge demonstrations. I went with them. Like them, I wore a chador whenever I participated in demonstrations in Aliabad and Shiraz. Not convinced that the chador hid my foreign features and fearful that others might not like an American present in the anti-Shah, anti-American imperialism demonstrations, my village friends clung tightly to my hands during the Shiraz marches and hurried me forward whenever someone turned to talk to me. Sometimes my companions tied a corner of their chadors to mine to make sure the crowds wouldn't separate us. On January 8, about a month before the February 11 Revolution, when we went in for a second Shiraz march, one Aliabad friend urged me to say I was French and had converted to Islam, if anyone should ask. Another added with a laugh, "And tell them you've just come from the side of Imam Khomeini" (who was still in Paris).[15] Following the events of January 5 to 8, the women went into Shiraz regularly to participate in the almost daily demonstrations in the city. They were supported in their revolutionary involvement by their kin and neighborhood network of women.

During rituals of revolution—marches (often in protest and mourning for martyrs of the Revolution), demonstrations and especially the Tasua and Ashura processions—Aliabad men, like other participants, were so moved by feelings and attitudes of jubilation, unity and brotherhood that they gained a sense of ebullient commitment and confidence.[16] Victory was certain, they believed. They proceeded to act on this assumption. After the Tasua and Ashura marches, many Aliabad men and boys attended marches and demonstrations in Shiraz on a regular basis. Starting January 7, some lower neighborhood women and girls went too. The fall of the regime was just a matter of time, they felt.

The new revolutionary rituals—processions and demonstrations—further unified the revolutionary movement and inspired ever greater commitment. The rituals constituted a show of strength, causing government forces to quail and draw back. The message of Ashura 1978 was clear for Aliabadis as well as for Iranians elsewhere: government forces and agents had lost control over the Husein rituals and over the population. Government political power had rapidly deteriorated.

After Tasua and Ashura, the country saw widespread, almost daily marches of thousands and thousands of people shouting "Death to the Shah" until the Shah's departure from the country on January 16, 1979; the return of Ayatollah Khomeini—the de facto leader of the Revolution—from exile in Paris on February 1, 1979; and then the fall of the Shah's government on February 11, 1979. In this war of numbers and morale, the processions and demonstrations involving millions of people—both women and men—succeeded in bringing about the collapse of the Shah's regime.

The Final Day—February 11, 1979

On February 11, the day of the final overthrow of the monarchy, many villagers traveled to Shiraz to take part in widespread demonstrations taking place there—as throughout the country. Many village men and boys joined the confrontations against the central police station, government troops in the old Zand Prison and smaller police stations throughout the city. After the fall of the Pahlavi regime and the revolutionary movement's takeover of media, villagers joined the joyous celebrations of victory. Later, many returned to the village in a large convoy of vehicles, noisily proclaiming their new power. They marched through the village shouting revolutionary couplets.

The Aliabad women I knew did not go into Shiraz on February 11 to take part in the final uprising. When women attempted to leave Aliabad to search for their sons and brothers, well-meaning people at the village gate stopped them, saying it was too dangerous for women. Only one woman I knew of was able to avoid the blockade and make her way into the city to search the streets for her son. Other women congregated in village alleys, pumping each new arrival from Shiraz: "What's going on? Did you see Mahmud or Ali or Yusef? Where is he? Is he alright?"

Later in the afternoon of February 11, Esmat and I made our way toward the mosque for evening prayers. She kept up a constant mutter of exhortations to the Imams: "Oh, Ali! Oh, Husein! Protect my brother, don't let harm come to him." Upon seeing a young man blackened from smoke coming in through the village gate, forgetting her usual modesty, she rushed up to him and pleaded, "Did anyone see my brother, is he alright?"

Few men were in the mosque for evening prayers on February 11, due to the demonstrations and clashes in Shiraz. The mulla asked the women to come out from behind the curtain separating the women's section from the men's and perform their prayers in rows behind the men. It didn't look right to have such a small group praying behind the mulla.

Attack on Kurosh's Stepfather-Uncle

The final day of the Revolution brought another eruption in Aliabad too. Perhaps Mehdi thought the chaos in Shiraz and the whole nation would provide cover for another attack on Kurosh.

In spite of Mashd Yusef's promise after the stabbing of Kurosh to stop his son and Haj Khodabakhsh's sons from further fighting, problems had continued. Again Mehdi had sent after his abused wife, Kurosh's sister. Again Kurosh had refused to consider sending her until Mehdi himself came and discussed the matter.

When Kurosh next saw Mehdi in front of the village gate, he asked him, "Why don't you come yourself instead of sending women?" Mehdi said he hadn't sent any women and starting cursing Kurosh. A fight broke out between them. Others separated them. Both Kurosh and Mehdi went into Shiraz, probably to find relatives for support, but apparently no further conflict took place at that time.

But then, on February 11, 1979, the same day the Pahlavi Shah's government fell, Mehdi rounded up his brother and Haj Khodabakhsh's two sons. He and his three relatives went to Kurosh's courtyard to attack him again. Not finding him, they dealt Kurosh's elderly uncle, who was also Kurosh's stepfather,[17] a severe blow on the head with an iron bar. They hit his wife too, with a chain, and even hit their little child, according to villagers. The wife, Kurosh's mother, screamed, alerting people outside in the alleyway to what was happening. They rushed in to intervene. People took Kurosh's stepfather-uncle to the hospital in Shiraz.

FIGURE 6. Kurosh Amini's mother, spring 1979. She is pounding dried balls of yogurt that have been soaked in water to reconstitute them for use in food.

Villagers had gone in to Shiraz that day for the huge demonstration against the Shah's government. When they came back from the turmoil and victory celebrations in Shiraz and heard about the attack on Kurosh's stepfather-uncle, Kurosh's taifeh, joined by other outraged villagers, fell on the shop of Haj Khodabakhsh, Mehdi's uncle and the father of the cousins who had joined Mehdi in attacking Kurosh's stepfather. Villagers were "disgusted" by their attack on the old man.

Haj Khodabakhsh was the only successful shopkeeper in Aliabad who was not pro-Khomeini. He had gone on haj (the pilgrimage to Mecca) only the year before, far later in his career than any other shopkeeper, and according to villagers was not religious.

The Aliabad population vented their rage against Mehdi and his close relatives by tearing apart his uncle's shop and wrecking all of the goods. They broke Haj Khodabakhsh's shop windows and threw the merchandize on the ground. People pulled down the roof of the shop and tore up chadors brought from Mecca as I watched. Children took his candy. They attempted some destruction on the home as well but were counseled against it by several of the leaders of the resistance, so they only broke some windows and did some other minor damage.

Then Kurosh's entire taifeh packed into Mehdi's courtyard, planning to wreak their vengeance there as well. They found Mehdi's brother and struck him. Mr. Rohani, the visiting mulla from Qom, came to admonish them. "They have done wrong; don't you do so too." So they left without doing much.

For a time, Mehdi and his relatives stayed away from the village. Yet, by March 1979, only a month later, Haj Khodabakhsh's shop in the open area just inside the village gate, close to the mosque, was once again in operation, and Mehdi was coming and going freely in the village. Mehdi and his group had come over to the pro-resistance side, on the surface anyway, basically admitting that they were outnumbered and defeated and must kowtow to the new power-monopolizing regime.

Taifeh-Keshi and the 1978–1979 Iranian Revolution

In spite of the apparent importance of Shia mythology, symbolic complexes and clerics for recruitment to the revolutionary movement, the taifeh-keshi worldview and political policies heavily influenced attitudes of Aliabad villagers toward the Revolution and their decisions about their own involvement. When people talked about the Revolution, they used terms also used to discuss taifeh-keshi. Villagers compared the conflict between the Shah and Khomeini with pre–land reform taifeh-keshi factionalism over the position of kadkhoda:

Taifeh-keshi is when people threw rocks at each other. They fought over being kadkhoda. Like the Shah and Khomeini are doing now.

At first Mulla Ali was rich. He had horses and lots of servants. Then he and his family used it all up. Pretty soon the people didn't want him—like now people don't want the Shah.

Although villagers enjoyed more economic freedom—allowed by the employment alternatives of the oil boom economy—and the resulting greater political freedom, ideological alternatives, and access to information about political repression and socioeconomic inequality, the majority did not become involved in the revolutionary movement until outrageous incidents of violence made the movement meaningful, relevant and imperative for them. Just as previous taifeh-keshi conflicts over the position of kadkhoda and control of the village were prompted by incidents of violence, outrageous events—violence perpetrated by government forces against fellow Iranians—provided occasions for the swift and public shift in sentiment and support of the village majority from one side (or acquiescence to the rule of the dominant faction) to the other. This and many other similarities to the earlier process of taifeh-keshi in the political position of kadkhoda and in control of Aliabad resources became apparent during the process of the Revolution.

Taifeh-Keshi Process and the Revolution

The people of Aliabad predicted and interpreted actions related to the revolutionary conflict according to the taifeh-keshi processual paradigm that was long part of political life in their village. The process of involvement in the Revolution, reasons for changing sides, means by which people transferred alliance, sudden shift of public opinion and support after "outrageous acts," destruction of property of vanquished foes, forced declaration of allegiance to the new regime, fleeing of foes from the village and even eventual reincorporation of foes into the village community—all these aspects of the revolutionary process in Aliabad bore a remarkable resemblance to the local cognitive system and political process of taifeh-keshi. Looking back at the eight stages of taifeh-keshi delineated in Chapter 1, we can see how the steps of the revolutionary conflict among Aliabadis largely replicated the steps of taifeh-keshi political process during the period of landownership by the Qavams.

1. *People work to develop useful ties.* While the Askari brothers spent time and resources courting outside central government agents, during the 1960s and 1970s other Aliabad people were also developing contacts outside the village, among bazar and shop personnel, fellow students, workmates, and relatives and friends in Shiraz—although initially they may not have been aware of the political implications of such ties. They gained interaction with revolutionary-minded people in Shiraz, even with Marxist classmates at Tehran University in the case of one young man, and felt connected with religious leaders such as Ayatollah Mahallati and other clerics in Shiraz. Their families and relatives often held similar attitudes toward the Shah versus Khomeini standoff, and as they interacted, these ties were strengthened. Young Aliabad revolutionaries, sharing bonds of common resistance to the Shah's government, hung out together. During this stage, clever politicians developed connections with both sides, using raft-o-amad, gifts and donations.[18] To play it both ways, Seyyid Ibn Ali Askari sought out connections with Shiraz clerics. Innovative elements of this first stage of the revolutionary process included generational differences influenced by differences in exposure to new schooling, work and more modern ways of life; the great significance of contacts with the world outside Aliabad and development of the two opposing Aliabad groups, which mirrored the national-level opposing forces.[19]

2. *A contender gathers resources.* Under the large landlord, potential contenders for the position of kadkhoda had built up their economic resources through trade—and then used those resources to develop village support by strengthening their own taifeh and developing a coalition of taifeh through pulling in in-laws and others. In the revolutionary process, the emerging opposition in Aliabad built up resources through schooling and work outside of Aliabad, in Shiraz or at work sites between Shiraz and Aliabad. They built up their resources in terms of fervor, morale, anger and confidence through participation in protests, revolutionary activities, processions and other gatherings. Media and speeches in Shiraz became resources, and so did study, discussion and ritual groups. A new element in this

stage of revolutionary political process was the lack of a single contender at the local level, although Ayatollah Khomeini was able to
emerge as the single leader of the anti-Shah resistance at the national
level. Many villagers were building up a diversity of resources, not
just one or a few, and their resources would lead not to getting rid
of the local incumbent and replacing him with a new kadkhoda and
getting control over Aliabad agricultural land and politics, but to
becoming politically independent from the village elite and getting
rid of the national leader and his regime—which would then bring
about a change in local leaders as well.

3. *Clashes occur between the contender and the incumbent.* During the
revolutionary process, in contrast to earlier taifeh-keshi conflict over
the position of kadkhoda, Aliabad people could not risk clashes inside Aliabad. They knew they were no match for the Askaris backed
by gendarmerie support. Rather, Aliabadis' clashes with the powers-
that-be initially took place in the Shiraz arena.[20] Aliabad commuters participated in the rising tide of processions, with people being
killed by government armed forces, followed by more mourning
processions. With more clashes and the death toll rising, Aliabadis,
especially commuters and their social circles, paid attention to the
shifting balance of power in Shiraz and the nation.

4. *The incumbent (or someone belonging to his group) performs an outrageous act.* In Shiraz, commuters observed acts of violence on the
part of government forces that so outraged them they felt willing to
do anything to get rid of the Shah and forces responsible. Then, in
Aliabad, the village witnessed the outrageous behavior of pro-Shah
personnel in the stone throwing, the stabbing of Kurosh and the
injury of Kurosh's old stepfather-uncle. Aliabadis were horrified by
violence perpetrated by Shah supporters against fellow Iranian in
Aliabad and all over Iran.

5. *The opposition, outraged, grows in numbers and resolve.* Traditionally,
an attack against a taifeh member had instigated factional mobilization, or taifeh-keshi. Members of the taifeh gathered to seek revenge
for this injury and protect themselves from further attack by demonstrating they were not to be fooled with. During the 1978–1979
revolutionary process, commuters became effective "culture brokers"
because once they became involved and then were threatened or

harmed, those near and dear to them likewise became personally involved in the struggle.

After the stone throwing and the stabbing of Kurosh, when villagers witnessed the brutality of government forces and suffered the anguish of a severe injury to a relative, friend and co-villager, the shift in Aliabad public opinion against the Shah and his regime was precipitous. Korosh's taifeh pulled in other taifeh, often by means of connections through women. At the national level as well, one reason for the Revolution, according to villagers, was that people wanted revenge for the martyrs—those killed by government forces during marches and demonstrations.

An event of outrage, the common attitude of *az khod gozashteh* and a large group of people gathered together to demonstrate or take action provided occasion for the swift public shift in sentiment and support of the village majority from one faction (or acquiescence to the rule of that dominant faction) to another so people could cross to the other side in the company of the majority, with relatively little risk to their own well-being. Since revolutionary participation was mainly through physical presence—almost like sangar, held in streets and religious centers—people could monitor the balance of power through the visual impact of relative numbers of supporters. From their own observations, word-of-mouth and media, Aliabadis were also well aware that the tide of support was moving away from the Shah's regime and toward the revolutionary movement, in Shiraz and all over Iran, as well as in Aliabad. Those who were more pragmatically concerned about their political futures watched the proceedings and shifted sides when the outcome became clear, thereby adding to the abrupt swing in support.

6. *A final confrontation demonstrates the victory of the contender.* Even after the stone throwing, the stabbing of Kurosh and the beating of his stepfather-uncle, Aliabad people apparently still did not feel up to confronting the Askari brothers. The battle could not be fought at the local level. In the aftermath of the stone throwing, Seyyid Yaqub and his main backers fled, but no one attacked their homes. After Mehdi and his brother and cousins beat up Kurosh's elderly stepfather-uncle, when Kurosh's taifeh came back from the Ashura procession in Shiraz and found out about it, they did trash Haj Khodabakhsh's shop. They started in on his and Mehdi's homes too

but were stopped. They stayed away from the homes of Seyyid Yaqub and his closest allies.

The decisive revolutionary confrontation of Aliabadis took place in Shiraz. Seyyid Yaqub tried to keep village men in Aliabad for the traditional Ashura chest-beating mourning procession for Imam Husein, which also signified allegiance to the local political structure. But the great majority of men went into Shiraz to join the wildly victorious Tasua and Ashura processions, then brought the victory back to the village, parading euphorically through Aliabad alleyways, chanting revolutionary couplets with fervor and delight. After Tasua and Ashura, it was just a matter of time until the final day, February 11, 1979, when the Shah's regime succumbed to the revolutionary forces.

7. *The village is reunited under the new leader.* After the culmination of the Revolution and the takeover of power by the new national leader, Ayatollah Khomeini, everyone in Aliabad—and the rest of Iran—was forced to acquiesce to the new regime. When Kurosh's allies threatened some people on the other side, they pledged allegiance to the new power. People utilized traditional means of changing sides and announcing change in alliance: presenting oneself at demonstrations, offering to cooperate, making apologies, publicly recognizing one's "mistakes," acting out rituals of deference, putting up symbols of allegiance to the other side, presenting gifts and making visits to oppositional leaders. Seyyid Yaqub, for example, came to the Aliabad mosque when a Shiraz cleric visited and scolded those responsible for the stone throwing. According to his wife, he began to do his prayers more faithfully. He grudgingly said "marg bar shah" once within my hearing. He put up a large picture of Ayatollah Khomeini over his courtyard entrance. His associates did too. Seyyid Yaqub presented a gift to the visiting mulla from Qom for New Year's Day of March 1979, and so did his son, Seyyid Muslem. Meanwhile, in Shiraz, his brother, Seyyid Ibn Ali, continued efforts to get on the good side of the Shiraz Shia establishment.

Opposition was not a legitimate option; everyone was required to come under the new regime, at the national as well as the local level. At the referendum on the Islamic Republic held on March 30 and 31, 1979, no alternative was offered. The vote could be only a yes or a no, and in front of everyone, who would dare vote no?[21]

Just as Seyyid Yaqub and his allies had controlled Aliabad mourning processions in the past, during Moharram 1979 the newly victorious village faction—supporters of Ayatollah Khomeini and the Revolution—completely monopolized the more extravagant rituals of mourning. Anyone who did not publicly align themselves with the new regime could not take part in these most significant Shia religious ceremonies.[22]

8. *People live politically, whether or not they are aware of it.* To demonstrate their political affiliation with the new regime, people had to do more than accept hospitality, bring gifts, participate in elite-sponsored religious rituals and act out rituals of deference as before. Views of people outside Aliabad about what one should believe and how one should think, dress and behave became significant. People had to be careful about their associations, Islamic education and knowledge, donations and how they spoke in public. They were forced to modify their dress, speech, knowledge, comportment and attendance at places and gatherings, among other required displays of alignment.

More and more, in contrast to taifeh-keshi under Qavam ownership, after the Revolution, political life extended beyond trying to form effective relations with Aliabad people who controlled one's livelihood. Much of how one lived one's life became political. Elements of everyday life, such as dress—neckties for men and forms of *hejab*,[23] or coverings, for women—language, street names, photos on walls in homes and workspaces, children's names, religious rituals, mosque attendance, men's facial hair, music, food, drink and more took on political meaning.

Those who wished to resist the regime—if they were willing to risk being lashed or imprisoned or losing their jobs, education or even their lives—could choose among many means, ways and symbols, either declining to act out required behavior, or choosing innovative ways of demonstrating defiance and alignment with other dissidents. Some found subtle, less self-threatening ways of registering their nonconformity.[24] More than just fostering associations with people currently in power—as in earlier taifeh-keshi—as time went on after 1979, living politically also became a matter of consciously following or diverging from the words, dress and behavior judged Islamically correct by the leaders currently at the forefront of Islamic Republic power. People from opposing factions used different rather than similar signs of affiliation with their respective stances. Further, just as other spheres of Aliabadi life tended to be guided by influences from outside Aliabad, so did Aliabadi people's political lives, and all aspects of daily life, which had been newly endowed with political meaning.

Wielding the Weapon of Sangar Once Again

The first sangar since 1964 started the night Kurosh was stabbed, December 8, 1978, and continued both in the hospital in Shiraz and in Kurosh's Aliabad courtyard. The second sangar began on February 11, 1979, the day Mehdi attacked Kurosh's stepfather-uncle and the Pahlavi Shah's government fell in Shiraz and elsewhere in Iran. Fearing another attack, taifeh members stayed in Kurosh's courtyard for a week. They ate at Kurosh's home only once or twice, not wishing to cause a financial burden or trouble for Kurosh's mother, otherwise returning to their own homes for meals. One relative, Haidar's son Behnam, who was employed by the government Office of Electricity in Shiraz, even took three days of leave.

When Kurosh's taifeh went to the courtyard of Kurosh's brother-in-law Mehdi, Kurosh's assailant, after they returned from the February 11 demonstrations and celebration of the fall of the Shah's regime furious about the attack on Kurosh's stepfather-uncle, no sangar of Mehdi's supporters was there to stop them. Mehdi and his allies did not hold a sangar or conduct taifeh-keshi at any point, at least not openly; they realized they were in no position to fight against Kurosh's taifeh and supporters. Instead, they escaped from the village. Kurosh's assailant, Mehdi, and his close relatives stayed away from Aliabad for a few weeks and then kept a low profile for a while.

The reemergence of the institution of sangar, in the two sangar held by Kurosh's supporters, indicated decline of central government strength, retreat of the gendarmes and transfer of political power in Aliabad back to taifeh. The processions and gatherings at shrines and mosques in Shiraz and elsewhere in Iran can also be seen as a sort of sangar: assembling people who are politically affiliated for the purpose of showing force and protecting themselves. The increasing size, frequency and geographic spread of such marches and gatherings and the enthusiasm, determination and confidence of the crowds served as the most crucial implements to overthrow the Pahlavi monarchy.

Women and Politics in Taifeh-Keshi and in the Revolution

In other publications, I have pointed out how the framing of revolutionary involvement as religious activity enabled women from more socially conservative backgrounds to participate.[25] In addition, Aliabad women who took an active part in revolutionary efforts had been prepared for national political activity by their work in earlier taifeh-keshi politics.

As in taifeh-keshi politics before land reform, women's revolutionary participation was valued and encouraged. In the same way, women's revolutionary involvement seemed proportional to the seriousness and importance of the situation. Although women often equaled men in number, men were the organizers and visible leaders of the marches; women's revolutionary involvement was seen as secondary and supportive of men's.

As in earlier taifeh-keshi politics, Aliabad women's political methods in the Revolution mainly entailed use of their verbal and social abilities, emotional displays and physical presence to show support. In the village, they carried on their political activities of information gathering and distributing, discussion and listening to revolutionary tapes and the radio and then passing on what they heard. After the stone throwing and the stabbing of Kurosh, seyyid women and other women—family members, relatives and neighbors—reacted with great distress, screaming and moaning, venting their outrage and grief, showing support for the victims, condemning the perpetrators through physical presence and arousing the emotions and resistance of others. They reacted emotionally to the martyrdom of others as well, both the few from Aliabad and victims they did not know in Shiraz and elsewhere in the country. They showed support through physical presence at Kurosh's courtyard, but also for the Revolution and its leader, Ayatollah Khomeini, at marches in Aliabad and gatherings at mosques, shrines and processions in Shiraz.

During their revolutionary activities, Aliabad women followed the usual constraints on their behavior. They did not disobey their husbands or fathers in order to participate; village men approved of their wives' and daughters' involvement, sometimes traveling into Shiraz with them before separating to march with the men. Revolutionary marches did not prevent tending to children, husbands and households. Women's activities could be spontaneous, informal, sporadic and subject to other responsibilities. Children were often taken on marches by their mothers, who could then drop out to feed a child or let her rest. Men who worked outside the village usually did not come home for lunch, and women could do their cooking for the evening meal before they set off for Shiraz. Involvement did not bring women into improper contact with nonrelated men; they went with their female relatives and neighbors and marched, properly covered with their chadors, in the company of their network of companions. In Shiraz processions, women marched in groups separate from men.

Aliabad seyyid women's activism in the Iranian Revolution followed lines of traditional methods, traditional constraints on women's activities and traditional concerns. As in earlier taifeh-keshi politics, women worked for the interests of their own family members. They hoped for improved justice and safety for their families and for restoration of peace and well-being in Aliabad and in the nation as a whole.

In contrast to women's political work in local taifeh-keshi, though, Aliabad women's contributions to the Revolution were openly acknowledged by both women and men, just as was women's participation in general in the Iranian Revolution. Further, the local level was no longer the level at which policy and forces determined the safety and welfare of their family and relatives, women could see. Although they applied taifeh-keshi culture and experience to the revolutionary movement, women, like men, redirected their resentment and political activities away from the local level and toward the national-level political conflict. In hopes of having effects on national politics and thereby on the safety and welfare of family, relatives and Iranians in general, Aliabad seyyid women initiated anti-Shah demonstrations in Aliabad on January 5, 1979, and after that traveled into Shiraz on a regular basis to demonstrate in the revolutionary movement, like many Aliabad men had already been doing.

Taifeh-Keshi Political Culture and Expectations of Political Process

Kurosh was among the more educated of the young village men (although he had not attended university). According to statements in his interview, he believed that everyone should benefit from the Islamic Republic—not just its supporters. He believed that people shouldn't take revenge, that no one should be harmed, that this would be against Islam. He believed in freedom, yet he apparently approved of his friends going after members of the village opposition to beat them up in order to force them into "unity." His taifeh trashed Haj Khodabakhsh's shop and starting to wreck his and Mehdi's homes before they were stopped.

Kurosh spoke about the importance of unity both at the local and the national level. Insistence on unity to the point of intimidation through violence or threatened violence by the dominant taifeh or faction hardly encourages consideration of minority opinion, meaningful political participation by all, legitimate opposition or even voicing of alternative views. In spite of his professed beliefs, it seems Kurosh was influenced by some of the concerns of taifeh-keshi ethos and worldview.

For some villagers, such as the majority of peasants, taifeh-keshi worldview informed their interpretation of the Revolution relatively unmodified by other ideologies. For other villagers, such as traders and commuters, ideas and policies derived from the concept of taifeh-keshi combined with worldviews and political policies from other ideologies and symbolic systems. For example, Seyyid Kazem Askari combined taifeh-keshi and the modified Shia ideology of revolution to explain for himself the process of the revolutionary movement.

Among villagers, only Shaikh Rahim Kazemi and his sons, some other teachers and a few others held more complex and diverse attitudes toward political process. Although originally activists in the revolutionary movement against the Pahlavi regime, Shaikh Rahim and his associates soon became disillusioned with governmental political control after the Revolution, which was even more extreme than under the Shah's government. They retired from political activity.

The great majority of villagers, influenced by the processual paradigm of their local political competition and conflict, expected extreme political hierarchy, one all-powerful leader, monopolization of political power and authority, punishment of dissidents and forced unification under the new regime. They did not expect a transformation in political process. They did not expect discussion among people supporting different political policies and philosophies, or even competing political parties and leaders with the possibility of ongoing existence of oppositional groups after the victory of one group at a certain point. The main aim of the Revolution was to get rid of the Shah; the most important slogan that participants shouted was "marg bar shah," "Death to the Shah." Aliabad villagers condemned the present leader, but the great majority wanted another strong leader to replace him. Even Mostafa seemed to feel that Iranians could be a good people only if they had a good leader.[26]

According to taifeh-keshi culture, the leader was expected to provide for villagers, protecting them and fulfilling their needs. In past examples of Aliabad taifeh-keshi, people complained about lack of competent and caring service, to the extent that they wanted a new leader. They held high expectations for the conditions to be provided by the new kadkhoda. During the 1978–1979 revolutionary process, most villagers wisely stayed out of the struggle until infuriated by "outrageous acts" that intolerably violated village norms for acceptable behavior and threatened or harmed friends and relatives. They saw the government and its agents as failing to live up to minimal standards of decency and responsibility.[27] Revolutionary-minded villagers complained about the uncaring tyranny of the local Askari regime and the inadequate, unequal and partial assistance that the central government provided to them. As in former village taifeh-keshi, most Aliabadis expected a change in personnel from the revolutionary process, a leader who would be more just and better protect them and provide for their needs.

Although the Shah had brought some degree of modernization and westernization to Iran, efforts had not been made in the area of political modernization. The Resurgence Party—the only party allowed—and "elections," with only one candidate from the one-party system standing for each position, were only window dressings. In spite of economic development and (selective) modernization, the great majority of Aliabad people had no other political culture, no political alternatives to the taifeh-keshi paradigm.

ALTHOUGH MANY ALIABAD PEOPLE became staunch supporters of the national-level revolutionary movement, participating in marches, demonstrations and strikes in Shiraz and even in Aliabad, the worldview and processual paradigm of taifeh-keshi still channeled their attitudes and behavior. The great majority of villagers applied taifeh-keshi understandings, analysis, decision making and action to the national-level Shah–revolutionary forces conflict.[28]

After the Shah's centralization program was carried out, power over villagers' lives lay at higher levels. With the merging of local and national politics during the violence of December 7 and 8, 1978, in Aliabad, both women and men realized that the target of their political activism must also be higher levels. For both men and women, the two main changes from earlier taifeh-keshi politics to their 1978–1978 revolutionary political participation were the *locus* of their activity—Shiraz as well as Aliabad—and its *focus*—national rather than local politics.

6

After the Revolution
The Local Uprising

DURING THE REVOLUTIONARY PERIOD, politically astute persons began developing connections with both sides, in order to pave the way for beneficial relations with whichever side ultimately prevailed. As early as fall 1978, Seyyid Ibn Ali Askari began courting revolutionary religious personnel in Shiraz. He professed his devotion to Ayatollah Khomeini. Shortly after the Revolution, he ingratiated himself with new Shiraz religious authorities by visits and donations. Similarly, Seyyid Yaqub Askari's son Seyyid Muslem had been building up his revolutionary credentials for some months. After the fall of the Pahlavi Shah's government on February 11, 1979, thanks to these efforts, he became the main Aliabad contact for the new Shiraz clerical authorities.

After the Revolution, villagers at first assumed the new government would be structurally similar to the old one, that Ayatollah Khomeini's political role and performance would be similar to those of the Shah. Many people expected a similar secret service organization in the Khomeini regime, and the same type of political organization. All power and authority would continue to emanate from the central government and the central figure of Ayatollah Khomeini. Since Seyyid Yaqub's son had done well ingratiating himself with the other side, he would be able to maintain the Askari advantage under the new government. Now, they assumed, the visiting mulla from Qom, the religious capital of Iran, would delegate authority to Seyyid Muslem Askari for local administration.

Villagers expected the new authorities to reward those who had helped bring about their victory. Because of his central role in revolutionary organizing, Seyyid Muslem should be able to protect his father from summary revolutionary justice. This protection, along with the older Askari's public apology, would result in forgiveness, as had been customary when joining forces with a victorious contender in the past, the Askaris foresaw.

Political activity was based on these assumptions for several months after the Revolution. Many people called on the visiting mulla, in the customary show of deference and allegiance to a superior, on Noruz, New Year's Day, March 21, 1979, and brought him gifts. Even persons from other villages came to the mulla with their problems and disputes. The mulla worked closely with Seyyid Muslem and was frequently a guest at his home. Seyyid Muslem took charge of organizing village men to guard the village every night. When Shiraz authorities provided food rations for night sentries to the mulla, he handed them over to Seyyid Muslem for distribution. Observing these connections and remembering the disastrous results of attempted revolts against the Askaris during the 1950s and 1960s, villagers were afraid to act against the Askaris.

Gradually, however, both mulla and people realized the situation was not as they had expected. The mulla did not have backing from higher up during the unsettled post-Revolution period to enforce his decisions, help people with problems or resolve conflicts. Dissatisfied with lack of obedience to his rulings, the mulla eventually left.

When the gendarmes came back to their Qodratabad station after the Revolution, fearing revenge for their past brutal treatment of villagers, they stayed at their post, refusing to involve themselves in village affairs; the Askaris lost their all-important armed gendarmerie backup. The new Revolutionary Guards in Shiraz—unorganized, inexperienced, unwilling to jeopardize their popularity, and too few in number—had little effect on security at that point. Unsure of what new policies would be, government personnel were reluctant to take any action. Religious leaders feared taking initiative that might lead to further dissension and strife. They were not prepared to champion such an unpopular family as the Askaris, even if some members *had* participated in the Revolution.

Shortly after the Revolution, with gendarmes out of the picture, educators, religious figures and heads of oppositional taifeh who had long been enemies of the Askaris resumed efforts to seek justice regarding the Askaris' past deeds. At first, assuming continuation of central government power, they filed complaints with government offices in Shiraz. They even traveled to Tehran to confer with land reform officials. These efforts, however, brought no results. Gradually, the oppositional faction realized that central government offices and personnel no longer possessed the power to rule directly.

Local political support had become more important for village-level political process, the Askaris also realized, than it had been for many years. Because of their lack of coercive power, wish to maintain popular support and need to maintain order with a minimum of effort and expense, authorities were again forced to accept the results of local power plays to a greater degree.

Gaining political influence with Shiraz religious authorities entailed a double strategy, similar to that of aspiring kadkhodas during Qavam ownership. First, local politicians had to demonstrate victory in local struggles and a larger group of followers in competitive displays to Shiraz authorities. Second, they had to persuade Shiraz religious authorities that one's faction and leaders shared the religious authorities' ideology, were willing to serve and protect Shiraz authorities' interests and were capable of doing so better than rivals. The long-restrained local dissidents—from Mosaddeq, strike and land reform conflicts—attempted to rally other reluctant villagers against Seyyid Ibn Ali Askari.

Tests of Strength and Power Transformations

It was not until several dramatic demonstrations of the Askari's power deficiency after the Revolution, and the government's failure to come to their aid, that the more cautious villagers began to think maybe the Askaris weren't so powerful anymore.

The Noruz Visitation That Didn't Happen

On Noruz, March 21, 1979, villagers boycotted the customary New Year's visitation to the home of the former village boss, Seyyid Yaqub Askari. Although his double doors were opened wide to the village alleyway to show he was prepared for visitors, no one came to congratulate Seyyid Yaqub on the New Year. Not even all members of his immediate family ate the traditional Noruz meal of fish and dill and fava bean rice with him. His daughter and family came for the day. His brother Seyyid Asadollah stopped by for a while. Otherwise, we, the suspect Americans, whom the gendarmerie captain had placed in his courtyard, were the only outsiders enjoying his hospitality!

The evening before, Seyyid Ayyub had told me he himself would not be receiving well-wishers this year—because his son Mostafa was not in the village. After presenting this rationale, he went on: "To tell the truth, people don't feel like going to Seyyid Yaqub's. But if I were receiving, everyone would come, down to kids Karima's age." (My daughter, Karima, was 21 months old then.)

When I visited the home of Rana, daughter-in-law of Seyyid Yaqub's sister, she asked if anyone had come to Seyyid Yaqub's that morning. When I answered, "No one," she commented,

Usually everyone goes to their house in the morning right after the New Year comes in. For a few years, Noruz coincided with Moharram, so it wasn't celebrated at all. But the last two years people really went all out. This year people aren't celebrating much—because of the martyrs.

When I returned to Seyyid Yaqub's courtyard, his wife asked me what was going on in the village. She said, "Last year at this time our courtyard was full. Everyone in Aliabad was here—men and women." Then she added the excuse for the humiliating lack of Noruz well-wishers: "But this year people aren't celebrating New Year's because of the martyrs."

Other villagers asked what had happened at Seyyid Yaqub's and commented on the lack of attendance, depending on their attitude toward him. Seyyid Mostafa, a supporter of the mellat, the anti-Askari faction, in spite of the fact that he was a son of Seyyid Ayyub and of Seyyid Yaqub's father's brother, said in a derogatory tone, "In the past, everyone from Aliabad went and kissed Seyyid Yaqub's hand, but not this year, thank God."

Six days after Noruz, when Rana finally dropped in for a Noruz visit, Rezvan, Seyyid Yaqub's wife, complained endlessly to her about the lack of Noruz visitors. "Seyyid Asadollah's son-in-law didn't even come," she sputtered. "Thank goodness Seyyid Enayat [Rana's husband] came over the other day since no one else came."

The complete boycott of the Noruz visitation at Seyyid Yaqub's on March 21, 1979, provided a dramatic demonstration of the lack of support for him in Aliabad. In a May 30th interview a couple of months later, Seyyid Kazem Askari, another son of Seyyid Ayyub and therefore Seyyid Yaqub's cousin, surely had Seyyid Yaqub's failed Noruz reception in mind when he talked about how political leaders could tell if people supported them:

It's obvious. You can tell if someone is being nice to you. You can tell by raft-o-amad. If I hadn't welcomed you the first time you came here, you wouldn't have come back.

Seyyid Ibn Ali and Seyyid Yaqub will hear from other people whether I say good things or bad things about them. If someone treats you disrespectfully, you know you can't expect his help in the future. If I pay attention to you and talk with you, you'll treat me well in return—we'll have warm raft-o-amad. If a *kuchik* [inferior, person of lower status] doesn't go to the home of a *bozorg* [superior] at Noruz, the superior will know they've grown apart.

Although no one paid the customary and required visit of congratulations to Seyyid Yaqub on New Year's Day, many people did call on the visiting mulla. Such visits indicated the villagers' recognition of the mulla's political preeminence, as a representative of the new government. By taking Noruz gifts to the mulla, villagers hoped to get on his good side and then be granted special consideration in future times of trouble. Seyyid Yaqub and his wife later presented Mr. Rohani with a blanket, and their son Seyyid Muslem gave him a large container of honey from his own beehives.

Attack on Seyyid Muslem Askari

After the Revolution, as villagers became more aware of the Askaris' lack of gendarmerie backup, minor attacks against Askari property went unpunished. In May, a young man actually assaulted Seyyid Muslem. The gendarmes failed to make an immediate appearance to arrest the young man. The Askaris, for their part, speedily and cheerfully patched up the quarrel.

Seyyid Yaqub had rented some rooms to a builder who used them to store cement. The man's construction business was not doing very well; he did not wish to pay the six months' rent. Seyyid Yaqub could take the cement stored in the rooms instead, he said. But then the builder sold the cement to a Rezai family member for 1,000 toman. On May 14, 1979, when Seyyid Yaqub went to tell the buyer that the cement actually belonged to him, a quarrel developed. Seyyid Muslem came to defend his father. Seyyid Muslem and the 17- or 18-year-old brother of Fazlollah Rezai got into a fight and gave each other at least one blow. The young man split open the skin on the back of Seyyid Muslem's head from ear to ear, people said. Seyyid Muslem was taken to the local clinic, where they bandaged his cut. According to another version, they took him to the hospital in Shiraz, where they stitched up his cut.

Several relatives immediately went to Seyyid Muslem's house: Seyyid Asadollah, another son of Seyyid Yaqub, at least two of Seyyid Ayyub's sons,

Mohammad Amini (Mashd Yusef Amini's son and Seyyid Muslem's brother-in-law), Seyyid Yaqub's wife (who was also Seyyid Muslem's mother) and others.

Even Seyyid Ayyub's wife, Ezzat, went, although Seyyid Ayyub's family was on bad terms with Seyyid Yaqub's family. On May 9, Seyyid Yaqub had discovered that extensive damage had been done to an orchard owned by the Askari relatives. Earlier, Seyyid Ayyub had accused Seyyid Yaqub of refusing to divide up the orchard among the owners. He suspected Seyyid Yaqub of keeping more than his share of the fruit during the process of administering the orchard on behalf of all of the relatives. When Seyyid Yaqub found that trees had been chopped down and burned, walls torn down and electricity wires cut from this orchard, he jumped to conclusions because of this quarrel and accused Seyyid Ayyub's son Mostafa of committing the vandalism. Mostafa and his family were outraged and deeply offended by this accusation. Several lively exchanges had taken place between members of Seyyid Ayyub's family and members of Seyyid Yaqub's family. Ezzat, Mostafa's mother, was livid and could talk of nothing else but Seyyid Yaqub's accusation.

Nevertheless, she went to Seyyid Muslem's home to show her solidarity. There, she could not restrain herself from a stream of sarcasm: "I certainly hope Mostafa isn't the one who did this, since Mostafa is the enemy. Rezvan doesn't have any enemies other than Mostafa. Are you sure it wasn't Mostafa? Maybe Mostafa gave the order to do this."

Rezvan spent her time that day at her son Seyyid Muslem's home. When she was not there herself, she was anxious to know who other visitors were. It was not an impressive sangar—hardly one to strike terror into the hearts of the Rezais and their supporters. Only some male descendants of Seyyid Ayyub and sons of Seyyid Ayyub's sister, the Amini brothers who were opium smugglers, came to show their support. Even fewer women were present. This small, short-lived sangar held by the Askari taifeh following the attack against Seyyid Muslem, and the cautious, do-nothing policy of the Askaris epitomized their loss of village power and authority. Clearly such a showing did not warrant a clash with the Rezais.

Amazingly, the attack against Seyyid Muslem Askari, Seyyid Yaqub's son, went unpunished! Askaris and supporters did not gather in order to prepare for conflict. Rather, they made efforts to settle the issue peacefully. Askari reaction to this second major post-Revolution test of backing for the Askaris—the physical attack on Seyyid Muslem—demonstrated their realization of a new political reality. They were on their own. They could no longer count on Qodratabad gendarmes and government offices in Shiraz to assist them in maintaining their rule in Aliabad.

According to Rezvan, Seyyid Yaqub had this to say about village political conditions: "What kind of situation is it when gendarmes can't do anything, when you can't call for gendarmes?"

Rezvan herself fumed:

Who can we go and complain to? The courts? Mr. Rohani? The revolutionary committees?[1]

Before, we would have taken this person to the gendarmes, and they would have put him in prison right away. Now we can't do anything. Things are terrible now. Back then there were gendarmes, there were policemen, there were prisons. Today there's nothing. What sort of life is this?

Several village peacemakers, including at least three seyyids, sons of Seyyid Ayyub, immediately urged Seyyid Muslem and the Rezai youth to make up. They made peace with each other the very same day, shaking hands and kissing each other on the cheeks. The Askaris' small sangar lasted not even a full day. Other Askari taifeh women (who had failed to appear at the sangar) were pleased and relieved to see the conflict end without further violence.

One of Seyyid Ayyub's sons who had served as a peacemaker complained about the dissatisfaction of Haj Aqa Amini, brother of Ali Reza and Mashd Yusef Amini. He hadn't wanted the men to make up but rather had wanted "to do them in." The peacemaker, a successful village shopkeeper, had no interest in supporting Seyyid Muslem and Seyyid Yaqub in a confrontation with the Rezais. The reaction of the small gathering of relatives at Seyyid Ayyub's home to the complaint revealed how most Askari relatives saw their situation:

Here someone does a good deed, and people complain. There's religious credit for making peace. The other side has a lot of supporters. What does Haj Aqa mean, he doesn't want to make up, wants to use the opportunity to teach those people a lesson, wants to draw blood? We're hardly in a position to do that.

The fight was really over land, people said. They used the cement as an excuse. The Rezai taifeh had been on bad terms with the Askaris since the land reform conflict. The night before, Seyyid Yaqub had caught Fazlollah

Rezai and his brothers cutting grass and wheat from Seyyid Yaqub's and Seyyid Ibn Ali's land. They had no right to do this, he told them, and cursed them. But they hadn't answered, most likely believing the land did not rightfully belong to the Askaris anyway.

Some members of the Askari taifeh, especially sons of Seyyid Ayyub's sister—the Amini brothers—wanted to go and get guns for revenge. Seyyid Yaqub and one of Seyyid Ayyub's sons stopped them. From the city, Seyyid Ibn Ali sent word that they shouldn't go to complain, they shouldn't do anything.

The incident became the main topic of conversation in Aliabad for several weeks. People repeated over and over, "This never could have happened before."

These two significant tests of the level of support for the Askaris after the Revolution—failure of villagers to show deference and loyalty to Seyyid Yaqub through the customary Noruz visitation, and lack of gendarmerie intervention and taifeh support for Seyyid Yaqub after the attack on his son—revealed the current powerlessness of Seyyid Yaqub's regime. For the first time since the suppression of the land reform uprising, Aliabad people really realized that Seyyid Yaqub no longer enjoyed central government support.

Village Opposition to Seyyid Ibn Ali Gains Momentum

Dissatisfied people had practiced taifeh-keshi in the past—before they were squelched following the land reform conflict—to overthrow an incumbent kadkhoda and his power and authority structure and bring a new leader into power. It might be possible, once again, to organize an uprising against Seyyid Yaqub, his Shiraz-based brother Seyyid Ibn Ali and their local power and authority structure, some villagers thought.

Appealing to the New Religious Authorities

Aliabad activists concentrated on arousing village support and eliciting participation in anti-Askari struggle. Even after the two tests of strength, however, most villagers were still afraid of the Askaris. It was one thing to go to Shiraz to join a swelling revolutionary movement in company with millions of other Iranians, but quite another to revolt directly against the local rulers.

Given local reluctance, activists had to find ways to calm fears. To appeal to the new Shia Muslim political authorities and motivate villagers to act against the local political elites, local activists clothed their political revolt and long-standing antipathy toward the Askaris in the new revolutionary interpretation of Shia Islam. Aiming to get both village- and Shiraz-level support, local activists began to apply Islamic frameworks and imagery used in the anti-Shah struggle to the local-level struggle against Seyyid Ibn Ali. They began to use Islamic terms, rhetoric, symbols, political categories and activities developed during the course of the Revolution to legitimize their actions for themselves, potential supporters and government authorities. In this they replicated the strategy of local activists and those persuaded to join them in the national revolutionary process, who had turned to revolutionary Shia rhetoric *after* deciding to join the revolutionary movement.

Activists began to point to local meanings of the reformist and revolutionary emphasis in Shia Islam, attempting to legitimize their local struggle by setting it in the context of the new political elite's ideology and political rhetoric. The Shia injunction to struggle against injustice, oppression and tyrants, activists argued, could apply to situations other than ridding the country of the Shah. Just as they had with the Shah, activists and other villagers began to compare Seyyid Ibn Ali with Yazid, the caliph who had ordered the battle against revered Shia Imam Husein, resulting in his 680 CE martyrdom. Villagers began discussing the past exploits and characteristics of the notorious Seyyid Ibn Ali in the victorious revolutionaries' vocabulary: *zolm* (oppression), *zur* (force), *taqhuti* (decadent, idolatrous), *zed-e enqelab* (antirevolutionary), *estebdad* (tyranny), *mofsed* (corrupter), *reshveh-khor* (bribe eater) and *savaki* (SAVAK personnel—the hated and feared secret police agency of the Pahlavi regime).

Villagers also referred to Islam's socialist aspects. Men and women commented positively on the simple life led by Imam Ali,[2] then muttered it wasn't Islamic for some people (like Seyyid Ibn Ali) to have hundreds of acres of land while others had none whatsoever, for some people (like Seyyid Ibn Ali) to own whole apartment buildings in Shiraz while others had not even a home to their name.

Through discussion and education, the number of people in the anti–Seyyid Ibn Ali alliance increased during summer 1979. Observing growing village sentiment against Seyyid Ibn Ali, oppositional activists became bolder in their struggle. Former neutrals decided their interests would best be served by joining oppositional forces. Nominal allies of Seyyid Ibn Ali deserted him, some even throwing support to the opposition. Eventually, the overwhelming strength of the oppositional movement intimidated even some die-hard Ibn Ali supporters. They retreated from their stance of vociferous defense.

Seyyid Ibn Ali Askari's Attempt to Distribute Land

Grasping that his situation had become precarious and now depended on the goodwill of Aliabad people, Seyyid Ibn Ali strategized to mend relations with villagers. He attempted to form an association of seyyids to consolidate his own taifeh. Hoping that the men whose antagonism he had earned through his appropriation of their land and water would forgive his past transgressions, Seyyid Ibn Ali ran the pumps for his well four days during a dry period in summer 1979 to provide water for their orchards.

In the conflict over land that occurred after the 1979 Revolution, Seyyid Ibn Ali again maintained support of khordeh-malek—the small owners—and their families for a while. If the peasant faction took over his land, Seyyid Ibn Ali warned khordeh-malek, they would also take over other small owners' land. Only after repeated assurances by riyat faction leaders that the khordeh-malek land was not in danger of seizure, and only after their own observations that peasants were not bothering their land, did the other small owners' support for Seyyid Ibn Ali subside.

Aiming to demonstrate his religiosity and piousness to Shiraz religious authorities and win back approval of Aliabad residents at the same time, Seyyid Ibn Ali planned to divide some 40,000 square meters of land among 40 village *mostazafin* (poor and oppressed). He came to the village on October 2, 1979, accompanied by four revolutionary guards and some engineers, and attempted to distribute some land. This move—calculated to win him the Shiraz religious hierarchy's sympathy—backfired, further unifying the opposition and mobilizing it into action against him. Upon learning the landlord planned to give away land that village activists believed actually belonging to peasants to so-called mostazafin (who were in fact his own relatives, supporters and a few influential persons whom he hoped to buy off), villagers were outraged. They protested furiously and prevented the land distribution. The revolutionary guards and engineers, innocent of contention over the land, stopped their work and asked protestors to explain their case at court the following Saturday.

Anti-Askari Demonstrations and
the Arrest of Seyyid Ibn Ali

As the Askari decline of power became obvious, activists were able to draw more supporters. Early on Saturday morning, October 6, several hundred irate men left in buses, pickups, taxis and private cars to chant in front of the governor's office and the court in Shiraz and swear out more than 100 complaints against Seyyid Ibn Ali, including four accusations of murder. Authorities arrested Seyyid Ibn Ali the same day. Several days in a row, Aliabad men commuted into Shiraz to shout slogans and chants in front of government offices and religious figures' homes, and to add to the file against Seyyid Ibn Ali (perhaps not always accurately). Seyyid Muslem organized the Askaris for a competitive show of force, but they were badly outnumbered and outshouted.

Apparently in hopes that Seyyid Ibn Ali would be able to reach a compromise with the riyat (actually mainly their sons now working in jobs outside of Aliabad), authorities let him out of jail on October 10. Accompanied by his relatives and other supporters in a noisy caravan of cars, Seyyid Ibn Ali drove back to Aliabad with the aim of pacifying his enemies. But the population reacted with outrage, crowding into the village square and even shouting in anger at a jeep full of then normally revered revolutionary guards sent to preserve the peace: "You think we're still back in the Shah's time so you should stick up for tyranny?"

At 6:00 the next morning the mosque loudspeaker broadcast the message to gather for another trip to Shiraz: "Don't be afraid! Fight for your rights!" Several hundred men repeated their trek to Shiraz to shout chants in front of the governor's office. Leaders spoke with the governor's representative, explaining why Aliabad people wanted Seyyid Ibn Ali put back in prison. The authorities again seized Seyyid Ibn Ali, this time in the process of arranging to leave the country.

With this second imprisonment, more people in Aliabad, who at first had been reluctant to openly defy Seyyid Ibn Ali, allowed themselves to be persuaded of their "Islamic duty" and joined forces with the opposition. The Shiraz court eventually acquiesced to continuous pressure and granted activists explicit written permission to farm those areas of Seyyid Ibn Ali's land that he himself hadn't planted yet. (Allowing villagers to sow land not currently farmed was a general policy designed to encourage agricultural productivity.) Armed with this document and optimistic about the final outcome of the dispute over land, opposition leaders announced that on

November 1 and 2, all married males native to Aliabad who wanted to receive land should register at the mosque. With those natives currently living in Shiraz also eligible, the signatories totaled some 800 men.

Taking Over and Cultivating Land
Seized from Seyyid Ibn Ali

By Friday, November 2, 1979, leaders of the peasant faction had gathered enough support to take over and sow the first section of Seyyid Ibn Ali's land, unjustly taken by him before land reform, they judged. On Friday morning, crowds of men gathered at the mosque, then marched out to a large section of land controlled by Seyyid Ibn Ali on the other side of the highway from the walled village. In the forefront, young men carried the green flag of Islam. Two groups chanted the alternating phrases of a revolutionary couplet, as had been customary in large national marches and demonstrations against the Shah. At the site, they planted the green flag of Islam in the ground. Men took turns sowing by hand while elated onlookers shouted "Allah o akbar" (God is great) and other inspiring slogans. Still subdued by community and kin pressures and hesitant to confront the for-

FIGURE 7. Euphoric young men surround an old peasant on the land taken over and sown by the people's faction on Friday, November 2, 1979.

merly powerful Askaris directly, they did not stage demonstrations against Askaris in the village or march inside the village walls.

Since it was late in the winter wheat season, rather than waste precious time dividing up land at this point, they would farm the land jointly that year, activists decided. They hired ten men to do the agricultural work. Activist leaders took over organization of the community. They taxed each new shareholder 400 toman to defray agricultural expenses. (In November 1979 the rate was about 17 toman to a US dollar.) They expected all shareholders to participate in necessary communal activities, such as cleaning out the irrigation ditch.

Villagers took over agricultural land in other areas of Iran too. Even by March 1979, sharecroppers and landless laborers in villages throughout the country were seizing land. In the northwest, Kurdish organizations promoted political autonomy, peasant resistance against landlords and land expropriations. In the northeast, Turkmen tribal-ethnic people established peasant councils to serve as regional authorities.[3]

Outrageous Askari Behavior and Local Resistance

Ultimately, it was because of outrageous Askari behavior toward villagers that resistance leaders succeeded in persuading Aliabad people to confront the Askaris directly in the fight over village land controlled by Seyyid Ibn Ali Askari—just as the stone throwing and stabbing of Kurosh had outraged villagers into supporting the revolutionary movement.

The Ditch Cleaning: Askari Malice and Mellat Outrage

Two weeks after the takeover of Seyyid Ibn Ali's land, at 7:30 in the morning, November 16, 1979, the mosque loudspeaker called all those who had signed up to receive land to come and help clean out the irrigation ditch bringing water to Aliabad land from Darab, the neighboring village. As it was not the right time of year for this task, the leaders clearly aimed to stage one more show of oppositional strength. With shovels and picks, the peasant faction marched off to remove obstructions from the ditch, widen it and rebuild walls where necessary. Once outside the village walls, they shouted such couplets as

zarein piruz ast. zamindar nabud ast.

The peasants have won. The landlord has been annihilated.

FIGURE 8. Young men of the peasant faction cleaning out the irrigation ditch that brought water to Aliabad from Darab, Friday, November 16, 1979.

Even then they did not say the name Askari or mention specific names of Askari taifeh members, nor did they march or shout their slogans inside the village walls. Several hundred men worked their way up the ditch toward Darab, enjoying their cooperative effort and celebration of strength in numbers and cohesion. But just outside Darab a large, angry mob from that village came out to meet them, all carrying clubs, rifles and other weapons.

Just short of an attack the two groups came to an understanding. The Aliabadis asked why the Darabis brandished weapons when the Aliabadis had come merely to clean out the irrigation ditch. Early that morning, the Darabis told them, Seyyid Yaqub and his sons and supporters had come to warn them of an impending attack by a large mob from Aliabad. According to informants, Seyyid Yaqub and his supporters then hid in trees and walled orchards. Reportedly, they planned to shoot the riyat faction leaders once the anticipated fighting started between Aliabad men and Darab men. Subsequent investigators would then assume Darabis to be responsible for the killings. Upon hearing this, the Aliabad men became outraged.

Ritual of Revolution
Against the Former Village Authorities

Furious, the peasant faction rushed back toward Aliabad. They gathered near the graveyard to make a unified entry into the village. Then they marched together toward the village gateway, carrying their shovels and picks like weapons and thunderously shouting couplets, for the first time naming names, in a direct verbal attack against the Askari taifeh:

marg bar se mofsed-e mahali: Seyyid Yaqub o Ali Reza o Ibn Ali.

Death to the three local corrupters: Seyyid Yaqub, Ali Reza and lbn Ali.

During revolutionary period marches in Shiraz, activists had shouted,

marg bar se mofsedin-e donyai: Amrika o Israil o Pahlavi.

Death to the three corrupters on earth: America, Israel and Pahlavi.

By borrowing from an anti-Shah, anti-imperialist couplet, the opposition claimed the legitimacy of their cause. For the first time, the peasant taifeh marched in unison right through the village gateway and then around the

FIGURE 9. The furious peasant taifeh rushing back to march through Aliabad after hearing from Darabis that the Askaris planned to assassinate their leaders, Friday, November 16, 1979.

village alleyways inside, shouting their fury and contempt. When they came near Seyyid Yaqub's home, several Askari women taunted and cursed the crowd. When they reached the Askari courtyard wall, about ten or twelve Askari supporters gathered in sangar threw stones and shot Colts down at them from their rooftop vantage point, infuriating the protesters even more. Fighting broke out between the two groups. Several men from both sides were wounded. The opposition went to bring gendarmes and policemen, with the complaint that the Askaris fired weapons down on the unarmed crowd.

Routing Out the Askari Taifeh

In a dramatic reversal from the Shah period, the riyat faction called the gendarmes. They came and arrested those of the Askari taifeh who were not able to escape and took them to the Qodratabad station. Reportedly the gendarmes beat and imprisoned some members of the Askari taifeh. Seyyid Muslem (Seyyid Yaqub's son) and Naser Amini (Mashd Yusef's son) were able to get away. Those who escaped hid out in Shiraz, moving from house to house to avoid being caught.

Gendarmes later released Seyyid Yaqub, his sons, Seyyid Ibn Ali's sons, Ali Reza Amini and Seyyid Rahman Askari, son of another deceased brother of Seyyid Ayyub who supported Seyyid Ibn Ali. Shiraz authorities warned them not to return to Aliabad. Virtually exiled and fearful for their safety, they remained in hiding. Other supporters did not dare return to the village but instead stayed with friends or relatives in Shiraz.

The furious villagers put aside kinship and community ties with the Askaris and turned against the Askari taifeh with a vengeance. Askaris had committed outrageous acts; villagers were prepared for direct confrontation.

Bereft of outside support and intimidated by the now unbridled anger of fellow villagers, the Askaris suffered deterioration in morale, strength and backing. They had hoped their scheme of an ambush at the ditch near Darab would turn the tide by ridding them of opposition leaders. The Askaris had also hoped they could provoke an attack on the Askari women and then complain about it to the authorities. This is why Mashd Yusef's wife cursed and swore at the peasant taifeh from the village alleyway, and why Seyyid Yaqub's wife and grandniece did so from their roof during the peasant taifeh march to Seyyid Yaqub's home, I was told.

Instead, the oppositional riyat faction, now backed by gendarmes, had routed out the small band of Askari supporters—Seyyid Yaqub, Ali Reza Amini and his brother Mashd Yusef, Seyyid Yaqub's sons, Seyyid Ibn Ali's sons, Seyyid Rahman and Mashd Yusef's son Naser. (Mashd Yusef's other son, Mohammad, who sympathized with the mellat, was not present on Seyyid Yaqub's roof when Seyyid Yaqub's taifeh attacked the peasant taifeh during their march into the village.)

Seyyid Ibn Ali's supporters were reduced to eight to ten men, mainly his own family and his cousins the opium smugglers, villagers estimated. The opposition reportedly had grown to some 1,000 members.

After the events of November 16, 1979, villagers were no longer restrained from open conflict with this small group by fear, kinship bonds or other ties. Eventually, even some previously hot-headed and determined partisans of Seyyid Ibn Ali withdrew from active involvement.

Seyyid Akbar Shifts to the Peasant Faction

Seyyid Akbar Askari was a vehement Seyyid Ibn Ali supporter. He and his family lived in the same alleyway with Seyyid Yaqub and other seyyids. Seyyid Akbar and at least one son had even been on the roof of Seyyid Yaqub's home along with other close allies of the Askari brothers on Friday, November 16, when violence broke out between the two factions.

On the evening of the next day, Seyyid Akbar changed sides. My friend Esmat Ajami commented,

Night before last, Seyyid Akbar came to the mosque. This shows he's with the people. The people didn't say, "You're bad." Rather, they said, "Your sons did a bad thing when they threw stones down on the people from Seyyid Yaqub's roof. They shouldn't have done that."

Seyyid Akbar's father-in-law had been the one to persuade him to leave Seyyid Ibn Ali and join the mellat. Seyyid Akbar's connection with the mellat through his father-in-law gave him a graceful way of giving in to forceful pressure.

Seyyid Akbar had been a shoemaker and trader, specializing in trade with migrating tribespeople, but had recently shifted to the Eshtad Motor factory between Shiraz and Aliabad. Unless he changed sides, the mellat had announced over the mosque loudspeaker, he would not be allowed to go to work. The many men from Aliabad working at Eshtad Motor actually did prevent him from entering the factory. He was afraid even to venture far enough out into the village alleyways to buy meat from the butcher. Due to mellat members' ability to come between him and his job and prevent him from coming and going, his decision to change sides was practical. His connection with the mellat through marriage provided him with a culturally approved reason for the switch, as well as a sponsor to introduce him to the mellat as a welcome new supporter.

Other villagers commented on Seyyid Akbar's move to join the opposition, saying he explained to them his past apparent support of the Askari taifeh and the reasons for his shift, and they predicted his future behavior and rationales, demonstrating how thoroughly taifeh-keshi culture permeated villagers' political analysis and behavior:

Seyyid Akbar said, "I wasn't on the roof to help the Askaris throw stones at the people, but to stop anything from happening, to stop them from throwing stones or shooting at the people."

Some people are afraid. They attach themselves to whichever side seems to be winning. Like Seyyid Akbar: He was on the other side, but then he saw they just weren't going to make it—they were going to be defeated. So he came over to this side. (From an interview on November 23, 1979, with a member of the mellat)

Another informant, daughter of Mashd Yadollah Saedi, explained,

Some people are fakes and scaredy-cats. They join up with whichever side is getting ahead. Like Seyyid Akbar: At first he was on the other side, but then he saw that they aren't strong enough and that they'll be beaten, so he came over to this side. He had Hamid the kadkhoda bring him to the mosque. Hamid told people, "Seyyid Akbar has come to help you. From now on he'll have nothing to do with the other side. He's on your side."

No one said anything. Seyyid Akbar came to the side of the people because he was afraid—afraid they'd beat him up. They actually did beat up his son.

Seyyid Akbar needs to go to the butcher shop and buy meat. He has to go to work. He has to get along with everybody else in the village. Maybe privately he isn't in agreement, but on the surface he's now on the side of the people. (From an interview on December 6, 1979, with a son of Haidar Amini)

From now on, Seyyid Akbar is on the side of the people. But if Seyyid Ibn Ali and Seyyid Yaqub win, then he might go back to their side again. Many people do this—go to whichever side is winning. Then, if Ibn Ali is victorious and Seyyid Akbar goes back to them and they ask him, "Why did you go to the mosque with the people?" he won't say, "I went to the mosque in order to join the people." Rather, he'll say, "I went to learn what their plans are."

In earlier decades, the village kadkhoda controlled the access of most village men to their livelihoods and therefore controlled their political allegiance. In this case, the mellat was, in effect, in control of Seyyid Akbar's access to his livelihood, and could therefore control his political alliance.

Villagers monitored all indications of the changing balance of power between Seyyid Ibn Ali's faction and the mellat faction. The Noruz sitting, the testing of Askari power through the attack against Seyyid Muslem, various sangar or failure to hold a sangar, sponsoring and attending rituals and Seyyid Akbar's dramatic shift to the mellat—villagers analyzed them all in hopes of predicting the eventual outcome of the conflict—and whose side they should therefore be on.

A combination of sentiment and need to get along with fellow villagers who could provide one with many necessities of life and a satisfactory social existence served to mute and postpone confrontation within the village. Villagers hesitated to offend those whose goodwill seemed necessary. But when the Askari side, in desperation, went to unacceptable lengths— unacceptable to villagers now free from gendarmerie intimidation—in an attempt to salvage their situation during the ditch cleaning, the population became outraged and lost their hesitation to clash with fellow villagers. When the opposition's ultimate victory seemed apparent or when they actually applied force, the same need for approval from one's fellow villagers resulted in a swing of support to the opposition faction.

Political Developments on Tasua and Ashura 1979

On Wednesday, November 28, 1979, the day before Tasua, authorities released Seyyid Ibn Ali from prison, causing further politicization of the mourning days.

A group of perhaps 50 of Seyyid Ibn Ali's supporters had gone to court, introducing themselves as peasants, some people told me. Seyyid Ibn Ali had given them land, they told court officials, and they therefore agreed to Seyyid Ibn Ali's release and would sign a paper indicating so. Seyyid Yaqub and Ali Reza had bribed the head of the court system, according to another story. Yet another version had Seyyid Ibn Ali's relatives seeking help from a tribal leader with whom the Askaris had dealings in the past; this man interceded for Seyyid Ibn Ali. Seyyid Ibn Ali wished only to be allowed 24 hours to see his wife and children, he apparently told court officials. To guarantee his return, he promised to pay 7,000 toman, about 400 US dollars at the time, should he fail to appear at the set hour.

He was released at about 6:00 on the eve of Tasua. Pointing to Seyyid Ibn Ali's political acumen in leaving prison at such a time, several people analyzed his thinking in this way: Tasua and Ashura, as important Shia religious days, were holidays. Therefore all government offices would be closed. There would be no place for people to go to protest Seyyid Ibn Ali's release. Sunday and Monday were also holidays to allow people to go and vote in the referendum for the Constitution of the Islamic Republic. The last time he had gotten out of prison, someone remembered, there had been a two-day holiday too. Perhaps included in Seyyid Ibn Ali's calculations about the timing of his release was the assumption that on Tasua and Ashura, the most important days of the religious year, Aliabad people would be too involved in mourning rituals to take political action. (In fact, one older woman spoke unfavorably of the neglect of mourning rituals to run after Seyyid Ibn Ali. "People shouldn't have left the self-flagellation procession to go into the city" (in efforts to have Seyyid Ibn Ali arrested again, she contended).

As Seyyid Ibn Ali walked out of prison, he flung a careless "Good-bye, Old Boy" at one of the prison guards who happened to be from Aliabad. By the next morning, the morning of Tasua, this guard brought word to the Aliabad opposition that Seyyid Ibn Ali had been freed from prison.

A crowd of men and boys and even some women and older girls had been marching around the village behind several opposition leaders carrying green flags of Islam and black flags of mourning. As they marched, they chanted Moharram and anti-American couplets:

Moharram: mah-e khun, mah-e shahadat
Amrika: mazhar-e zolm va janayat

Moharram: Month of Blood, Month of Martyrs
America: Manifestation of tyranny and crime

The crowd circled twice around the alleyway inside the village walls. Then news of Seyyid Ibn Ali's release reached them. Suddenly all was chaos. Men and boys rushed out through the village gate passageway shouting anti–Seyyid Ibn Ali slogans. Everyone piled into available vehicles—cars, taxis, pickups. The crowd went to the gendarme station down the road in

Qodratabad. There the opposition leaders complained vociferously about Seyyid Ibn Ali, demanding to know why he was released. "You must listen to the cry of the people."

The gendarme station was pretty much closed, with only a few gendarmes present. They claimed ignorance of the whole matter. The crowd should go to Shiraz to take care of their business, they suggested. Leaders of the riyat faction told women to return to Aliabad while they made further investigations.

At 2:00 in the afternoon a call came from the mosque loudspeaker that all should convene at the mosque for efforts to track down Seyyid Ibn Ali. By the time I reached the edge of the square, the volatile crowd of activists was emerging from the mosque, led by main opposition organizers. They were carrying the green flag of Islam and shouting:

marg bar seh mofsed-e mahali: Seyyid Yaqub o Ali Reza o Ibn Ali.
Death to the three local corrupters: Seyyid Yaqub and Ali Reza and Ibn Ali.

Protestors marched around the village shouting anti–Seyyid Ibn Ali slogans with fervent determination, then loaded themselves into taxis, cars, pickups and a minibus and headed for the city. The remaining crowd, mainly older girls but also a few women, men and boys, stood about, talking excitedly. In addition to more general political slogans, including anti-American couplets, they shouted anti–Ibn Ali slogans such as

be ganun-e asasi Ibn Ali-ye Askari edam bayad gardad.
According to the Constitution, Ibn Ali Askari must be executed.

In the city, the Aliabadis met with a satisfactory reception at Dastgheib's home. Seyyid Ibn Ali was a criminal, this leading religious figure recognized in his speech. He should not have been released from prison. Dastgheib apparently phoned the court to reprimand them for releasing Seyyid Ibn Ali and ordered his re-detainment. The dissidents called the Shiraz gendarme station, but the gendarmes knew nothing of the matter. They called the revolutionary guards office. A tribal leader had intervened to have him released, officials there reported, and Seyyid Ibn Ali was at home. When they called this tribal leader, he acknowledged he'd been instrumental in Seyyid Ibn Ali's release but hadn't realized he was a bad man. He promised to hand over Seyyid Ibn Ali the next morning. Two Aliabad men were to accompany four armed revolutionary guards to lead them to the tribal leader's home.

Satisfied with the promise, the Aliabadis traveled back to the village, where people had been impatiently waiting for them. They arrived after 10:00 in the evening. All was well, several different voices announced from the mosque loudspeaker. Seyyid Ibn Ali had been arrested once again. Everyone should eat dinner in a hurry and then gather at the mosque for the mourning procession of Tasua. But nothing more happened. Men did not convene for self-flagellation mourning rituals that evening after all. "But no matter," concluded a friend, expressing common sentiment. "It was more worthy to go after a tyrant and bring him to justice than to passively mourn the martyrdom of Husein."

Assured that Seyyid Ibn Ali would be arrested again, villagers felt able to go ahead the next day, the 10th of Moharram, November 29, with mourning processions and self-flagellation from before 8:00 in the morning until noon in remembrance of the eve of Imam Husein's martyrdom. Many Aliabadis living in Shiraz came to join them. As had been the case since the beginning of the month of Moharram, the most important leaders of the oppositional alliance directed groups of flagellants, each using a loudspeaker to lead his group's chants, and generally taking charge of the proceedings.

At noon the men ended their self-flagellation mourning procession on the far side of the village. They then labored with picks and shovels to destroy the brick walls around Seyyid Ibn Ali's apricot orchard. With that task accomplished, the large contingent of men and boys walked back to the village, where three men, all members of the peasant faction, sponsored feasts for the flagellants.

Taifeh-Keshi and the Post-Revolution Uprising Against the Askaris

People applied their taifeh-keshi political culture, ethos and processual paradigm during the 1979 summer and fall local uprising against the Askaris. Taifeh-keshi political concepts and process became active during times of lack of consolidated government authority. In the post-Revolution context, the central government lacked power to enforce decisions at the local level. It took a while for authority structures to become reestablished. Seyyid Kazem Askari, a son of Seyyid Ayyub, analyzed the changes in taifeh after the Revolution:

Today taifeh are as important as they were in the past. Why? Because now you have to depend on your taifeh to solve things for you. Well, actually, taifeh haven't really become more important than during the time of the Shah, but figuring out strategy is different now. Now, if our taifeh should have a fight with another taifeh, we have to remember that the gendarmes aren't around. We have to defend ourselves on our own.

We have only ourselves. No one from outside will come and help us. If we feel that we can get somewhere by ourselves, we'll go ahead. If not, we won't try it. If we feel we can't win a conflict without the help of the gendarmes, we'll just give in. We don't have any hope for assistance.

In the 1979 land seizure and local revolution against the Askaris, people wielded traditional cultural modes to demonstrate and mobilize political support. Noruz visitation, control over rituals, physical presence to indicate support, sangar and meetings of faction members all became instrumental again. Now too, both factions—Askaris and mellat—attempted to demonstrate to the outside authorities—now the clerical administration, with their Shia rhetoric and ideology—that they had the largest group and could serve the administration's interests better than the opposition, as contenders for kadkhoda had done before land reform. People saw and talked about the conflict as taifeh-keshi. They based their views, explanations, terminology and predictions on a taifeh-keshi worldview.

When after the Revolution the Askaris could no longer rely on the gendarmes to back them in their advantaged position, they attempted once again to utilize ties of taifeh common interest and dependence. They attempted to resurrect their kinship ties to recreate taifeh association, unity and a strong fighting force. The Askaris stressed their common identity as seyyids with a sizable minority of villagers and emphasized their kinship relations, directly or indirectly, with most villagers. In the words of one villager:

Before, Seyyid Yaqub's taifeh brought in armed tribal horsemen, martial law and gendarmes. Now his taifeh isn't so important anymore. The taifeh of the peasants, of the mostazafin, is more important. All of a sudden the Askaris are saying hello, how are you and shaking hands with their relatives. They're getting along with them and not cursing them. They're all seyyids.

They gather them together and tell them, "I'll give you homes and land. We're relatives. We're all descendants of the Prophet. You must help me. The others are saying that the seyyids are *khoms-khor* [alms-eaters].[4] They're out after all of us. They lie to people and try to trick them into being on their side."

This strategy served to postpone the fall of Seyyid Ibn Ali and the takeover of his land. Due, however, to earlier reliance of the Askaris on the gendarmes and other government agencies, their resulting failure to maintain the support of the majority of the villagers during the period before the Revolution, and the many men who would gain from seizure of Seyyid Ibn Ali's land, this strategy was ultimately unsuccessful. Although previously unable to rebel, too many villagers had become resentful of the Askaris due to mistreatment by them. They took advantage of the failure of the gendarmes and the government to back the Askaris, and eventually rose against them.

Taifeh-Keshi Stages in the Local Uprising

The process and sequence of the struggle replicated earlier pre–land reform taifeh battles, as comparison with the eight stages of typical taifeh-keshi politics shows. Both sides sought out useful ties. A change in balance of resources and support began the process. In earlier years, balance of power might shift because a contender for office built up greater wealth and more supporters. In this case, the Askaris lost their outside government support, and the opposition could claim affiliation with the now-prominent Shia ideology and aims.

Taifeh members and community residents were an attentive audience to political events and conditions, attempting to predict the eventual outcome in order to decide on their own behavior. People were cautious about offending a political figure who still had not been demonstrably and soundly defeated. The process of resisting the current political power began slowly, extended over a relatively long period and included a number of skirmishes and tests of strength. Then, when the Askari faction apparently planned to assassinate some opposition leaders, under cover of an attack on them by Darab villagers that the Askaris attempted to instigate, opposition men became furious. A precipitous swing of support occurred as the men perceived the Askari faction's behavior to be outrageous and intolerable, and marched into the village. The Askari faction's shooting of firearms against the opposition made them even angrier. The gendarmes took the Askaries they could capture into custody, and the others fled.

This event of outrage and its results demonstrated the defeat of the current political leader, so most people rushed to join the other faction. Closer relatives and associates stuck with the Askaris a while longer. Eventually, however, most realized the necessity of getting along with community members if they wished to continue living in the village. After a period, most were reintegrated into the community. Some were actually forced into leaving the Askari taifeh and joining the mellat. They had to come to terms with the new status quo. Monopolization of political power was taken over by the newly victorious faction. Village unity was reestablished, as in pre–land reform taifeh-keshi.

Taifeh Alignment Decision Making

As in earlier taifeh-keshi, people had alternative ties. They needed to analyze which ties were of greater significance and make alignment decisions accordingly. An actual kinship relation was not always the most important. For example, two opium smugglers in the village, although "in their hearts" they supported the mellat in the struggle against Seyyid Ibn Ali, could not participate openly because of their association with the Askaris in their smuggling activities. Informants explained their actions as follows:

Sasan is in the middle. He's related to Haj Nuri, who's very much on the side of the people. All of the Baqeris, his relatives, are with the people. Sasan is probably with the people 100%, but he's a smuggler so he's not open about it. He doesn't get involved.

Oseh Ibrahim doesn't get involved on one side or another. He doesn't support Seyyid Ibn Ali because all of the people against Seyyid Ibn Ali are relatives of his wife. But he can't join them, because he's a smuggler. The other smugglers support Seyyid Ibn Ali because they're his relatives.

Yet another villager supported Seyyid Ibn Ali, though he had been expected to support the riyat faction, reportedly because Seyyid Ibn Ali had used his connections to intervene and save the son of this man from execution for smuggling heroin.

Those with relatives on both sides of the Askari-mellat conflict after the Revolution were fortunate, villagers mused: "The people with relatives on both sides are the ones who are well-off. They will be all right no matter which side wins: who would wish his own brother harm?"

Similar to pre–land reform days, people watched the balance of power between contending factions. As Seyyid Ibn Ali's side began to appear less successful, his supporters began to drift away, some even joining the opposition. Reasons and rationalizations put forth for changing sides were similar to those of earlier struggles in Aliabad. The opposition charged corruption and violence. Some of Seyyid Ibn Ali's own relatives complained about his lack of generosity and began to fear he would not be able to protect them from the opposition.

In discussing people's shift of support from Seyyid Ibn Ali to the riyat faction, Aliabad observers noted decision-making processes similar to those in earlier taifeh-keshi processes:

These days, some people are on one side one day and on the other side the next, as when some people were for the Shah until they saw he was losing, and then they went over to Aqa's [Khomeini's] side. Some people were on Seyyid Ibn Ali's side as long as he was winning. But when they see he's in prison and has been defeated, they go over to the other side. They look after themselves. They look to their own interests and become supporters of the mellat.

It was the same during the time of Mosaddeq. Haj Ibrahim, who's now for Seyyid Ibn Ali, was for Mosaddeq, and so were Haj Qodrat Ranai and many others too. But then when Mosaddeq lost, when there was a coup d'etat, when all of Mosaddeq's supporters were put in prison, people got frightened. (From an interview on November 12, 1979, with Esmat Ajami)

Seyyid Ibn Ali's supporters were his relatives or people he had helped. Some were people who had gotten land from land reform although they weren't actually share-croppers. They were afraid the mellat would take their land.

At first Haj Al Morad was with Seyyid Ibn Ali. He went to court on his behalf. At first he thought Seyyid Ibn Ali would win. He had raft-o-amad and supported him at first, but now he doesn't. He's come over to the side of the people.

Seyyid Ali's son [the one who had been a Seyyid Ibn Ali supporter] and Seyyid Ayyub's youngest son, Hadi, don't involve themselves any more. Hadi now comes and goes freely in the village.

Seyyid Rahman used to get furious when the mellat shouted slogans against Seyyid Ibn Ali. Now he doesn't say so much—he's afraid people will beat him up.

The kadkhoda, Hamid Jehangiri, who had given his daughter in marriage to a son of Ali Reza Amini, was dependent upon the Askaris for his tenure in office, as well as for other economic and political advantages resulting from his political alliance with the Askaris and the Amini brothers. As it was common for political allies and business associates to intermarry, persons were often economically or politically dependent to one degree or another upon in-laws and were hesitant, just as in the case of blood relatives, to jeopardize an important relationship.[5] During the post-Revolution local struggle against Seyyid Ibn Ali, Hamid Jehangiri withdrew his support from the Askari faction and joined the peasant faction only when it seemed sure that the latter would be victorious. Some informants suspected him of maintaining his connection with the Askaris, perhaps telling them that he was just taking part in various gatherings of the peasant faction because he felt pressured into it and not because he actually supported that faction. He could thereby maintain a connection with both sides, protecting his own interests no matter what the final outcome of the conflict.

Means of switching sides had changed little. Men used in-law relations, cross-cutting ties or earlier alliances, or they were introduced by an important opposition leader as new supporters who should be accepted because they had now seen the light. People wishing to join the opposition might participate in a demonstration, go to a gathering or cooperate in a task in order to declare their new alliance. Other means of announcing a change in allegiance, as in earlier confrontations, could be through one's own or a sponsor's verbal announcement or being seen with the oppositional group.

As in pre–land reform taifeh-keshi, the oppositional faction gratefully accepted defectors. Faction members publicly explained the switch using socially and culturally acceptable rationales such as "He now understands what a tyrant Seyyid Ibn Ali is" or "His brother-in-law talked with him and then he saw the light" or "He had always supported the peasants in the past and finally realized that he should now too." In private, at least in some cases, people suspected the defectors of choosing the forecasted winner, straddling the fence or serving as spies.

Taifeh-Keshi Strategies in the Local Uprising

As was usual in taifeh-keshi, both sides considered themselves to be in the right. Seyyid Ibn Ali's relatives defended him. He had bought the land, they pointed out, and it was therefore rightfully his. Imam Khomeini wouldn't like it if he knew what was happening in Aliabad. Private property must be respected, the Islamic authorities had proclaimed. The opposing side was lying in their presentation of the situation to the authorities.

Members of the opposing faction took a different viewpoint. Seyyid Ibn Ali had wrongfully taken the land. He had stolen land belonging to the people. Therefore it must be returned to the people. He was a corrupt and violent person and should be imprisoned, if not executed. In any case, according to Islam, great disparities in wealth should not exist. The mostazafin must receive assistance. Members of each side demonstrated remarkable similarity in their explanations of why the mellat should not have taken over Seyyid Ibn Ali's land and had no right to it (according to the seyyids) or why it was entirely right to have done so (according to the mellat).

Both sides used strategies of psychological warfare. When Seyyid Ibn All persuaded the authorities to allow him out of prison during the post-Revolution local conflict to attempt a reconciliation with the mellat, his relatives had been notified beforehand. As he entered the village accompanied by many vehicles filled with his supporters, his relatives and associates honked their horns victoriously and shouted, and the women ululated, taking great satisfaction in demonstrating Seyyid Ibn Ali's political strength in the form of the connections that had freed him. In chagrin and irritation, other villagers compared the display to the bringing of a bride from another village.

Shows of taifeh strength could occur during demonstrations, marches, gatherings at the home of a person involved in a fight or quarrel (sangar) and religious rituals such as the commemorations of the martyrdom of Imam Husein. The noisy procession of the riyat faction to take over and sow Seyyid Ibn Ali's land, complete with Islamic flags and shouting of slogans, in fall 1979 was just such a show of strength, power and unity. The large gathering of men, including many villagers residing in Shiraz, to clean the several kilometers of irrigation ditch two weeks later was another example of psychological warfare. It wasn't even an important time of the year to clean out the irrigation ditch, one relatively uninvolved villager commented. He compared the activity to the Islamic Republic leadership's frequent calling for marches and demonstrations as a show of strength, a means of keeping levels of commitment and enthusiasm high and a warning to opponents.

When Seyyid Ibn Ali was imprisoned, members of the peasant faction spread the story that he was being beaten in prison and his head had been shaved. This was a lie, the seyyids countered; members of the peasant faction were saying this in hopes of discouraging Seyyid Ibn Ali supporters.

Aliabad Women and the Post-Revolution Uprising

Women became active during this struggle, as they had been in pre–land reform taifeh-keshi. They gathered and disseminated intelligence, did emotional and social relations-maintenance work, showed support through presence and maintained unity and commitment through condemning the other side. Many maintained communication with the opposite side, which eventually helped ease reestablishment of relations.

For example, during the height of the post-Revolution local struggle, the bathhouse was closed during the hours normally reserved for men. The bathhouse operators feared an outbreak of violence between the men of the two factions as they entered the one-room bathhouse to bathe themselves. The bathhouse generally remained open during the women's hours, but it was closed for women's hours during the several days of violence between the two factions, in fear of attacks on the bathhouse, which might result in harm to women inside. There was no concern about a potential clash among the women themselves.

A daughter of Ali Reza's sister had been married to a nephew of Mashd Musa Saedi. She died in fall 1979 when the struggle between Seyyid Ibn Ali and other villagers was escalating. The men's *fateheh-khuni* (gathering for prayers for the dead) in the mosque to mark the 40th day after her death was cancelled. Since all of Ali Reza's and all of Mashd Musa Saedi's relatives would have been present, fighting might have broken out. Women, however, from both the riyat faction and the Askari faction, met to mourn as usual at the home of the deceased.

Although a few women openly displayed their anger and antipathy toward some members of the opposite faction, some even entering swearing matches with a man or woman from the other side, women usually chose to disclaim involvement and continue social interaction as usual.

During the height of the post-Revolution conflict, Ehteram, the granddaughter of Fatimeh, sister of the Askari brothers, and Sakineh, daughter of Seyyid Ayyub—both teachers of the local kindergarten—continued to attend rozeh at the home of Esmat Ajami, whose husband had been a Saedi and who fervently supported the peasant faction. Esmat gave the following reply when I asked her how she behaved with the two young Askari women:

I talk in such a way that I don't come into conflict with them. I don't curse Seyyid Ibn Ali in front of Ehteram and Sakineh, and they don't curse my family in front of me. Mainly we avoid the subject. Or I say, "What do the conflicts, the cutting off of relationships or the peacemaking of men have to do with women? What do women have to do with this situation? I'm not on either side."

Ehteram and Sakineh come to rozehs at my house. They are for Seyyid Ibn Ali, and they know I'm not. We just don't say anything. We just act polite. And then if the two sides make up, we'll be on good terms with each other.

Women might continue interaction with friends and relatives from the opposite side in an attempt to learn about the activities or plans of the contending faction, some people suspected.

The Post-Revolution Uprising and Sangar

In spite of their efforts, support for the Askaris dwindled steadily in late fall 1978 and the following year. The shifting balance of power can be followed through events calling for sangar and was further influenced by sangar as villagers could see for themselves the degree of support retained by the Askaris. They made political decisions under the influence of this perception.

As far as I am aware, sangar occurred four times in Aliabad during my fieldwork from early September 1978 to early December 1979. Just as politically telling as when sangar were held were those occasions that called for sangar but Askaris did not stage them. The stone throwing of December 7, 1978, was the first event calling for sangar, but the Askaris did not hold one. The first and second sangar occurred to support Kurosh after attacks by Mehdi, a policeman and Shah supporter, and his three relatives on Kurosh and then on Kurosh's stepfather-uncle. Mehdi and his relatives did not even attempt to stage a sangar or activate taifeh-keshi, showing how well they realized they didn't have a chance in a fight against the now great majority against the Shah's regime and its local representatives.

A third sangar took place in summer 1979 when the opposition against the Askaris' local rule was gathering steam. This was the small and short-lived sangar—not even a full day long—of the Askari taifeh following the blow against Seyyid Muslem. One could in fact hardly call it a sangar. Although in the face of attack against Seyyid Muslem, the Askaris and their supporters could have been expected to hold a sangar, relatives and supporters made the decision not to gather for defense and planning strategy, but rather to cheerfully make peace.

The longest period of sangar took place during the local uprising against Seyyid Ibn Ali in fall and winter 1979. For several months, relatives and supporters visited Seyyid Ibn Ali's Shiraz home and Seyyid Yaqub's home in Aliabad. At crisis points, the number of people present increased. Ardent supporters visited most regularly and stayed longest, eating meals and even sleeping at Seyyid Ibn Ali's home at night. They were most energetic in protests of loyalty, willingness to assist and denunciation of the other side.

The Post-Revolution Aliabad Sangar and Taifeh-Keshi—
Old and New

In many ways, the sangar held by Seyyid Ibn Ali and his supporters
in fall 1979 and his taifeh-keshi were reminiscent of sangar and taifeh-keshi
before land reform. The reason given by Askari relatives themselves for their
fierce defense of Seyyid Ibn Ali—just because he was a relative—harkened
back to taifeh sentiment, *taasob-e taifeh,* an effective pressure in earlier
struggles. Other villagers' explanations—that relatives' support of Seyyid
Ibn Ali because of their visiting at his home, acceptance of hospitality at his
table and other economic assistance forced them into that stance—recalled
the earlier pressures of raft-o-amad, hospitality accepted and economic dependence. In the words of villagers:

People who have raft-o-amad with political leaders are forced into assisting them when
there is a fight.

Seyyid Ayyub's wife has been eating at their table for years—they've been giving her
wheat and money—and she goes there too. We don't go there.

My friend Akhtar told me,

Seyyid Ibn Ali's wife can't say to me, "You've eaten in our home, you've eaten our fat,
we've given you wheat, so why are you cursing me now?" We haven't gone to their
house, so now we are free to say what we want. Seyyid Ayyub's wife curses them in private, but she can't in public because she's been eating out of their hands. [Even though
Akhtar was married to Seyyid Ali Askari and a cousin of Seyyid Ibn Ali and Seyyid
Yaqub, she and her husband did not support them.]

Seyyid Ibn Ali's supporters were close, dependent associates—relatives
who felt economically dependent on Seyyid Ibn Ali to some extent or
needed his support, or other villagers who felt they needed Seyyid Ibn
Ali's assistance or for whom he had done favors. The sangar was held at
Seyyid Ibn Ali's Shiraz home or, on occasion, at his base in Aliabad, his
brother Seyyid Yaqub's home. Several times the sangar was to physically
protect Seyyid Ibn Ali or other taifeh combatants. November 16, 1979,
taifeh members gathered at Seyyid Yaqub's village home, bringing rifles,
clubs and food supplies and collecting taifeh womenfolk in a courtyard
room, supposedly to protect them against attack by the opposing forces.
When the opposition marched by, the Askaris attacked them, firing down
on the crowd from the roof with stones and rifles.

Taifeh members often slept at Seyyid Ibn Ali's home. He had meals served to all who were present, including those who came just for the day. Seyyid Ibn Ali was recognized as head of the group. Taifeh members were not present to cooperatively plan strategy, but rather to respond to the taifeh head's suggestions and wishes. Members came to indicate support and readiness to assist their head. Women taifeh members were part of the assembly too.

The opposition was organized differently. The group included men opposed to the Askaris and the Pahlavi government from a variety of kinship groups. There was not one recognized leader or head. Rather, a number of men served as organizers, and members were not economically dependent on them. Meetings were not held in only one person's home; the gathering moved from home to home on successive evenings or convened in the village mosque. A great deal of arguing went on during the sessions as members presented different views and defended different strategy plans.

Women did not come for the purpose of showing support. The only women present were relatives of the host who assisted with serving tea. Although women relatives of the peasant taifeh generally agreed with group aims, most of the time they did not attend meetings; it would have been improper to go to an unrelated person's home or to a home where they were not frequent visitors. The lack of women demonstrates that this group was not primarily kinship-based.

The differences in sangar organization, process and aims between the Askari taifeh and the riyat taifeh represented the differences between an older and a newer order. The Askari sangar and taifeh organization, process and aims shared much with pre–land reform taifeh political organization. Their purpose was primarily to protect the person and interests of the taifeh head and his control of Aliabad and its resources. Supporters hoped they would also thereby be protecting their own interests.

The organization, operation and aims of the riyat taifeh, however, were a remarkable mixture of traditional and new elements. As in earlier efforts of coalitions to remove a village kadkhoda and take control of village land, the main purpose of the opposition was to evict Seyyid Ibn Ali from his position of political power, even to ruin him—in this case to imprison him rather than force him to flee to another village—and to take his land. Seyyid Ibn Ali was put in prison, although he later escaped and fled, probably leaving the country. The peasant coalition did take over Seyyid Ibn Ali's land.

In contrast to the results of pre–land reform conflicts, however, a replacement head did not take over the position and the control of land. Rather, all married male members of the riyat faction were to share the land equally. In fall 1979 they planted the land cooperatively, hiring some village agriculturalists to do the work. The produce was to be divided equally among the new owners. The following year, according to mutual decision, the peasant faction was to divide up the land. Also in contrast to the pre–land reform period, contended resources would not provide the living of taifeh members. Peasant faction adherents—actually mainly the sons of former sharecroppers and of traders—worked outside the agricultural sector. They had been pushed out of agriculture because of land reform and insufficient land to support the population explosion, and they had been pulled away by factories and construction outside the village and many new job opportunities in Shiraz. Even all of Seyyid Ibn Ali's land—more than half the village—if divided among all of these young men, would merely provide some wheat for bread or a little extra cash from sale of produce to build a home, or it could be sold to others for this purpose.

In the case of the Askari faction, internal structure, leadership, composition, aims and the process of sangar quite closely paralleled those aspects of earlier taifeh struggles over the position of kadkhoda and control over land. The workings of the peasant taifeh, however, indicated the radical changes that had taken place in the last quarter-century. No one person was in charge. No one held all meetings in his own home, or spent heavily to provide hospitality. Members were economically independent of leaders as they mainly worked outside the village. Independent jobs, lack of great economic interest in the outcome for any one member and lack of economic and political control by any one political leader translated into a more egalitarian interest group.

As time wore on and Seyyid Ibn Ali escaped and his whereabouts were not known, activity at Seyyid Ibn Ali's home declined. Even close relatives and supporters began to lose their obsessive interest in the matter. When I left the field, Seyyid Ibn Ali and his taifeh seemed doomed to defeat.

HAVING MANAGED TO STAY IN IRAN for the entire 18 months of my research grant period, I left in December 1979, several weeks after young revolutionary activists entered the American Embassy in Tehran on November 4 and took American personnel there hostage, beginning a 444-day standoff between the Iranian and American governments. Given the relations of enmity between Iran and the United States after my departure, I was basically cut off from Aliabad friends. Only when I was finally able to return to Aliabad—almost a quarter of a century later—did I learn how the Askari-mellat conflict had proceeded and what had happened to the land seized from Seyyid Ibn Ali Askari in November 1979.

7

Aliabad
Thirty-Four Years Later

MAY 2013. It is now more than 33 years since I left Aliabad in December 1979 after my first research trip there. Because of another four research trips to Aliabad in the 21st century, totaling six and a half months, I have been able to examine the directions of change. Many other sources of information are available as well—the Internet, written and phone communication with friends in Iran and visits with travelers and expatriates from Iran in the United States. From Iranian American friends in California who have visited Tehran recently I hear observations: Conspicuous consumption is getting more extreme among those who can afford it and even those who cannot. The materialist global culture is spreading, even in the Islamic Republic. In spite of government policy, most people like American culture, and Americans. What the Islamic Republic government expects and how people actually behave can be quite different.

Women friends tell me about the colorful scarves and *manto*, or covering tunics, women are required to wear, how tight and short they have gotten, and how elegant women's makeup and hair styles are, and quite visible under their scarves. Iran is the nose job capital of the world.[1] Upperclass Iranians travel to Europe for shopping and vacations. Middle-class tourists flood into the Iranian Persian Gulf island of Kish for shopping and relief from Islamic Republic restrictions on dress and behavior. Both go to Europe, the United States and Canada to visit if they have children and grandchildren or sisters, brothers and other relatives living there. On a trip to Istanbul in August 2012, I was struck with how much Persian I heard spoken; Iranian businesspeople, tourists and political refugees throng to their neighboring country. At an outdoor café in Istanbul, I saw an Iranian family enjoying personal freedoms; the wife was casually resting her leg over her husband's leg, and the teenage daughter was dressed in a spaghetti-strap top, neither wearing a headscarf, of course. During my 2012 visits to Hyderabad, India and Istanbul, Turkey, I learned about the thousands of Iranian young people attending universities in those countries. As the Philippines is relatively affordable, many students go there as well. I have heard of Iranians getting apartments in Tajikistan.

The high unemployment rate, steep inflation, corruption, drastic drop in the value of the Iranian rial and sanctions against Iran have caused financial problems, especially among the less well-off. Industry has waned; both in the United States and in Iran, a friend commented, much of what one buys is from China—with the difference that the imports from China to the United States are better quality and more expensive.[2]

People talk about palpable economic and political discontent. Disillusionment and anger against the Islamic Republic government have increased all the more in recent years, especially since the 2009 presidential election—even without considering those who voted with their feet by leaving Iran. The Iranian diaspora—four million strong or more—is scattered all over the world, mostly in the Middle East, Pakistan, India, the United States, Canada and Europe.

The Islamic Republic has its enthusiastic supporters, and many others who in their hearts may feel critical know it is in their best interests to appear devoted. The class, religious and political divide between the less and more modernized and globalized sectors of the population, apparent in the 1960s and 1970s before the Revolution, has been growing more extreme.[3]

Similar to the way Seyyid Yaqub Askari used gendarmerie repression and the buying-off of some former rebels against the land reform outcome to prevent overt dissent in Aliabad from 1964 to 1979, the Islamic Republic government tries to prevent dissent. Many people cover their dissatisfaction with cynicism and apathy and—young people especially—try to entertain themselves with whatever they can find. Rates of drug addiction have soared.

Many Iranians, especially the young, are not very devoted to Muslim beliefs and practices. The elderly blame the government and say religion is not to be forced. Many people have become more secular—believing that religion and government should be separate, bringing Islamic practices and attitudes into fewer spheres of life or losing interest in Islam. The Islamic Republic has turned more Iranians secular than the Shah ever could have done, I have heard people inside and outside of the country say. Interest in Zoroastrianism and Christianity has grown.

The word I get from Aliabad is not always reassuring. When I returned in 2003, most of my friends were enjoying a much higher standard of living than they had 25 years earlier. Many people had been able to sell some land and build a nice home. Since I had not seen these people since December 1979, some shared their stored-up frustrations with me—and seemed to feel comfortable doing so in the less restrictive atmosphere of Mohammad Khatami's presidency—but I could see for myself their much modernized lifestyles. By December 2012, however, many had already sold their land, the real estate market was less active and the sanctions[4] against Iran from the outside and bad economic planning from the inside had brought about economic pressures and insecurities and a sharp drop in fortunes. Further, many Aliabadis were even more disillusioned with Iranian politics.

Aliabad is now an altogether different place, even more so than at the time of my 2008 visit, I hear. Not many of the Aliabadis I knew are still there. The old ones are dead, and the young have moved away. Anyone who can afford it gets out; people have gone to Shiraz, Tehran, Turkey, Europe, even Malaysia, people have told me. Most of Aliabad is filled with people from rural areas further out. People are having a hard time economically—which is getting worse, especially for those who didn't own land in the first place.

On November 4, 1979, young radicals rushed the American Embassy and took hostages. They held 52 embassy personnel until January 20, 1981. In December 1979, at the end of my 18-month research grant, I reluctantly left Aliabad with my two-and-a-half-year-old daughter for the United States, planning on returning for more research after a short visit with family—which was prevented by the ongoing hostage crisis. Iraq invaded Iran on September 22, 1980, starting a war that lasted eight years. The United States supported President Saddam Hussein and Iraq as a counter against the now anti-US Islamic Republic of Iran. The Iran-Iraq War was a terrible one, reminiscent of World War I, with trenches, bayonets, barbed wire and human wave attacks. Those living in Iranian cities attacked by Iraqi missiles were especially traumatized. Saddam Hussein deployed chemical weapons against Iranians[5] and Iraqi Kurdish settlements—most notably Halabja, close to the Iranian border, on March 16, 1988.[6]

Then, on July 3, 1988, an American navy cruiser in Iranian waters in the Persian Gulf shot down an Iranian passenger airliner, claiming it was accidental, and killed 290 passengers and crew.[7] Relations between the Iranian and American governments deteriorated further.[8] The Iraq-Iran war finally ended on August 20, 1988. The war left half a million people, soldiers and civilians, dead in Iraq and Iran, and many more injured. Many Iranians suffered from depression during the Iraq-Iran War, of course, and rates of depression have continued to be high.

After the war, Iranians continued to encounter crises, altercations and challenging conditions. Political executions and imprisonment rose sharply after the 1979 Revolution.[9] The Islamic Republic government felt entitled to exert control over most aspects of people's lives.

During his presidency (1997–2005), Mohammad Khatami worked for reforms and liberalization, bringing hope to those who wanted a more open and progressive society, but in the face of lack of support from many government clerics, he was not able to accomplish as much as he and his supporters hoped. When Mahmoud Ahmadinejad—much more of a conservative and hardliner—became president in 2005, he brought back more restrictions and has been criticized for not handling the economy well. During the 2009 presidential elections, accusations of election fraud erupted. Many believed that Ahmadinejad's opponent, Mir Hussein Mousavi, had actually won, in spite of the announced victory for Ahmadinejad. Mass protests broke out. "Green Movement" demonstrations supporting Mousavi and more political freedom continued for some months, but the government used enough force to curb them.[10] Many books have been published on the course of events in Iran during the past several decades.[11]

Like Iranians elsewhere, people in Aliabad[12] suffered through all of this. By the end of the eight-year Iran-Iraq War, some 33 young martyrs were buried in the Aliabad cemetery next to the shrine at the right of the highway.

Because of antagonistic relations between the US and Iranian governments, maintaining contact with Aliabad friends, other than exchange of a few letters, proved to be difficult between December 1979 and September 2003. At one point, in 1999, I was able to get a visa, but both of my parents were ill. It was not until September 2003 that I was able to get another visa and go to Iran for two weeks. During my almost 24-year absence, Aliabad had gone through dramatic changes. It had changed from a village into a suburb of Shiraz.[13] Since 2003, I have been able to spend another six and a half months in Iran, mainly in Aliabad and Shiraz.

Driving out from Shiraz to Aliabad in September 2003 brought shocks to my senses. Gone were the walled orchards on the outskirts of

Shiraz. In their place, residential areas had been built. Suburban residential centers had been constructed on the previously bare areas on the way to Aliabad. After the boundary between Qodratabad and Aliabad land, shops and businesses lined the highway, with some breaks. The old village gate, entryway passage and wall all the way around with a turret at each of the four corners were no more. Inside the old village area, many courtyards and homes were in a state of ruin. Not many villagers lived there anymore. A few people rented their old homes to outsiders who had flooded into Aliabad. People had built houses above and below the old village area and on both sides of the highway. Streets were arranged in rows, with people's courtyards and homes behind high walls, as had been the usual urban practice. People had built large courtyards and homes of fired rather than sun-dried brick. On both sides of the highway, many shops and even a gas station had been put up. There were new boys' and girls' primary and high schools, a kindergarten building, a huge *Huseiniyyeh* (religious gathering place) built in memory of a war martyr by his father, a religious seminary and center and health, natural gas and other government buildings. All over I saw large homes and other buildings under construction.

The vineyards that used to surround the village were gone. In the area behind the old village, going up to the hills, stumps of grapevines stuck up awkwardly, cut off in preparation for building homes in that area too. Not much of the original agricultural land remained. Rather, immediately upon coming to the border of Aliabad land, one could see walled-in gardens and huge villas on land sold by villagers to outsiders.

My friend Esmat had sent word after her mother died. I cried when I read the letter, written by her son. But now I heard about other deaths. Seyyid Yaqub Askari had died and so had his wife, cousins and close supporters, Haj Ali Reza Amini and Mashd Yusef Amini, Mohammad's father. Seyyid Yaqub's son Muslem had moved into Shiraz, and none of his other children lived in Aliabad either. The old titular head of the Askari taifeh, Seyyid Ayyub, had passed on, and his wife, Ezzat—so active before—had turned into a very old lady—physically at least; she still had her sharp mind. Forced to live with her children, she missed her old home, work and independence. When I visited Shaikh Rahim's family—he had been politically active along with his family during the Mosaddeq era and then again initially during the revolutionary period, I wept, hating the loss of this historical figure and enlightened person. Haidar Amini—head of the Amini taifeh—was gone too. He had allowed me to interview him only once, but I had been at his home often, and found it hard to take that I would not be able to see him again. Others had of course ceased to mourn and had gotten accustomed to absences, but they were fresh wounds for me. I wished I could go back in time.

Haidar Amini's son Behnam had moved into Shiraz some years earlier. His first child, born while I was in Aliabad the first time and my little daughter's playmate, had earned her MA in English translating and was teaching English. Four more children had been born to him and his wife. Aliabad children had grown up, had children of their own and become grandparents.

Aliabad's population had grown from perhaps 3,000 in 1978–1979 to maybe 7,000 by 2003, villagers estimated. (No accurate statistics are available.) Many people had moved into Shiraz, but many others had come to Aliabad. The construction business was booming, and with its walled orchards, villas and many services, shops and businesses providing employment, Aliabad was considered a place of opportunity by people from rural areas further out and Afghans. Economics, family and kin systems, social relations, religion, politics—all had gone through dramatic transformation.

Land Ownership and Economic Activities

Seyyid Ibn Ali Askari had returned from abroad or come out of hiding and lived in Shiraz again. He and his sons didn't come to Aliabad. The struggle over Aliabad land had continued. Both sides went through periods of having the upper hand, but Seyyid Ibn Ali hadn't been able to attain his goal of getting back the seized land.

For years the land taken over by Aliabadis in November 1979 was held communally. Men were hired to work it, and the crops were distributed. Finally, in 2001, the land seized in 1979 was divided among some 3,000 married village men. Because the original signees had so many sons who had grown to maturation in 25 years—and because some men got more than their share from the 2001 distribution, there was not much land for each—just enough to build a courtyard and home. Many men sold their land to start a little business, buy a car and ferry passengers or buy opium. All of the land going on the market attracted the attention of Shiraz people and caused a real estate boom. Land prices skyrocketed. Aliabad residents who came to own village land through land reform or purchase could become wealthy and build large, elegant urban-style homes, some farther outside the village area in new residential neighbor-hoods. Outsiders bought land for speculation or to build a weekend re-treat, a walled-in area with perhaps an orchard and a house. People who got involved with land sales made a killing. Eventually, 70 or more real estate offices operated in Aliabad. Outside governmental bodies took over areas of Aliabad land out toward the hills to build little cities for govern-ment employees. By 2008, the real estate market was slowing down. But even in 2012, people remarked on the high prices and chic streets of the Garden City residential area on Aliabad land between Aliabad proper and the border with Qodratabad. Most villagers who had owned land had sold all or portions of it. By 2003–2004, villagers estimated, 80% of village land had passed into the hands of outsiders. By 2008, villagers told me, 90% had been bought by outsiders.

Many people in Aliabad were distressed about how much land had passed into the hands of outsiders. People talked a lot about the Garden City area of walled orchards, which used to be wheatland. Most of it has been sold to outsiders who have turned their walled plots of land into recreational retreats. Often people, especially outsiders, build houses and swimming pools in their walled gardens. They come on Fridays and holi-days, sometimes inviting friends and relatives. By now the area next to Qodratabad has become an up-scale residential neighborhood, famous in the region, according to some Aliabadis. When I look at the Garden City area on a Google map, I see it has grown much larger than Aliabad proper. In 2008, Aliabad people who owned a walled orchard there or elsewhere enjoyed cooking food and going on picnics for a relaxing day.

In fall 2012, I talked by phone with a middle-aged man from Aliabad who criticized what people had done with the land next to Qodratabad:

Some Lur guy comes along and buys it. Those gardens are just for having a good time. They don't really produce any fruit, like for export. They just eat it or throw it away. It's really nothing. There is just enough for themselves or maybe not even enough for them. Before it was all wheat. Aliabad agriculture is ruined. Now it is nothing.

Agriculture has become a thing of the past. By 2003–2004, only two or three village men earned their living through agriculture. Villagers have built homes on prime irrigated agricultural land. Those who own dryland now find it of little use to sow wheat on it. Most of it is just left fallow. Young men are no longer available to obediently go out and work on the land when their fathers tell them to, as was the case in 1978–1979.

In the last several years, due to the poor economy, some men have revived interest in cultivation. In fall 2010, about 10 men used tractors to plow their dry land next to the hills, sowed wheat or lentils by hand and planned to use a combine to harvest. They sold their crops; women don't make their own bread anymore. There isn't even a flour mill in the village. People buy their bread from the village bakeries, increased from three to six in recent years.

In November 2012, Seyyid Ibn Ali Askari, at least 90 by then, again made a move to regain some of the land seized by Aliabad people back in 1979, people have told me. He complained to the court in Shiraz that the Aliabad people had taken over his land to plant wheat but instead had used it to make walled recreational gardens for themselves. (To increase grain production, in 1979 the central government was allowing people to cultivate abandoned land; Aliabad people used this argument to support their takeover of Seyyid Ibn Ali's land.) Aliabad people had to go back to court to defend themselves against Seyyid Ibn Ali's charge.

A couple of men continued to raise animals and became well-off, due to the high price of meat. Middle-aged men might continue to work in the newer vineyards and in their orchards, some even coming back from Shiraz to irrigate and prune, if they had moved into the city. They use the fruit in their own families, give some away and sell any extra. Usually sons refused to help their fathers with fruit trees and grapevines, feeling it below their dignity and preferring more entertaining and relaxing activities. In the last few years, though, in the face of the current declining real estate market and scarcity of other money sources, some young men have been working in orchards again, hoping to earn some cash by selling the fruit.

Other employed village men drive taxis or other vehicles for conveying passengers or goods. Others serve as government employees in schools or offices, own or operate small businesses or shops or work at factories or construction sites in Aliabad or Shiraz or in between. A number of government job opportunities exist right in the village—schools, the kindergarten, the health office and a 24-hour clinic. In summer 2008 there were many clothing stores, household supply stores and "supermarkets"—little stores selling groceries and other items. The grocery stores have large glassed-in refrigerated areas for packaged milk, yogurt and other perishables. People say that anything you might need to build a home or business you can buy right in Aliabad. By 2010, some men who had been running shops in Shiraz or were retired from government offices started businesses in Aliabad. Observing Aliabad's exploding population, they thought it provided better business opportunities than Shiraz.

People rent their old houses or rooms in their homes to outsiders. A number of apartment buildings have sprung up. People get money from renting out shops too.

From an agricultural village and base for itinerant traders until the early 1960s, Aliabad has transitioned into a town, a commercial and business center, and from a self-sufficient productive agricultural unit into a population of consumers.

Modern Lifestyle and Urban Identity

The lifestyles of Aliabad people have changed from quite "traditional" to similar to those of middle-class urbanites. Before, most villagers lived in rooms of mudbrick with a mud and straw protective coating, crowded around a dirt courtyard that usually housed farm animals. Fortunate women had access to a water spigot in the courtyard, where they joined neighbors to wash dishes and clothes in cold water. Other women had to carry clothes to the stream to wash and then spread them on stones in the cemetery next to it to dry. Women did not have kitchens but cooked over an *aladin,* or natural gas burner, in the courtyard, a shed or, in winter, the living room to provide warmth. During meals, a plastic tablecloth spread on the floor turned the one room usually available for a family into the dining room, and at night, sleeping mats and blankets brought down from a stack at the side of the room turned it into the bedroom. Although men wore Western clothing outside the house, most women still wore regional dress: wide, loose pants under a long gathered skirt, covered with a long tunic, and a gossamer scarf over the head. Of course all women put on a chador to go outside. Girls older than nine or so did too, except when dressed in their uniforms on the way to and from school. Children wore simple homemade pants and tops.

Now many people live in fine, urban-style nuclear family homes with air conditioning; decorative plaster or mirror work (designs made from small pieces of mirror) on ceilings; a clean, tiled toilet room with wash basin out in the tiled courtyard; a living room, bedrooms and shower room; and a modern kitchen equipped with counters, refrigerator, freezer, sometimes electrical appliances and hot and cold running water for the sink. Women have vacuum cleaners and clothes washers. Before, no one in Aliabad had a phone. Now everyone has a cell phones.

By 2008 only a few old women wore regional dress. Shopping for clothes has become a main preoccupation. Some women buy new outfits for each season. Some people have moved from Shiraz back to Aliabad because, they say, life there isn't much different from urban living in Shiraz.

In earlier years, there was one car in Aliabad, and a few shopkeepers had an old pickup. Now most families own at least one car. Well-off villagers have late-model cars with all the latest gadgets. Teenage boys roam around on motorcycles. Taxi offices operate in Aliabad, and one needs only to make a telephone call for a car to come right to one's door. The high volume of traffic on the highway dividing Aliabad has driven accident casualty rates up. The bus leaves for Shiraz every half hour and is inexpensive. People go to Shiraz often for shopping and other errands. Many people have moved to Shiraz or to the new suburban areas between Aliabad and Shiraz. They may come back often for visits. People travel more. They go on excursions to parks and tourist spots in Fars Province. Pilgrimages to Mashad, with a side trip to other areas such as Isfahan and the Caspian Sea added on, to Mecca and Medina in Saudi Arabia and to Syria and Iraq—during more secure periods—have become popular.

Because of land sales, government loans for different purposes (including marriage), government employment, service jobs and business activities, Aliabad people enjoy a much higher standard of living today. Nevertheless, people are dissatisfied. They have even higher levels of expectation for how they and their children should live. They are worried about the future of their children, given rising unemployment rates recently. Yet pressure to spend money on living a certain lifestyle—such as engagement parties, weddings, homes and furnishings—are growing ever greater. There is never enough money for what is needed to maintain appearances.

Shiraz has been growing outward—almost all the way to Aliabad by 2008. The Shiraz mayor's office has incorporated Aliabad's neighboring village, Qodratabad. It looks as if it may be only a matter of time before Shiraz incorporates Aliabad as well. Aliabad is expanding toward Shiraz too. The upscale Garden City residential area stretches to the edge of Aliabad land.

When in 2012 I asked a friend why young people from Aliabad families I know go into Shiraz for school, she responded,

Because there are so many children from the surrounding regions, so the schools here aren't good any more. Aliabad is a good place, they think, so they move here. There are Turks [Qashqais], Lurs, Afghans, people from Darab, Beyza, Kelistun. Now all of the former vineyard areas have buildings on them. They are even fixing up inside the old village area.

Sometimes during my visits, older people waxed nostalgic about the old days and bemoaned the loss of Aliabad land, the influx of outsiders and the lack of togetherness they previously shared. They talked about the close ties and frequent interaction of the past and said now people don't take time to see each other. They said Aliabad no longer has a separate identity, that it is in the process of becoming just another neighborhood of Shiraz. People sometimes have tried to fight the looming incorporation, such as when the mayor of Shiraz ordered a temporary ban on land sales because of hour-to-hour real estate inflation in 2001. Aliabad people staged a demonstration, arguing that Aliabad was not under his control (and some likely didn't want their land sale profits to be cut off).

The identification of many Aliabad people with Shiraz became symbolized during the 2006 Moharram season of mourning for Imam Husein and his band. On Ashura, Aliabad self-flagellants went into Shiraz to take their turn in the procession of flagellant groups from Shiraz neighborhoods into the courtyard of Shah-e Cheragh shrine. Like flagellant groups from various Shiraz neighborhoods, they performed their self-flagellation while chanting mourning couplets at the shrine. Their performance at Shah-e Cheragh with the other flagellant groups of Shiraz was symbolic of their place among Shirazis. A few women from Aliabad, including me, went into Shiraz to watch the flagellant groups in the large Shah-e Cheragh courtyard. After the Aliabad self-flagellant group exited the courtyard, they were guests for a meal at a Shiraz mosque, like flagellant groups from other Shiraz neighborhoods.

In 2006 I rode in a small service bus with a young woman, originally from Aliabad, whose family had moved into Shiraz, to her university more than two hours outside Shiraz. As we passed Aliabad, I started to point out familiar places. She shushed me. Later she explained she didn't want the other students to know she had rural origins, because it would lower her status with them. She identified herself as Shirazi.[14]

Aliabad people now feel much more connected with Shiraz. Because of improvements in transportation and education, rising standards of living, exposure to outside influences and ideas and interaction with people in Shiraz and elsewhere, the outlooks and lifestyles of Aliabad middle-class people have become similar to those of middle-class urbanites who experienced modernization in earlier decades. Aliabad middle-class residents are becoming citified, less involved with Aliabad and more identified with Shiraz, Iran in general and the larger world. Their jobs, side enterprises, government loans and sale of village land brought villagers the financial resources for a much higher standard of living, enabling them to take on urban lifestyles. The recent economic downturn due to sanctions and worldwide economic problems, though, is cutting back on some Aliabadis' ability to compete in materialism.

In government documents, Aliabad is now considered a town (*shahrak*). It also serves as the administrative center for several surrounding villages. People do not see themselves as living in a village. They don't even use the name *Aliabad* much at all; they use the names of its neighborhoods instead. If they refer to the old village, they say, "the Inner Village."

"An old woman like me," my friend Esmat said, "may sometimes miss the old Aliabad, but the young don't. Who knows what they think? The young people think about new things and the present."

Young People and Gender Dynamics

In 1978–1979, children—especially girls, and in agricultural families, boys too—were expected to be obedient and help their parents. Children did not have store-bought things. Now middle-class Aliabad society has become child centered. Children want the latest in clothes and toys, and parents spend money on them. Children like TV, satellite disks, smuggled videos and DVDs, computer games, rock music, the Internet, brand-name running shoes and tee-shirts with English words or American movie stars printed on them. Parents may designate a bedroom for even a young child, even if she usually sleeps with them. I have seen rooms furnished with shelves and closets; lots of toys, dolls and stuffed animals; and a computer with desk and chair. Before, I remember, children did not have toys, unless fashioned by themselves from sticks and stones and maybe an old bicycle wheel.[15]

These days, middle-class mothers may take even preschool children into Shiraz for English lessons. Teens and even younger girls may supplement their village schooling by going to classes in English, computer, swimming or other subjects in Shiraz, though this may have changed since 2008 because of the bad economy. Many children go into Shiraz for schooling, even starting with preschool. From seeing children as workers helping the family and hoping therefore to have as many as possible, especially boys, families now have few children and focus on getting them advantages, education, jobs and spouses.

Young people expect their parents to provide money for their modern lifestyles. Girls must have new, fashionable clothing, makeup and money for haircuts, hair dying and beauty parlour visits before weddings and other important occasions. Boys must have fashionable clothing; late-model expensive cars, ideally, or at the very least motorcycles; and plenty of pocket money. These days, children are expensive and time-consuming— one more reason to have fewer of them.

Many young men, bored and—with current high rates of unemployment—often discouraged about their future, use opium and other drugs. As elsewhere in Iran, addiction is a great problem in Aliabad, in spite of classes and workshops for addicts. In the past, people said, a few old men smoked opium. They knew how to use it safely, and the quality of the opium was good. Now, however, addiction is widespread, especially among the young, but not limited to them. People don't know how to handle opium, and the quality is poor, people say. When I asked how many men in Aliabad were addicted, people would say, don't ask how many are addicted. Rather, ask how many are not. Death from overdose has become common. Now opium smoking is so common that people don't even talk about addiction to opium. They use the word *addiction* to refer to worse drugs, like heroin.[16]

Many young people, unable to find jobs, or jobs at the level they want, do not work, even when they are no longer in school. Their parents must support them.

Like the strength of political and generational hierarchies, the strength of Aliabad gender hierarchy has declined in the last 34 years. These days, people seem to value girls as much as boys. Little girls are often active and talkative and may tease and disrupt adult activities rather than sitting quietly and motionless in front of adults as was typical earlier. Although girls are still expected to act more responsibly and help at home more than their brothers, they do not work as hard for their mothers as in the past. Many teenage girls speak up freely, offer advice and guidance to adults, openly express their ideas and argue, even outside their own families.

Unmarried males spend most of their time out with their friends. Young women—even those who live in Shiraz—are still expected to spend their time with the family, at least in 2008. Any outside socializing is with female cousins. They may be openly critical of their lot, which was not the case 34 years ago. Life in Aliabad is stultifying, a young, unmarried woman complained. There is nothing for her except to accompany her mother on visits to relatives' homes.

People in Aliabad expect girls to earn at least their high school diploma before marriage. Girls do better at school than boys, and more girls than boys pass the difficult *concur,* the university entrance examination, and continue their education at higher rates, as do girls throughout Iran. They gain admittance to universities in smaller cities in Fars Province, in Shiraz or even in Tehran.

The percentage of females in Iranian universities has reached more than 60%. Recently, however, gender segregation in Iranian higher education has become stricter; females are barred from fields of study considered not proper for them, and the quota system of 50% of spaces each for males and females in other fields will probably cut back on the education advantage women now hold.[17]

Female high school graduates now see preparation for the concur as a main goal. I was in Aliabad in late summer 2004 during announcements about concur results. An Aliabad girl who passed was ecstatic, and one who failed was heartbroken. She cried for days before pulling herself together. With her mother's help she spent the next three months recovering. She vowed she would study and pass the following year, and she did.[18]

Teenage and even younger girls wear lipstick, makeup and nail polish, instead of waiting until their wedding day to wear makeup for the first time, as girls did 34 years ago. When they go outside, instead of a chador, they wear a scarf and a tunic over pants, as colorful, tight and minimal as they can get away with. Girls and younger married women wear sophisticated, revealing Western dresses for weddings—by 2008, often strapless and very short—covered by hejab, of course, on the way to the rented hall or garden wedding party venue. Young people dance enthusiastically in Western style to Western-influenced music.

Girls have more education—often more than the groom—and are older when they marry. The age gap between bride and groom is less, now about two years, rather than five, ten or more. The engaged couples with whom I have spent time in Aliabad in recent years spend time together. They seem to feel more at ease with each other and interact on a more egalitarian basis than engaged couples years ago.[19] (Because of Aliabad's proximity to Shiraz and its land sales, long-time residents of Aliabad are generally quite well-off. For many other more conservative or less well-off

Iranians, such behavior and conspicuous consumption for person, home and wedding would not be the case.)

Instead of sitting motionless and speechless, looking down and abstaining from eating or drinking during the wedding celebration festivities as they did before the Revolution, brides now walk around, eat whatever they want, hold the groom's arm and talk and dance with him. They display no demure, shy, frightened demeanor whatsoever, but behave in an everyday, assertive, confident manner. Generally young couples put off having children, and when they do have children, they keep their families small.[20]

Although Aliabad females have gained relative power, a husband still has legal right of permission over his wife's forays outside the home and over whether or not she will work. Very few married women work outside the home even now. Most fathers and husbands still see female employment as insulting their capability to support their family and as a threat against their authority. Few families among the long-time residents of Aliabad were so poor as to require females to bring in some money, and the idea of females working outside the home would be all the more reprehensible in the culture of the families at low income levels. Part of the reason for this low female employment rate is lack of appropriate opportunities, especially for middle-class females, which is how most young village females see themselves. Working at home, where a woman will not be interacting with strange males, is less of a problem. Aliabadis no longer wear simple homemade clothes, so sewing is less of a possibility, but a few women have opened a small beauty shop at home. A widow who lost her husband at an early age and wanted to keep custody of her children and thus could not remarry, or the very rare case of an abandoned wife, might work, but she would keep her low-status job—such as caring for very young children or house cleaning in Shiraz—a secret. Several young, unmarried women did work in Aliabad shops and in the 24-hour clinic. Several married women found professional positions in government employment in Aliabad or Shiraz. One older unmarried woman worked as a nurse in Shiraz, living with and caring for her elderly parents. Among several better-off families who had moved to Shiraz, female education, even postgraduate, and professional work are gaining acceptance. However, it remains to be seen what will happen with marriage and children, or if single or at least childless life will be necessary for a sustained career.

Decline of Extended Family and Kinship Bonds

Seniors and extended family members have far less authority over juniors[21] than before land reform. Back then, more fathers controlled access to their sons' livelihood—either farming or trading. Extended-family seniors met to make decisions and plan young people's lives. Fathers controlled funds, resources and initiative to obtain wives for their sons. Parents chose their children's marriage partners rather than allowing their children to choose on the basis of their own attractions. When a family got a bride for a son, they brought her to live in the family compound, in a room in the courtyard set aside for the bridal couple. There she worked under the supervision of her mother-in-law. Brides spent time with the other women in the household while the men were off working. Usually one or more of a father's brothers and their families and their sons' wives and children lived in the same courtyard. Fathers expected young men to obey them without question and to follow their directions for work. A young man listened to his parents and was expected to minimize his emotional attachment and daytime contact with his wife. Husband and wife did not show attention to each other in front of the older generation, in order to demonstrate respect for them. Married couples barely spoke to each other in public. At weddings and funeral gatherings, males and females sat in separate rooms or houses. To communicate with each other, husbands and wives sent messages through their children.

These days, young people get an education, a high school degree—at least for females—whereas their parents may be barely literate or have only a few years of schooling. Men who do find jobs earn money and are away from fathers' influence. Young men often work in office jobs, government positions or electronics shops, which are not in their fathers' experience. Younger men and women have education, experiences, exposure to new ideas and access to means of communication different from those of their parents and in-laws. Young people live in an almost different world from their seniors.

Young people do not face as much economic, financial or social pressure to acquiesce to the demands of the older generation. For example, one young villager broke his engagement, deciding on his own to marry someone else. His parents were completely against this. He went ahead with this marriage. His parents and most of his extended family did not speak to him for several years. With a well-paying white collar job in the city, he managed fine without the support of his relatives. Eventually his relatives began to interact with him and his new family.

In 2003 and 2004, several middle-aged people made comments to me such as:

Back then our fathers told us what work to do on a certain day. No way could we disagree. We just went and did it. Now young men might say, "No, I can't do that today." Now our children tell *us* what to do. Back then it was rule of the fathers. Now it is rule of the progeny.

Marriage and family dynamics are influenced by greater gender parity and serve as arenas in which females negotiate for more power. Girls now may refuse young men their parents choose for them. They may say they do not wish to marry, that they want to study. Often young people make their own marriage decisions, although their parents then do the negotiating and arranging. Age of marriage is rising for Aliabad girls as elsewhere in Iran. Girls and their families may refuse to go ahead with the wedding until a separate home is ready and furnished.

These days, the goal is a companionate marriage. Now young people get to know each other before marriage. In order to maintain propriety while being alone with each other, couples go through the marriage contract ceremony privately with their families. Engaged couples go together to relatives' homes. They go into Shiraz. They visit in each other's homes and may even stay overnight for a week or more. They travel together, taking with them the certificate of their marriage contract ceremony to show any morality police who might stop them. As engaged couples spend time with each other, begin to treat each other with affection and have plenty of opportunity to talk, some of their relationship development process occurs before the wedding. Couples negotiate about lifestyle, behavior and decisions even before the wedding, ideally leading to a more intimate marital relationship.

As couples spend time with each other and have opportunity to be alone with each other, initiation into sexual activity is more gradual than in earlier years and is expected to be accompanied by emotional closeness. Aliabad young couples are engaged and have the marriage contract ceremony but not necessarily the wedding celebration party before becoming sexually intimate, or at least they did in 2008.[22] Young couples no longer experience the emotional distancing that results from a possibly traumatic wedding-night sexual initiation, as often happened decades ago.

Several young, unmarried girls whose families live in Shiraz don't like going to the village. One said *she* would not spend one minute living in a mother-in-law's home. She contrasted herself to Aliabad girls who, she said, are trained and willing to tolerate their mother-in-law's authority. This actually was not true. Aliabad brides run their own homes and kitchens and do not want their mother-in-law to tell them what to do. Several older women have made comments to me such as, "Back when we were brides, it was the rule of the mother-in-law. Now that we are mothers-in-law, it is the rule of the brides."

Most often, young couples live in their own nuclear family home.[23] They stay at home together or go places with each other more rather than with same-sex relatives and friends.[24] Now when young people marry, even their *hejleh*, their bridal bower,[25] is in their new, separate, urban-style home, or perhaps in a separate apartment in the same building as the groom's parents—or even the bride's parents.

This emphasis on the marital relationship and nuclear family cuts into generational hierarchy and extended family bonds and authority. As a newly married couple moves to their own home, the groom's parents lose influence over the couple's lives. Married couples devote time, attention and resources to each other and their own children and home rather than to the husband's parents.

However, sons and daughters rely on parental assistance to help provide engagement and wedding expenses, the new home, car and home furnishings to start their marriage. Parents feel duty-bound to find appropriate spouses for their children. A mother is required to provide all the necessities for her daughter's first child, now practically until the grandchild reaches adulthood. Parents are subject to social pressure, and concern for their own reputations, to spend heavily for their children, although this means they use up their own resources. Yet grown children apparently do not feel much social pressure to provide for their parents when they are old.[26]

Thirty-four years ago, not one Aliabad widow lived by herself. Now some 50% of widows live alone in their own homes, like older widows elsewhere in Iran.[27] Some Aliabad widows stay with children part of the time. Sometimes married children who live in Shiraz come and spend their Friday off with their parents in Aliabad.[28]

Younger people take on changing lifestyles more readily than older people. Children, especially Shiraz residents, want pizza and sandwiches and not dishes their grandmothers cook. Often children and young people find it boring to spend time with their Aliabad grandparents.

The generational difference in lifestyle is one more reason for older people's declining authority. Middle-aged and younger people now do not give grandparents the attention and deference they expect on the basis of their own experiences with grandparents when they were youngsters. Grandparents may remark that the children ignore them, are noisy and talkative or busy with their cell phones. When grandparents enter the room, children now do not stand and give them their silent, undivided attention.[29]

Grandparents most often live in their own separate homes, their children do as they want without consulting them[30] and they are no longer integrated into their children's lives. As their adult children and, even more so their grandchildren, live in a different world from the one the grandparents grew up in, old people and young people may not have much to say to each other. Much less are grandparents in a position to give sound advice about the present world.

Instead of ordering the world of their family and kin, older parents are left on the sidelines. They hope for visits from their children. In contrast to the earlier strict generational hierarchy and extended kin authority, Aliabadis now focus on the marital relationship and individual and nuclear family autonomy and interests.[31]

Taifeh-Keshi in the 21st Century?

The political struggle between the Askari seyyid relatives and the peasant faction over the land seized from Seyyid Ibn Ali in November 1979 continued through the next decades. Both sides got people together to lobby various Shiraz officials, clergy and government bodies. Both sides even traveled to Tehran to defend their positions. The conflict got so bad that a number of more vociferous Seyyid Ibn Ali defenders felt forced to move into Shiraz.

When I returned in 2003 and 2004, Seyyid Ibn Ali was still attempting to regain the seized land, supported by his Aliabad relatives, the Askari seyyids. The other villagers stood firm in their demands to hold on to this land.

By 2003, other than supporting Seyyid Ibn Ali Askari in his attempt to regain the land, and their condemnation of the peasant faction holding on to this land, the Askari taifeh did not have much to do with village political affairs. They had lost their political power over Aliabad. Seyyid Yaqub Askari had died some years earlier. Other close colleagues who had worked with him in managing village affairs in 1978–1979 had died or moved into Shiraz. A few of them lived quietly in Aliabad.

By 2008, five years later, even Seyyid Ibn Ali's relatives had dropped out of his fight over Aliabad land. He didn't do anything for them, they had decided, not even inviting them to his grandchildren's weddings. Several more relatives who had fled to Shiraz during the conflict over the land seized in fall 1979 moved back to Aliabad or to newer residential areas on Aliabad land.

In 1999, the central government had instituted councils as local administrative bodies. In the council elections, Aliabad residents voted in representatives who had been active in the people's uprising against Seyyid Ibn Ali after the Revolution. However, the council had limited power and held little authority over villagers' lives. Local councils were supposedly responsible for settling conflicts—which the kadkhodas and taifeh-keshi process had handled with more or less force and violence before land reform—and for making improvements in village life. According to my informants, though, the council's influence was restricted to some administrational, bureaucratic and service issues; they did not perform such tasks as mediating in family or neighborhood conflicts. Members collected money to asphalt streets and alleyways, put up street lights and lay out streets and gas and water lines for developing sections of Aliabad.

Much as people had blamed kadkhodas in pre–land reform days and government representatives and village bosses in the post–land reform period, in 2003, 2004 and 2005–2006, people complained about council members. They promise things before they are elected, people charged, but then they don't do anything. They collect so much money to pave alleyways and build streets, but then things go very slowly. They don't provide any financial records. Whoever becomes a member of the village council, people pointed out, builds a large, elegant home. They give precedence to their own family and relatives and to people they like. They even take their families for trips to Europe. They are worse than the old landlord![32]

In summer 2008, a friend shared his views of the village council:

Now there isn't a kadkhoda; instead there is a *shora* [local council]. Because of conditions, people with character, with education, don't come forward. They don't want their reputations to be ruined. So the field is open for people who don't have any ability, education or character. They don't know how to do anything.

Taifeh-keshi is not practiced these days to handle concerns of Aliabad residents. Although the taifeh-keshi system surged up again when the central government and gendarmes lost control during the revolutionary chaos, with the reemergence of central government control and the destruction of the taifeh-keshi economic base, taifeh-keshi force and process are no longer in effect. Many aspects of taifeh-keshi culture are losing salience.

When land was distributed during land reform and in 2001 or sold to villagers as private property, and when villagers sold these plots of land or used them to build homes, the agricultural economic base of the village—and of the taifeh-keshi political system—was destroyed. With the rapidly inflating prices of land in the Aliabad real estate market, people could sell their land profitably and build a home or business, making them even more independent from any village or family authority.

In 2008, instead of relying on relationships with blood relatives, in-laws and taifeh members, people formed connections with others who shared common interests. An example was the association formed to improve living conditions in the area of Aliabad land bordering on Qodratabad where people were building walled garden areas in rows along new streets connected to the highway, called Garden City. In August 2008, Haidar Amini's son Hushang told me about the new organization:

We have formed an association and have 45 representatives, from Aliabad and other places too, for about 1,000 persons. We counted 13 streets, and each has 110 plots of 2,000 square meters, so that makes at least 1,000 men. I am the president. We want to get piped natural gas, pesticides and tractors, electricity, health facilities—all of the amenities. We want to make it like a town.

There is not much of a culture of cooperation, though. In the village, people have the concept of helping others in the household, but to cooperate with a large group is something new for them. But on each street there are three or four men who are active and want to meet.

Now most of the gardens have light at night. But some don't have electricity; they aren't any good at night. So we want access to electricity. During the meeting on Friday, we collected 70 million to put in the bank. We need one or two billion toman to get electricity. We have to give 120,000 at first for permission, and the rest is for wiring and so on. The money goes to the government Office of Electricity. The government doesn't do this for us; they say a new region has to pay in order to get on the electrical grid—as if the government doesn't have money, doesn't export natural gas and oil.

It all depends on people organizing. There is inflation; every day things get more expensive. The sooner people pay up, the sooner we can get the electricity.

Some of us from Aliabad think if we get an electrical grid put in, we ourselves should be in charge of it. Then, if others want it, they will need to get it from us, or we won't connect them. If we pay for it and then others come and get it free, that isn't good. Many men from Aliabad think, "Let's not give money. Let others pay the money, and then we will come and use the connection for free."

The way it is now, even if we pay to get connected to the electrical grid, the Office of Electricity can sell connections to the other people here. So we sent a letter to the Office of Electricity to try to change that. We have to form a cooperative for electricity.

When we asphalted the streets, one Aliabad man didn't pay his share. We ourselves paid for it, but he didn't give any money. Before, the streets were dirty and dusty—sand and stones all over. Now it is easy to come and go. Everyone should help.

In this newly formed association, some men from Aliabad were members, including some of Hushang's relatives through his mother, daughter of Seyyid Ayyub Askari. He specifically mentioned two of Seyyid Yaqub's sons, whom previously he saw very little, as outstanding participants. But only people who owned gardens in this area were included, whether originally from Aliabad or from elsewhere. Membership was not kinship-based, although it seems that some of the Aliabad people worked together especially well.

By no means is Aliabad now a unit of power and hierarchical authority as during the landlord period. No one center of power is able to manage Aliabad residents' lives. Residents of Aliabad largely manage their own lives. Rather than the hierarchical and dependency relationships characteristic of the taifeh-keshi political system, relationships have become more egalitarian.[33]

Before the 1979 Revolution, although authority structures were becoming less compelling, individuals at lower levels still camouflaged their own wishes and personalities to an extent behind a persona acceptable to those in positions of authority. Now, though, children, females, young people and adults all feel less pressure to present an attentive, respectful, obedient demeanor to superiors.

"Taifeh Culture Is leaving, and City Culture Is Taking Over"

In summer 2008, when I asked people about taifeh, if there was any more taifeh-keshi in Aliabad, person after person responded that now conflicts are *within* families rather than among the kinship-based taifeh. They talked about a decline in people's emotional attachments and feelings of partisanship for their taifeh. They said now brothers fight with each other over land, so with whom could they form a taifeh? And since most of the land has been sold, over what would people do taifeh-keshi?

During my visit to Iran in summer 2008, I was able to get Hushang Amini—a can-do person busy with his government employment, family with four children, courtyard in Aliabad, walled orchard and house in the new Garden City and community activism in the Garden City community—to spare some time to talk with me about taifeh. Not surprisingly, as a person from a large, successful taifeh, Hushang regretted the loss of positive aspects of taifeh culture and organization. Highly intelligent and perceptive, Hushang tended to think critically about conditions in Aliabad and the country and was less hesitant than others to share his thoughts, even in the more cautious atmosphere of 2008:

The taifeh has been abandoned. Before, incomes were very low. Agriculture was important to people, so people were forced to help each other, and the taifeh took shape. If you wanted to plant a large piece of land, you couldn't do it by yourself. You got help from brothers, father's brothers, sons of father's brothers to do this, so the taifeh became strong. If others wanted to come and get this land, you had to fight with them. Back then, people who put their hearts and hands into it made progress.

Now only a few people are in agriculture. So people depend on themselves; they think only about themselves and their families. Now relatives don't get together, they don't support each other. If only they would join in and clean out the water channel together, the orchards would do very well. Now there are only a few people my age whose hearts mourn for agriculture.

When we were young, we had to work. I went to do harvesting [with a handheld sickle] from the time I was three or four years old, in the heat of summer. I know the value of land, but the young people don't know its value because they haven't worked it. They haven't put any effort into it.

Now, in every family, the young go after cars, satellite dishes, houses—and the only way to get them is to sell land.

My heart burns when I wonder why things have become like this. I feel bad, not for myself but for the country. I send the children to study, but what do those who study get? The young people who don't study will buy and sell land and get rich. My children tell me, "Why do you go to the Office [of Education]? Come and sell land."

But I think about what I can do that is good for my country, for my society. Buying and selling land so that the price goes up because of speculation does nothing. I am glad the government put a ban on buying and selling land four months ago. I hope land will become worthless like it was before.

MARY: Why do you think the young generation is like this?

HUSHANG: It's the responsibility of the government. Everything comes without much effort—communications, the Internet, satellite dishes, luxuries. But this is not the way to work for the progress of the country. This is misfortune.

The government made loan programs because they didn't have a plan to make jobs so that people will be productive. All of the factories have gone. The motor factory has left; they made farm equipment. The cable factory is leaving; it employed 2,000 people.

It is all consumption and no productivity. There is nothing that produces very much. The traditional system of production was agriculture, and now it is not there.

The new conditions, urban living and city culture mean everyone has to go after his own interests. Now some are government employees, and many go after buying and selling. There are so many real estate offices, 100 at least. Each person puts his own income in his pocket. No one depends on anyone else for his living, so the taifeh is vanishing. Taifeh culture is leaving and city culture is taking over. Now there are so many opportunities for entertainment, so many toys for play. There are so many computers for playing games; they are in every house. It is so changed.

Living is so different. You saw it yourself 30 years ago: ten families living together in one courtyard. Now even two men [and their families] don't live together in one house. My children are unhappy that they don't have a room each.

There isn't any vision, any idealism. If there is, people make fun of it. They say, "What? Think about your own life."

We are losing our culture. The city culture is destroying the old culture and putting in its place a culture of consumption and luxury. You have seen it yourself. Before, there was productivity in Aliabad, before the Revolution. But not now. If you had gone to the area of Sepidan—they raised lentils, onions; the chickpeas were famous. The whole area between Shiraz and Sepidan produced so much. Now it has all become one big area of [walled] gardens, like a city park. People go to the gardens and engage in corruption. They are not going there to pray; they drink, take drugs, engage in illicit activities. There are so many addicts.

Those real estate agents—it is really a dirty job.[34] If I buy something from you cheap and sell it to someone else, what value is there in that? A person has to have peace of conscience.

Many persons sold their land for almost nothing, bought a car, the car got wrecked, and now where is their land? Ten years from now, the people will be poor and unfortunate because the one thing they had they have sold, and it is gone.

Most of this is also happening to the majority of villages in the whole country. It's criminal. The government should wake up. Or they should leave.

By 2008, taifeh and taifeh-keshi were out of the picture, many people in Aliabad felt. Later I thought I would ask some young people about taifeh, to see if they even knew what it means. When I asked two of them about taifeh and taifeh-keshi by phone in 2012, they did not seem familiar with the terms. According to the 14- and 16-year-old I asked, as well as other adults, people don't even say the word *taifeh* anymore. They don't talk about the taifeh of Seyyid Ibn Ali or the people's or peasant taifeh or the taifeh of so and so. To talk about relatives, they use the word *famil* (family, relatives).

After her grandmother and I had explained to my young Aliabad friend Yasamin the meaning of taifeh and taifeh-keshi, she told me (with some prompting from her grandmother),

Now people take care of their own problems. They don't do taifeh-keshi. The culture has changed now; it is much better. People don't fight any more. Now you can hardly see taifeh any more. In Shiraz there isn't taifeh-keshi anymore. It was a long, long time ago. Maybe in other places in Iran there are taifeh,[35] but now there aren't in Shiraz. Now it is city living. Now there are such difficult problems that people don't have the time or energy to do taifeh.

It's not like before, when people had taifeh. Now there are jobs. People don't have time. Now people are busy with the family, with education, going to school, money, the children, a lot of unemployment, the economy is a problem, sometimes people in a family have problems with each other—there are so many problems. People try to solve their problems, and they don't have time for taifeh-keshi.

If we can take these responses as an indication, taifeh and taifeh-keshi seem to be exiting from Aliabad culture and collective memory. Aliabad people now think of themselves rather than of the common interests of a taifeh, is the feeling among those with whom I have spoken.

Taifeh culture is disappearing, along with many other aspects of Aliabad culture—men's and even women's regional dress, regional circle "handkerchief" dancing and the music that went with it, male stick dancing at weddings, regional culinary specialties. Since weddings are now held at rented gardens or urban halls and the food is catered, women no longer gather at a home a couple of weeks or more before a wedding to help out cleaning rice and yellow split peas; they no longer sing the regional wedding ditties together, and girls don't learn them. The old people whose only language was the regional vernacular, a Luri dialect,[36] have died. Older people who do know it are embarrassed to speak it, and the young people don't know it. Well on their way out too are the formal, deferential phrases, postures and behavior that people in lower positions—females, children, political and economic inferiors—had to use with higher-status persons.[37] As Hushang Amini pointed out, urban culture is taking over—and really, global culture, sometimes modified for the Iranian setting.

As I read over this section, I feel called upon to make a few personal comments. I am sorry too about so much of Aliabad land now being in the hands of strangers, and like older Aliabadis, I feel nostalgic for the Aliabad of 1978–1979 and perhaps idealize it a bit. But the complaints I heard from so many people about how people don't take time to see each other now, I myself have not seen it. When I am in Aliabad and Shiraz, I have a wonderful time—there are gatherings; lunches, dinners and picnics in walled gardens; weddings; engagement parties; rituals at shrines and in houses; visits to homes; outings to Shiraz parks, old mansions and monuments; and morning and evening prayers at a nearby shrine. Even mourning ceremonies in the mosque and the Huseiniyyeh are occasions to see friends and enjoy treats. I see neighbors visiting each other, sisters dropping in on each other, parents and grandparents spending time with the young and trying their best to help them enjoy life and prepare for a good future. I see loving, affectionate, supportive relationships between husbands and wives, in families and among relatives.[38]

Many people in Aliabad seemed to be of two minds when they thought about the present versus the past. Most people I heard bemoaning the loss of Aliabad land to outsiders enjoyed a much higher standard of living, usually in large part due to their own sale of land to outsiders. They decried the disappearance of agriculture, but they themselves were not cultivating grain on their land. The people who pointed to so much less interaction with relatives were themselves very busy with their own interests and nuclear families. They benefit from their new freedoms: Which adult son would want to be under his father's orders again? Which daughter-in-law would like to have her life supervised by her mother-in-law? And in actuality, Aliabad in 1978–1979 and before land reform was a fractious and divided community. I can remember people, especially women, complaining about how everyone knew everyone else's business, and how they would like to move to Shiraz to get away from all this. When I asked people what they like and don't like about present conditions, even the elderly who missed the past—when their children were around them—talked about the nice modern conveniences.[39]

From Kinship-Based Taifeh to Individual and Nuclear Family Interests

Because the village as a unit does not control resources, people do not feel encouraged to maintain extended kinship ties to help protect their interests. In a transformation that has also been happening in many other places around the world, extended kinship networks have been allowed to lapse, and the individual and the nuclear family are becoming supreme. A man can go for a year or more, people say, without getting together with his brother. People go into their nuclear family homes and shut the door behind them, people say. People talk about how no one takes the time to socialize with relatives anymore, how people aren't close and kind to each other anymore.

Now Aliabad is no longer a village of people all related to each other and unified in their use of the surrounding land. People of the old Aliabad live among the many strangers who have come into their midst. Even the visual boundary between Aliabad and the outside world—the high village walls—are no longer. People no longer unite with their taifeh to fight over resources and power in Aliabad to hopefully benefit the group. Rather, people want to use the money, land and orchards of Aliabad to attain higher positions for themselves and their nuclear families in the wider world.

Because land became individually owned and valuable, people who earlier would have been each other's strongest allies are cast against each other as enemies. Now that there is valuable land to inherit, almost all families argue over the inheritance when a father dies, people told me. I learned about quite a number of cases of brothers and sisters wrangling over the inheritance, even taking the case to the Shiraz courts. One brother may be appointed executor and may take more than his share of the land, or the others assume he has. Sisters are no longer willing to allow their brothers to keep the half shares of their fathers' property allowed to daughters by law. A husband might pressure his wife to go after her half share. Earlier, the excuse for not letting females inherit land was that women can't do agricultural work. Now that land has monetary value and can be sold, sisters don't have to farm it to get any use out of it. But often brothers do not want to give up the half shares due to their sisters. Or under threat of a sister going to court—which some do—brothers give her land, but perhaps not—in the sister's or her husband's view—her rightful share. One brother may have died before the father, and then the other brothers say his children don't have the right to inherit when their grandfather dies. But the orphans might take the case to court or at least ask for their share. If they do not get it, they might not stay on good terms with their father's relatives. One brother may have depended on farming land in Aliabad while the others were working elsewhere, but then, when their father dies, those who have worked elsewhere may still want the equal share of the property stipulated by law when a father dies without a will. Mothers might get involved, taking the side of one of their children and becoming alienated from the others.

In many families, people broke off relations with each other over land, I learned during research trips between 2003 and 2008. These days, land pushes relatives apart rather than pulling them together in cooperation.

Over the last half-century, modernization of the infrastructure—piped gas and water, electricity, radio and television, schools, health services and regular transportation facilities—have brought Aliabad closer to Shiraz in both ease of travel and way of life. The economic shift from sharecropping to jobs and outside cultural influences have allowed villagers to move away from local political control by others.[40] Without the need to struggle for access to agricultural land, and encouraged by materialism, a wealth of consumer goods imported from China and examples of modern, up-scale living all around, from Aliabad neighbors to Tehrangeles (the large Iranian-American population in Los Angeles) and worldwide TV, Aliabadis are using their time, labor and resources for themselves and their own nuclear families. Individuals and nuclear families are salient social, political and economic units, instead of the kin-based factions and extended families so significant before land reform. Tending to taifeh relations and taifeh-keshi are things of the past.[41]

Hierarchies in all arenas of life have weakened. Those previously lower in status don't engage in rituals of deference and displays of obedience as before. Offspring to father, daughter-in-law to mother-in-law, wife to husband, sister to brother, and even in religion, people who formerly would have been underlings are far less willing to acquiesce. Some former hierarchical relationships don't even exist anymore, such as peasants versus landlord and sharecroppers versus kadkhoda. Even the taifeh head versus taifeh member power relationship is gone. Hierarchies of control have faded, allowing individuals to pursue their self-interests[42] and interact with others on a more egalitarian and openly negotiable basis.[43]

One can appreciate the positive aspects of all of this change, but Aliabad people also bemoan the loss of frequent interaction among relatives—even living together in one courtyard, the sense of community and taifeh members' cooperation and helpfulness toward each other—which they needed previously to make the most of opportunities and resources at the time. Some parents complain about how young people these days don't listen; they just want to eat and sleep. The older generation, both males and females, talk about how hard they used to work. They take pride in that ability. They look down on the young because the young want to take it easy and enjoy themselves. The young want everything, the parents say, but they don't make any efforts themselves. Fathers feel under great pressure to try to provide for their families at the levels expected and to support even young adult offspring, especially in the face of their demands and comments about how their friends have various items—cars, motorcycles, nose jobs—and why can't they?

Aliabadis know their children will have to make it on their own, using their own skills, work, status and cleverness. In spite of some parents' complaints, I saw many parents and children in cordial, cooperative interaction with their children. It would be going against their culture to talk to others about their children's achievements or outstanding characteristics, although it is probably the main aim of most parents to help their offspring toward a good future. Members of nuclear families keep their time, labor and resources for themselves, to keep up appearances, raise their children and try to provide them with what they will need to be successful in this new world.

Middle-class Aliabad villagers have gone through a cognitive shift. They have moved away from taifeh-keshi culture based on hierarchy, kinship and local political power toward the global world of individualism, nuclear family supremacy, child-centeredness, modern lifestyle, investment and financial cleverness and climbing the ladder of material success. Aliabadis have become more urbanized, secularized and worldly, with closer connections with Shiraz, the provincial capital. The central government's religiously and politically conservative attitudes and isolationist policies have not prevented Aliabadis from experiencing modernization and globalization.

Evolution of Political Attitudes
Since the 1979 Revolution

Early international trade led to socioeconomic differentiation within the village, as well as fluctuations in economic standing and political insecurity, competition and conflict. Before the 1962 land reform, government and landlord policy encouraged taifeh factionalism. Villagers were able, in effect, to choose their own kadkhodas through taifeh-keshi process. This policy, although it encouraged expenditures, insecurity and conflict,[44] did have the result of placing a ceiling, high though it might be, on tyranny,[45] corruption and partiality, and it encouraged kadkhodas, to some extent, to protect and redistribute. After political centralization and gendarmerie control of Aliabad, local representatives of the Shah's government experienced no such ceilings or encouragement. Because of local administrators' unjust behavior and gendarmes' brutality, villagers' resentment continued to build.

With the exit of the large Qavam landlords and sharecropping from Aliabad and the plethora of new economic opportunities outside the village's economic and political structure in the 1960s and 1970s, Aliabad villagers were able to emerge from feudal-like economic and political relationships. Because the gendarmes backed Askari village bosses, Aliabad men still could not revolt against these local authorities. They now blamed the Shah's central government for their problems anyway. Aliabadis found political space in Shiraz. They aimed their resentment and political activism against the national government during the 1978 and 1979 revolutionary movement.

During the Pahlavi regime, the central government made great strides in modernizing education; health care; the military, police and secret service; the oil industry; governmental bureaucracies; infrastructure; clothing and urban upper- and middle-class lifestyles. However, political modernization was not on the agenda. In spite of Aliabad villagers' participation in national politics during the 1978–1979 Revolution, the majority had only their local taifeh-keshi political culture to guide them. Lacking experience with other types of political cultures or systems, most Aliabad villagers applied their taifeh-keshi processual paradigm to their understanding, decision making and activities in the 1978–1979 revolutionary movement and in the post-Revolution uprising against the Askaris. Only after deciding to join the revolutionary forces, on the basis of taifeh-keshi analysis—and then later the local uprising did most villagers begin to use the rhetoric and symbolism of modified revolutionary Shia Islam. People holding a variety of political philosophies joined together under the revolutionary Shia umbrella, as the only political framework available, to get rid of the dictatorial Shah and his American backing.

In Aliabad, in spite of many economic changes, development, and involvement of villagers in national politics, Aliabadis' political culture—the taifeh-keshi ethos and processual paradigm—and actions had not significantly evolved. Traditional political culture, with its allowance for the stances of acquiescence and shifting sides (depending on the forecast outcome of the struggle) and revolt (for the purpose of getting a more benevolent ruler rather than profoundly altering the system), retained influence.

Unlike the majority of Aliabadis, who supported the revolutionary movement, a small group of people—educators and a few others who had supported Prime Minister Mosaddeq and the Tudeh party in the 1950s—seemed to question the political system, distribution of authority and existing political relationships. The very different organization of the people's faction against Seyyid Ibn Ali Askari after the Revolution may have been partially the result of their different attitude toward political authority—its different political culture—as well as the very different economic and power relationships among these men compared with the earlier political organization of kadkhodas and their taifeh. The leadership of this small group in the Aliabad peasant taifeh, dominant nine months after the Revolution, did not last long. By Moharram of December 1979, Shaikh Rahim Kazemi and his associates were no longer involved with the people's faction. Fazlollah Rezai and his family and other traders took over leadership roles. Given the course of events in Iran after December 1979, Shaikh Rahim's and his friends' efforts to change the distribution of authority did not have lasting success.

Since the establishment of the Islamic Republic, along with other social changes and transformations, many people in Aliabad and elsewhere have learned more about alternative political perspectives and systems. In some ways, Islamic Republic officials have displayed some interest in the views and welfare of the population. Their rhetoric has raised expectations of some degree of participatory government. They have held elections. Although the Council of Experts vets candidates and prevents large numbers of people from running for president and the Parliament, elections—before the 2009 presidential election—have seemed relatively free of corruption. Further, rates of literacy and education have increased tremendously since the 1979 Iranian Revolution. Foreign travel has become common, and the media bring Iranians day-to-day news from abroad—even in Persian, such as the BBC Persian language service and, most important, the Iranian-American TV stations in Los Angeles and elsewhere by means of satellite dishes. (Although satellite dishes are illegal, people manage to get away with having them.) Communication by telephone and visits home of the many people living outside Iran have also allowed

Iranians to learn about other countries and other political systems. From what I have seen in Aliabad and learned about elsewhere in Iran, with the greater freedom from relationships of required deference and obedience and with exposure to more egalitarian social, economic and political systems, Iranians have been working toward more egalitarian and negotiable relationships in all spheres of life.[46] Culture is changing for all types of relationships, from the bottom up. At the grassroots level, people have been refusing to go along with formerly salient systems of authority and hierarchy and have been pushing for their voices to be heard. This is so for political culture as well as for family, gender, community and extended family culture.

By my last trip in summer 2008, it seemed, the individuation and decline in dependency relationships and in strength of hierarchies in all areas of life apparent to me in Aliabad—and in Iranian society in general—might be paving the way for opening up the political system. Along with other Iranians, Aliabadis have gained more acquaintance with national politics, events and dynamics outside Iran, decision making about voting, critiquing the national government in light of its claims, and what goes on in politics in other countries. Aliabadis have higher expectations about political participation.

More Aliabadis are beginning to move beyond the familiar political perspective that if they are dissatisfied with one leader, the course of action is to shift support to another though similar alternative, as many did in earlier local politics and in the 1979 Revolution.[47] More so than during the 1979 Revolution, Aliabad people now consider the somewhat different philosophies and policies advocated by different political personages and candidates for office rather than just supporting an alternative leader in a similar structural position who will hopefully provide better for their needs. While some people enjoy government bodies' patronage in return for loyal support, many other people feel they do not need to enter into feudal-like dependency relationships; they have their own sources of access to a livelihood.

However, the Islamic Republic government is resisting this push for a culture of greater participatory government, especially dramatically during and after the 2009 presidential election—in spite of the fact that this push is in part an unintended result of Islamic Republic policies and programs. The majority of Iranians' additional political experience, knowledge and expectations, gleaned from the events, transformations and communications of the past 60 years shed light on the background for the massive demonstrations about alleged corruption in the June 2009 elections and the Green Movement.

Iranians want and expect to have political influence on the government—more than merely getting rid of one set of personnel and putting another set in place. People expect to have their voices heard and their votes count. When Iranians felt this was not happening during the 2009 Iranian presidential election, they took to the streets to demonstrate.

According to some expatriates and recent emigrants, many people from Aliabad voted against Ahmadinejad in the 2009 presidential election.[48] A few even participated in the Shiraz protests against election corruption and for the Green Movement. Other Aliabadis supported Ahmadinejad. Aliabad Mousavi supporters believe there was cheating in the election and call it a "selection," not an election. Before the presidential election, they say, Ahmadinejad went to many villages, paying villagers money and promising them many things. Still, many if not most of the younger generation, even in Aliabad, voted for Mousavi. Some of the former Ahmadinejad supporters in Aliabad, I've been told, have recently been complaining, especially because of inflation. They say they were fooled into voting for him. Like Iranians elsewhere, Aliabad Mousavi supporters are distressed that he and his wife, Zahra Rahnavard,[49] have been under house arrest.

With this Islamic Republic government repression—and materialism, extravagance, desire for entertainment and distraction, corruption, bad economy and political apathy, unsurprising in light of the present political and socioeconomic conditions—it is hard to see where all of the decline in hierarchy and from-the-bottom-up political culture change will go. Since the scandalous irregularities in the 2009 Iranian presidential election[50] and the subsequent brutal squashing of protests—as well as the recent tightening of sanctions[51] and disastrous economy, international brouhaha over nuclear development and threats from Israel, it is difficult to be as optimistic about the near future.

One has to remember too that millions of Iranians do support the current government. For many of them, the political executions and imprisonment, human rights shortcomings, clampdown on communications and problematic election behavior that are so reprehensive to many other Iranians, inside and outside of the country, are irrelevant. And, they feel, if they are necessary for a government that stands for the correct version of Shia Islam to maintain power, as well as to the interests of the population devoted to that government and the correct version of Islam, so be it. My research in recent years has mostly not been among such people. I do not understand the current Iranian government and its philosophies, doings and supporters. I am here sharing the results of my fieldwork and interviews and trying to convey the current culture, worldviews and criticisms of the many people of Aliabad who in general have hopes for a less autocratic and more participatory government and more open society.

Thinking about my friends in Aliabad and Shiraz, I can't help but wonder and worry about the future. The Islamic Republic government faces many challenges and both secular and religious opposition. Within the government and among the Shia clergy, different factions are at odds with each other. Some are even more hardline than the current rulers, and other groups are more progressive. Just as there are varying interpretations of other religions, such as Christianity, there are different readings of Shia Islam. The Revolutionary Guards, initially a paramilitary and semi-official group, have gained a great deal of political and economic power—one more worry for progressive forces in Iran.[52] At this point it is uncertain how the June 2013 election of moderate Hassan Rouhani as president will affect conditions in Iran. For the short run, it is hard to know in what direction Iranian society—and Aliabad—will move. For the long run, though, people will surely continue pushing toward a more participatory and less hierarchical political system.

Glossary

In most cases, the given pronunciations and meanings are those common in Aliabad in 1978–1979.

akhund   Lower-level clergyman; synonymous with *mulla*

allah o akbar   "God is great."

aqa   Respectful title meaning Mr. or Sir; also used to refer to Ayatollah Khomeini.

Ashura   Tenth day of the month of Moharram; anniversary of the martyrdom of Imam Husein, the most important holy day for Shia.

az khod gozashteh   Outraged to the point of no longer caring about one's own welfare or the consequences of one's actions for oneself.

bazar   Traditional market area with shops lining narrow alleyways; sometimes covered.

bozorg   A superior, an influential man.

bozorgha   The most influential men.

chador   Veil in the shape of a semicircle that women and girls wrap around their bodies to cover themselves from head to foot, with only their face and hands visible.

dero   Harvesting with a handheld sickle.

durud bar Khomeini   "Hail to Khomeini" or "Long live Khomeini."

dang   One-sixth of the agricultural land of a village.

famil   Family, relatives.

gaw or *gav*   A share of agricultural land worked under a sharecropping agreement.

Haj   Title given to those who have made the *haj*, or pilgrimage to Mecca; *haji* is a person who has made the Mecca pilgrimage.

hajat   Prayer for the fulfillment of wishes.

hejab Modesty and covering of women, usually seen as part of religious duty among traditional Muslims.

hejleh Decorated bridal chamber.

herateh or heraseh (also *boneh*) Organized group of sharecroppers who might work their area of land cooperatively.

imam In Shia Islam, one of the twelve successive leaders of the Shia after the death of the Prophet Mohammad in 632 CE; also the cleric stationed at a mosque or a prayer leader.

javid shah "Hail to the Shah" or "Long live the Shah."

jehad Holy war or war against evil in one's self.

kadkhoda Village headman; before land reform, in charge of village sharecroppers and agricultural land and intermediary between sharecroppers and landlord.

Kerbala Karbala in present-day Iraq. Site of the martyrdom of Imam Husein in 680 CE.

khan Tribal chief; sometimes used as a term to show respect.

khanum Respectful title meaning Miss or Mrs.

khoms From Arabic: a fifth, referring to the expectation that Muslims give one-fifth of their income as religious donations.

khoms-khor Alms-eater, a person who lives off alms. Since seyyids, as descendants of the Prophet Mohammad, are appropriate recipients for almsgiving, they might be spoken of in this derogatory manner.

Khordad The third month in the Iranian calendar, begins with the New Year on March 21.

khordeh-malek Small landowner; in Aliabad, the people who bought land formerly owned by Khanum Khorshid Kola Qavam.

khoshneshin Villager with no access to agricultural land.

Majles The Iranian Parliament.

man Unit of weight equivalent to 2.97 kilograms.

manto Tunic-like garment that, with a scarf and leg coverings, presently fulfills modesty regulations for women instituted after the 1977 Revolution; the modern substitute for the chador.

marg bar shah "Death to the Shah."

Mashd Short for *Mashhadi*, title given to people who have made the pilgrimage to Mashhad, where the tomb of Imam Reza is located.

mellat The people; in Aliabad, often used to refer to the anti-Seyyid Ibn Ali Askari faction or taifeh after the Revolution.

mirzai In Aliabad, offspring of a female seyyid.

mojahedin Soldiers for the Faith, warriors for religion, often used to mean the revolutionary activists.

mostazafin The poor, helpless and oppressed.

mulla Low-level clergyman; synonymous with *akhund.*

namaz The five prayers a day required of Muslims, completed in three sessions by Shia; one of the five pillars of Islam, along with statement of belief in God and his Prophet Mohammad, alms, fasting during daylight hours during the month of Ramadan and pilgrimage to Mecca for those who can afford it.

noheh Mourning couplet chanted during the sineh-zani and zanjir-zani commemorating the martyrdom of Imam Husein.

Noruz Iranian New Year, March 21.

Qom Relatives, kin.

Qoran The Holy Book of Islam, considered by Muslims to be the direct word of God.

raft-o-amad Social interaction, visiting, coming and going.

reshveh-khor Bribe-eater, someone who expects and takes bribes.

rial Unit of currency in Iran, a tenth of a *toman;* one US dollar was equivalent to 75 rials during my 1978–1979 fieldwork.

rish-sefid Head of an agricultural group.

riyat Sharecropper, peasant; in Aliabad, often used to refer to those who received land under the 1962 land reform and to the anti-Seyyid Ibn Ali Askari faction or taifeh after the Revolution.

riyati Sharecropping rights, rights of cultivation.

salavat Set prayer responses.

sangar Gathering of members of a taifeh or faction in times of conflict for fortification or entrenchment, for mutual protection and to plan strategy.

sineh-zani Beating the chest with one's hand in mourning for Imam Husein.

seyyid Descendant of the Prophet through his daughter Fatimeh (he had no surviving sons) and then through the male line.

shahrak A town, more than a village, a settlement with amenities.

shaikh Learned clergyman, religious head of a community or an honorary title.

Shia One of the two main branches of Islam. The Shia believe in the special spiritual powers of descendants of the Prophet Mohammad and that he chose them as successors to the Prophet rather than electing the successors, as the Sunni believe should be done. Iran is the only country where both the majority of the population and the government are Shia. Before the institution of the Islamic Republic of Iran, though, Shia clergy stayed out of formal government positions.

shobeh Before land reform, a rural trading branch or concession for sale of government-controlled commodities that brought financial benefits to its operator.

shora Local council. The Islamic Republic central government instituted elected local councils in 1999.

sineh-zani   Beating the chest with one's hand in mourning for Imam Husein.

Sunni   One of the two main branches of Islam. Most countries in the Middle East and North Africa are Sunni. Sunni clergy hold their positions as government employees.

taasob-e taifeh   Taifeh sentiment, emotional attachment to one's taifeh.

taghuti   A decadent, idolatrous person—a condemning insult used during the revolutionary period and afterward.

taifeh   Kinship-based group, mobilized in Aliabad during periods of weak central government as the main political institution.

taifeh-dar   Head of a strong, political taifeh.

taifeh-keshi   Political competition and conflict among kinship-based factions.

Tasua   Ninth day of the month of Moharram; anniversary of the eve of the martyrdom of Imam Husein.

taziyeh   Dramatization of the events surrounding the martyrdom of Imam Husein.

toman   Ten rials; 7.5 toman were equivalent to one US dollar during my 1978–1979 fieldwork. From 2003 to 2012, the official rate went up from 800 toman to 1,100 to the dollar; by May 2013, about 1,230 toman were equivalent to one US dollar. Most Iranians have to pay almost three times that on the street for dollars.

Tudehi   A person belonging to or supporting the Tudeh Party of Iran.

zanjir-zani   Beating the back with a chain, a form of self-mortification, in mourning for Imam Husein; similar to the self-flagellation that originated in Italy in the 11th century, and practiced by Christian medieval guilds and even now by some Catholics in the Philippines, Latin America, the Iberian Peninsula and the southwest United States, such as the Penitentes in northern New Mexico.

Notes

Preface

1. In Aliabad, *Mashd* is short for the title *Mashhadi,* meaning a person who has made the pilgrimage to the shrine of Imam Reza, eighth Imam, or leader, of the Shias, who was martyred in 818 CE in Mashhad, Iran.

2. *Seyyid* is a title for a person who self-identifies as a descendant of the Prophet Mohammad through his daughter Fatimah Zahra, as the Prophet Mohammad did not have any surviving sons.

3. Aliabadis used the word *hayat* (courtyard) to mean the entire space inside the high walls of a residential compound, including all of the rooms around it as well as the open space in the middle.

4. Also see Beeman and Bhattacharyya 1978.

5. By "the Revolution," I generally mean the revolutionary process of at least two years leading up to the day the regime of Mohammad Reza Shah Pahlavi fell. Occasionally, for convenience, I use *Revolution* to refer only to February 11, 1979, the day the revolutionary movement was successful in overthrowing the Shah's government.

6. *Khanum* is a title meaning "Miss" or "Mrs." When it is used with a female's first name, it can come either before or after the name, with the later being less formal and more familiar. Although generally used whenever addressing or referring to a woman, by 2003, with less formal social relations, Aliabad people were using it less often.

7. For more about Esmat Ajami, see Hegland 2003a and 2008.

8. Reza Shah Pahlavi, an army officer who supported a coup against the former Qajar dynasty, became Shah in 1925. In 1941, dissatisfied with the Shah's tolerance of the German presence in Iran, British and Soviet troops deposed and exiled him. The Americans and British then put his son, Mohammad Reza Pahlavi, in his place as Shah. Mohammad Reza Shah fled the country briefly in 1953, until a British and American CIA-engineered coup overthrew Prime Minister Mosaddeq and brought the Shah back to power. With strong American backing, he then ruled as a dictator until fleeing the country on January 16, 1979. His government fell on February 11, 1979.

9. Shapour Bakhtiar had been a strong critic of the Shah's regime as a moderate and activist in the National Front, an opposition coalition founded by Mohammad Mosaddeq and others. Bakhtiar had served in the government during Mosaddeq's tenure as prime minister and was subsequently imprisoned repeatedly by the Shah's government. At the end of December 1978, in hopes of appeasing the revolutionary forces, the Shah appointed Bakhtiar prime minister to make the shift from a military to a civilian government. Bakhtiar accepted this position, although as a result he was evicted from the National Front, because he feared what might happen should the Revolution be successful—such as religious fundamentalists gaining power. Ayatollah Khomeini, who returned from France to Iran on February 1, 1979, refused to compromise. After the government fell, Bakhtiar left for France. He escaped one assassination attempt but was murdered in his home on August 7, 1991.

10. Muslims belong to one of two major groups: the Sunni and the Shia. Sunni countries are in the majority in the Middle East. Iranians, however, are mainly Shia, and the Islamic Republic of Iran is a Shia government, though some of the tribal-ethnic groups close to the borders are Sunni. The more northern Kurds are Sunni, although further south, as in the Province of Kermanshah, most are Shia.

11. The title Haj means *haji*, a person who has made the pilgrimage to Mecca required of every Muslim who meets the financial qualifications. Sometimes the word is used to indicate respect to an older person.

12. The 12th and last Shia Imam or leader of the Shia—all descendants of the Prophet Mohammad through his daughter Fatimah—was born in 868 CE. Also called the Mahdi or Hidden Imam, in 874 CE he was made invisible, or occulted, by God for his protection, according to Shia belief. All of the other 11 imams were martyred. When the Hidden Imam reappears, a number of Shia have told me, he will be accompanied by Jesus Christ.

Cast of Characters

1. Although normally a title meaning acceptance by peers as a high-level and learned religious leader, *Ayatollah* was used as a proper name in Aliabad.

2. Although normally a title, *Aqa* was also used as a proper name in Aliabad.

Introduction

1. See Ringer's (2000) discussion of modernization, including differentiation from westernization. Patricia Higgins has made helpful comments to me in this regard.

2. Others have also criticized the explanation of rapid modernization for the Revolution. See Abrahamian 1983:426, 427; Bayat 2007; Halliday 1979; Katouzian 1981 and 2003 and Keddie 1981.

3. Also see Abrahamian 1983:426, 427.

4. Also see Abrahamian 1983:426, 427, 435–446 and Bayat 2007:22.

5. Although *mulla* generally means "preacher," here it is the title for kadkhoda. At one period in Aliabad history, a kadkhoda was referred to as *mulla*, an honorific implying literacy.

6. The title Haj means *haji*, a person who has made the pilgrimage to Mecca required of every Muslim who meets the financial qualifications. Sometimes the word is used to indicate respect to an older person.

7. *Am* is short for *amu*, which means "father's brother." It is also used as a respectful term of address for older men.

8. The Qavams were descendants of a merchant who came to Shiraz from Gazvin. He supposedly was from a family originally from Shiraz. His son became very wealthy from profits earned by trading in the ports of Bandar Abass and Kharak. The Qavams became prominent, with members of the family acting as mayors, governors, ministers and senators (Barth 1961:86–87). They married into other prominent families, including the Pahlavi royal family. Their great wealth, from trade with India and the opium trade, and political prominence led them to become tax farmers for Aliabad and many other villages, and then to take over ownership of large rural areas. The family basically took over control of Shiraz and the region, and even added the port of Bushire to their area of influence. For more information on the Qavams, see Barth 1961, S. Cronin 2007, Karandish 2011 and Royce 1981.

9. On similar political systems, see Bailey 2001a, Black-Michaud 1986, Barth 1968, Keiser 1991, Knudsen 2009, Lindholm 1982, R. Loeffler 1978 and Wright 1986.

10. I will deal with influences on the historical development of the taifeh-keshi political system in a later publication.

11. My mentor, the late Richard Antoun, gave a graduate course in political anthropology that helped sensitize me to taifeh political process, as did his guidance and deep interest when I returned from Aliabad field research in December 1979. Most helpful in working with my materials have been books by Antoun (1979), Bailey (2001a), Barth (1968), Black-Michaud (1986), Cohen (1976, 1981), Gerlach and Hine (1981), Keiser (1991), Kertzer (1980), Knudsen (2009) and Lindholm (1982).

12. Moavieh, accepted by Sunnis as the fifth caliph, and Yazid, the sixth caliph, vied for leadership of the Muslim community with the sons of Imam Ali, son-in-law of the Prophet Mohammad. In 680 CE, the forces of Yazid fought against Imam Husein, son of Imam Ali and accepted by Shia Muslims as the third Imam or head of the Muslim community after the death of the Prophet Mohammad in 632 CE. Imam Husein was martyred at this time, and Shia still mourn during the anniversary of his death in the month of Moharram.

13. As much as possible, I try to avoid adding an *s* to Persian words to indicate plural. In informal spoken Persian, a singular noun is often used for the plural as well.

14. In this book I use the word *peasant* to mean sharecropper or *riyat*—those villagers who hold agricultural rights to land. After land reform, the sharecroppers at the time were to become owners of land distributed under the land reform.

15. Turner (1978a:37–44 and 1978b) lays out four phases in his "processual analysis" of "social dramas." Perhaps knowledge of this helped me to discern the phases of taifeh-keshi.

16. In her study of the founding of Sherpa monasteries, anthropologist Sherry Ortner (1990) discussed the economic and political influences involved. Although she assumed her political economy argument to be correct, Ortner also found it "incomplete" and "impoverished," because both the cultural and the human elements were missing (68).

17. Cultural models or paradigms are also reproduced through practice. See Ortner (1990:63), who follows Pierre Bourdieu's (1992) "theory of practice."

18. Bourdieu 1992 and Ortner 1990.

19. Although anthropologists have not specifically studied the political socialization

and enculturation of Iranian children, anthropologist Erika Friedl's book *Children of Deh Koh: Young Life in an Iranian Village* (1997) demonstrates aspects of children's cultural learning that would be relevant for taifeh-keshi politics.

20. Geertz (1973:3) defines a people's ethos as "the tone, character, and quality of their life, its moral and aesthetic style and mood," and their worldview as "the picture they have of the way things in sheer actuality are, their most comprehensive ideas of order."

21. Such cultural beaten paths or processual paradigms (Also see Vincent 1995:356) are similar to the "root paradigms" or "cultural models" discussed by Victor Turner (1978b:64, 96) which provide models for people's behavior. The phases of "social dramas" during times of conflict, Turner argues, result not from people's instincts, but rather from "models and metaphors carried in the actors' heads" (1978a:36, 37). Ortner (1990:60) defines key scenarios as "preorganized schemes of action, symbolic programs for the staging and playing out of standard social interactions in a particular culture." What Turner terms social dramas and Ortner key scenarios or cultural schema may be compared to the process of taifeh-keshi in Aliabad. Such an approach has been used widely in the field of psychology. See Corr and Matthews 2009:238-241, for example.

22. According to Ortner, cultural schemas such as a myth or story may be in the background and lacking motivational force, but "at moments in the course of events the story seems to make sense of a person's circumstances and is thus appropriated and internalized" (1990:89). Ortner has worked on ways to analyze the channeling of behavior by such cultural schema while still allowing more room for individual agency (1990:89, 90).

23. See Hegland 1983b and 1983c.

24. See Katouzian's (2003) discussion of "the repetitive cycle of arbitrary rule and public rebellion and disorder followed by arbitrary rule" (131) which, he argues, has been prevalent in Iran and is somewhat similar, at the national level, to Aliabad's local process of taifeh-keshi.

25. Loeffler worked at Shiraz University Medical School among doctors, professors and students, observed doctors in their practices and at home, and talked extensively with laypeople. In spite of Shiraz University Medical School's historic close connection with the University of Pennsylvania, the school's high percentage of foreign doctors and professors before the 1979 Iranian Revolution (90%) and their allopathic medical training, traditional Iranian views about health and healing continued to influence doctors' views and practices. They rejected those aspects of allopathic ideas and practices that seemed illogical or inappropriate in the context of Iranian culture (Loeffler 2013).

26. See, for example, Ortner 1989 and 1990.

27. Ohnuki-Tierney 1990:8. Also see Friedl 1991.

28. Bayat (2007) also argues that "the language of dissent and protests was largely antimonarchy, anti-imperialist, Third Worldist, and even nationalist," which turned "*in the end* to religious discourse" (22, emphasis added).

29. Reza Shah Pahlavi changed the name of the country from Persia to Iran in 1935.

30. See S. Cronin 2010b.

31. Abrahamian 1983 and 2013, Bill 1989, de Bellaigue 2013, Gasiorowski and Bryne 2004, Katouzian 1999, Kinzer 2008 and Wilber 2006.

Chapter 1

1. Also see Lambton 1969a:102.

2. Although Persians switched from drinking coffee to drinking tea in the 19th century (Matthee 1996), the term *qaveh khaneh*, which means coffee house, is still used for a place that serves tea.

3. Shrines in Iran are generally the burial place of a descendant of a Shia imam, who is thus also a descendent of the Prophet Mohammad and therefore is a seyyid.

4. See Lambton 1969a:139–140 for discussion of how tax farmers tended to usurp as their own private property agricultural land that had been granted to them by the Shah or other government personnel as tax farms from which to collect taxes for the government and as a substitute for salaries for administering and collecting revenues from these lands.

5. Here Darab is the name of an actual region, whereas elsewhere in the text, Darab is the pseudonym for a village close to Aliabad.

6. The Qashqai "shah" was Solat ed-Doleh Qashqai, head of the Qashqai tribespeople and father of Naser Khan and Khosrow Khan Qashqai, leaders of the Qashqai at the time of my fieldwork. The Shaikh "shah" was Shaikh Khazal, head of the Arab tribes and active in the political process in Khuzistan and Fars during the early decades of the 20th century. It is revealing that all three "shahs" of the region were the heads of important tribal confederacies. The Qavams were not tribal people themselves. However, between 1860 and 1865, Ali Mohammad Khan Qavam ol-Molk put together the Khamseh tribal coalition to contravene the political influence of the Qashqai. See Barth 1961:86–88 and Abrahamian 1982:45, 46. Before centralization of the government and development of the army, police and gendarmes—made possible by oil money—to enforce the rule of the central government, tribesmen were necessarily the armed forces of the provincial "shahs," because of their tribal organization and mobility, riding and shooting expertise and fearlessness. Ali Mohammad Khan Qavam ol-Molk became the first head of the Khamseh Confederacy. When Habibollah Qavam ol-Molk, head of the Khamseh Confederacy in 1916, died in a hunting accident, his son Ibrahim Khan Qavam ol-Molk took over until Reza Shah took away his position in 1933 for a time. See Karandish 2011.

7. See Royce 1981:253 and Barth 1961:86–88.

8. Abrahamian 1983:197.

9. Arab was from the Arab Shaibani family, leaders of the Arab tribe, one of the five groups put together into the Khamseh Confederation by Ali Khan Qavam ol-Molk (Lambton 1969a:159; Barth 1961:86).

10. Royce 1981:253. Although Khanum Khorshid Kolah Qavam was formally owner of Aliabad, villagers sometimes referred to Arab as the owner. Females could own property. According to Islamic law, a daughter should inherit property along with sons, in a ratio of a half share to every share for a male offspring. A widow should inherit one-eighth of her husband's property, with the rest going to the children. However, often females did not actually obtain their inheritance, or if a female did hold title, a male family member, such as her husband, would manage it and often be able to use the proceeds as he wished.

11. Also see di Leonardo 1987; Hale 1986 and 1996; Hegland 1986, 1991, 1998a and 2003a; Joseph 1979 and 1983; Peteet 1986 and 1992 and Tucker 1986.

12. See Alberts 1963, C. Cronin 1981, Goodell 1977 and 1986, Spooner 1965 and 1966 and Thompson 1979.

13. In his study of a Kohistani community, Keiser (1991) found that when roads made possible gaining cash from potatoes and lumber, leading to purchase of guns and then to increased violent confrontations and vengeance, men could mobilize their mothers' and wives' kin, as well as take on friends and people with other types of ties, for conflict. Social organization became somewhat more like a "personal network": "the significance of lineages withered in politics. Kohistanis borrowed *dala* (the Pushto word meaning 'political faction') to refer to such networks, and *dalabasi* (roughly, the confrontation between *dala*) became the Kohistani word for politics" (92). Kinship "inconsistencies and ambiguities," Keiser found, "unfold options, establish possibilities for negotiation, and create opportunities to exploit weaknesses and strengths" (84).

14. Both males and females could enter into a kinlike relationship with a close friend. In an example of literature borrowing from cultural reality, in the novel *A Persian Requiem* by Simin Daneshvar (1991), set in Shiraz in the midst of the British occupation during WWII, two women swore loyalty to each other as sisters. Close family friends are often addressed with a kinship term, such as uncle or aunt.

15. See Bailey 2001a.

16. In the absence of parents able to do this, a brother was often expected to take on this responsibility.

17. Many other anthropologists have discussed the significance of social interaction, visiting and attending rituals, life-cycle commemorations and other social occasions and the commensality that takes place at these times in the formation and maintenance of political ties. See, for example, Abu-Zahra 1974, Antoun 1979, Barth 1968, Cohen 1976 and 1981 and Kertzer 1980.

18. As Spooner (1965) has noted, "A kin tie will need to take on the values of a personal friendship before it is really reliable or important. Uncles and cousins are felt as an important part of the family only in proportion to their physical (and social) proximity" (30).

19. Seyyid Enayat was also son of the sister of the carpet workshop owners, Seyyid Ibn Ali Askari and Seyyid Yaqub Askari. This relationship is most likely why Seyyid Enayat and his wife, Rana, were friendly with the carpet workshop manager and his wife, outsiders from Kerman, in the first place.

20. Loeffler 1978:168.

21. Also see Bailey 2001a:48.

22. The term *politics of hospitality* was coined by the late Richard Antoun (1979:98, 207). Also see Barth 1968:79–81, Loeffler 1978:154 and Nakhleh 1975:505.

23. The central event of Shia Islam was the 680 CE martyrdom of its leader, Imam Husein, along with 72 male members of his band, on the plains of Karbala in present-day Iraq, and the taking of the womenfolk into captivity. The Persian theater tradition, *taziyeh*, developed around this event. In earlier years, Aliabad kadkhodas hosted players from Shiraz to act out these stories on consecutive evenings during Moharram, the month of mourning for the Karbala martyrs.

24. Several political aspects of hospitality brought up by Antoun (1979) are relevant to politics in the Iranian village of Aliabad.

25. Antoun (1979) called this political strategy "passive confrontation." "One way of adding to clan prestige is to pack clan guest houses full of one's own clansmen on appropriate occasions—religious festivals, weddings, funerals, circumcision celebrations, etc." (37).

26. *Mashd* is short for the title *Mashhadi,* meaning a person who has made the pilgrimage to the shrine of Imam Reza, eighth Imam, or leader, of the Shia, who was martyred in 818 CE in Mashhad, Iran.

27. Also see Antoun 1979:98.

28. Also see Ahmed 1976:59 and Antoun 1976:59.

29. Also see Bailey 2001a:38.

30. Also see Nakhleh 1975:508.

31. A *man* equals 2.97 kilos.

32. Compare this account with C. Cronin's (1970) study of the bilateral kinship system of Sicilian villagers whose preference for matrilateral kin increased as a new wife pursued her connections with her own kin. Cronin also notes the correspondence between kinship and contact: "The general rule is: more contact more relatedness" (47).

33. Once when I visited my friend Rana she was rolling out the large, round, thin sheets of homemade Aliabad bread and baking them on a large, round sheet of metal over several gas flames. She was making it for her brother who lived in the city, she said, and had to do it while her husband was away since he didn't like her to bake bread for her brother.

34. Erika Friedl (1981:15) also stresses this point.

35. Abu-Lughod (1985) also points to the close relationship between mother and daughter among the Awlad Ali Bedouins in Egypt.

36. Loeffler (1978) also states, "A man receiving a woman in marriage incurs a stringent and lasting obligation toward his father-in-law; he becomes, as the Lurs say, the servant of his father-in-law" (162). Other anthropologists have noted the effectiveness of kinship or other normative obligations in maintaining bonds between political leaders and followers or cohesion of a group (Cohen 1976:60 and Bailey 2001a:43, 44, 48), and enabling a higher-level person to better exploit a person below them in status or power (Asad 1972:91).

37. Compare to Barbara Aswad's (1967) study of women's roles in the noble lineage of an Arab village community on the Syrian-Turkish border. Aswad found women's communication networks to be more informal and less constrained by factional divisions than men's interaction. Women's communications were more direct and specific than those of men, and their circle of contacts, although not as wide as men's and restricted to the locality, tended to be more intense within the geographical limitation (1967:149–151). Also see Wright 1978 and several of the ethnographic short stories in Friedl 1991.

38. The expression "the work of kinship" was, I believe, coined by di Leonardo (1987).

39. As Suad Joseph (1979:552 and 1983) and Barbara Aswad (1967:149, 150) have also noted in their respective studies of a Beirut neighborhood and an Arab village community on the Syrian-Turkish border, women, more so than men, tended to maintain interaction with individuals from opposing political groups.

40. See Papanek 1973.

41. Much of this section is taken from Hegland 1991:215–230 and 1998a:211–225. I am grateful to the editors and presses for allowing me to use this material. The discussion on women and politics in Aliabad was first published in a special issue of *MERIP Middle East Report* (Hegland 1986a) featuring pioneering research on Middle Eastern women's grass-roots political work, such as that by Sondra Hale, Suad Joseph, Julie Peteet and Judith Tucker. Also see Betteridge 1985 and 2000, di Leonardo 1987, Hale 1996, Hegland 2003a, Joseph 1979 and 1983, Kaplan 1982 and 1987, Nashat 1983 and Peteet 1992.

42. The term *core* was significant in F. G. Bailey's framework for political analysis (2001a:44–49). My use of the term corresponds roughly to his.

43. *White beard* referred to the assumption that these positions were held by older, more experienced men.

44. Evans-Pritchard 1949 and 1969, and Gellner 1969. Developed with the influence of Robertson-Smith (1885) and others, the segmentary lineage model of political process provided a way to look at how stateless societies managed without strong leadership: segments of patrilineal corporate kinship groups at the different descent levels acted as political units in complementary opposition to, hopefully, prevent higher-level warfare.

45. Many of the points raised by Bailey in his seminal book *Stratagems and Spoils* (2001a), such as taifeh leaders' exhortations about the moral quality of relationships in order to get relatives to work for leaders' interests, could also be seen in the operation of Aliabad taifeh.

46. In a study of Iranian taifeh, Behnam (1971) notes, "Each *ta'ife* is placed under the direction of a chief" (122).

47. Stirling (1965:27) and Hinderink and Kiray (1970:196, 7) also mention that poor and uninfluential Turkish villagers do not maintain lineage ties. Behnam (1971:122) brings up this point as well.

48. For similar dependence on lineages and lineage heads in Turkey, see Stirling 1965:27, 167, 168, 169; and Hinderink and Kiray 1970:196, 197.

49. *Herateh* corresponds to the term *haraseh*, used in the city of Jahrom for sharecropper work units (Lambton 1969a:300). In some other areas of Iran, the term used for agricultural groups was *boneh* (Ajami 1993 and Hooglund 1981b).

50. Large absentee landlords were particularly common in Fars. Annual redistribution of irrigated land among sharecroppers was also especially common in Fars. See Lambton 1969a:171 and 1969b:7.

Chapter 2

1. The Allies deposed Reza Shah Pahlavi in 1941, replacing him with his son Mohammad Reza Shah Pahlavi, who was under the influence of the United States until his departure from Iran on January 16, 1979, during the revolutionary upheaval.

2. See Abrahamian 2008, Beeman 2008, Gasiorowski 1991, Gasiorowski and Byrne 2004, Katouzian 1981 and 2003, Keddie 2006 and Kinzer 2007 and 2008.

3. See Abrahamian 1983, 2008 and 2013; Katouzian 1999; Keddie 2006 and Kinzer 2008.

4. See Atabaki 1993.

5. Also see Abrahamian 1983:302.

6. See Abrahamian 1983, 2008 and 2013; Katouzian 1999; Keddie 2006 and Kinzer 2007 and 2008.

7. According to village informants, *Murashes* was the name of the ship sent to take British citizens back to England. British gunboats were sent to the Gulf to "protect British lives and property" after Tudeh protests in April 1951 (Abrahamian 1983:266). The British evacuated their oil technicians and closed their oil installations in September 1951 (Abrahamian 1983:266, 268). *Murashes* is the HMS Mauritius, which took the last of the British nationals from Abadan across the Shatt-al-Arab to Basra on October 4, 1951 (Kinzer 2008:121).

8. Abrahamian 2008.

9. See Abrahamian 2013.

10. Abrahamian 1983:324, 325 and Keddie 2006:130. Tudeh leaders did ask Mosaddeq to call for a broad alliance to resist the coup, but Mosaddeq didn't want such bloodshed (Abrahamian 1983:325) and feared foreign intervention (Abrahamian 2013:107). The military governor of Tehran told Tudeh and National Front leaders that Mosaddeq said to "stay off the streets" (Abrahamian 2013:191). According to Kinzer (2008:179, 180), another reason the Tudeh did not support Mosaddeq on August 19 was their indecisiveness—for which they criticized themselves later (Keddie 2006:130).

11. Abrahamian 1983:267–280. Also see Abrahamian 2013, Cottam 1979 and 2006, Katouzian 1999, Keddie 2006 and Kinzer 2007 and 2008 for treatments of the Tudeh and Mosaddeq era.

12. See Abrahamian 1983:325 and 2013:213 and Kinzer 2008:176–194.

13. *Gau*, pronounced "gav" (meaning cow or ox) in other parts of Iran, generally refers to the amount of land a pair of oxen can plow in a day. See Hooglund 1982 and Lambton 1969a and 1969b.

14. See Hassanpour 2012, Elm 1992:274, Keddie 2006:126 and Moaddel 1993:48.

15. Hassanpour 2012. Also see S. Cronin 2010a:264. Interestingly, this long period of resistance, although recorded in US State Department documents and even in *New York Times* articles, has been given little scholarly attention, Hassanpour points out. Surely sharecroppers elsewhere in Iran went on strike or rose up against landlords at this time as well. The reasons for the Mukri Kurdistan peasant uprisings—such as brutal repression after the overthrow of Mosaddeq, government censorship of the media in Iran, self-censorship and the censoring of theoretical perspectives (Hassanpour 2012)—may be the same reasons that prevented awareness of other peasant resistance during this period.

16. For treatments of the 1960s Iranian land reform, see Farazmand 1989, Hooglund 1982, Lambton 1969b, Moghadam 1996 and Najmabadi 1988.

17. A *dang* is a sixth of a village. Three dang would therefore be half of the land attached to the village of Aliabad. Also see Lambton 1969a:426.

18. See Lambton 1969b:71 and Hooglund 1975:88, 89.

19. In the 1960s, one dollar was equal to 7.575 toman, or 75.75 rials.

20. Land reform was part of a six-point reform plan, the "White Revolution," the Shah—pressured by the Kennedy administration to fend off communist successes and Soviet influence—introduced in 1962. See Halliday 1979:104, Abrahamian 1983:421, 422 and

Hooglund 1982:47, 50. A main purpose of land reform was to break down the large land-lords' power as part of the centralization project (Lambton 1969b:64).

21. For information about land reform in Fars, see Lambton 1969b:93, 101–102, 120–122, 149ff, 218–222. Also see Hooglund 1982.

22. See Lampton 1969b and Hooglund 1982.

23. Majd 2000:186, cited by S. Cronin 2010:264.

24. The Lurs are a large ethnic group from southwest Iran. In years past, many Lurs were nomadic and tribally organized, although now they are mainly settled in villages. See Amanollahi 1985. Erika Friedl's and Reinhold Loeffler's publications are based on fieldwork in a Luri village several hours up the valley from Aliabad. The village of Delli, mainly popu-lated by Persianized Lurs, lies closer to Aliabad. It was apparently home to the Banu Delli Lur group, who helped Sayyid Ibn Ali then (personal communication from Erika Friedl).

25. The dollar was equal to 75.75 rials or 7.575 toman in 1962.

26. Also see Ajami 2005 and Hooglund 1982.

27. Also see Hooglund 1975:210–214.

28. Also see Lambton 1969a:263, 264.

29. See Keddie 2006, Lambton 1969b and Hooglund 1982.

30. Although after land reform agriculturalists and landholders in Aliabad were no longer sharecroppers but owners or agricultural laborers, people still often used the word *riyat* to refer to those who had received land during land reform.

31. They had made the pilgrimage to Mecca, demonstrating their religious worthiness and financial success.

32. Also see Antoun 1976:16, Hooglund 1975:200, Miller 1964:489, 490 and Ashraf and Safai 1977:53–55.

33. Also see Antoun 1979:98, Loeffler 1973:1084, 1085 and Alberts 1963:750.

34. Also see Beeman 1976:32, 33.

35. Also see Ashraf and Safai 1977:54.

36. For discussion of earlier elite-sponsored rituals in Aliabad, see Hegland 1983b and 1983c.

Chapter 3

1. Keddie 2006:158–169.

2. See Antoun 1976 for analysis of how a landlord kinship group in northeastern Iran maintained their status as a political and economic elite after land reform through capital investment, higher education, monopoly of local government offices and connections with government officials. Also see Hooglund 1975:190, Inayatullah 1972:85, 86, Keddie 1972:397, H. Mahdavi 1965:140–142 and Miller 1964:489, 494.

3. Also see Okazaki 1969 and Antoun 1981.

4. I use the word *agriculturalist* to refer to a person actually performing agricultural work.

5. Other researchers have found this to be the case in other areas as well. For example, Hooglund (1981a) states, "75% of all peasants who acquired land [under land reform] ob-tained holdings inadequate for basic subsistence" (16). Kazemi's (1980) study focuses on the urban poor forced to out-migrate because of poverty from the disruption of agriculture.

6. Using the agricultural census of 1973, Parvin Ghorayshi (1981:29) says that 51% of all agricultural units in Iran did not sell a significant proportion of what they produced, and another 26.7% of units sold less than half.

7. Households generally needed from 100 to 500 *man* of wheat for a year's supply of bread, depending on the number of persons in the household.

8. Ten women who earned money are included in the sample, but the 20 to 30 girls who worked in Seyyid Ibn Ali and Seyyid Yaqub Askari's carpet shop are not, as it was temporary work that would end when they became engaged.

9. Other researchers have made similar comments: "The allegiance of the poor peasants and the farm laborers to their masters is . . . based on the objective fact of their dependence on their masters for their continued livelihood. . . . [The poor peasant] finds himself and his family totally dependent upon his master for their livelihood. . . . He is unable to rise, by himself, against the system" (Alavi 1973a:332, 333). Also see J. Black 1972, Bradburd 1983 and 1994; Hooglund 1981a:16 and Kazemi and Abrahamian 1978.

10. Other researchers have pointed to the similarities between the situations of peasants and khoshneshin before land reform and small owners after land reform. "Faced with so many problems in selling their labor power, the mass of the landless population or the small owner-cultivators, just like the majority of the khwushneshin population before land reform, had to continue their reliance on old feudalistic ties, live on charity, and be satisfied with their marginal life" (Ghorayshi 1981:30). Also see Hooglund 1981a:16.

11. As they came to Aliabad infrequently, I did not include six Aliabad men who had shops in the Beyza area further to the north. Four of them lived there with their wives from Aliabad, and two had married Beyza women.

12. Also see Loeffler 1976 for similar new opportunities in a Luri village.

13. Only government employees received pensions after retirement. Thus, except for the two retired teachers, by retired I mean no longer working.

14. The men who were Shiraz policemen and in the army tended to support the Shah's government during the revolutionary period, more likely because of this central government association than because of fear of and economic dependence on the Askaris.

15. Also see Hill 1991, for example.

16. Aliabadis not aligned with the Askaris were afraid of and hated the gendarmes. The Askaris, however, had close relations with the gendarmes in Qodratabad. They had long been close personal friends with the old head of the gendarmerie station located only minutes away from Aliabad. Pictures of this person appeared often in Seyyid Yaqub's family picture album. He had frequently been present in their home and at their social gatherings. Seyyid Yaqub told stories illustrating their great friendship. When the old head retired and a new head was appointed, the new head and his wife and child lived with Seyyid Yaqub and his family until they found a home in Qodratabad. Visiting between the families continued, and the new captain of the station and other gendarmes were frequent dinner guests in Seyyid Yaqub's home. Seyyid Muslem Askari was especially close friends with the new young captain and other officers from the gendarmerie station. Villagers were aware of this close personal relationship between the Askaris and the gendarmes and had learned from bitter experience that the gendarmes always came down firmly on the side of the Askaris in

any dispute. Seyyid Yaqub immediately sent for the gendarmes when any problem arose. The gendarmes arrived with dispatch and arrested on the spot or physically punished any person who was giving the Askaris or their supporters any difficulty. The gendarmerie station was hardly the place to take complaints about mistreatment by the Askaris, villagers learned. For example, Seyyid Muslem had refused to pay a young villager for 20 days of agricultural labor and had struck him with a chain when he requested payment. The young man went to the gendarmerie station to complain. The captain beat this villager on the soles of his feet after soaking them in cold water and then ordered him to do another 20 days of labor for Seyyid Muslem without pay.

Chapter 4

1. See Betteridge 1992 for discussions of Shiraz shrines.

2. Hegland 1983b. Also see Fischer 2003. Influenced by the lay theologian Ali Shariati, this perspective stresses struggling against injustice in this world. See Abrahamian 1989, Shari'ati 1982 and Sachedina 1981. Because I plan to focus my next book on the significance of the Shia martyrdom paradigm in the Iranian Revolution and elsewhere, I do not include much about it here. Of course the new Shia ideology of revolution was not the only revolutionary ideology coming into the village. Ideas such as liberal democracy and Marxist views influenced a minority. In the Revolution in general, people holding a wide spectrum of political ideologies came together to act under the umbrella of Shia ideology. Among the placards carried in marches were some portraits of Iranian writer Samad Behrangi. See Behrangi 1987.

3. See Gerlach and Hine 1981:56, 79. Also see Curry and Goedl 2012:338.

4. See Gerlach and Hine 1981:88. Also see Curry and Goedl, 2012.

5. See Hegland 1991, 1998a, 1998b and 1998c and 2003a for information on women's networking and verbal work.

6. Hegland 1987.

7. Although villagers of course found it challenging to follow Muslim law, women especially were expected to follow purification rituals, such as after sex, menstruation and childbirth.

8. Also see Tarrow 2006:71–90 and McAdam 1999:59.

9. Abrahamian 1989:31–34.

10. Also see Abrahamian 1989:33. On Ashura (the tenth of the Arab month of Moharram and anniversary of the martyrdom of Imam Husein) 1963, which fell that year on the 15th of the Iranian month of Khordad, June 4, Ayatollah Khomeini was arrested. He was exiled in 1964. A great deal of conflict took place in Shiraz between clerics and religious groups on the one hand and government forces on the other. Some villagers could describe aspects of this conflict, and a few had even been personally involved. Ayatollah Mahallati of Shiraz was also imprisoned during this period. See Keddie 1981:158 for a brief account of the arrest of Ayatollah Khomeini. Also see Cottam 1979:308 and Abrahamian 1983:424–426.

11. I appreciate Eric Hooglund's effort in translating this essay.

12. Gerlach and Hine 1981:156. For further discussion of identity in social movements, see Stryker, Owens and White 2001.

13. Seyyid Yaqub's sons did not speak with him for a period during the height of revo-

lutionary fervor, but in this case there were considerations of trying to play both sides of the political fence, at least on the part of his son Seyyid Muslem. An older son by Seyyid Yaqub's earlier wife, though, was definitely an advocate of Ayatollah Khomeini and the revolutionary movement.

14. Or "an altered view of self and some degree of cognitive restructuring" (Gerlach and Hine 1981:135). Also see Curry and Goedl forthcoming:120.

15. For more information on women in the Revolution, see Hegland 1998a and 1991.

16. Some of the material in the following two sections was previously printed in Hegland 1998a:211–225. I am grateful to the editor and press for allowing me to use it.

17. The Bahai religion was founded in Iran. As the leader and others had previously been Muslims, Muslim Iranians considered them to be apostates, people who had access to the messages of Islam but left. Practicing Muslims generally consider leaving the faith to be a very serious act against Islam.

18. I am grateful to Eric Hooglund for repeating this conversation for me.

19. At the time, many Iranians from a variety of backgrounds, classes and levels of education, not only Aliabad villagers, believed that an Islamic government would bring freedom and rights for people.

20. Also see Tarrow 2006:111, 112.

21. According to McAdam (1999), the factors that "facilitate movement generation" include "expanding political opportunities, indigenous organizational strength, and the presence of certain shared cognitions . . . and the shifting control response of other groups" (59). I would also include the responses of grassroots people to outrageous acts of pro–status quo personnel.

22. Aliabadis' sudden shift in allegiance to the side of the revolutionary forces, based on villagers' perceptions of the two sides in the conflict, can be compared with political process among the Swat Pathans in the North-West Frontier Province of Pakistan, as studied by Fredrik Barth (1968). Also see Bailey 2001a:91, 92 and 2001b:20–21 and Banfield 1967.

23. Also see the Gerlach and Hine 1981 discussion of the decision to embrace a movement, perhaps brought about by "an experience of excessive police force" (119), as a transformation, "an identity-altering experience" (142).

24. Also see Polletta 1998.

25. Hegland 1983b.

26. See Turner 1978b on "root paradigms in people's heads that become objectivated models for future behavior"(96).

27. Also see Gerlach and Hine 1981:102, 148 and Curry and Goedl 2012:69.

28. Also see Goodwin, Jasper and Polletta (2003) for further discussion of emotions in social movements.

Chapter 5

1. Some of the material in this chapter is drawn from Hegland 1998a. I appreciate the permission of the book editor and press to use it.

2. The report of Special Correspondent (1982:27–28) about another area in southwest Iran indicates that peasants in that area as well were not enthusiastic about the Revolution.

The relatively low level of involvement of poorer peasants in the Iranian Revolution tends to support the conclusions of Wolf (1973:290–91) and Alavi (1971:123, 332–334) that poorer rural groups generally do not have the resources and therefore are usually unable to risk revolutionary involvement.

3. In Pakistan and India, Shia women may practice self-flagellation (Hegland 1998b, 1998c and 2003b), although they are not expected to shed blood. During my visit to Iran during Moharram of 2006, I was surprised to witness Aliabad women practicing rhythmic beating of their chests with their hands during women's mourning rituals (Hegland 2006), which I had not seen during 1978–1979. Presumably, such women's chest-beating was introduced from Pakistan or India. In Iraq, chest-beating was also practiced among women of some Shia communities.

4. Self-flagellation and mourning for Imam Husein are also assumed to bring religious credit and Imam Husein's friendship and therefore his willingness to help the petitioner. See Hegland 1983b. Recently, it seems as if Moharram rituals, gatherings and self-flagellation have shifted to being cultural rituals, to a degree, for some people, somewhat as people of Christian background or even those lacking such a background celebrate Christmas with decorated trees, cocktail parties and gifts, without paying much attention to the religious origin. In fact, some young people in Tehran have begun the practice of "Hussein parties"—rather like street festivals in which they gather in "mod" dress and do "chic mourning," in a parody of the usual religious Moharram rituals (Khosravi 2008:144, 145).

5. For further discussion of the significance of processions and demonstrations for the success of the Iranian Revolution, see Abrahamian 2009 and 2011.

6. See Geertz 1973:3.

7. Dr. Karim Sanjabi, head of the National Front during the 1978–1979 revolutionary period, pushed for democracy after the overthrow of the Shah's government. Eventually, opposed to Ayatollah Khomeini's Islamic Republic, he had to flee Iran.

8. Manoukian (2012:135–139, 147–149) provides information on these leading Shiraz religious families, the Mahallatis and the Dastgheibs.

9. Shia place a prepared stone or small tablet of pressed earth on their prayer rug on which to rest their foreheads during the part of the prayer sequence when they are on their knees and then bow forward to touch their foreheads to the ground.

10. Muslims are supposed to perform five sets of prayers a day. Shia accomplish all five in only three sessions. In addition to these obligatory prayers, or *namaz*, the *hajat*—prayer for the fulfillment of wishes—is optional. It may be performed in times of fear or need, in the late night hours or at other times. Hopefully it will help bring one closer to God. The ablutions necessary before the obligatory prayers are not required for hajat.

11. Mostafa was not a practicing Muslim. He suddenly decided to join in the Tasua procession when he saw the great crowds, not due to any pull from political Islam. Yet, when others prayed, he was also pulled in—another example of Islamic framing added on *after* the decision to participate. Also see Bayat 2007:17–32.

12. Before the 1979 Revolution, some 80,000 Jews lived in Iran, of which about 8,000 were in Shiraz. The Jewish community in Persia is one of the oldest in the diaspora. When Kurosh (Cyrus) the Great of Persia conquered Babylon in 539 BCE, he freed the Jewish cap-

tives and allowed them to return home if they wished, but some chose to stay. They became scattered in various areas of present-day Iraq and Iran. Since the Iranian Revolution, many more Jews have left. Now perhaps 25,000 remain in Iran, the second largest number in the Middle East after Israel. Some 300,000 to 350,000 people with Iranian Jewish ancestry live in Israel mainly but also in the United States. See "The Jews of Iran," Jewish Virtual Library, a Division of the American-Israel Cooperative Enterprise, http://www.jewishvirtuallibrary .org/jsource/anti-semitism/iranjews.html, site visited March 20, 2012.

13. I am grateful to Eric Hooglund for passing on this incident.

14. Some of the material in this section was previously printed in Hegland 1998a:211–225. I am grateful to the editor and press for allowing me to use it.

15. My father was a Lutheran pastor and my mother the daughter, granddaughter and great granddaughter of Lutheran pastors. My upbringing makes it difficult for me to lie, so I didn't follow their advice.

16. Gerlach and Hine 1979:102.

17. When Kurosh's father was killed in the fight over water with Darab, his brother married the widow, a common practice. That way, she could stay in the family and keep her son. If a widow married a man outside her first husband's family, she would have to leave her children with her first husband's family.

18. Of course wealthy American businessmen and corporate leaders may contribute generously to both political parties as well.

19. This had also happened during the Tudeh/National Front/Mosaddeq era.

20. In Mohammad Amini's account of his participation in the June 5, 1978 confrontation with police at his teachers' training college, it is interesting to note, the Aliabad policemen protected him, as expected of connections during taifeh-keshi.

21. There were two boxes out in the open at polling stations, one marked yes and the other no. The vote was 98.2% in favor of an Islamic Republic, according to government sources. The referendum on the Constitution of the Islamic Republic was held on December 2 and 3, 1979, again with only a yes-or-no option.

22. Hegland 1983c, 1986b.

23. Wearing hejab is religiously required according to many Muslims and varies according to period, place and source of the requirement.

24. Also see Khosravi 2008, P. Mahdavi 2009 and Moaveni 2005 and 2009.

25. See Hegland 1983a and 1998a.

26. Compare with the work of sociologist Asef Bayat (2007), who believes that "protest or insurrectionary movements, as occurred in Iran in 1978, aim solely to negate the existing order" (22). He contrasts insurrectionary movements, which do not have a long life-span but, as in Iran, are "aimed at capturing state power," with social movements, which "function over a longer time span, during which people can ask questions, debate key issues, and clarify the movement's aims" (21). Also see Katouzian (2003), who sees the 1979 Iranian Revolution as resistance against "arbitrary rule," "every bit like traditional Iranian revolts against unjust rulers" (25, 26). Also see Moore (1978): "Essentially [the traditionalist form of criticism] accepts the existence of hierarchy and authority while attempting to make it conform to an idealized pattern of how it should behave" (510). Also, in Gluckman's (1959)

differentiation between revolution and rebellion, the stance of most villagers toward the Iranian Revolution can be judged to be rebellious: "A revolution aims to alter the nature of political offices and of the social structure in which they function, and not merely to change the incumbents in persisting offices" (28). Also see Gluckman 2004a and 2004b. All four authors point to two kinds of political criticism and uprising, one aiming at a deep transformation in political systems, the other at overthrowing the personnel, if they do not live up to expectations, while holding on to the same system of authority and hierarchy. For the majority of Aliabadis, participation in the Iranian Revolution was of the latter type.

27. Compare with Moore 1978: "In many different times and places popular criticism of authority has been to the effect that authority has not lived up to its obligation to take care of its subjects, that it has oppressed and plundered where it should have cherished and protected. . . . Anger at the failure of authority to live up to its obligations, to keep its word and faith with the subjects, can be among the most potent of human emotions and topple thrones" (509, 510). Also see Bayat 2007, who refers to "a sense of injustice in many sectors of Iranian society" (22), and Katouzian 2003:26.

28. As such, the Aliabad taifeh-keshi processual paradigm fits into Clifford Geertz's well-know formulation of cultural patterns as "models"—as "theory or chart" which is both "a model *of* reality" and "a model *for* reality" (Geertz 1973:7).

Chapter 6

1. When the police and armed forces lost control during the revolutionary period, semiautonomous armed groups developed at different levels to police neighborhoods and perform other functions related to maintaining control. They became powerful after the Revolution, and people grew to fear them.

2. Ali was the first Imam of the Muslim community, the successor to the Prophet Mohammad, in the Shia view, and his son-in-law and blood relative.

3. S. Cronin 2010a:264. Also see Paul 1982:22 and Bakhash 1985:197–201. Farazmand (1989) talks about peasants "in several hundreds of villages" expropriating the land of absentee landlords (207, 208).

4. One of the five pillars of Islam is to give alms. Ideally people should give a fifth of their income, so *khoms*—five in Arabic—is used to refer to this obligation. Giving alms to seyyids, people believed, brought religious blessing. Some people, however, spoke in derogatory fashion about seyyids who take advantage of this belief to enjoy an easy income from other people's work.

5. In this case, the father-in-law of the groom had lower political status and was dependent upon the father, relatives and other political allies of the son-in-law. In spite of the cultural imperative to obey a father-in-law, when the son-in-law and his family were in a more powerful political and economic situation, it was the father-in-law who was more beholden to them and under pressure to follow their wishes.

Chapter 7

1. Although elsewhere people usually want to keep plastic surgery to themselves, in Iran, rhinoplasty has become so popular and such a sign of status that those who have gone

under the knife—and even some who have not—are happy to display the telltale bandage on the nose. They consider small Western noses to be more beautiful.

2. See "The Latest Invasion: Iranians See Burgeoning Trade with China as a Mixed Blessing," *Economist*, August 18, 2012. The cheap goods from China that are flooding the market have hurt Iranian businesses, such as tailor shops and shoemakers. People have lost their jobs, and businesses have gone bankrupt.

3. Personal communication from Erika Friedl, November 26, 2012. Historian Nikki Keddie (1981:183 and 2006:170) points to the separation of Iranians into two cultures, "different cultures for the elite and the masses," which developed during the era of the two Pahlavi Shahs (1925–1979). Because most people in Aliabad had become quite well-off by 2003—and I have interacted very little with the less well-off people who have moved into Aliabad since 1979—the two cultures are not so obvious to me from personal observation.

4. Since 1979, when the American Embassy was taken over and American hostages were held by radical students, the United States has been imposing sanctions on Iran. After Iraq invaded Iran in 1980, sanctions on Iran increased, prohibiting weapons from going to Iran or any other assistance from being given. The United States cannot import any goods or services from Iran since President Reagan instituted that measure in 1987. Since 2006, the United States, with the assistance of the UN Security Council, has been putting more sanctions in place, to discourage Iran from developing its nuclear program. The European Union has joined in, banning the import of crude oil from Iran and freezing the assets of the Iranian bank in the European Union.

5. See "Iran-Iraq War (1980–1988)," GobalSecurity.org, http://www.globalsecurity.org/military/world/war/Iran-Iran.htm, November 7, 2011, site visited March 30, 2012.

6. The chemical attack on Halabja, a city of about 80,000, then in the hands of Kurdish and Iranian troops, killed some 3,000 to 5,000 people, most of them civilians, injured 7,000 to 10,000 and eventually killed many more thousands from disease, complications, miscarriages and birth defects. Some 75% of victims were women and children, reports indicated. The attack started with rockets and napalm for two days and then continued with a five-hour chemical weapons bombardment. A variety of chemicals were used, with mustard gas predominating. Materials for production of chemical weapons in Iraq came from firms in Germany and other countries. (See "Thousands Die in Halabja Gas Attack," BBC, March 16, 1988, site visited March 30, 2012.) The Iraqi army was then able to retake Halabja from Kurdish and Iranian troops. They razed the town with explosives and bulldozers. The US government, allied with Saddam Hussein in his war against Iran, stated that the devastated town strewn with bodies that was shown in a video broadcast could not be attributed to Iraqi action, and officially charged Iran with responsibility. The Halabja massacre was condemned by the Canadian Parliament as a crime against humanity and on March 1, 2010, was declared by the Iraqi High Criminal Court to be genocide. The Saddam Hussein regime carried out a program of genocide called the Anfal Campaign against the Kurds and other minorities in Northern Iraq between 1986 and 1989 to stamp out Kurdish insurgence and autonomy efforts. The Anfal Campaign included concentration camps and mass executions. It destroyed some 4,000 Kurdish villages out of a total of about 4,500, killed some 1,100,000 to 2,150,000 people, exposed some 250 villages and

282 Notes to Chapter 7

towns to chemical weapons and displaced close to a third of the estimated 3.5 million Iraqi Kurdish population. See Black 1993. In 2005 a court in the Hague ruled this campaign to be genocide. See "Killing of Iraq Kurds 'Genocide,'" *BBC News*, December 23, 2005, http://news.bbc.co.uk/2/hi/europe/4555000.stm, site visited March 29, 2012.

7. The US warship the USS Vincennes, equipped with all of the most advanced electronic and radar gear "of the Navy's surface arsenal," shot two heat-seeking missiles at the A300 Airbus, made in Europe, that was Iran Air Flight 655 on its regular time and course from Bandar Abbas on the coast of southwestern Iran to Dubai. It was claimed that the warship crew thought the airbus was an Iranian F14 fighter trying to attack the two US warships. See "Navy Missile Downs Iranian Jetliner," by George C. Wilson, *Washington Post*, Monday, July 4, 1988, p. A01.

8. For a treatment of relations between Iran and the United States by an anthropologist, see Beeman 2008.

9. The government executed some 10,000 oppositional people in 1988 alone, after the end of the Iran-Iraq War.

10. See Bayat 2013. (Green had been Mousavi's campaign color.)

11. Some particularly enlightening ones are Ervand Abrahamian's *Iran Between Two Revolutions (1983)*, *Tortured Confessions: Prisons and Public Recantations in Modern Iran* (1999), *A History of Modern Iran* (2008) and *The Coup: 1953, the CIA, and the Roots of Modern U.S.-Iranian Relations* (2013); Janet Afary's *Sexual Politics in Modern Iran* (2009); Asef Bayat's *Street Politics: Poor People's Movements in Iran* (1997), *Making Islam Democratic: Social Movements and the Post-Islamist Turn* (2007) and *Life as Politics: How Ordinary People Change the Middle East* (2010); William Beeman's *The 'Great Satan' vs. the 'Mad Mullahs': How the United States and Iran Demonize Each Other* (2008); Erika Friedl's *Women of Deh Koh: Lives in an Iranian Village* (1991), *Children of Deh Koh: Young Lives in an Iranian Village* (1997) and *Sparrow's Song: Everyday Culture and Cosmology in Folktales of Tribal Iran* (2013); Mark Gasiorowski and Malcolm Byrne's *Mohammad Mosaddeq and the 1953 Coup in Iran* (2004); Ali Gheissari's *Iranian Intellectuals in the 20th Century* (1998) and *Contemporary Iran: Economy, Society, Politics* (2009); Ali Gheissari and Vali Nasr's *Democracy in Iran: History and the Quest for Liberty* (2009); Homa Katouzian's *The Political Economy of Modern Iran: Despotism and Pseudo-Modernism, 1926–1979* (1981), *Mosaddiq and the Struggle for Power in Iran* (1999) and *Iranian History and Politics: The Dialectic of State and Society* (2003); Nikki Keddie's *Modern Iran: Roots and Results of Revolution* (2003); Arang Keshavarzian's *Bazaar and State in Iran: The Politics of the Tehran Marketplace* (2009); Shahram Khosravi's *Young and Defiant in Tehran* (2008); Stephen Kinzer's *All the Shah's Men: An American Coup and the Roots of Middle East Terror* (2008); Agnes Loeffler's *Health and Medical Practice in Iran: Traditional Culture and Modern Medicine* (2013); Reinhold Loeffler's *Islam in Practice: Religious Beliefs in a Persian Village* (1988); Pardis Mahdavi's *Passionate Uprisings: Iran's Sexual Revolution* (2009); Farzaneh Milani's *Veils and Words: The Emerging Voices of Iranian Women Writers* (1992) and *Words Not Swords: Iranian Women Writers and the Freedom of Movement* (2011); Azadeh Moaveni's *Lipstick Jihad: A Memoir of Growing Up Iranian in America and American in Iran* (2005) and *Honeymoon in Tehran: Two Years of Love and Danger in Iran* (2010); Haideh Moghissi's *Populism and Feminism in Iran: Women's*

Struggle in a Male-Defined Revolutionary Movement (1997)and *Feminism and Islamic Fundamentalism: The Limits of Postmodern Analysis* (1999); Amy Motlagh's *Burying the Beloved: Marriage, Realism, and Reform in Modern Iran* (2011); Afsaneh Najmabadi's *Women with Mustaches and Men Without Beards: Gender and Sexual Anxieties of Iranian Modernity* (1995); Arzoo Osanloo's *The Politics of Women's Rights in Iran* (2009); Marjane Satrapi's *Persepolis: The Story of a Childhood* (2004) and *Persepolis 2: The Story of a Return* (2005) and Shahla Talebi's *Ghosts of Revolution: Rekindled Memories of Imprisonment in Iran* (2011).

12. By Aliabad people I mean the people from Aliabad who lived in the village in 1978–1979, as well as their relatives who had moved to Shiraz. Because of my limited time in Aliabad during visits in the 21st century, I have not been able to work with the many people who moved there since 1979. Although friendly to newcomers who rent rooms from them, work for them or are their neighbors, Aliabad people class them as outsiders and have little else to do with them.

13. Parts of this chapter were previously published in Hegland 2011. I am grateful to the editor for permission to use them.

14. Interestingly, in 2008, when I took caution to keep from others the Aliabad origins of my friends, my friends told me no, it is alright. Now Aliabadis had the reputation of being wealthy, due to the escalating prices of their land and the fame of the Garden City residential area, so Aliabad origins enhanced rather than detracted from status.

15. Also see Friedl 1997.

16. Some Aliabadis say the government does not try that hard to lower addiction rates, hoping that use of opium and other drugs will keep people from political dissent. Some say similar things about conspicuous consumption, competitive materialism and use of alcohol.

17. See Shahrokni and Dokouhaki 2012.

18. Also see Hegland 2009.

19. Other research has also uncovered more egalitarian relations among young educated Iranian females in contemporary marriages. See, for example, Kurzman 2008.

20. In August 2012, though, the Iranian government announced it had dropped its extremely successful population control program. (The rural birth rate had made an astounding drop from 8.1 to 2.1 births per woman in just one generation.) Much of this was due to rising standards of living and rising expectations for children, with the need therefore to provide more opportunities for them and spend more time, money and effort on them. The desire to make progress and to appear modern was perhaps just as important as, if not more important than, the government ads, birth control education and provision of birth control methods. (Also see Loeffler and Friedl 2009.) Now concerned that the Iranian population is rapidly aging, the government is trying to encourage people to have more children. See Farzaneh Roudi, "Iran Reverses Family Planning, Calls for More Children," *Iran Primer,* United States Institute of Peace, August 29, 2012, http://iranprimer.usip.org/blog/2012/aug/29/iran-reverses-family-planning-calls-more-children-0.

21. Also see Friedl 2009.

22. Casual sexual relations—as described by Bayat 2010, Khosravi 2008, Pardis Mahdavi 2009, Moaveni 2010 and Sadeghi 2010 for Tehran—did not occur in Aliabad by 2008.

23. Also see Friedl 2002.

24. Also see Friedl 2009.

25. In 1978–1979, young male relatives of the couple to be married decorated a room in the groom's father's home, covering walls with cloth, to turn it into the *hejleh*. Consummation of the marriage took place here. The bride sat in this room for several days receiving congratulating guests. The hejleh usually became the room assigned to the bride and groom in his father's courtyard. In 2003, I saw only one or two *hejleh* in a groom's parents' home, still decorated several months after the wedding, now with more extravagant and commercial decorations, including strings of lights, bedroom furniture, satin bed covers, heart-shaped pillows, and handmade paper wall decorations. Now wedding couples most often go to their own home even for the first night of marriage.

26. In the last few decades, homes for the elderly, previously unheard of, have been coming into existence in Iran. As women work outside the home, middle-class homes no longer have servants, people live longer, wives resist pressures to care for their husbands' mothers, the nuclear family has become more significant and life is more modern, caring for elderly parents has become a problem. Although more common in Tehran, several government and private elderly care establishments had opened in Shiraz by 2008. No Aliabad elderly had been placed in Shiraz nursing homes by then. Even if children had wanted to do this, social pressure would not have allowed it. Some elderly women living in their own home or a son's courtyard could have benefitted from better care. See Hegland with Sarraf and Shahbazi 2008.

27. Because of the typically large age gap between bride and groom in Aliabad—and in Iran in general—in earlier years, husbands often preceded their wives in death by quite a few years.

28. In Iran, instead of Saturday and Sunday, Friday is the typical day off.

29. Hegland with Sarraf and Shahbazi 2008.

30. Also see Antoun 1965, Ammar 1966, Arensberg 1968, Cohen 1972, Hinderink and Kiray 1970, Magnarella 1974, Peters 1963, Rosenfeld 1968 and Stirling 1976, where independent sources of a living allowed young people more freedom from control of the older generation.

31. For analysis of decline in hierarchy and development of relationships based more on "friendship and equality" within the family in another southwestern Iranian village, see Friedl 2009.

32. When I was last in Aliabad, in summer 2008, a new council was functioning under the new *shahrak* organization, after two four-year terms with other elected members. I do not know the issues this new council membership addressed or what people say about them.

33. Elsewhere in Iran, many indications demonstrate decline in hierarchical political relations and growth of more democratic political attitudes. For example, in her study of Iranian youth, Fatemeh Sadeghi (2008) found younger Iranians to be more democratic than older Iranians.

34. In addition to buying and selling land, some of the men in the real estate offices were in the illegal opium business.

35. In fact, among the Fars Province Mamasani Lurs, anthropologist Soheila Shahshahani (2012) found that in more rural areas people were still turning to relatives for assistance and even fighting among various kinship-based groups during parliamentary

elections, hoping to get in a representative who would favor their own faction. They also used taifeh terminology.

36. As I do not know Luri, I didn't realize this was the local language elderly people spoke in 1978–1979 until Friedl informed me.

37. See Beeman 1976, 1977 and 1986 for more discussion of such issues.

38. Many of these gatherings, I realize, were for my sake—and I appreciated them very much. After one large dinner of an extended family held at the old parental home in Aliabad, I told one of the family how delighted I was to be able to be there with all of them. That had been the first time they had all been together for years, she told me; there had been disagreements that had pulled the relatives apart.

39. I am indebted to Erika Friedl and Patricia Higgins for urging me not to leave out contradictions and divisions in Aliabad and Iranian society in general.

40. Other researchers have also pointed to the connections between economic dependence and political control on the one hand and economic independence and more freedom of political action on the other. Compare Alavi 1971, 1973a and 1973b to Hill 1972, for example.

41. Others have documented factional conflict similar to taifeh-keshi elsewhere in the Middle East, usually among kinship-based groups. See, for example, Fredrik Barth (1968) on the Swat Pathan, Charles Lindholm (1982) also on the Pathan and, in Iran, Reinhold Loeffler (1978), Black (1972) Black-Michaud (1986) and Sue Wright (1986) on Lurs. The publications of these anthropologists have not, however, included books on transformations in local economic, kinship, political and cultural systems as people adapt to modernization, a changing national economy and politics.

My initial study took place after the oil boom and government policy had significantly changed the political economy in Aliabad. Because the Revolution occurred while I was there, I could observe the resurgence of taifeh-keshi during the revolutionary chaos. When I returned after 24 years, when agricultural land had been transformed into real estate and men had urban jobs, I could see that modernization and outside economic and political changes had again brought about a decline in the taifeh-keshi system.

Much of the change, spanning both the Pahlavi and the Islamic Republic eras, is due to Iranian oil export revenues that have allowed the government to develop armed forces, police, gendarmerie and secret police to control even rural areas, and enabled men to make a living outside Aliabad and get involved in consumerism for themselves and their own nuclear families. In other places where patterns of factional struggle similar to taifeh-keshi have been studied, such as among the Pathan in Pakistan and Afghanistan, an oil boom economy has not developed. Central government weakness, political instability and insecure access to land have continued, and with them, the need for local groups to manage their own protection and access to resources.

In a Kohistani area of northern Pakistan, when building roads enabled sale of lumber and crops to the outside and then purchase of arms, death vengeance in factional conflict increased radically, Lincoln Keiser (1991) found. Of course in Afghanistan the decades of war and insecurity have exacerbated tribal factional conflict all the more, and the influx of money and arms from outside powers has made factional conflict more deadly.

42. This is not to say that previously people had not worked for their own interests and had not strategized and negotiated toward their own aims. Of course people had wielded what Scott (1987 and 1992) refers to as "weapons of the weak." However, their forms of resistance and spheres of actions had been more constricted. See Friedl 1991 for ethnographic short stories of how illiterate women in a Luri village cleverly strategized and wielded aspects of their culture, within highly restrictive parameters, to work toward their goals.

43. Also see Friedl 2002 and 2009 and the books by Bayat, Mahdavi, Moaveni and Khosravi listed in the Bibliography for examples from gender, family and generational arenas. In general, one can expect transformations in relationships in all arenas of life during periods of change, with some conflict between those who previously held the advantage and those pushing for change. When I ran into some comments by Virginia Woolf (1882–1941), I was struck with the parallels to what has been happening in Aliabad—and in Iran in general: "in or about December 1910 human character changed. . . . All human relations have shifted—those between masters and servants, husbands and wives, parents and children. And when human relations change there is at the same time a change in religion, conduct, politics, and literature." See Woolf 1924. In recent American history, the movements and transformations in relationships of the 1960s and 1970s provide other examples.

44. Although political systems in the Qavams' many other villages quite possibly may have been similar to the one in Aliabad, one can't of course automatically generalize findings from one village to other Iranian villages. In Loeffler's village research site in the Luri area of Boir Ahmad, for example, instead of another person like Seyyid Ibn Ali Askari going after his own interests regardless of harm to others, a very enlightened "representative mediator" struggled to improve conditions for villagers. Luri villagers were able to fight off the acquisitive Boir Ahmad chiefs. The village now has many more educated people and a much better political economy than Aliabad. See Loeffler 1971 and 2011.

45. As Katouzian (2003: 31) comments, revolts against the national "arbitrary rule" in Persia and Iran erupted "when it was deemed not to be 'just', or, more often, to be too 'unjust'" (31).

46. Of course usually it does not come about without effort. Generally, those in the formerly dominant positions do not wish to give up their authority. See Friedl 2002 and 2009 for examples of how wives and offspring in a Luri tribal village struggled for more egalitarian relationships, bringing strife into the family.

47. Also see Arlacchi 1983, Banfield 1967, Bayat 2007, Bodemann 1982, Gluckman 1959, Katouzian 2003 and Moore 1978 for other examples of this type of political system.

48. Of course some may have voted for Mousavi, the candidate thought to be more of a reformist, with the mind-set—to one degree or another—of getting rid of one ruler and substituting another, hopefully more responsive one, without much thought about a different system of government and distribution of authority. (Although Mousavi is thought of as a reformist these days, he was prime minister between 1981 and 1989, when many thousands of people were executed.)

49. Iranian women do not take their husband's last name upon marriage.

50. As a US citizen, I also am distressed by attempts in the United States to prevent people from voting or their votes from counting, such as during the 2004 and 2012 presidential elections.

51. The controversial sanctions against Iran, led by the United States and fueled by Israeli attitudes, are aimed at discouraging Iran from developing its nuclear capacity to the extent that it might be able to make nuclear weapons. Israel is the only country in the Middle East that has nuclear weapons. In 2011, the United States imposed even stricter sanctions against Iran's petroleum industry, preventing any efforts to help enhance petroleum resources, even with insurance, financing, brokering and shipping. According to some reports, the tightening of sanctions on Iran during the these past years has had a "devastating" effect. With the European Union embargo on oil, Iranian exports dropped 50%. See Adrian Blomfield, "Iran Sanctions 'Having Devastating Effect,'" *Telegraph*, September 27, 2012. A November 2012 report indicated Iran is losing some $100 million a day in oil revenues, due to the sanctions. See David Blair, "Sanctions Costing Iran $100 Million Every Day," *Telegraph*, November 13, 2012. Although hitting all sectors, the sanctions are especially detrimental for the ill, who cannot get the drugs and medical supplies they need because of the ban on financial transactions with the outside and transportation problems due to lack of parts. See Najmeh Bozormehr, "In Iran, Sanctions Take Toll on the Sick," *Washington Post*, September 4, 2012, and Thomas Erdbrink, "Iran Sanctions Take Unexpected Toll on Medical Imports," *New York Times*, November 2, 2012. Because of inability to get replacement parts, airliners are not safe and a number have crashed, causing quite a number of civilian deaths. The sanctions are seriously interfering with humanitarian work in Iran and are significantly detrimental for the general population because of their effects on the economy and the shortages of necessities, such as medicine, Ban Ki-moon, UN Secretary-General, told the UN. See Saeed Kamali Dehghan, "Iran Sanctions 'Putting Millions of Lives at Risk,'" *Guardian*, October 17, 2012. I know my friends in Aliabad are badly affected by the sanctions in many ways. For example, a man studying in Turkey who is married to a young woman from Aliabad cannot afford an apartment for his family in Turkey because of the troubled Iranian economy. The family is separated; the man's wife and baby have had to stay behind in Iran. Due to rising unemployment and business failures—because people don't have as much money for purchases—other Aliabadis are now facing severe financial problems. Since December 2012, the US Congress has been working to pass legislation for even more severe sanctions on Iran.

52. See Alfoneh 2008.

Bibliography

Abrahamian, Ervand. 1982. "Shari'ati and the Iranian Revolution." *MERIP Reports* no. 87, pp. 24–30.

———. 1983. *Iran Between Two Revolutions.* Princeton, NJ: Princeton University Press.

———. 1989. *The Iranian Mojahedin.* New Haven, CT: Yale University Press.

———. 1999. *Tortured Confessions: Prisons and Public Recantations in Modern Iran.* Berkeley: University of California Press.

———. 2008. *A History of Modern Iran.* Cambridge, UK: Cambridge University Press.

———. 2009. "The Crowd in the Iranian Revolution." *The Iranian Revolution Turns Thirty, a Special Issue of Radical History Review* 105:13–38.

———. 2011. "Mass Protests in the Iranian Revolution, 1977–1979." In A. Roberts and T. Ash (eds.), *Civil Resistance and Power Politics: The Experience of Non-violent Action from Gandhi to the Present.* London: Oxford University Press.

———. 2013. *The Coup: 1953, the CIA, and the Roots of Modern U.S.-Iranian Relations.* New York: New Press.

Abu-Lughod, Lila. 1985. "A Community of Secrets: The Separate World of Bedouin Women." *Signs* 10:637–657.

Abu-Zahra, Nadia. 1974. "Material Power, Honour, Friendship, and the Etiquette of Visiting." *Anthropological Quarterly* 47:120–132.

Afary, Janet. 2009. *Sexual Politics in Modern Iran.* Cambridge, UK: Cambridge University Press.

Ahmed, Akbar. 1976. *Millennium and Charisma among Pathans: A Critical Essay in Social Anthropology.* London: Routledge and Kegan Paul.

Ajami, Amir. 1993. "The Boneh System in Iran's Rural Society." *Iran Nameh* VIII.

———. 2005. "From Peasant to Farmer: A Study of Agrarian Transformation in an Iranian Village, 1967–2002." *International Journal Of Middle East Studies* 37:327–349.

Alavi, Hamzeh. 1971. "The Politics of Dependence: A Village in West Punjab." *South Asian Review* 4:111–128.

———. 1973a. "Peasants and Revolution." In K. Gough and H. Sharma (eds.), *Imperialism and Revolt in South Asia.* New York: Monthly Review Press.

———. 1973b. "Peasant Classes and Primordial Loyalties." *Journal of Peasant Studies* 1:23–61.

Alberts, Robert. 1963. "Social Structure and Cultural Change in an Iranian Village." Ph.D. dissertation, University of Wisconsin.

Alfoneh, Ali. 2008. "The Revolutionary Guards' Role in Iranian Politics." *Middle East Quarterly* 15(4):3–14.

Amanollahi, Sekardar. 1985. "The Lurs of Iran." *Cultural Survival Quarterly* 9(1):65–69.

Antoun, Richard. 1965. "Conservatism and Change in the Village Community: A Jordanian Case Study." *Human Organization* 24:4–16.

———. 1976. "The Gentry of a Traditional Peasant Community Undergoing Rapid Technological Change: An Iranian Case Study." *Iranian Studies* 9:7–21.

———. 1979. *Low-Key Politics: Local-Level Leadership and Change in the Middle East.* Albany: State University of New York Press.

———. 1981. "The Complexity of the Lowest Stratum: Sharecroppers and Rural Wage-Laborers in an Iranian Village." *Iranian Studies* 14:215–246.

Ammar, Hamid. 1966. *Growing Up in an Egyptian Village: Silwa, Province of Aswan.* New York: Octagon.

Arensberg, Conrad. 1968. *The Irish Countryman.* New York: Doubleday.

Arlacchi, Pino. 1983. *Mafia, Peasants and Great Estates.* Cambridge, UK: Cambridge University Press.

Asad, Talal. 1972. "Market Model, Class Structure and Consent: A Reconsideration of Swat Political Organisation." *Man* 7:74–94.

Ashraf, Ahmad, and Marsha Safai. 1977. *The Role of Rural Organizations in Rural Development: The Case of Iran.* Tehran: Bureau of Research and Planning.

Aswad, Barbara C. 1967. "Key and Peripheral Roles of Noble Women in a Middle Eastern Plains Village." *Anthropological Quarterly* 40:139–152.

———. 1974. "Visiting Patterns among Women of the Elite in a Small Turkish City." *Anthropological Quarterly* 47:9–27.

Atabaki, Touraj. 1993. *Azerbaijan: Ethnicity and Autonomy in Twentieth-Century Iran.* London: I.B. Tauris.

Bailey, F. 1970. *Politics and Social Change: Orissa in 1955.* Berkeley: University of California Press.

———. 2001a. *Stratagems and Spoils: A Social Anthropology of Politics.* Boulder, CO: Westview Press.

———. 2001b. *Treasons, Stratagems, and Spoils: How Leaders Make Practical Use of Beliefs and Values.* Boulder, CO: Westview Press.

Bakhash, Shawl. 1985. *The Reign of the Ayatollahs: Iran and the Islamic Revolution.* London: I.B. Tauris.

Banfield, Edward. 1967. *The Moral Basis of a Backward Society.* New York: Free Press.

Barth, Fredrik. 1961. *Nomads of South Persia: The Basseri Tribe of the Khamseh Confederacy.* Prospect Heights, IL: Waveland Press.

———. 1968. *Political Leadership among Swat Pathans*. London: Athlone Press.

Bayat, Asef. 1997. *Street Politics: Poor People's Movements in Iran*. New York: Columbia University Press.

———. 2007. *Making Islam Democratic: Social Movements and the Post-Islamist Turn*. Stanford, CA: Stanford University Press.

———. 2013. *Life as Politics: How Ordinary People Change the Middle East*. Stanford, CA: Stanford University Press.

Beeman, William. 1976. "Status, Style and Strategy in Iranian Interaction." *Anthropological Linguistics* 18:305–322.

———. 1977. "The Hows and Whys of Persian Style: A Pragmatic Approach." In R. Fasold and R. Shuy (eds.), *Studies in Language Variation*. Washington, DC: Georgetown University Press.

———. 1986. *Language, Status, and Power in Iran*. Bloomington: Indiana University Press.

———. 2008. *The "Great Satan" vs. the "Mad Mullahs": How the United States and Iran Demonize Each Other*. Chicago: University of Chicago Press.

Beeman, William, and Amit Bhattacharyya. 1978. "Toward an Assessment of the Social Role of Rural Midwives and Its Implication for the Family Planning Program: An Iranian Case Study. *Human Organization* 37(3):295–300.

Behnam, Djamchid. 1971. "Nuclear Families and Kinship Groups in Iran." *Diogenes* 76:115–131.

Behrangi, Samad. 1987. *The Little Black Fish and Other Modern Persian Stories*. Trans. M. Hegland and E. Hooglund. Boulder, CO: Lynne Rienner.

Betteridge, Anne. 1985. "Gift Exchange in Iran: The Locus of Self-Identity in Social Interaction." *Anthropological Quarterly* 58(4):190–202.

———. 1992. "Specialists in Miraculous Action: Some Shrines in Shiraz." In A. Morinis (ed.), *Sacred Journeys: The Anthropology of Pilgrimage*. Westport, CT: Greenwood Press.

———. 2000. "The Controversial Vows of Urban Muslim Women in Iran." In N. Falk and R. Cross (eds.), *Unspoken Worlds: Women's Religious Lives in Non-Western Cultures*. Independence, KY: Cengage.

Bill, James. 1989. *The Eagle and the Lion: The Tragedy of American-Iranian Relations*. New Haven, CT: Yale University Press.

Black, George, 1993. *Genocide in Iraq: The Anfal Campaign Against the Kurds*. New York: Human Rights Watch.

Black, Jacob. 1972. "Tyranny as a Strategy for Survival in an 'Egalitarian' Society: Luri Facts Versus an Anthropological Mystique." *Man* 7:614–634.

Black-Michaud, Jacob. 1986. *Sheep and Land: The Economics of Power in a Tribal Society*. Cambridge, UK: Cambridge University Press.

Bodemann, Michal. 1982. "Class Rule as Patronage: Kinship, Local Ruling Cliques and the State in Rural Sardinia." *Journal of Peasant Studies* 9(2):147–175.

Bourdieu, Pierre. 1992. *Outline of a Theory of Practice*. Cambridge, UK: Cambridge University Press.

Bradburd, Daniel. 1983. "National Conditions and Local-Level Political Structures: Patronage in Prerevolutionary Iran." *American Ethnologist* 10(1):23–40.

————. 1994. "Historical Bases of the Political Economy of Kermani Pastoralists: Tribe and World Markets in the Nineteenth and Early Twentieth Centuries." In C. Chang and H. Foster (eds.), *Pastoralists at the Periphery: Herders in a Capitalist World.* Tucson: University of Arizona Press.

Cohen, Abner. 1972. *Arab Border-Villages in Israel: A Study of Continuity and Change in Social Organization.* Manchester, UK: Manchester University Press.

————. 1976. *Two-Dimensional Man: An Essay on the Anthropology of Power and Symbolism in Complex Society.* Berkeley: University of California Press.

————. 1981. *The Politics of Elite Culture: Explorations in the Dramaturgy of Power in a Modern African Society.* Berkeley: University of California Press.

————. 2003. *Custom and Politics in Urban Africa: A Study of Hausa Migrants in Yoruba Towns.* Berkeley: University of California Press.

Corr, Philip, and Gerald Matthews. 2009. *The Cambridge Handbook of Personality Psychology.* Cambridge, UK: Cambridge University Press.

Cottam, Richard 1979. *Nationalism in Iran: Updated Through 1978.* Pittsburgh, PA: University of Pittsburgh Press.

————. 2006. *Iran and the United States: A Cold War Case Study.* Pittsburgh, PA: University of Pittsburgh Press.

Cronin, Constance. 1970. *The Sting of Change: Sicilians in Sicily and Australia.* Chicago: University of Chicago Press.

————. 1981. "The Effect of Development on the Urban Family." In M. Bonine and N. Keddie (eds.), *Modern Iran: The Dialectics of Continuity and Change.* Albany: State University of New York Press.

Cronin, Stephanie. 2007. *Tribal Politics in Iran: Rural Conflict and the New State, 1921–1941.* New York: Routledge.

————. 2010a. *Soldiers, Shahs and Subalterns in Iran: Opposition, Protest and Revolt, 1921–1941.* New York: Palgrave Macmillan.

————. 2010b. "Popular Politics, the New State and the Birth of the Iranian Working Class: The 1929 Abadan Oil Refinery Strike." *Middle Eastern Studies* 46:699–732.

Curry, Jane, and Doris Goedl. 2012. *"Together We Are Strong": Stories of People in the People's Revolutions: Serbia, 2000; Georgia, 2003 and Ukraine, 2004."* Unpublished manuscript.

Daneshvar, Simin. 1991. *A Persian Requiem.* Trans. Roxane Zand. London: Peter Halban.

Davis, Gerald, Doug McAdam, Richard Scott, and Mayer Zald (eds.). 2005. *Social Movements and Organizations.* New York: Cambridge University Press.

de Bellaigue, Christopher. 2013. *Patriot of Persia: Muhammad Mossadegh and a Tragic Anglo-American Coup.* New York: Harper Perennial.

de Certeau, Michel. 1988. *The Practice of Everyday Life.* Berkeley: University of California Press.

di Leonardo, Micaela. 1987. "The Female World of Cards and Holidays: Women, Families, and the Work of Kinship." *Signs* 12(3):444–453.

Diani, Mario, and Doug McAdam (eds.). 2003. *Social Movements and Networks: Relational Approaches to Collective Action.* Oxford, UK: Oxford University Press.

Elm, Mostafa. 1992. *Oil, Power, and Principle: Iran's Oil Nationalization and Its Aftermath.* Syracuse, NY: Syracuse University Press.

Evans-Pritchard, E. 1949. *The Sanusi of Cyrenaica.* Oxford: Clarendon Press.

———. 1969. *The Nuer: A Description of the Modes of Livelihood and Political Institutions of a Nilotic People.* London: Oxford University Press.

Fakhouri, Hani. 1972. *Kafr el-Elow: An Egyptian Village in Transition.* New York: Holt, Rinehart and Winston.

Farazmand, Ali. 1989. *The State, Bureaucracy, and Revolution in Modern Iran: Agrarian Reforms and Regime Politics.* New York: Praeger.

Fischer, Michael. 2003. *From Religious Dispute to Revolution.* Madison: University of Wisconsin Press.

Friedl, Erika. 1981. "Division of Labor in an Iranian Village." *MERIP Reports* no. 55:12–18, 31.

———. 1991. *Women of Deh Koh: Lives in an Iranian Village.* New York: Penguin Books.

———. 1997. *Children of Deh Koh: Young Life in an Iranian Village.* Syracuse, NY: Syracuse University Press.

———. 2002. "A Thorny State of Marriage in Iran." In D. Bowen and E. Early (eds.), *Everyday Life in the Muslim Middle East,* 2nd ed. Bloomington: Indiana University Press.

———. (2009). "New Friends: Gender Relations within the Family." *Iranian Studies* 42(1):27–43.

———. 2013. *Sparrow's Song: Everyday Culture and Cosmology in Folktales of Tribal Iran.* London: I.B. Tauris.

Gasiorowski, Mark. 1991. *U.S. Foreign Policy and the Shah: Building a Client State in Iran.* Ithaca, NY: Cornel University Press.

Gasiorowski, Mark, and Malcolm Byrne (eds.). 2004. *Mohammad Mosaddeq and the 1953 Coup in Iran.* Syracuse, NY: Syracuse University Press

Geertz, Clifford. 1973. "Religion as a Cultural System." In M. Banton (ed.), *Anthropological Approaches to the Study of Religion.* London: Tavistock.

Gellner, Ernest. 1969. *Saints of the Atlas.* Chicago: University of Chicago Press.

Gerlach, Luther, and Virginia Hine. 1981. *People, Power, Change: Movements of Social Transformation.* Indianapolis: Bobbs-Merrill.

Gheissari, Ali. 1998. *Iranian Intellectuals in the 20th Century.* Austin: University of Texas Press.

———. (ed). 2009. *Contemporary Iran: Economy, Society, Politics.* New York: Oxford University Press.

Gheissari, Ali, and Vali Nasr. 2009. *Democracy in Iran: History and the Quest for Liberty.* New York: Oxford University Press.

Ghorayshi, Parvin. 1981. "Capitalism in Rural Iran." *MERIP Reports* no. 93:28–30.

Gluckman, Max. 1959. "The Frailty of Authority." In M. Gluckman (ed.), *Custom and Conflict in Africa.* Glencoe, IL: Free Press.

———. 2004a. "Rituals of Rebellion in Southeast Africa." In M. Gluckman (ed.), *Order and Rebellion in Tribal Africa.* New York: Routledge.

———. 2004b. "Introduction." In M. Gluckman (ed.), *Order and Rebellion in Tribal Africa.* New York: Routledge.

Goodell, Grace. 1977. "The Elementary Structures of Political Life." Ph.D. dissertation, Columbia University.

———. 1986. *The Elementary Structures of Political Life: Rural Development in Pahlavi Iran.* New York: Oxford University Press.

Goodwin, Jeff, James Jasper and Francesca Polletta. 2001. *Passionate Politics: Emotions and Social Movements.* Chicago: University of Chicago Press.

Hale, Sondra. 1986. "The Wing of the Patriarch: Sudanese Women and Revolutionary Parties." *MERIP Reports* no. 38:25–30.

———. 1996. *Gender Politics in Sudan: Islamism, Socialism, and the State.* Boulder, CO: Westview Press.

Halliday, Fred. 1979. *Iran: Dictatorship and Development.* New York: Penguin Books.

Hassanpour, Amir. 2012. "The Absence of Peasant Revolts in the Middle East: A Historiographic Myth." Unpublished manuscript.

Hegland, Mary. 1983a. "Aliabad Women: Revolution as Religious Activity." In G. Nashat (ed.), *Women and the Iranian Revolution.* Boulder, CO: Westview Press.

———. 1983b. "Two Images of Husain: Accommodation and Revolution in an Iranian Village." In N. Keddie (ed.), *Religion and Politics in Iran: Shi'ism from Quietism to Revolution.* New Haven, CT: Yale University Press.

———. 1983c. "Ritual and Revolution in Iran." In M. Aronoff (ed.), *Political Anthropology. Volume II: Culture and Political Change.* New Brunswick, NJ: Transaction Books.

———. 1986a. "The Political Roles of Iranian Village Women." *MERIP Reports* no. 138:14–19, 46.

———. 1986b. "Imam Khomeini's Village: Recruitment to Revolution." Ph.D. dissertation, Department of Anthropology, SUNY Binghamton.

———. 1987. "Islamic Revival or Political and Cultural Revolution? An Iranian Case Study." In R. Antoun and M. Hegland (eds.), *Religious Resurgence: Contemporary Cases in Islam, Christianity, and Judaism.* Syracuse, NY: Syracuse University Press.

———. 1991. "Political Roles of Aliabad Women: The Public/Private Dichotomy Transcended." In N. Keddie and B. Baron (eds.), *Shifting Boundaries: Gender Roles in the Middle East, Past and Present.* New Haven, CT: Yale University Press.

———. 1998a. Women and the Iranian Revolution: A Village Case Study." In M. Diamond (ed.), *Women and Revolution: Global Expressions.* Dordrecht: Kluwer.

———. 1998b. "The Power Paradox in Muslim Women's *Majales:* North-West Pakistani Mourning Rituals as Sites of Contestation over Religious Politics, Ethnicity, and Gender." *Signs* 23(2):391–428.

———. 1998c "Flagellation and Fundamentalism: (trans)Forming Meaning, Identity, and Gender Through Pakistani Women's Rituals of Mourning." *American Ethnologist* 25(2):240–266.

———. 2003a. "Talking Politics: A Village Widow in Iran." In L. Walbridge and A. Sievert (eds.), *Personal Encounters: A Reader in Cultural Anthropology.* Boston: McGraw-Hill.

———. 2003b. "Shi'a Women's Rituals in Northwest Pakistan: The Shortcomings and Significance of Resistance." *Anthropological Quarterly* 76(3):411–442.

———. 2006. "Secularization and Reformation Trends in Shi'i Iran: Changing Beliefs in an Iranian Village." Paper presented at 8th Annual Middle East Studies Conference: The Resurgence of Shi'ism, University of California, Santa Barbara, March 25.

———. 2008. "Esmat Khanum and a Life of Travail: 'God, Help Me.'" In F. Trix, J. Walbridge and L. Walbridge (eds.), *Muslim Voices and Lives in the Contemporary World*. New York: Palgrave Macmillan.

———. 2009. "Educating Young Women: Culture, Conflict, and New Identities in an Iranian Village." *Iranian Studies* 42(1):45–78.

———. 2011. "Aliabad of Shiraz: Transformation from Village to Suburban Town." *Anthropology of the Middle East* 6(2):21–39.

Hegland, Mary, with Zahra Sarraf and Mohammad Shahbazi. 2008. "Modernization and Social Change: The Impact on Iranian Elderly Social Networks and Care Systems." *Anthropology of the Middle East* 2(5):55–74.

Hill, Christopher. 1991. *The World Turned Upside Down: Radical Ideas During the English Revolution*. New York: Penguin.

Hillmann, Michael. 1981. "Language and Social Distinctions in Iran." In M. Bonine and N. Keddie (eds.), *Modern Iran: The Dialectics of Continuity and Change*. Albany: State University of New York Press.

Hinderink, Jan, and Mubeccel Kiray. 1970. *Social Stratification as an Obstacle to Development: A Study of Four Turkish Villages*. New York: Praeger.

Hooglund, Eric. 1975. "The Effects of the Land Reform Program on Rural Iran, 1962–1972." Ph.D. dissertation, Johns Hopkins University.

———. 1981a. "Iran's Agricultural Inheritance." *MERIP Reports* no. 99:15–19.

———. 1981b. "Rural Socioeconomic Organization in Transition: The Case of Iran's Bonehs." In M. Bonine and N. Keddie (eds.), *Modern Iran: The Dialectics of Continuity and Change*. Albany: State University of New York.

———. 1982. *Land and Revolution in Iran, 1960–1980*. Austin: University of Texas Press

Inayatullah. 1972. *Cooperatives and Development in Asia: A Study of Cooperatives in Fourteen Rural Communities of Iran, Pakistan and Ceylon*, Vol. VI. Geneva: United Nations Research Institute of Social Development, Rural Institutions and Planned Change.

Jayawardena, Chandra. 1968. "Ideology and Conflict in Lower Class Communities." *Society and History* 10:413–446.

Joseph, Suad. 1979. "Women and the Neighborhood Street in Borj Hammound, Lebanon." In L. Beck and N. Keddie (eds.), *Women in the Muslim World*. Cambridge, MA: Harvard University Press.

———. 1983. "Working-Class Women's Networks in a Sectarian State: A Political Paradox." *American Ethnologist* 10:1–22.

Kaplan, Temma. 1982. "Female Consciousness and Collective Action in Barcelona, 1910–1918." *Signs* 7(3):545–566.

———. 1987. "Women and Communal Strikes in the Crisis of 1917–1922." In R. Bridenthal, C. Koonz and S. Stuart (eds.), *Becoming Visible*. Boston: Houghton Mifflin.

Karandish, Javad. 2011. *State and Tribes in Persia, 1919–1925: A Case Study on Political Role of the Great Tribes in Southern Persia*. Ph.D. dissertation, Free University of Berlin, Dissertations Online, University Library.

Katouzian, Homa. 1981. *The Political Economy of Modern Iran: Despotism and Pseudo-Modernism, 1926–1979*. London: MacMillan.

———. 1999. *Musaddiq and the Struggle for Power in Iran.* London: I.B. Tauris.

———. 2003. *Iranian History and Politics: The Dialectic of State and Society.* London: Routledge.

———. 2004. "The Short-Term Society: A Study in the Problems of Long-Term Political and Economic Development in Iran." *Middle Eastern Studies* 40(1):1–22.

Kazemi, Farhad. 1980. *Poverty and Revolution in Iran: The Migrant Poor, Urban Marginality and Politics.* New York: New York University Press.

Kazemi, Farhad, and Ervand Abrahamian. 1978. "The Nonrevolutionary Peasantry of Modern Iran." *Iranian Studies* 11:259–304.

Keddie, Nikki. 1972. "Stratification, Social Control, and Capitalism in Iranian Villages: Before and After Land Reform." In R. Antoun and I. Harik (eds.), *Rural Politics and Social Change in the Middle East.* Bloomington: Indiana University Press.

———. 1981. *Roots of Revolution: An Interpretive History of Modern Iran.* New Haven, CT: Yale University Press.

———. 2006. *Modern Iran: Roots and Results of Revolution.* New Haven: Yale University Press.

Keiser, Lincoln. 1991. *Friend by Day, Enemy by Night: Organized Vengeance in a Kohistani Community.* Fort Worth, TX: Holt, Rinehart and Winston.

Kertzer, David. 1980. *Comrades and Christians: Religion and Political Struggle in Communist Italy.* Cambridge, UK: Cambridge University Press.

Keshavarzian, Arang. 2009. *Bazaar and State in Iran: The Politics of the Tehran Marketplace.* Cambridge, UK: Cambridge University Press.

Khosravi, Shahram. 2008. *Young and Defiant in Tehran.* Philadelphia: University of Pennsylvania Press.

Kinzer, Stephen. 2007. *Overthrow: America's Century of Regime Change from Hawaii to Iraq.* New York: Times Books.

———. 2008. *All the Shah's Men: An American Coup and the Roots of Middle East Terror.* Hoboken, NJ: Wiley.

Knudsen, Are. 2009. *Violence and Belonging: Land, Love and Lethal Conflict in the North-West Frontier Province of Pakistan.*

Kurzman, Charles. 2004. *The Unthinkable Revolution in Iran.* Cambridge, MA: Harvard University Press.

———. 2008. "A Feminist Generation in Iran?" *Iranian Studies* 41(3):297–321.

Lambton, Ann. 1969a. *Landlord and Peasant in Persia: A Study of Land Tenure and Land Revenue Administration.* London: Oxford University Press.

———. 1969b. *The Persian Land Reform, 1942–1966.* London: Oxford University Press.

Lindisfarne (Tapper), Nancy. 1979. "The Women's Subsociety among the Shabsevan Nomads of Iran." In L. Beck and N. Keddie (eds.), *Women in the Muslim World.* Cambridge, MA: Harvard University Press.

———. 1980. "Matrons and Mistresses: Women and Boundaries in Two Middle Eastern Tribal Societies." *European Journal of Sociology* 21:59–79.

Lindholm, Charles. 1982. *Generosity and Jealousy: The Swat Pukhtun of Northern Pakistan.* New York: Columbia University Press.

Loeffler, Agnes. 2013. *Health and Medical Practice in Iran: Traditional Culture and Modern Medicine*. London: I.B. Taurus.

Loeffler, Agnes, and Erika Friedl. 2009. "Cultural Parameters of a 'Miraculous' Birth Rate Drop." *Anthropology News* 50(3):14–15.

Loeffler, Reinhold. 1971. "The Representative Mediator and the New Peasant." *American Anthropologist* 73(2):1077–1091.

———. 1973. "The National Integration of the Boir Ahmad." *Iranian Studies* 6(2–3):127–135.

———. 1976. "Recent Economic Changes in Boir Ahmed: Regional Growth Without Development." *Iranian Studies* 9(4):266–287.

———. 1978. "Tribal Order and the State: The Political Organization of Boir Ahmed." *Iranian Studies* 11:145–171.

———. 1988. *Islam in Practice: Religious Beliefs in a Persian Village*. Albany: State University of New York Press.

———. 2011. "The Ethos of Progress in a Village in Iran." *Anthropology of the Middle East* 6(2):1–13.

Magnarella, Paul. 1974. *Tradition and Change in a Turkish Town*. New York: Wiley.

Mahdavi, Hossein. 1965. "The Coming Crisis in Iran." *Foreign Affairs* 44:134–146.

Mahdavi, Pardis. 2009. *Passionate Uprisings: Iran's Sexual Revolution*. Stanford, CA: Stanford University Press.

Majd, Mohammad. 2000. *Resistance to the Shah: Landowners and Ulama in Iran*. Gainsville: University Press of Florida.

Manoukian, Setrag. 2012. *City of Knowledge in Twentieth Century Iran: Shiraz, History and Poetry*. New York: Routledge.

Matthee, Rudolph. 1996. "From Coffee to Tea: Shifting Patterns of Consumption in Qajar Iran." *Journal of World History* 7(2):199–230.

McAdam, Doug. 1999. *Political Process and the Development of Black Insurgency, 1930–1970*. Chicago: University of Chicago Press.

Milani, Farzaneh. 1992. *Veils and Words: The Emerging Voices of Iranian Women Writers*. Syracuse, NY: Syracuse University Press.

———. 2011. *Words, Not Swords: Iranian Women Writers and the Freedom of Movement*. Syracuse, NY: Syracuse University Press.

Miller, William. 1964. "Hosseinabad: A Persian Village." *Middle East Journal* 18:483–498.

Moaddel, Mansoor. 1993. *Class, Politics, and Ideology in the Iranian Revolution*. New York: Columbia University Press.

Moaveni, Azadeh. 2005. *Lipstick Jihad: A Memoir of Growing Up Iranian in America and American in Iran*. New York: Public Affairs.

———. 2010. *Honeymoon in Tehran: Two Years of Love and Danger in Iran*. New York: Random House.

Moghadam, Fatemeh. 1996. *From Land Reform to Revolution: Political Economy of Agricultural Development in Iran, 1962–1979*. London: I.B. Tauris.

Moghissi, Haideh, 1997. *Populism and Feminism in Iran: Women's Struggle in a Male-Defined Revolutionary Movement*. New York: St. Martin's Press.

———. 1999. *Feminism and Islamic Fundamentalism: The Limits of Postmodern Analysis*. London: Zed Books.

Moore, Barrington, Jr. 1978. *Injustice: The Social Bases of Obedience and Revolt*. White Plains, NY: M. E. Sharpe.

Motlagh, Amy. 2011. *Burying the Beloved: Marriage, Realism, and Reform in Modern Iran*. Stanford, CA: Stanford University Press.

Nakhleh, Khalil. 1975. "The Direction of Local-Level Conflict in Two Arab Villages in Israel." *American Ethnologist* 2(3):497–516.

Najmabadi, Afsaneh. 1988. *Land Reform and Social Change in Iran*. Salt Lake City: University of Utah Press.

———. 1995. *Women with Mustaches and Men without Beards: Gender and Sexual Anxieties of Iranian Modernity*. Berkeley: University of California Press.

Nashat, Guity (ed.). 1983. *Women and Revolution in Iran*. Boulder, CO: Westview Press.

Ohnuki-Tierney, Emiko (ed.). 1990. *Culture Through Time: Anthropological Approaches*. Stanford, CA: Stanford University Press.

Okazaki, Shoko. 1969. "Shirang-Sofla: The Economics of a Northeast Iranian Village." *The Developing Economics* 7:261–283.

Ortner, Sherry. 1989. *High Religion: A Cultural and Political History of Sherpa Buddhism*. Princeton, NJ: Princeton University Press.

———. 1990. "The Political Economy of Monastery Founding." In E. Ohnuki-Tierney (ed.), *Culture Through Time: Anthropological Approaches*. Stanford, CA: Stanford University Press.

Osanloo, Arzoo. 2009. *The Politics of Women's Rights in Iran*. Princeton, NJ: Princeton University Press.

Paivandi, Saeed. "Iranian Youth Vis a Vis an Ideological Education System." *Iran Nameh* 25(4).

Papanek, Hannah. 1973. "Men, Women, and Work: Reflections on the Two-Person Career." *American Journal of Sociology* 78(4):852–872.

Paul, Jim. 1982. "Iran's Peasants and the Revolution: An Introduction." *MERIP Reports* no. 99:22, 23.

Peteet, Julie. 1986. "Women and the Palestinian Movement: No Going Back?" *MERIP Reports* no. 138:20–24, 44.

———. 1992. *Gender in Crisis: Women and the Palestinian Resistance Movement*. New York: Columbia University Press.

Peters, Emrys. 1963. "Aspects of Rank and Status among Muslims in a Lebanese Village." In J. Pitt-Rivers (ed.), *Mediterranean Countrymen*. Paris: Mouton.

Pierce, Joe. 1964. *Life in a Turkish Village*. New York; Holt, Rinehart and Winston.

Polletta, Francesca. 1998. *It Was Like a Fever: Storytelling in Protest and Politics*. Chicago: Chicago University Press.

Ringer, Monica. 2000. "The Discourse on Modernization and the Problem of Cultural Integrity in Nineteenth-Century Iran." In R. Matthee and B. Baron (eds.), *Iran and Beyond: Essays in Middle Eastern History in Honor of Nikki R. Keddie*. Costa Mesa, CA: Mazda Publishers.

Robertson-Smith, W. 1885. *Kinship and Marriage in Early Arabia.* Cambridge, UK: Cambridge University Press.

Rosenfeld, Henry. 1968. "Change, Barriers to Change, and Contradictions in the Arab Village Family." *American Anthropologist* 70(4):732-752.

Royce, William. 1981. "The Shirazi Provincial Elite: Status Maintenance and Change." In M. Bonine and N. Keddie (eds.), *Continuity and Change in Modern Iran.* Albany: State University of New York Press.

Sachedina, Abulaziz Abdulhussein. 1981. *Islamic Messianism: The Idea of the Mahdi in Twelver Shi'ism.* Albany: State University of New York Press.

Sadeghi, Fatemeh. 2010. "Negotiating with Modernity: Young Women and Sexuality in Iran." In L. Herrera and A. Bayat (eds.), *Being Young and Muslim.* London: Oxford University Press.

Satrapi, Marjane. 2004. *Persepolis: The Story of a Childhood.* New York: Pantheon Books.

———. 2005. *Persepolis 2: The Story of a Return.* New York: Pantheon Books.

Scott, James. 1987. *Weapons of the Weak: Everyday Forms of Peasant Resistance.* New Haven, CT: Yale University Press.

———. 1992. *Domination and the Arts of Resistance: Hidden Transcripts.* New Haven, CT: Yale University Press.

Shahrokni, Nazanin, and Parastou Dokouhaki. 2012. "A Separation at Iranian Universities." *MERIP MER Online,* October 18.

Shahshahani, Soheila. 2012 "Longitudinal Study of Oyun, with an Emphasis on Kinship and Law." Paper presented at the Ninth Biennial Conference of the International Society for Iranian Studies, Istanbul.

Shari'ati, Ali. 1979. *On the Sociology of Islam.* Trans. Hamid Algar. Berkeley, CA: Mizan Press.

———. 1982. *Fatima Is Fatima.* New York: Tahrike Tarsile Qur'an.

Special Correspondent. 1982. "Report from an Iranian Village." *MERIP Reports* no. 104:26–29.

Spooner, Brian. 1965. "Kinship and Marriage in Eastern Persia. *Sociologus* 15:22–31.

———. 1966. "Iranian Kinship and Marriage." *Iran* 4:51–60.

Stirling, Paul. 1965. *Turkish Village.* New York: Wiley.

———. 1976. "Cause, Knowledge and Change: Turkish Village Revisited." In W. Hale (ed.), *Aspects of Modern Turkey.* London: Bowker.

Stryker, Sheldon, Timothy Owens and Robert White, eds. 2001. *Self, Identity, and Social Movements.* Minneapolis: University of Minnesota Press.

Talebi, Shahla. 2011. *Ghosts of Revolution: Rekindled Memories of Imprisonment in Iran.* Stanford, CA: Stanford University Press.

Tarrow, Sydney. 2006. *Power in Movement: Social Movements and Contentious Politics.* Cambridge: Cambridge University Press.

"Tehran Radio on Land Reform and Struggles in the Countryside" and "The Government Fully Respects Ownership." *MERIP Reports* no. 97:17.

Thompson, Charles. 1979. "A Persian Miniature: The Value of Tradition in a Mazandaran Village." Ph.D. dissertation, University of Texas at Austin.

Tucker, Judith. 1986. "Insurrectionary Women: Women and Politics in Nineteenth-Century Egypt." *MERIP Reports* no. 138:9–14.

Turner, Victor. 1978a. "Social Dramas and Ritual Metaphors." In V. Turner (ed.), *Dramas, Fields, and Metaphors: Symbolic Action in Human Society*. Ithaca, NY: Cornell University Press.

———. 1978b. "Religious Paradigms and Political Action: Thomas Becket at the Council of Northampton." In V. Turner (ed.), *Dramas, Fields, and Metaphors: Symbolic Action in Human Society*. Ithaca, NY: Cornell University Press.

Upadhyaya, Ashok. 1980. "Peasant Movements: Class Struggle in Rural Maharashtra (India): Towards a New Perspective." *Journal of Peasant Studies* 7:213–223.

Varzi, Roxanne. 2006. *Warring Souls: Youth, Media and Martyrdom in Post-Revolutionary Iran*. Durham, NC: Duke University Press.

Vincent, Joan. 1995. *Anthropology and Politics: Visions, Traditions, and Trends*. Tucson: University of Arizona Press.

———. (ed.). 2002. *The Anthropology of Politics*. Malden, MA: Wiley-Blackwell.

Wilber, Donald. 2006. *The CIA in Iran: The 1953 Coup and the Origins of the US-Iran Divide*. Washington, D.C.: America Free Press.

Wolf, Eric. 1973. *Peasant Wars of the Twentieth Century*. New York: Harper & Row.

Woolf, Virginia. 1924. *Mr. Bennett and Mrs. Brown*. London: Hogarth Press.

Wright, Sue. 1978. "Prattle and Politics: The Position of Women in Doshman-Ziari." *Anthropological Society of Oxford Journal* 9(2):98–112.

———. 1986 "Identities and Influence: Political Organization in Doshman Ziāri, Mamasani, Iran." Ph.D. Dissertation, University of Oxford.

Index

Note: page numbers in italics refer to figures. Those followed by n refer to notes, with note number.

agriculture in Aliabad: as basis of *taifeh-keshi* system, 247, 249; capital and credit shortages and, 99–101; command hierarchy of, 48–49, 104–5, 107–12; decline in, and food prices, 93–94; decline of employment in, 88, 91, 101, 102–3; declining profitability of, 73–74, 89–90, 91–103; grain production, decline in profitability of, 101–3; history of, 20; labor shortages and, 101; land shortages, 72, 89, 91–95; sharecroppers' farming methods, 49; water shortages and, 95–99. *See also entries under* land
Ahmadinejad, Mahmoud, 230, 259
airliner, Iranian, U.S. downing of (1988), 229–30, 282n7
Ajami, Esmat: on Aliabad of 21st century, 238; character and background, xiv; correspondence with author, 231; on required visits on Iranian New Year (*Noruz*), 33; and revolutionary unrest, xiv, 158; on Tudeh Party, rejection of, 58; on winning side, switch to, 209; and women's protest marches, 174; and women's role in maintaining social relations, 221

Ajami, Jamshid, Mullah, 3–6, 33, 48, 61, 148
Ajami family, and village uprising against Ibn Ali Askari, xiv
Ajami home, as center of activity, xiv
Alam, Asadollah, 68, 91
Alavi, Hamzeh, 277–78n2
Aliabad: in 1970s, described, 20–22, *21*; author's accommodations in, xii, xiv, xv, xx, 77, 157, 173, 195; economic conditions in, 20; economy, history of, 24; grain storage rooms, 21; history of, 22–24; Iran-Iraq War and, 230; lifestyle of in 1970s, 235–38; maps of, *xxxiv–xxxv*; as model village, xiii; modern political opinions in, 259, 260; population of, xii; relative prosperity of, xii–xiii; road to Shiraz, described, 19; trends in, generalizability of, 286n44
Aliabad of 21st century: agricultural lands, disappearance of, 231, 233; agriculture, small number employed in, 233–34; children and family life in, 238–39; city culture, rise of, 248–52; decline of extended family and kinship bonds, 242–45; drug use in, 239; economic activities, 232–35; economic stress in, 229;

301

houses in Aliabad, in 1970s *vs.* 21st century, 235

Husein, Imam, 9, 159, 267n12, 270n23, 278n4. *See also* Moharram

Hussein, Saddam, 229, 281–82n6

individualism, rise of, 253–55

inequality, Iranian resentment of, as cause of Revolution, 1–2, 118, 119

inheritance: disputes over, in modern Aliabad, 253–54; laws, and women, 34–35, 253, 269n10

in-laws: and kinship system, 26; obligations to, 36–37, 218, 271n36; *taifeh* structure and, 43

Iran, 21st-century life in: dissent, government suppression of, 228; drug use, 228, 239; economic problems, 228, 229; materialist culture, spread of, 227–28, 254; Muslim beliefs, declining interest in, 228–29; political life, 230; public discontent, 228; sources of information on, 227; travel and leisure, 227–28, 236; wealth gap, increase in, 228, 281n3. *See also* Islamic Republic

Iranian New Year. *See Noruz*

Iran-Iraq War, 229–30, 281–82n6

irrigated land: productivity *vs.* dry lands, 20, 93; Seyyid Ibn Ali's control of, 63, 69–70, 104; shortages of after land reform, 63, 72, 89, 91–95; suburban homes built on, 233

irrigation system: collapse of agreements on, after land reform, 95–99; control of, 16, 49, 53; failed efforts to improve, 100–101; maintenance of, 53, 73, 96–97, 205–6, *206*, 220; peasants' dependence on Askari protection of, 105; Tudeh Party takeover in Darab and, 53, 56–57, 143

Islamic Republic: elections of 2009, 228, 230, 257, 259; flight from (Iranian diaspora), 228; future of, as unclear, 259–60; increasing political awareness of citizens in, 257–60; internal strife in, 260; and local government, early weakness of, 194–95, 214, 280n1; and local government, 21st-century ineffectiveness of,

246; politicized daily life in, 186–87; population control program, 283n20; referendum on, 185; repressive rule of, 230; resistance to greater participatory government, 258; support for, 259–60; villagers' expectations of, 141, 189–91, 193–94, 277n19; villagers' socialist inclinations and, 201, 219. See also Iran, 21st-century life in

Jafari, Majid, 69, 76, 105

Jehangiri, Hamid, 75–76, 77, 135, 162, 218–19

Jehangiri *taifeh*, power of under Shah's government, 75, 82

Jews: in Iran, 278–79n12; in Shiraz, Revolution and, 164

Joseph, Suad, 271n39

kadkhoda (village headman): after land reform, as government official, 74; armed forces under command of, 48; control of agriculture by, 48–49, 90; control of trade by, 90; corruption of, under Shah's government, 78; defeated, fate of, 11, 12, 14, 44–46, *45*; dependents of, 43; exploitation of weak by, 100; locally-chosen, replacement by Shah's government official, 2–3, 16–18, 51–52, 71; power of before land reform, 12–13; reduction from 2 to 1, after peasants' strike, 61; required peasant visits to, on Iranian New Year (*Noruz*), 32–33; role in *taifeh*, 43; selection of, through *taifeh-keshi*, 3–6; *taifeh* of, privileges enjoyed by, 6

Katouzian, Homa, 279–80n26

Kazemi, Abbas, Shaikh, 54

Kazemi, Karim, Shaikh, 54, 55, 56, 59

Kazemi, Rahim, Shaikh: author's contact with, xiv; death of, 231–32; as long-time Askari opponent, 157; and mourning etiquette, 136; and peasants' strike, 60; and peasant *taifeh*, 257; on political chants during oil nationalization crisis, 54; and protest marches, participation in, 161, 164; Seyyid Yaqub's views on, 77; Tudeh Party and, 54, 55, 57–58; views on